FIELDS of PLAY

SPORT,
RACE,
and
MEMORY
in the
STEEL CITY

FIELDS

ROBERT T. HAYASHI

of **PLAY**

University of Pittsburgh Press

Published by the University of Pittsburgh Press, Pittsburgh, Pa., 15260
This paperback edition, Copyright © 2025, University of Pittsburgh Press
Copyright © 2023, University of Pittsburgh Press
All rights reserved
Manufactured in the United States of America
Printed on acid-free paper
10 9 8 7 6 5 4 3 2 1

Cataloging-in-Publication data is available from the Library of Congress

ISBN 13: 978-0-8229-6744-6
ISBN 10: 0-8229-6744-8

Jacket Art: (*Top to bottom, left to right*) Charles "Teenie" Harris, *Five hunters gathered around car with woman seated on roof and two dead deer lying on hood*, c. 1941–1946. Black-and-white, Ansco safety film, 4 × 5 in. (10.20 × 12.70 cm). Carnegie Museum of Art, Pittsburgh: Heinz Family Fund, 2001.35.3115; *Group portrait of four male boxers, including unknown, Jimmy Eichelberger, Bob Lundy, and Charley Burley, standing in boxing ring in Centre Avenue YMCA for All-Star boxing show*, November 1946. Black-and-white, Ansco safety film, 4 × 5 in. (10.20 × 12.70 cm). Carnegie Museum of Art, Pittsburgh: Heinz Family Fund, 2001.35.1008; *Three football players and manager on Homewood field*, c. 1950–1970. Black-and-white, Kodak safety film, 4 × 5 in. (10.20 × 12.70 cm). Carnegie Museum of Art, Pittsburgh: Heinz Family Fund, 2001.35.696; *Portrait of female golfer, wearing light colored baseball cap, light colored shirt, and large shorts, swinging golf club on golf course, possibly in South Park, with trees in background*, c. 1952. Black- and-white, Kodak safety film, 4 × 5 in. (10.20 × 12.70 cm). Carnegie Museum of Art, Pittsburgh: Heinz Family Fund, 2001.35.40993; *Lifeguard teaching boy to swim, with Thomas Strawder and Thomas McDaniels to left, in Highland Park swimming pool*, 1951. Black-and-white, Kodak safety film, 4 × 5 in. (10.20 × 12.70 cm). Carnegie Museum of Art, Pittsburgh: Heinz Family Fund, 2001.35.3073.

Jacket Design: Joel W. Coggins

I would try to make him know that just as American history is longer, larger, more various, more beautiful and more terrible than anything anyone has ever said about it, so is the world larger, more daring, more beautiful and more terrible, but principally larger— and that it belongs to him . . .

—James Baldwin, "A Talk to Teachers"

CONTENTS

PREFACE
Shady Avenue — ix

1 **FROM NATIONS YOU KNOW NOT**
Race, Labor, and Play in Western Pennsylvania — 3

2 **CORNER KICKS AND COAL**
Soccer, Community, and Recalling a Coal Mining Past — 34

3 **POACHED TROUT**
Fishing and Hunting in Penn's Woods — 72

4 **BASKETBALLS, BUNK BEDS, AND BRIDGES**
The Irene Kaufmann Settlement House and Its Neighbors — 118

5 **TERRIBLE TOWELS AND SIXTY-MINUTE MEN**
The Pittsburgh Steelers and Remembering a Black
(and Yellow) Past — 165

ACKNOWLEDGMENTS — 217

NOTES — 219

BIBLIOGRAPHY — 245

INDEX — 265

PREFACE

Shady Avenue

The satellite trucks and crowds that coalesce around American tragedies are gone. A newly installed gate, a chain-link fence adorned with paper stars, some with the message "Keep Strong," remains. After the mass shooting at Pittsburgh's Tree of Life Synagogue, a local designer developed a logo consisting of three colored hypocycloids—red, blue, and yellow pointed stars—like those long adorning the helmet of our city's beloved professional football team, the Pittsburgh Steelers. Only now one was a golden Star of David. The phrase "Stronger Than Hate" accompanied the image, and this message was quickly embraced by the grieving city. The symbol was an ideal blending of Pittsburgh's identity: toughness forged in a defining industrial past. We are blue collar and immigrant, an identity manifest in our play, the teams we worship. As the designer noted on his Facebook page, "It was a perfect basis for an image of hope." The logo soon spread across the Internet and onto thousands of T-shirts sold to aid victims' families or to make a quick buck. I ordered four.

As an embodied cultural practice, sport is replete with both personal meaning and social significance, and few places more dramatically exemplify the meaning of sport to a community than Pittsburgh, Pennsylvania. The iconic Pittsburgh Steelers often stand as proxy for the city's identity despite the steel industry's near complete disappearance from its riverbanks—the exodus of its workers. That its fan base calls itself a nation, the Steeler Nation, underscores the role of modern spectator sport in providing the invented histories, practices, and symbols that unite disparate peoples into a collective, a nation of remembrance. Pittsburghers of my generation are, after all, a diaspora. Sport operates as a substitute for home: the landscape with its rivers and bridges and hollers, the secular and once sacred that bound us, the cultural glue flowing from communal institutions and their inherited narratives. The games we play and watch now feed collective desires to remember Pittsburgh and define ourselves, our community, and what we hope to be. Sport offers an escape from a world of unremitting change, shifting borders, but one that often involves forgetting who and what we really have been.

This book narrates the social and economic evolution of the greater Pittsburgh area through the lens of sport. Drawing from a range of sources—institutional records, newspaper accounts, legislation, court cases, oral histories, literature, and photographs—I describe how the region's dominant institutions utilized sport to define and enforce visions of identity and community that promoted white supremacy, unchecked capitalism, and racial segregation. These influential institutions touted genteel white outdoorsmen, compliant immigrant industrial workers, and heroic male athletes, while they excluded and demonized those unlike them, justifying their denial.

I analyze how, with varying agendas, sometimes clashing visions, state and local government agencies, media, corporations, fans, religious organizations, and players shaped the meaning of our play, who we are. Institutions sought to mold productive workers, true sportsmen, and proper girls, and to maintain their leaders' interests. Others resisted, and our soccer pitches, hunting grounds, rivers, basketball courts, pools, and playgrounds have been sites of contestation: over the meaning of our play and, most of all, over who can play.

The general failure in media and sports writing to clarify how historical forces such as systemic racism, global capitalism, and politics influenced who got in the game normalizes the limited representation of Asians and others. Many Americans view sport as defined by meritocracy and assume a group's absence is due to their lack of something—cultural, biological. We disappear, outside the reach of history's narrative voice. Unless one explores such axes in the historical record, bias can seem but natural evolution and the hagiographies of sports idols accurate chronicles of America's past.

This history of western Pennsylvania begins then with the earliest

Asian migrants to the region, the Chinese. I recount their experiences in chapter 1, "From Nations You Know Not: Race, Labor, and Play in Western Pennsylvania." Asian experiences frame the book's exploration of the intersections of sport, identity, and memory because of the unique positioning of Asians in American society. Asians' presence drove American society to define the legal, physical, and social boundaries to opportunity—migration, labor, citizenship, civil rights, and recreation. Our presence has insisted on the questions: What is race? Whiteness? What is possible? The answer for Asians was: not much in the Pittsburgh region. But it was not for lack of game.

Chinese arrived in the area in the late 1800s, first as replacement workers for a local factory, and this role as antagonists to white workers defines local history, with Asians, African Americans too—demarcating the boundaries of the racial and industrial order. The region's powerful labor unions and lawmakers lobbied for and enacted legislation and boycotts targeting the Chinese and their businesses, mainly laundries and restaurants. Media portrayed Chinese men as predators and the Pittsburgh City Council sought to bar white women and girls from the alleged vipers' dens: Chinese restaurants. Chinatown was a neglected, impoverished neighborhood cut off from the expanding recreational opportunities available in Pittsburgh. Racial segregation of public space was the rule. Yet a set of privileged Asian and Pacific Islander athletes excelled in local venues and enjoyed both unique social mobility and media acclaim. This group included a crack baseball team of mainly ethnic Chinese from Hawaii who barnstormed the area from 1912 to 1916 and whupped a lot of local college, amateur, and semiprofessional teams. Several members settled in Pennsylvania and were talented enough to receive major league offers, but not white enough to leap the color line. Their opportunity remained constrained, like Asians in Pittsburgh, even if they were clearly capable and willing to succeed, just as formerly incarcerated Japanese Americans were.

By the late 1800s, Asians were excluded from the financial and social rewards of Pittsburgh's industrial boom and expanding recreational opportunities. White residents too were not a monolith and the area's economic growth established and reinforced disparities in wealth and power between the ruling mainly WASPish elite and the largely southern and eastern European immigrant laboring class. No other industry better exemplified the vast inequities of industrial capitalism than coal mining, the subject of chapter 2, "Corner Kicks and Coal: Soccer, Community, and Recalling a Coal Mining Past." Coal towns were racially segregated fiefdoms in the stranglehold of coal companies that employed their own private police force, the despised Coal and Iron Police. Accidents and violent strikes defined the industry, and topflight, physical soccer. The coal industry's labor and social conditions in southwest Pennsylvania spurred the development of a robust soccer community during the first half of the twentieth century. Local amateurs became national champions and Olympians, and media widely promoted the local game and exploits of the popular teams and star players. Many teams were founded by coal companies, and the class and community-specific nature of soccer here and its ties to a bloody industrial past challenges common narratives of the game's allegedly suburban or mainly ethnic roots in the United States. Soccer in the area was much more American than we acknowledge—its growth tied to industry, mass media, and social inequality.

The region's famed industrial expansion fueled by coal radically reshaped the social and natural worlds: enriching and empowering a select few, warping American democratic ideals, and destroying the rich native flora and fauna. It also spurred the expansion of fishing and hunting in Pennsylvania, the focus chapter 3, "Poached Trout: Fishing and Hunting in Penn's Woods." The Commonwealth played a key role in the history of outdoor sports, home to the country's earliest fishing and hunting clubs and lodges, getaways for eastern elites including Pittsburgh's industrial and banking magnates. I detail how in the early 1900s these powerful interests and allies used their economic, social, and political capital to develop the state's game agencies and ground them in core beliefs: science-based game management practices, public access, and gentlemanly recreation for WASP sportsmen. Media and state agencies presented the region's southern and eastern Europeans as dangerous threats to the natural environment, and Pennsylvania passed laws barring them from hunting or fishing. They viewed Black people as menaces as well, and I focus specifically on the rarely acknowledged history of Pittsburgh's African American hunters and anglers. The practices and experiences of these men and women expand the history of conservation beyond nostalgic narratives centered in whiteness, maleness, and industrial philanthropy and can inform current efforts to increase participation in these waning sports that are crucial to the preservation of natural resources.

Recreation in the Three Rivers region was often segregated by class, gender, race, and faith, but it also provided opportunities for residents to connect across such boundaries, including conservation efforts and interracial coalitions to combat racism. Pittsburgh's dramatic landscape of bridges and steep hillsides, coupled with urban planning, housing segregation, and suburbanization, however, led to entrenched racial segregation, including in recreation. In the first half of the twentieth century, philanthropists, social service agencies, industry and city planners argued for and expanded the recreational infrastructure of the city and the opportunities for its residents—founding parks, playgrounds, stadia, swimming pools, and professional and amateur sports teams, competitions, and leagues. When residents were denied access, they created separate institutions such as the Bucktails Fishing and Hunting Club and the Irene Kaufmann Settlement House (IKS), the focus of chapter 4, "Basketballs, Bunk Beds and Bridges: The Irene Kaufmann Settlement House and Its Neighbors." I analyze the settlement's evolution amid the pressures of Americanization and racial integration as its surrounding community transformed. The IKS was originally a women's organization in Pittsburgh's Hill District, serving Jewish girls' spiritual needs, which expanded into a community organization serving an ethnically and spiritually diverse neighborhood. The settlement's recreation programs, especially competitive athletics, grew increasingly robust and settlement staff invested in sport to mold the physical and moral character of members. Some in the Jewish community, however, argued that this emphasis on sport instead promoted the secularization of Jewish youth and questioned its growth.

The IKS offered athletic opportunities for girls and women, but they were secondary and declined as the organization struggled to integrate its increasingly Black clientele during the post–World War II era. The institution eventually relocated in the late 1960s, following the upwardly mobile Jewish community to the wealthy suburbs of East Pittsburgh. Like others, the community was streaming to Pittsburgh's expanding suburbs and seeking recreation even farther afield, in summer camps that were popping up across Pennsylvania. Outdoor recreation was increasingly touted as an antidote to industrial urban life, and local institutions increasingly provided resources and opportunities. Summer camps became widely popular in the Pittsburgh area but were limited almost entirely to white youth. The IKS's Camp Emma focused on the promotion and maintenance of Jewish identity, further separating Jewish kids from their nonwhite peers.

Local sporting practices demonstrated the region's entrenched racial segregation, but also interracial efforts to counter such ills. Progressive members of the Jewish community and other white citizens fought alongside Black residents in the 1950s and 1960s to integrate local municipal swimming pools such as Highland Park. Local law enforcement and anti-communist judges stymied their efforts, upholding the racial order, which became further embedded in the city's geography through the cumulative impact of rapid suburbanization, white flight, segregation, and urban redevelopment. Pittsburgh's business and political elite of the time fostered a series of ambitious projects in the city to address urban flooding, air quality, transportation, and business development, part of Pittsburgh's Renaissance period.

Unfortunately, Pittsburgh's once powerful industrial base began to implode, and in the 1970s and 1980s thousands of industrial workers left in search of new dreams elsewhere. In chapter 5, "Terrible Towels and Sixty-Minute Men: The Pittsburgh Steelers and Remembering a Black (and Yellow) Past," I recount how locals embraced the Pittsburgh Steelers, including African American athletes like Franco Harris, as symbols of white ethnic pride and blue-collar masculinity as the once woeful team became the most dominant in the NFL. As with soccer and coal mining in earlier generations, football and steel were bound together, if in mostly unacknowledged ways. The Steelers were a team dominated by Black athletes and possessed a progressive history of minority hiring. Steeler fans, in using Black athletes as celebratory symbols, divorced themselves from the historical challenges of local Black life, including police violence, and the steel industry's long mistreatment of African American workers. White fans and media failed to apprehend the deep, persistent costs of being a Black person in Pittsburgh that extended well beyond its playing fields and pools.

I end the narrative by returning to local Asian American history, discussing the life and career of the Pittsburgh Steelers star receiver Hines Ward and the recent influx of Asians that is again reshaping the local. The work and play of new Asian migrants challenge the region's imagined narrative of white identity promoted through sport, who we mean by yinz, the local form of the second-person plural that confounds outsiders. How serviceable are these inherited stories of identity for the Pittsburgh of today and tomorrow? The city is now an aging postindustrial metropolis, whose white working-class residents migrated out of the region en masse a generation ago. Its economy is now anchored in education, health care, finance, and technology sectors that attract international migrants from India, Nigeria, and the United Kingdom. Hines Ward, a biracial transnational migrant who became an international star due to his Black Korean heritage, illustrates the historical complexity of local identity in the modern world long defined by fluid borders, mass media, and persistent racial anxieties. His story and that of the city's other residents—coal mining soccer players, Jewish female hoopsters, Black summer campers, and Bhutanese refugee youth—offer complicated, multivocal notions of the local and a critical history to reconnect present Pittsburgh to its past.

I include my own narrative as an angler, athlete, fan, and Japanese American to underscore this ongoing contestation over the cultural meaning of sport in Pittsburgh, its legacy. My feelings of alienation, belonging, and nostalgia underscore the complex, even contradictory meanings of sport and western Pennsylvania. Though Pittsburghers, like other Americans, have characteristically portrayed sport as exemplifying hope, the promise of opportunity and tolerance in a democratic society, the region's history illustrates the inertial pull of racism, nativism, and capitalism that has run through our games. We made our play spaces exclusively white; passed laws to keep guns from immigrants; beat Black kids trying to swim; and dumped tens of millions of public dollars into corporate sports' infrastructures in the name of public welfare, while long impoverished communities continued to suffer.

Whether just a lazy swim on a hot summer day, a perfectly placed fly cast, a full volley buried into the upper corner of the net in double overtime, or a deflected pass barely caught and returned for the winning touchdown as the clock expires, the meaning of any sporting activity is fluid, despite simplistic, comforting stories in media and public history. Franco Harris's touchdown in 1972 against the despised Oakland Raiders was a spectacular play, but only became the Immaculate Reception in hindsight and was, despite later claims, ignored by many locals and ascended to holiness only over time. The term fit the assumed Christian character of the city, and was aspirational, an act of God's grace during a time of shared economic pain. For in sport we trust.

Sport entices us with the physical challenge it presents—to command our bodies, to overcome. We witness the possibility of the body. But, in these arenas and on our rivers and streets, they remain vulnerable to definitions we ascribe to them through the stories we tell about who we are, the meaning of our play.

FIELDS *of* PLAY

FROM NATIONS YOU KNOW NOT

Race, Labor, and Play in Western Pennsylvania

I should have just driven away in the hotel parking lot. But, when I saw the burgundy Jeep—a Steelers license plate frame holding Michigan tags with the message "CYINZ"—I had to wait around at least a little bit. I'm always too eager for that connection to home: an amiable chat with another Steelers fan about how "this will be the year" and "where'd yinz live at?" But now we're late. It's the naming ceremony of my wife's niece. "Shabbat Shalom," I respond to the stooped elderly man passing me on the gleaming marble floor, grateful for his greeting and smile. With a last adjustment of my kippah, I pull open the heavy doors as the family rushes in. Heads turn as we emerge into the sacred space where a young man speaks from the bimah. Wendy begins a quick, silent-as-can-be scurry along the back of the sanctuary to the far side where her sister-in-law's family sits chattering—loudly. Once seated, I'm grateful she assumes this is why slow glances are directed our way. But, I am listening, knowing we have emerged into a role, Exhibit 1A.

"It is time we face the Inconvenient Truth facing Judaism today . . . intermarriage!" inveighs the earnest Ivy League, Hillel kid addressing his home congregation. I smile to the faces staring back and am glad, despite the humid Maryland air, that I brought my best tailored-wool suit, accompanied by one of Dad's carefully curated 1960s bowties. Scary? I look sharp.

But Jewish Americans, like many other Americans, like many people back home in Pittsburgh, are scared. They are trying to hold on to a tribe thrown wide into the polyglot mix of modern America, riding the waves of assimilation, integration, and globalization—the still persistent hatreds so easily inflamed. The armed security outside was a reminder of that. Outmarriage is both a threat to and marker of Jewish success in riding those shock waves of America's and Pittsburgh's evolution. It is a focal point of deep and shared historical anxieties. An often-cited 2013 Pew study of Jewish Americans reported that 44 percent of those married had non-Jewish spouses, a trend that had dramatically accelerated over the past few decades.[1] Coupled with the increasing number of young Jewish Americans who are not religiously observant, this trend has some gravely concerned and fuels debates about the nature of Jewish identity.

In cities like Pittsburgh, even their strongest communities, sturdiest institutions, like the Jewish Community Center (JCC), face the challenges of such change, neighborhoods suddenly filled with peoples unlike them. The once predominantly Jewish section of East Pittsburgh, Squirrel Hill, has over the past few decades become nearly 20 percent Asian.[2] The JCC ran an advertising campaign announcing, "The JCC is for Every Body."[3] When I visited the center, elderly Jewish women were getting fit on the new elliptical machines, while little Chinese kids laughingly splashed about during their swim lesson. A recent article in a national foodie magazine about Pittsburgh's iconic Jewish neighborhood announced, "America's Next Great Chinatown Takes Root in Pittsburgh."[4] While the article is a bit of demographic and culinary hyperbole, you can get tasty noodles and dumplings made before your eyes by Taiwanese workers on H-1B visas, feast on sweet red bean cakes from a Chinese bakery down the street; and I never miss a chance to get some uni at the Japanese restaurant on the next block, across the street from a corner deli where I used to get hot fatty corned beef on rye. It's now an Indian place.

The Steel City's new Chinatown emerges seemingly sui generis: separate, but authentically and uncomplicatedly Chinese for non-Chinese to consume. But then, any Chinatown to Americans is, as Eric Liu notes, "not so much a place as it is a metaphor—an ideograph—for all the exotic mystery of the Orient . . . we believe in it, as surely as we believe in the ghetto or the suburb."[5] While openness to something more authentic than General Tso's chicken evidences a cosmopolitan Pittsburgh, the history of the Chinese, Asians in general, in the region has been one of exclusion. We have been antagonists to the area's core identity, one now promoted in popular film and Pittsburgh's professional sports franchises: industrial, lunch pail, white, and working class. Pittsburghers are steelworkers with guts and Slavic names in a town where you get what you earn. Guys who hunt deer and root for the Steelers, or Stillers in the local parlance. The early history of Asians in the region reveals how white people defined them as threats to the evolving industrial and racial order and how the world of sport reflected and reinforced that social structure, warping collective regional memory. Asian contributions and identities in the public sphere remain obscured, our unique narratives whited out and forgotten or turned into the colorful backdrop of a white tale. Pittsburgh's original Chinatown and its history have faded into hazy nostalgia: its businesses and residences long ago displaced by the city's redevelopment, like other ethnic enclaves of the Hill District and East Liberty would be decades later.

Endowed with Splendor

Pittsburgh's Chinatown, the region's early Asian American history, arguably originated in Germany—southwest Germany, from where a charismatic religious leader, Johann Georg Rapp, fled to America with followers to establish a communal, self-sustaining society preparing for the Second Coming. Beginning in 1804, Rapp and his followers established three utopian, if celibate, communities in the United States. The first, Harmonie (Harmony), was along the banks of Connoquenessing Creek, where years later I would fly-fish for smallmouth bass. The Harmony Society sold Harmonie to the Mennonites, but unlike Pennsylvania's more iconic Christian communal societies, Rapp's followers were far from ascetic isolates. They were model Jeffersonians, blending agriculture and industry. After relocating to Indiana, they again sold their varied assets and in 1825 established their final community, Ökonomie (Economy) along the Beaver River north of Pittsburgh. The Rappites developed extensive investments in railroads, steel, mining, and oil that spurred the region's industrial expansion and connected them to the developing global economy.[6] Rapp died in 1847, but a group of senior leaders continued to manage the society's diverse economic interests, which included one of the nation's first silk mills, a distillery, brewery, and a cutlery factory in nearby Beaver Falls, the future birthplace of Joe Namath, who would become known across America as "Broadway Joe."

The society purchased the land, plotted it out, and sold homes to the workers of the then robust manufacturing town, nearly entirely white: only 1 percent of its population listed as "colored" in the 1870 census. The

Beaver Falls Cutlery Company, which employed roughly 10 percent of the town's population then, was owned almost entirely by the society but managed by the nonmembers John and Henry Reeves. Concerned about maintaining the company's profitability under the pressures of high labor costs and European competition, the brothers decided to hire three hundred Chinese laborers to do the forging, grinding, polishing, and packing of the company's wares.[7]

Not surprisingly, the plan alarmed workers, suspicious of the company's motives, their fears fed by the national debate on banning Chinese labor. Beginning in the mid-1800s, the Chinese began immigrating in large numbers to the United States, mainly to the West Coast, some already under contract to American businesses looking for cheap, trouble-free workers. In Sierra Nevada railroad tunnels, Idaho placer mines, Bay Area tobacco shops, Alaskan salmon canneries and eastward, Chinese labored. And they were often feared, reviled. In the late 1800s the Chinese were run out of hundreds of towns across the West and scores were beaten, hanged, and shot—typically with no consequences—in infamous cases such as those in Los Angeles and Rock Springs, and at sites absent from public history and only recorded in suggestive news snippets: "Two Chinamen who confessed to being the murderers of Omera, in Delnorte county, were lynched by a mob at Happy Camp in that county."[8]

As early as 1870 Pittsburgh media warned about the threat of Chinese "coolie labor," although in 1862 Congress had already banned such workers from entry into the country. Noting the recent arrival of Chinese workers in Massachusetts and "negroes from Virginia," the *Pittsburgh Daily Post* warned, "The white laborers there must be filled with admiration for the Radical monopolists, who give them the choice of reduced wages or vagrancy. How long before the same thing is inaugurated here?" The paper reported "upon pretty good authority that steps are being taken to import a large number of Chinese to Pittsburgh," but it would be several years before Pittsburgh's population of Celestials surpassed that of tiny Beaver Falls, where in the mid-1870s hundreds lived.[9]

The first group of approximately one hundred workers, under four-year-term contracts, arrived in June 1872 and entered an angry town. The Mansion House, a large two-story stone building surrounded by a high fence, was their home in Beaver Falls, including during the initial "state of siege."[10] The men, between the ages of twelve and fifty-five, began work at 6:30 in the morning and labored until 6:00 p.m., six days a week and for a maximum of twenty-five gold dollars a month. White workers at the factory were paid between seventy and eighty dollars a month.[11] While management remained technically faithful to its pledge not to replace white workers with the Chinese, managers began to move some white workers into lower-paying jobs, replacing them with the now skilled Chinese. White workers quit. Locals established Anti-Coolie Labor Association groups in surrounding towns, including Pittsburgh, where the *Pittsburgh Post* decried the company's preference for "a lot of irreclaimable heathens" over "our own race of people."[12] The papers encouraged readers to assert their rejection of the Chinese by voting against Republican candidates in upcoming elections, and concerned residents around Beaver Falls held public meetings to organize an appeal to the Harmonist Society and the legislature. In January 1873, locals petitioned the United States Congress to bar Chinese laborers from entry into the United States; and in February 1873, a large meeting was held to discuss a series of resolutions to present to the Harmony Society, now winnowed down to about one hundred members, its ranks depleted since Rapp's death in 1847.

On February 1, the Council of Elders met with a delegation of locals, and the men, some speaking in German, appealed to their common ties as Germans and as Christians.[13] Though some in Penn's colony had viewed German immigration as a grave threat to its English character, Germans had by then melded into the fabric of the region's social life. But, the council's response, despite its Christian allusions, disappointed the delegates, for the Harmonists insisted on using Chinese labor. Elders noted that the company's directors had taken this business measure "as a last desperate effort to save it from utter ruin" and, thus, the Chinese were to be welcomed.[14] They cited scripture:

> Surely you will summon nations you know not
> and nations you do not know will come running to you,
> because of the LORD your God,
> the Holy One of Israel,
> for he has endowed you with splendor.[15]

To demonstrate their concern for the townspeople, the elders offered to donate the factory's profits over the next eight years to public works in Beaver Falls, but they warned that any unlawful acts against the company would be followed by their divestiture. Apparently, the people of Beaver Falls did not share the prophecy or feel any holy "splendor"; and on March 19, a resolution was introduced before the Pennsylvania Senate to bar Chinese labor. However, like its federal counterpart, the legislation died in committee. Workers in local towns called for a boycott of the company's products and the businesses of those who supported "Cooly labor." Residents in neighboring New Castle unanimously adopted a set of resolutions in April boycotting the company and committing to organize against the importation of Chinese workers, a "semi-civilized race . . . who can never become assimilated to Americans, who have no intention to become citizens, who will never defend our country against the wrongs of other nations . . . and who are content to work for a paltry pittance."[16]

Despite the company's efforts, the factory continued to lose money and by 1886 it shut down. Management's goal of employing three hundred Chinese workers had never been realized; no more than two hundred were employed there at a time. Despite their image as "industrious and peaceable," a contrast to the white workers who possessed a troubling "disposition to dictate in the management" of the factory, they turned out to be cheap—but not docile workers.[17] As early as December of 1872, they went on strike. And in June 1873, angered over the enforcement of the prohibition on gambling and opium smoking in their contract, nearly half the Chinese workers walked off the job and boarded a train to Pittsburgh, and many headed back to the Louisiana plantations. In June of the following year there was a dramatic confrontation between the labor boss, Ah Chuck, and a group of several dozen workers who attacked his home, armed with a rope, rocks, readily available knives, and pistols, too. Thirteen of the men were arrested but later released and promptly fired. The last of the Chinese cutlery workers left Beaver Falls by 1877, and in the 1880 census no Chinese were recorded there.

John Chinaman, Laundryman

With occupational opportunities limited to those that white people would allow them, the nearly all-male Chinese population in the US and locally concentrated in less desirable occupational niches in the industrial economy, service work. The local foment created by the Beaver Falls Chinese underscored societal anxieties about Chinese migration and restricted economic opportunities in the Steel City's expanding manufacturing base for nonwhites. The Pittsburgh Survey, one of the most impressive documentations of urban life in early twentieth-century America, was produced by the newly established Russell Sage Foundation in New York, which sent dozens of investigators to the burgeoning industrial city of diverse peoples from 1907 to 1908 to study living and working conditions. The survey did not record a single Chinese worker in the city's mills. But with increasing urbanization and industrialization, demand for laundry services increased, especially in urban centers as women left domestic work, and men's fashion trends and expanding wardrobes grew demand.[18]

Chinese laundrymen, as they had in rural Western mining towns, migrated to Eastern cities like Pittsburgh. In January 1874, the *Pittsburgh Daily Post* reported that a "colony of the Beaver Falls Chinese" in Pittsburgh—laundrymen. The article, "John Chinaman as a Policeman," laughingly recounted one of the Chinese grabbing a local boy who vandalized his store. "You throwee nother stone through my window me shootee you." The laundryman had brought the boy to the police station but hastily fled upon seeing the police enter "with seven or eight Ethiopians."[19]

By 1880 there were 7 Chinese-owned laundries in Pittsburgh and that number ballooned to 160 by 1930. They had a separate category in the city business directory.[20] The work was dirty, arduous; and although stigmatized, it was better paying and more autonomous than laboring in one of the region's smoky mills. The most thorough history of the region's Chinese population indicates that salaries of laundry workers were better than that of immigrant mill workers, at times exceedingly so. One laundry owner in Ambridge, the town the American Bridge Company purchased from the remaining Harmonists and renamed, returned to China with an impressive $35,000 in hand.[21]

With economic success, though, came the wrath of white residents especially as white women increasingly entered the laundry industry as steam laundries expanded. A labor-organizing hotbed, Pittsburgh was a center of gravity for anti-Chinese activism. Local papers supported federal measures to curtail Chinese immigration and, during its 1881 Pittsburgh Congress, the American Federation of Labor (AFL) passed a resolution in support of Chinese exclusion, a measure Congress had passed in 1878. President Hayes vetoed the legislation, which obviously violated the existing United States treaty agreement with China. In response Democrats tried unsuccessfully to impeach him and the "Chinese Problem" became an increasingly major point of debate in presidential politics. Locally, in 1888, the powerful Knights of Labor, which later explicitly banned Chinese from membership, held a joint meeting with laundry owners to organize a boycott and "drive out the Chinese laundries." During the meeting, the Knights reported information furnished by the National Laundrymen's Association that twenty-seven Chinese laundries had opened locally in just the past several months. A committee of laundry owners reported that the Chinese were "not organized labor. They work night and day, and their habits enable them to live cheaper and laundry [sic] clothes cheaper than possible for Americans."[22] This boycott was one of many during the period by labor groups targeting Chinese-operated laundries in the East. In 1899, there was another boycott push among the local cigar makers' union, inspired by

1.1 Chinese Laundry, Pittsburgh, 1939. Reproduced by permission from Pittsburgh City Photographer Collection, University of Pittsburgh.

the lead of Erie union brethren who were threatening "to exterminate the Chinese in that city." The secretary of the Pittsburgh assembly commended the Erie effort and expressed support for a widespread boycott of the Chinese. He noted the presence of over 684 Chinese laundry workers in the city: "Everyone knows they are of no benefit to the community."[23] However, "John does not intend to give up his laundry business. Oh, no."

To compete with the white-owned steam laundries, local Chinese considered organizing a trust, the Chinese Home Finished Laundry Company, to be owned by Chinese investors. The company would offer the innovation of delivery service, employing jobless Chinese as delivery drivers. This plan was an effort to "fight the steam laundries to the last ditch."[24] Nearly ten years earlier, in 1887, Yee Wah Sing, a "dapper-looking Celestial from Denver," had visited the city seeking support among local laundry owners to invest in a Chinese-run steam laundry that would not undersell American shops but use the same modern equipment. He derided his fellow Chinese for discouraging white patronage, placing their shops "in cellars, regular rat holes." His comments and plan, not surprisingly, were not embraced by his compatriots. A local laundryman, Da Quong, expressed both his offense at the Denver businessman's comments and fear of his plan's repercussions: "We build big laundly; Knights of Labor say Chinaman try to keep Melican gals from makes money to buy clings to eat. Then they say, 'Chinaman, you no goodee; get out of town, go back home.'"[25]

By that point, the United States government had done much to affect such an exodus, successfully passing a ban on Chinese labor that was signed into law in 1882. Ten years later the Geary Act extended the prohibition, and due to further amendments and legislation, Chinese immigration to the nation was essentially cut off well into the mid-twentieth century. The laws also prohibited the naturalization of Chinese residents in the US. And even the "natural" rights of citizenship held by their American-born children had to be fought for in the United States Supreme Court.[26] As a result of these and other prejudicial measures, the Chinese population in the United States dramatically declined in the early half of the twentieth century. In 1920 the number of Chinese laundry workers counted in the census was half the number in 1900.[27] Ending all Chinese immigration had long been supported by pro-labor groups and media in Pittsburgh that railed against the economic and moral threat posed by the Celestials. Even before any significant Chinese community was established, residents were warned: "Their presence here is a constant danger to the communities in which they live. . . . Better to check this evil in time, than allow it to get headway."[28]

Whereas Americans now rely on thousands of Chinese restaurants spread across the country to sate their love of savory egg rolls, sweet and sour pork, and lo mein, legislators, union officials, and media once waged a war against these now iconically American establishments. Chinese immigrants revolutionized our foodways: introducing new foods and flavors and offering cheap, filling food to dine on or to take out that was perfectly suited for the expanding urban working world. Chop suey houses became popular among white consumers who were attracted to their affordable food and exotic atmosphere. Like Chinese laundries, however, Chinese restaurants were also flashpoints of white anxieties about Chinese labor and the balefulness that allegedly defined the Chinese and other Asians.

Pittsburgh newspapers published salacious stories about white women falling prey to wily predatory "Chinamen" who led them to ruin via noodles and opium. Although opiates were lawfully used by scores of white Americans and found in numerous over-the-counter medications, media and others presented Chinese immigrants as the cause of society's opium abuse. In November 1908, one headline about a Chinese restaurant raid warned, "Police Raid in Pittsburgh Discloses Patronage of Place by Daughters of Good Families," girls who fell "prey to opium and Chinamen."[29] The wife of a wealthy Altoona manufacturer was allegedly drugged by her Chinese Sunday school pupil and kidnapped, ending up in the Steel City's Chinatown where she was rescued by police. Mrs. W. L. Reese recounted, "I had forgotten my home, my husband, my mother, and everyone else, and I looked upon the world and every one in it from Chinese eyes."[30] The 1909 murder in New York City of a female church worker, allegedly by one of her Chinese male Bible school students, captured national attention, and churches pulled female workers from outreach to the Chinese.[31] Pittsburgh media covered the lurid story in detail, and Yee Tang, the superintendent of the city's Second Presbyterian Sunday school reassuringly expressed his view that "Chinamen and American girls are thrown too much together in Sunday-schools," and he barred such future intermingling of the races.[32]

In the early 1900s, unions across the country announced boycotts targeting Chinese restaurants, and often those of other Asians, and insisted that members participate to quash the economic and moral threats posed by Chinese in America to white men and their protectees, white women.[33] Unions like the AFL had lobbied successfully for Chinese exclusion, but when boycotts proved ineffective, the union called for a strict prohibition on women frequenting or working in a Chinese restaurant. Despite its small and segregated Chinese population, in 1910 Pittsburgh city government passed legislation targeting Chinese restaurants where "young men and women describe . . . sights and sounds and incidents . . . which, if published would chill the blood of the right-minded citizen." Although the captain of detectives stated, "We never have any trouble with those restaurants,"[34] the city council overwhelmingly passed an especially harsh ordinance that would force the businesses to close by midnight, not serve alcohol, bar any girls and women from entry, and require licensure to only those of "good moral character."[35] The local Chinese-American Merchants' Association fought back: hiring an attorney to battle the measure, announcing their refusal to comply if the ordinance became law, and seeking the support of Chinese diplomats in Washington. However, that proved unnecessary when Mayor William A. Magee vetoed the legislation, calling it "class legislation" and "plainly illegal."[36] The proposed measure's history demonstrates the pernicious legal and extralegal means locals wielded to maintain the social order and how at this time Chinese and also newer white immigrant workers remained on the outside. After the measure's veto, the local district attorney in nearby Greensburg directed a ban on Chinese, French, and Italian restaurants and State Constabulary officers raided several, including "the finest in Greensburg" where "pretty French and Italian girls" served the "the youth of the town." The police confiscated liquor and arrested not only the owners but also "a large number of foreigners who are held as witnesses."[37]

Though local media, unions, and white laborers decried the presence of

Chinese in the Steel City, there were also those, as in Beaver Falls, who advocated for their right and fitness to join society. This was especially true of those who stood to profit from their inclusion, from the growing ties between China and the United States that flowed from American colonial expansion. During a meeting in 1893, the burgeoning Pittsburgh Chamber of Commerce passed a resolution denouncing the Geary Act, calling for its repeal. The resolution proclaimed that the legislation was "ill-advised and in bad faith toward a friendly nation and devoid of that statesmanship which should characterize American dealings with foreign powers." During the chamber's meeting, one member denounced the influence of West Coast politicians, in whose territory Chinese had been "murdered by the hundred, simply because they were Chinese," and he affirmed, "They have come here to dwell, they have helped to build this country."[38] When Lee Kin, a local merchant, was apprehended at the Canadian border attempting to reenter the United States, local businessmen appealed to their representative in Congress to intervene.[39] Outside of the business community, additional support for the Chinese came from religious leaders and institutions, such as the Eighth Street Reformed Presbyterian, East Liberty Presbyterian, and the Fourth Avenue Baptist Churches. During a meeting at the latter, Lee To, a missionary sent to work with local Chinese, reported that one-third of them were then attending Sunday school.[40] Outreach to the Chinese had begun over twenty years earlier when the Eighth Street Reformed in Allegheny began a Sabbath school to proselytize to the Chinese. To the charge that the Geary Act was un-American, these religious officials added the indictment of its being un-Christian. The pastor of the Eighth Street Church encouraged other Christians to "prepare to do earnest battle in behalf of the Chinese," whose rights were being trampled like "those of the negro" and "the Indian."[41] The embrace of Christianity by these "heathen" Chinese contradicted the popular portrayal of them as unassimilable, as did their willingness later to register for the draft. As early as 1877, before the Geary Act foreclosed this possibility, Chin Hock became the first naturalized Chinese in Allegheny County.[42]

Unfortunately for Hock and other Asian immigrants, including veterans of World War I, his citizenship would be lost as future legislation and court decisions concretized the conflicting and contrasting Asian nationalities and ethnicities of Asia into a single yellow race. The adjudication of Asian identity narrowed the number of those who could legally claim white identity and its privileged position, and "such discrimination was intended to increase the economic opportunities for whites."[43] Asians' conjoined status in American culture and in law has brought us together in the eyes of Americans but pulled us apart as we have sought to negotiate the racial hierarchy. In the 1890s, local Japanese attended an early meeting in Pittsburgh regarding the mandated federal registration of Chinese in lieu of the Geary Act.[44] The Chinese were resisting. Japanese likely wondered if they were next.

Japanese migration to the United States followed that of the Chinese, and initially they enjoyed less restrictive immigration laws than the Chinese due to the rise of Japan as an international power during the Meiji Restoration. The forced opening of Japan's society by American gunship diplomacy catalyzed a rapid modernization of Japan, including development of a military that soon proved its mettle in the Sino-Japanese War. More favorable immigration policies and Japan's careful monitoring of its emigrant flow resulted in a more diverse, better-educated, and more gender-balanced community in the US than that of the Chinese. Japanese first appear in Pittsburgh census records in 1900. They included English-speaking household servants and students training as electrical workers. By 1910, over three dozen appeared in the census, including the first Hayashi, a cook for a local family. Japanese, like that earlier Hayashi, served some of the area's most powerful and wealthy families. Fresa Fujikawa worked as a butler for William Larimer Mellon, the founder of Gulf Oil and brother of Andrew Mellon, the influential banker and future secretary of the Treasury.

In late 1909, a Japanese commercial delegation, touring the country for three months, visited the Steel City. The men examined a local steel mill, drove through the city's impressive parks, and were sent off with an elaborate gala, "one of the most brilliant social events in the history of the city." A delegate noted his changed impression of the city known best for its suffocating soot and smoke. Kanda Naibu, a member of the Amherst College class of 1879, remarked: "Of course, I expected to find your city smoky. I found it so. But I also found on top of this your educational institutions, your art and music, and your wonderful Carnegie Institute. . . . We should have had at least a day to look at the many beautiful things there."[45]

The delegation's visit was one of several government-sponsored trips to Pittsburgh as both Japanese and Americans sought beneficial relations during the period, with education and trade key foci. The Westinghouse Electric Corporation, founded in Pittsburgh in 1886, began business in Japan as early as 1890.[46] Six Japanese were working in local Westinghouse plants and offices by 1913.[47] The Japanese emperor later bestowed the third Order of the Rising Sun on Westinghouse's president.[48] The early presence of Japanese in local industries, as both blue- and white-collar workers, contrasted with the lives of their fellow Asians: the Chinese, who were mainly consigned to toil in sweltering laundries and restaurant kitchens.

Another Japanese delegation visited the city in late 1917, an educational commission, sponsored by a magazine published by the Japanese government, *Jutsugyono-Nippon* (Industrial Japan). The Japanese had developed a national educational system that borrowed heavily from Western models, including compulsory physical education training, which was part of this mission's investigatory agenda. At Naibu's alma mater, Amherst College—where I now teach—Edward "Doc" Hitchcock had instituted the country's first college physical education training program, one steeped in the doctrine of Muscular Christianity with its emphasis on the equipoise of body, mind, and morality that is most famously captured in the triangle of the influential Young Men's Christian Association (YMCA; the Y). Luther Gulick, the founding superintendent of the Physical Education Department of the International YMCA Training School from 1887 to 1900, developed the Y's particular form of physical education and its key symbol. Gulick stated: "It is quite evident that body, mind and spirit are not entirely separate. What the Triangle stands for is a balanced development, a powerful, sane development of all these aspects in relation to each other."[49] At the core of Doc Hitchcock's plan were mandated group exercises—rhythmic routines with light weights accompanied by music—and the careful and comprehensive measurement and monitoring of his charges' bodies. The Japanese government invited a disciple of Hitchcock's, George Leland, to Japan where he helped design Japan's educational program and teacher training school based on this doctrine of interconnectedness of mind, body, and spirit. The Japanese readily embraced the plan's emphasis on training the body and American games, too, especially baseball, which quickly took root across the Pacific.[50]

The Japanese educational system merged Western sporting practices with existing Japanese practices, such as judo. During their Pittsburgh visit, delegation members were pleased to hear that the American military trained fighting men in the martial art, for Japanese school gymnasiums too had become a site for the "fusion of the values of the samurai with the Victorian values of manliness."[51] The Japanese visitors' itinerary therefore included not only meetings with local public and college officials, but visits to the Carnegie Homestead steel plant, the site of a famous 1892 labor strike, and to a football game between the University of Pittsburgh and Carnegie Tech (later Carnegie Mellon University). The educators were evaluating college athletics in the US and considering what role American football might play in shaping Japanese youth for the new global era. They were impressed: "The game is, as you might say here in America, most stirring. We love its excitement and will make our report to our school system with the recommendation that the game as played in this country be introduced into Japan."[52]

Published accounts of football's evolution in Japan typically place Americans at the center of the story, and it is true that Americans in Japan were crucial to its development, but this delegation's response to the gridiron indicates an earlier embrace of the game. One Japanese teacher, Heita Okabe, was pivotal in establishing Japanese football. Okabe, an accomplished judo master and adept soccer, baseball, and tennis player, embodied the era's transnational cultural blending. He moved to Chicago to learn more about American sports at the University of Chicago, where the legendary Amos Alonzo Stagg was the football coach after leaving the International YMCA Training School in Springfield, Massachusetts. Okabe tried out for the freshman football team and the "little Jap" made quite an impression at his first practice when "in a few minutes he learned to like the tackling trick so well he would pull to earth the first man who got in his way."[53] Impressed with the Japanese teacher's "speed and aptitude in the gridiron melees ... on the practice field," Stagg put him on his freshman squad.[54]

Upon his return to Japan, Okabe became a one-man football evangelist. He taught the game to students, began publishing accounts of the sport, and in 1925 penned the first Japanese manual of the game.[55] However, it was a natural disaster that ultimately led to football's institutionalization: the Great Kantō Earthquake that killed over 140,000 Japanese in 1923. Western nations and institutions offered aid to the Japanese, including the YMCA, whose relief staff included an American missionary, Paul Rusch. In 1934, while teaching economics at Rikkyo University, Rusch organized the first collegiate football league. The sport's growth was further catalyzed by the influx of Americans to Japan, including young, second-generation Japanese Americans, the Nisei. The first official collegiate clash in Japan was appropriately held on Thanksgiving Day and witnessed by an enthusiastic twenty thousand fans. Over the next several years, the game's popularity grew, and an All-Star team of Japanese college players toured the US in 1936.

Chinatown, My Chinatown

In 1915, the American Quartet recorded an upbeat jazz tune, "Chinatown, My Chinatown." It became a number one record and eventually a standard recorded by the jazz stars Al Jolson, Louis Armstrong, Louis Prima, and Bing Crosby. With a cheery chorus—

Chinatown, my Chinatown,
Where the lights are low,
Hearts that know no other land,
Drifting to and fro,
Dreamy, dreamy Chinatown,
Almond eyes of brown,
Heart seems light and life seems bright,
In dreamy Chinatown.[56]

—it captured the resurrection of Chinatown in the American mind after its residents had been deemed outside of civic life, and in many cities, as in Pittsburgh, were vanishing. Local press had portrayed Chinatown as "the filthiest place in all of Christendom," but by the late 1920s Chinatown was a scenic relic of intriguing people.[57] It was like one of those elaborate dioramas at Andrew Carnegie's marble cultural palace where the Japanese hoped to linger. Immigration legislation and judicial decisions had by then deemed Chinese and other Asians ineligible for immigration and naturalization, literally "nonwhite" and the Chinese population in Pittsburgh and elsewhere began a steep decline.

Pittsburgh's Chinatown had been centered in various downtown locales but was eventually situated along Second and Third Avenues near Grant Street. It was a place filled with "the wall of strange music, the twang of voices lifted in weird choruses that clink like soft gongs." During the New Year "in the city where the mills of industrial civilization rumble, the yellow people of the east (were) very gay."[58] But, as with many Pittsburgh neighborhoods decades later, modernity mandated Chinatown's obsolescence. The construction in 1921 of the Boulevard of the Allies, running from downtown to the expanding Oakland district, resulted in the destruction of half the buildings in Chinatown. On the demolition of "picturesque" Chinatown, the *Pittsburgh Daily Post* noted, "the dingy shops will have to give way to greater structures in keeping with the widening project and the dignity of the boulevard."[59] The impact of the Great Depression in the following decade further depopulated Chinatown, by then "a desolate, dank corner under the approach to the Boulevard of the Allies."[60] Only a few hundred Chinese residents and a handful of businesses remained.

Progress also claimed the Chinese laundryman, as steam laundries supplanted the "picturesque Orientals." The number of Chinese laundries began declining from the 1920s onward, a trend that, as the *Pittsburgh Press* noted, was not all bad for John, for the change had "emancipated him from his slaving toil." The white consumer, however, was saddled with a laundry bill that would either "blind or stagger" him.[61] In later years local shops not only became romantic symbols of a bygone early Pittsburgh, but their operators prized craft workers in a technological era of impersonal mass production. In 1974, a newspaper reporter for the *Pittsburgh Post-Gazette*, one of the few city papers still printing, wrote an article recalling those "tiny shops standing in virtually every block of the more heavily industrialized parts of the city."[62] By this time, there were fewer than twenty Chinese laundries in the city, but dozens of Chinese restaurants.[63] Chinatown, once the city's "most romantic district," had only a few families.[64] And by the 1980s, when only a handful of Chinese-operated laundries remained, they catered to the city's elite, including the then mayor, Richard Caliguiri. Due to high demand, they typically refused new customers.[65]

In the late 1980s during Caliguiri's administration, the city's Urban Redevelopment Authority (URA) began negotiating with a local Chinese restaurateur and Hong Kong developers to create a new Asian Trade Center, dubbed a new Chinatown, on eight acres of waterfront property along Pittsburgh's North Shore, between the Seventh and Ninth Street Bridges, the spans later named after the local legends Andy Warhol and Rachel Carson. The URA emphasized its desire to develop solely housing on the site and rejected the proposal.[66] Today, it is home to the impressive undulating glass corporate office of Alcoa, looking out onto the now cleaned up Allegheny and out-of-town tourists taking riverboat cruises and selfies.

White Lines of Play

During Chinatown's demolition, a newspaper writer described finding among the ruins "three or four discarded hats, remnants of large dominoes, cards and other games."[67] Chinatown was long associated with such forms of recreation, and as early as 1880 there were two gambling houses "the Celestials frequent[ed] nightly."[68] Card games, including poker, as well as traditional games of chance such as fan-tan, pai gow, and mah-jongg, which many Jewish Americans later adopted, were popular diversions among local Chinese. At one time, as many as twenty gambling houses were catering to them.[69] By the 1890s local newspapers covered raids on Chinese gambling dens, including one where gamblers were "playing some kind of game with American cards."[70] At times such unfamiliarity with Chinese games alone led suspicious police to arrest players.[71]

Unlike in other regions with larger Chinese communities or less rigid social borders, such as Philadelphia, Chinese in Pittsburgh apparently rarely engaged with other locals in the burgeoning world of American recreation. In Kansas City in the 1890s, a Chinese laundry sponsored its own

Negro League Grays, the Walls Laundry Grays.[72] And among the class of Chinese still allowed temporary entry to the US—merchants, diplomats, and students—true sports stars emerged. By the late 1800s, Chinese and other Asians in the United States had not only adopted American sports like baseball, but athletes, sporting practices, coaching, and equipment were moving across transnational circuits throughout the Pacific. American politicians viewed sport as both a necessary recreation for its military and an important tool to shape the minds and souls of nonwhite residents across the Pacific. The sports historian Gerald Gems summarizes the role of baseball in America's empire: "Baseball taught American values inherent in the national game, such as teamwork on defense, individualism on offense, and the efficiency, order, and discipline imposed by an umpire."[73]

This cross-cultural exchange included young Chinese men and women who came to the US as part of government-sponsored educational programs: the Chinese Educational Mission and the Boxer Indemnity Scholarship Program. After the unsuccessful Boxer Rebellion to purge China of its Western colonizers and their influence, China paid over $300 million in reparations to the victors, including Uncle Sam. To compensate China's overpayment in reparations, President Roosevelt's administration established a fund to support Chinese study at American educational institutions. Americans hoped to influence the future development of China's ruling elite and curry favorable trade and diplomatic relations. Between 1909 and 1929, the fund supported the education of over 1,300 young men and women in places like Oberlin, Ohio State, Yale, and the University of Pittsburgh.[74] Many of them excelled in sport, especially soccer in collegiate competition and leagues across the country, including Pennsylvania and were covered in Pittsburgh media.

In an April 1911 article, "Chinese Are Adepts at the Soccer Game" the Pittsburgh Press recounted how the Chinese had "begun to show an athletic ability that was unsuspected before."[75] Later that year Yale's C. L. Tan was named an All-American. New York soon fielded all-Chinese teams with rosters composed of college students from the area.[76] And in 1920, an All-Chinese side began playing in the Bethlehem League.[77] The New York team was managed by the secretary of the United States Football Association and played in the National Challenge Cup, precursor to a national tournament that local sides would later win.[78] A match pitting the New Yorkers against a team of Bridgeport, Connecticut, all-stars was boldly touted then as "the greatest soccer game in the history of the Connecticut State Football Association," and pulled in six thousand fans.[79] The Chinese tied the local all-stars and, although "the Chinamen came . . .

as perfect strangers ... their brilliant and clever playing made them many friends in a very short time."[80] Their manager hoped they would soon be touring other cities, including Bethlehem and Pittsburgh.[81] It seems they never made it across the Alleghenies. However, Asian athletes moving along these transnational circuits did play in the Steel City region, participating in the rapidly expanding and various recreational platforms of the United States, which offered the chance to play at work and increasingly to play for work.

By the early 1900s, American military and cultural power had spread across the globe, extending the reach of the country's favored sports. None was more successful than baseball. By 1900 there were already connected but distinct sites of baseball play across the Pacific, especially between the US and Japan, and the game's cultural meaning was far more complicated than a one-way exchange of American values. As Sayuri Guthrie-Shimizu writes of the relationship between the two nations, "People from various social strata, along with capital, commodities, technology, and less visibly, ideas, knowledge, ambitions, and dreams, flowed between the two centralizing nation-states through increasingly layered and intertwined material, human and institutional networks."[82] American educators, military and religious officials, and commercial interests helped introduce baseball to Japan, where it was rapidly incorporated into the operations of the evolving nation-state and its structures. Though the game was an American import, its Japanese supporters associated it with "traditional Japanese virtues of loyalty, honor and manly courage."[83] Japanese immigrants then transmitted their baseball culture to the United States, so that baseball in these communities reflected a complex blending of cultural values not merely assimilation to American ones.[84]

As in China, educational institutions were crucial vehicles for this transcultural exchange and, by the turn of the century, Japanese students were not only studying in American colleges along with Chinese students but also traveling here to play ball. In 1890 a team from Keio University sailed to the US and matched up against college nines, including West Virginia University and Allegheny College, where the "Japs" beat the Americans "at their own game."[85] They were followed in 1901 by a team from Waseda University that had already battled the University of Wisconsin in Japan, as American college and professional teams were also now barnstorming the Pacific. Local media gave less attention to the Waseda team's sojourn but covered the development of Japanese baseball and the growing strength of its teams. The *Pittsburgh Press* informed readers "Baseball Is Thriving Now in Old Japan" and that its universities had

"Crackerjack Nines."[86] However, it was a traveling team from the nation's new territories that most impressed American media as to the potential of Asian athleticism and underscored the problematic racial boundaries that American sport promoted.

In December 1911, the *Pittsburgh Daily Post* announced "Chinks to Invade United States."[87] The writer alluded not to an impending military invasion, but to the upcoming mainland tour of a "Chinese baseball club" of Hawaiian university students.[88] The Hawaiian Islands were another site where American Protestant missionaries, military officials, and educators had spread the gospel of the baseball diamond. America's illegal annexation of the nation and deposing of its monarchy accelerated the decline of native sporting practices such as the allegedly amoral surfing—derided by American colonizers—and catalyzed the supremacy of American sports.[89] Due to white colonization and the labor demands of the plantation-based economy, the islands were a heterogeneous mix of Asians, Hawaiians, and haoles (white people), and so was Hawaiian baseball. The game was played across ethnic and racial lines in sometimes ugly clashes and it was dominated by Asian and mixed-race players.

The all-Chinese team was backed by prominent Chinese Hawaiians and local business leaders. The former sought to counter anti-Chinese racism and instill ethnic pride, while the latter sought financial investment in the emerging Hawaiian economy.[90] From 1912 to 1916, versions of the team toured the US mainland, playing a range of amateur, collegiate, semiprofessional and professional nines across the nation. They were wildly popular in some locales, played before crowds exceeding ten thousand, and won a lot of games with their aggressive baserunning and skillful pitching. During their inaugural tour "the University of Hawii [sic] team" was scheduled to play the University of Pittsburgh's nine on June 12 at the Pirates' lavish new park, Forbes Field.[91] The Pittsburgh Pirates were owned by the German Jewish immigrant Barney Dreyfuss, who built a stadium that anticipated the design of modern ballparks, the increasing popularity and commercialism of the game, and the evolution of the city, too. With its premium-priced tickets, box seats, inclined ramps, elevators, telephones, and tiered grandstands of concrete and steel, it set the standard for future ballparks and hinted at the contemporary monetized sports arena. Unfortunately for fans, it was announced in May that the team's management had canceled the match as "they were unable to secure other games in the section."[92] They did catch a thrilling doubleheader matchup of the Pirates against the cross-state rival Philadelphia Phillies in August.[93] Later they were on their way to Cleveland after being denied lodging in nearby

Franklin after "trouncing the local players."[94] The following month they played the local McBrides before five hundred fans in Homestead and against whom they "piled up ten runs."[95]

The following year "the Chinese team" was back in town, staying at the Seventh Avenue Hotel, their status as elite student athletes and Chinese Hawaiians allowing them unique mobility for nonwhite players. Next up was local Washington and Jefferson College. The Chinese won 14–3 and a few days later "outclassed" Allegheny College, after "the Celestials" suffered an "onslaught" upon Grove City College.[96] In early September they were back in town to see the Bucs again win both games of a doubleheader.[97] The Celestial Hawaiians, from a fictitious Hawaiian university, with rosters of an increasingly diverse ethnic makeup, continued to visit the area until their last tour in 1916.

The Hawaiians were always more popular in eastern Pennsylvania, and local coverage of their exploits waned over time. Their draw was due to novelty based in their loaded racialized and colonized identities as "alien" Asians and "exotic" Hawaiians, logic that also justified their exclusion from American institutions and spaces. These conceptions were apparent in the terminology media used to define them: their consistent habit of collapsing the players' ethnic, racial, national, linguistic, and cultural identities into an objectionable mass. One sportswriter expressed astonishment and more on witnessing the slick play and success of the Hawaiians against the Duquesne University Dukes: "Upon what food were the members of the Chinese university team of Honolulu raised that they perform such wonders upon the baseball battlefields of Uncle Sam's land? . . . Right here in the Smoky City the Orientals administered a defeat in a large dose to a team largely Irish. . . . They have an unnatural swiftness, which, at times, looks 'spooky.'"[98]

This writer's comment well defined the anxiety over race that the success of these Hawaiians incited within the institution of baseball. Since baseball had banned Black players via a contradictorily named gentleman's agreement, it was necessary to maintain a clear racial boundary in the national pastime. But in an increasingly racially diverse society incorporating millions of nonwhite people, who fell where? And who or what precisely were these athletes?

On January 29, 1915, readers of the *Pittsburgh Press* were warned that a "Yellow Peril" was trying out for the Chicago White Sox of major league baseball. Lai Tin, who had "been already dubbed by the fans—'The Yellow Peril,'" was a "clever fielder" and "crack batter"[99] who captained the Hawaiian barnstormers. The success of the island nine had received significant at-

1.2 Chinese Hawaiian Baseball Team, 1914. Courtesy of Bain News Service, Library of Congress Prints and Photographs Division.

tention from the nation's burgeoning sports media and several players attracted the interest of pro teams. Though the *Pittsburgh Press* writer's use of "Yellow Peril" may have been meant to be humorous, anti-Chinese hate was no joke. Allowing Chinese or any nonwhite players more than a transitory platform in the iconic American game was too much for many in the National Pastime.

Lang Akana, a player of Chinese and Hawaiian heritage, signed with the Spokane Indians of the Pacific Coast League at the same time as his teammate but reportedly would not travel back from his "home in the Philippine Islands" and was picked up by the Portland Beavers of the Pacific Coast League (PCL).[100] Settlers had established Oregon as a white refuge and enacted scores of measures to ban Black migrants and disempower nonwhite ones, including Asians. It is unsurprising given this history that PCL team members who had played in Hawaii began protesting the possible intrusion of the Hawaiian player and his ilk. Portland's manager, Walter McCredie, explained the team's decision to release "the foreigner."[101] Having heard from players that his "poi-eating prodigy" was "as dark as Jack Johnson," the Black reigning heavyweight boxing champion, the manager felt he had no choice. "His skin's too dark," McCredie told the press. The association of Akana with Jack Johnson was notable since Johnson was a trigger of white anxieties, having supplanted a white champion in the most masculine of sports and openly flaunting the racial and sexual boundaries of the era by consorting with white women. The Beavers manager regretted not only Akana's treatment, but the color line that matched the field's lines of play: "I don't think the color of the skin ought to be a barrier in baseball. . . . If I had my say, the negro would be welcome inside the fold."[102]

Like his teammates, Lai would never crack a major league lineup. Yet he and several others stayed on the mainland and played often stellar baseball on minor league, amateur and semiprofessional teams, especially in the Philadelphia and New York areas. In 1918, Lai, known then as Buck or Bill, was playing for the Bridgeport Americans of the Eastern League. In an exhibition game against the Pittsburgh Pirates, the "heathen Chinese . . . helped scuttle the Pirate ship."[103] This prompted the Pirates manager Hugo Bezdek to claim, "I cannot see any reason why Lai should not be in the big leagues."[104] Lai did not get another chance to make "The Show" until many years later, and in the meantime he worked for the Pennsylvania Railroad, raised his mixed-race family, and continued competing in baseball and other sports, such as track. At the annual Olympics of the Pennsylvania rail system in 1923, he incited a "tremor when he leaped over the sawdust pit for a distance of 22 feet 8 and 1/8th inches."[105] Despite his reputation as a gifted athlete, news of his signing with the New York Giants in 1928 incited familiar racist tropes. The popular baseball writer Will Wedge wrote: "You can't go into the nearest hand laundry and drag the Chink from behind the counter and find that he knows how to use a finger mitt. Most Chinks, if given a baseball bat, would think it was an overgrown chop stick [sic] and use it to fish wet wash out of the washtub."[106] The Hawaiian players like Lai, of course, were natural citizens of the American nation-state, many of them World War I veterans. Lai's former teammate, the spitballer Sergeant Apau Kau was killed by German gunfire in November 1918. Despite their range of exceptional skill and commitment to American life, they remained racially marked temporary workers in a transnational circuit of commercial baseball.

Like the Chinese and Japanese athletes in American colleges, these Hawaiian baseball players were also typically highly educated young men of means or the middle class. They and early Chinese residents of Pittsburgh arrived in time for the founding of the Pittsburgh Pirates and the building of municipal playgrounds and swimming pools—yet there is scant evidence that Chinese residents of the city took in a day at the Bucs' impressive ballpark. And participation was a rare exception available to that class of privileged Chinese migrants who could find a comfortable place in western Pennsylvania. The Homestead Steelworks' capable team included the second baseman Mon Chung, a Chinese employee who "was deluged with offers to sign with various league teams" after helping his nine claim the United States Steel Championship in 1913. Chung was from a wealthy family, working at the mill for experience and in no need of money and claimed he "only plays the game for the sport."[107] The young infielder and industrial worker was another Boxer Indemnity Scholar and an alumnus of Yale College. Yet even those in this acculturated set were suspicious given their, well, nature. And since by 1913 "scores" of "Orientals" were "here under such guise," the virulent anti-Asian commissioner general of immigration, Anthony Caminetti, argued that a "closer check be kept on Orientals admitted to the United States."[108]

From a Desolate, Dank Place

Not until the 1940s did the kind of outreach offered to kids in the Hill District and other neighborhoods, through settlement houses, philanthropic organizations, and government agencies, find the needy children of Pittsburgh's Chinatown. By then the growing incursions of Japan into China, including its 1931 invasion of Manchuria, had mushroomed into an all-out war in Asia. Given Japan's earlier invasion of China and the long history of conflict between China and Japan, local Chinese proved adept Japanese haters, at times out in front of their white counterparts. As early as 1932, Chinatown shops displayed signs: "Boycott Jap Goods," and the Japanese raid in Hawaii was met the next day with celebration in Chinatown.[109] Even laundrymen took the day off.[110] As the war progressed and American views of the Chinese softened, the Japanese, regardless of nationality, became the unredeemable Asians. Chinese locals, like the laundryman Yee Poo, signed up to fight them. Yee's picture appeared in the local news, where he declared his willingness to fight "because he hates the Japs so much."[111] The neighborhood always marked as apart was now filled with "great patriotism" as blue stars appeared next to hand-painted Chinese characters on the shop windows of anxious parents.[112] National and local media of the time portrayed the Chinese in increasingly sympathetic terms, and in 1940 Santa Claus's first venture into Pittsburgh's Chinatown was widely reported: "Slant eyes opened with wonder and shown with joy," upon meeting Saint Nick. Journalists expected the kids to be adorned in the "colorful ceremonial garb of the Orient."[113] But the "small Orientals" in the news photos were all in contemporaneous American fashions, including little Alvin Lee, "solemn in a black suit."[114] Despite the media's claims, an earlier Santa Claus had lived in the neighborhood. A. J. Lee, a successful restaurant owner, decades earlier had celebrated Christmas in Chinatown: tree, presents, and all. By the 1930s, Lee had returned to China and, in a news account of that time, reaction to his Yuletide practices was imagined from the perspective of his wife, "who clung to the old ways of old China and watched with silent bewilderment as new Chinatown applauded the dazzling, candlelit tree in her home."[115] The envisaged response of Mrs. Lee is exceptional in its rarity, as was she.

Another factor that impacted recreation opportunities among the local Chinese was the chronic absence of women. Not until 1888 did the city's putative first Chinese woman resident, a "feminine Mongol," and her "little four-year-old urchin" appear in public. A crowd gathered to witness her waiting on a street corner, "her black hair . . . redolent of perfume and shining with oil . . . decked with fantastic gold and silver pins." The equally florid and crude description captures well the historical American response to the Chinese: simultaneous fascination and repulsion. This woman's feet were particularly noteworthy due to their Lilliputian size, and "her face was a pleasant one, and were it not for the high cheek bones and almond-shaped eyes she would be considered good looking." The woman's husband, a "dried withered up specimen of humanity," was seemingly a merchant, free of the immigration restrictions barring his lower-class countrymen from entry, reentry, or family reunification. American immigration law was particularly harsh on Chinese women.[116] By 1875, Congress had passed a measure specifically targeting Chinese women, the Page Act, barring subjects of "China, Japan, or any other Oriental country" from entering "for lewd and immoral purposes."[117] In addition, many Western states adopted or modified anti-miscegenation laws, specifically barring Chinese or "Mongolians" from marrying white people. When my parents married in the 1950s, their union remained illegal in several states, and not until the 1967 Supreme Court *Loving v. Virginia* decision were such prejudicial laws voided.

In Pittsburgh, Chinese women were especially scarce, and not until 1930 do any appear in official census counts, at which point they made up only 13 percent of the local Chinese population.[118] Given the peripatetic life of many early Chinese immigrants, prejudicial immigration laws, and the related "illegal" immigration status of many, population estimates are, of course, only benchmarks. Newspaper accounts note that Chinese women resided in the city before 1930, but only three in Chinatown by 1903.[119] Their paucity, coupled with the unique character of the city's Chinese population, hindered the establishment of a robust Chinese community and related economic, political, cultural, and recreational resources. Most early Chinese migrants were not only from the same region of China, two counties in Guangdong (Canton), but also from just two families: Yee and Lee. The proscription of intermarriage within the family, coupled with the American social prescription against interracial marriage, meant that Chinese men had scant odds of finding wives in the Steel City. The most complete history of early Chinese in the region credits the "womanless" life of Chinese here with fostering the power of the two influential tongs—Hop Sing and On Leong—and their associated ills. "Without a family, early Chinese in Pittsburgh never had a sense of belonging. . . . Life was monotonous and the feeling of rootlessness was too much to bear. They needed diversions and some kind of recreation so that they might forget the agony and meaninglessness of life. Finally they were drawn closer and closer to the gambling houses where there was not only excitement and a chance to win money, but also companionship that the desolate Chinese needed most."[120]

The limited number of families among the Chinese also exacerbated the rapid population decline begun in the 1920s. By 1940, only 246 Chinese were officially recorded in the census.[121] A few families were left in shrinking Chinatown, with a few dozen children who had "no outdoor play space available."[122] Concerned with the children's situation, in early 1943 a college student from the community, Charles Lee, approached staff at the Irene Kaufmann Settlement House in the Hill District for help. Word of his inquiry eventually reached the secretary of the Community Councils who contacted Helen Green at the American Service Institute (ASI), a community organization founded in 1941 that for twenty years labored to build understanding and tolerance among Pittsburgh's diverse groups. The indefatigable Green soon organized a meeting of stakeholders and began an investigation of the neighborhood's recreational resources. Representatives from the Community Council, American Service Institute, YMCA, and Salvation Army, which had opened a mission to the Chinese in 1937—where Santa first appeared—met to discuss a recreational program for Chinatown's children. The Salvation Army offered its nearby facility, including its gymnasium and pool, and two slots at its summer camp.[123] None of the children had been to camp, had ever "sat on the porch railing in the bright light of the moon" as kids had at other local camps like Camp James Weldon Johnson or Camp Emma.

Representatives from the Young Women's Christian Association (YWCA) did not attend, but later wrote Green, noting that four Chinese girls were already enrolled in their swimming program, and they were willing to extend this opportunity to young boys. Though their summer camp, Camp Redwing, located along Connoquenessing Creek, was full, the YMCA was willing to place these girls on the waiting list in case any cancellations arose.[124] The offers to attend summer camp made by the Salvation Army and the YMCA were in sync with the increasing national and local efforts to democratize camp life: to integrate camps and use the fire council and basketball court to teach racial tolerance.[125]

The South Side–based Brashear Association agreed to supervise the program as a trial outreach effort, with students from the University of Pittsburgh's School of Applied Social Sciences as the boots on the ground. In July 1943 the program began with twenty-five kids, ages three to sixteen. The Salvation Army agreed to open its doors twice a week to the children who, like other deprived local youngsters, required some instruction in play: "Since the project was the first of its kind in the community and the first opportunity these children had for any organized leisure time play experience, the leaders had to proceed in a 'feel your way' process in introducing programs and working with the children."[126] Despite the particularly pressing needs of the Chinese, social agencies often repeated the goal that these efforts were to be community-focused, not exclusively for the benefit of Chinese American children. During the roughly two and a half years of the program's operation, it did include a handful of white children from the neighborhood, but it continued to serve mostly ethnic Chinese kids.

The children made craft projects, such as a lighted streetcar, developed their jitterbug moves, played in the army's indoor sandbox, and were introduced to the YMCA's wholesome invention, volleyball. They marched in War Bond parades, and a few also became members of the Brashear Association. However, the group was soon divided by gender, with boys participating in the more physically demanding activities like swimming and the girls focusing on cooking, dancing, and crafts. Gender segregation was also based on facilities: boys swam at the public Oliver Bath House on the South Side since the pool at the Salvation Army was closed during cold months and not initially available. While the program enforced its own gender restrictions, parents also limited girls' activities. When one mother complained about the filthiness of her daughter after playing in the gym, such play was ended. Another young girl who was an active member was "restricted by her parents' ideas of suitable activity."[127] All the kids relished outdoor ventures; they "preferred going where they could fish, or swim—Highland Park being their preference."[128] But by 1945 attendance was lagging.

Cooperation and support from the adults in Chinatown had always been a challenge, and in late 1945 interested parties of the Downtown Project met to review the modest program. The ambitious goals of expanding the "scope of experiences for these children by integrating others from the neighborhood, and by inviting Chinese children from other parts of the city" were never realized, especially the latter. Attempts at outreach were deemed fruitless. The committee noted that the lack of a liaison to the community—Charles Lee was working now in Ohio—was the crux of the issue. The distribution of brochures in English and Chinese to families, touting "healthy gaming and entertaining opportunities for Chinese kids," and other efforts had not built support.[129] They agreed to enlist the help of the Chinese Mission staff and penned a letter to the unofficial mayor of Chinatown, William Yot, seeking his help. But, as the secretary of the On Leong Association, Yot's reach was limited to only those families affiliated with On Leong. He never replied. Turnover of supervisory staff and conflicts with Mission staff also handicapped the project and evidenced preexisting tensions. Staff noted "conflicts" that were "inherited and created" and the bruised feelings of children who did understand the reason for the changes in staffing. Brashear was plagued then by staffing issues, including the loss of female staff who, as mandated, resigned upon marriage. Brashear's records also indicate the resistance of the Salvation Army Mission to allow the full use of its facility and concerns about the possible theft of its equipment.

The region's racial climate also meant the Downtown Project's reach would not extend much farther than across the river. One boy's desire to join the Boy Scouts was met with "moving in the direction of a troop exclusively for the Chinese Boys," a demographic and logistical impossibility. Meanwhile, the more consistently inclusive Girl Scouts did enroll a Chinatown girl. The well-intentioned project directors, like other peers in the city, also put themselves at odds with their charges when they insisted on defining play and its proper place. In 1945, the Chinese Mission had relocated to the building hosting the project, and its evangelical mission was likely seen as part and parcel of the Downtown Project. Heading for a swim up the street could now mean something ominous to elders, and "children felt uneasy when their activities at the Mission were mentioned." One other "possible source of conflict" noted in association records was "the game of Release": the game we used to call Kick the Can, which involved the taking of prisoners. The Brashear staff was cognizant of "the Salvation Army's objection to this type of activity—and to its questionable value over a period of time."[130] They explained to the children the game's inappropriate nature in a house of God and offered them alternatives. But the boys and girls just wanted to play—define fun for themselves.

Japs by Any Other Name

The increased focus on racial equity during and after World War II was not the only factor influencing the decision to offer play spaces to little Lees and Yees. Chinese had been the base metal from which Americans and their institutions, including sports media, formed subsequent Asian identities—like the catchall term "Mongolian" or "Oriental" that boxed in later Asian immigrants with the Chinese in legal codes and public imaginings. The cleaving of the world into Allied and Axis powers forced Americans to discern carefully among Asian ethnicities now that the Chinese were not adversaries, but partners in armed struggle. To this end, within weeks of Pearl Harbor, the influential *Life* magazine published an anthropological and morphological key to help its addled readers "distinguish friendly Chinese from enemy alien Japs."[131]

Unlike their counterparts along the West Coast and beyond, the few Japanese in Pittsburgh avoided mass incarceration when war broke out between the US and Japan. As in other eastern cities, World War II provided an opportunity to rapidly expand the Steel City's tiny Japanese American population, for local industries to look again for mobile Asians to meet their labor needs. The War Relocation Authority's (WRA) resettlement of released Japanese Americans had created new Nikkei communities in midwestern and eastern cities. The first effort to relocate Japanese Americans in Pittsburgh was initiated in March 1943 by the American Service Institute, acting upon a request by the YWCA.[132] Unfortunately for supporters, a board member, Colonel Shenkel, had leaked word of the plan to the press. Shenkel was also a board member and the Americanization director of the local American Legion. Although Pittsburgh papers were generally evenhanded in their coverage, they displayed confusion about who Japanese Americans were—Americans. The federal government's rationale for their mass removal and incarceration, that there were unidentified disloyals among them—despite the evidence of its own intelligence agencies—tainted public perceptions of Japanese Americans. It made them Japs: potential poisoners of our water supplies. Hirohito's spies. In a letter to a local paper, one woman described their likely reception: "The men in the mills would walk out in a body if only one filthy Jap was to step inside.... The students in school would just about pulverize any little Gremlin of a Jap that would dare show his ugly face."[133]

Jap. The monosyllabic spat-out-of-the-mouth slur. *McHale's Navy* banter. Descriptor of cheap steel. Of cars to bludgeon. Vincent Chin. A convenient abbreviation. What the man leaning out of his brown Cadillac on a leafy Fox Chapel street wanted to know. Was I one? The nickname of a Pirates player back in the day, of my soccer coach in mine. In my face before I even reached the sideline. "Bobby, what did you say to him?!" Trotting off . . . "I said 'In your face . . . white boy.'" Jap. The white noise of growing up.

Though Pittsburgh faced an "acute labor shortage" at the time, Colonel George E. A. Fairley, Pittsburgh's safety director, was opposed to any plan bringing "thousands of Japanese here."[134] The WRA and supporters never envisioned resettling thousands of incarcerated Japanese Americans locally, but noted that "several hundred evacuees could have been easily provided for."[135] After the uproar caused by Shenkel, efforts were put on hold until the following year as ASI and its allies built support, with the religious community taking the lead. A committee was formed that included a wide swath of Protestant religious organizations, Jewish leaders, social service agencies, business interests, and media. The city's prominent Black newspaper, the *Pittsburgh Courier*, and the columnist P. L. Prattis were early supporters. The committee enlisted backing from the local press to prevent repeating prior mishaps and to counter the damaged public image of Japanese Americans. A main vector of persuasion involved promoting the combat exploits of the all-Nisei 442nd Regimental Combat Team, which redeemed Japanese Americans through its bloody sacrifice. The unit's motto, "Go for Broke," said it all. They remain the most decorated military unit in American history.

With publications like "Fighting Nisei," the committee curried favor with labor unions, receiving support from the AFL, United Steelworkers, and Congress of Industrial Organizations leadership. However, despite his solid support, H. J. Heinz III, who had hosted the 1921 Japanese delegation at his home, would not offer positions at his food-processing plants. The company's earlier use of German prisoners of war had incited a backlash among local labor unions.[136] By the time the WRA office finally opened at the end of 1944, over 1,600 relocatees lived in nearby Cleveland; and Chicago had a burgeoning community of over 7,000, including my aunt's family. Despite the paranoid scenarios imagined by detractors, such as the letter writer to the *Pittsburgh Sun-Telegraph*, the first evacuee served by the Pittsburgh office, George Kimura, was successfully placed in the Carnegie-Illinois Steel Corporation's McKees Rocks plant: "His relationships there from the standpoint of the mill were most satisfactory, and the industrial relationship department indicated their willingness to employ as many evacuees as might apply for work."[137] Later, Masao Nozaki was hired by the mill. Kimura left the mill to be with his family after his brother was killed in Italy fighting with the 442nd Regimental Combat Team, but later returned to the area to attend the University of Pittsburgh. Like many other eastern schools, Pitt had opened its doors to Nisei college kids seeking to resume their studies. Penn State University, however, resisted enrolling these men and women until later in the war.[138]

Numerous offers from companies, including Westinghouse, remained unfilled, as resistance to employing the formerly incarcerated Americans continued. In general, smaller mills refused to cooperate with the plan, and in Tarentum and McKeesport, locals protested the proposed use of "Japanese laborers in the steel mills."[139] The demonstrations echoed earlier public outcries to the Chinese and were fueled by similar grievances and racist thoughts. ASI's final report on resettlement bluntly stated: "Pittsburgh is a very cosmopolitan city with major racial and national groups from most every section of the world. Nevertheless, relationships between these national groups have left much to be desired. Intolerance, bigotry, race and national discriminations have been very strong in this section of Pennsylvania."[140]

Robert Collum, the relocation supervisor, described to a key Pittsburgh Citizens Committee member, Arthur Kingsolving of Calvary Episcopal Church, the moral challenge resettlement posed: "The vigor with which the larger American community moves to repair this damage is a real measure of its good faith. That is, I think, the essential of the program in which we are engaged. Its importance is to be gauged not only in the lives of the people with whom we are directly working, but also in the moral life of our country."[141] The mass incarceration of over 112,000 people of Japanese ancestry due to "broad historical causes . . . race prejudice, war hysteria and a failure of political leadership," however dramatic, was but a point along a historical arc in which Asians had been shuffled around the map under the inertial pull of a society organized by race and capital.[142]

The few Asians remaining in the Steel City recount in oral interviews being barred entry at local recreation sites, including popular Kennywood Park's expansive pool upon its opening.[143] They report, in general, being "verbally and physically assaulted" in public spaces.[144] In the 1970s, a young angler trying his luck in the dirty Monongahela River was approached by a police officer who asked to see his license. "You borrowed it from someone else, didn't you?" Although the young man had a valid fishing license, the officer asked him for further identification; he offered his college ID. That seemed finally to assure the cop of this Chinese American's right to wet a line, for the cop walked off, "leaving the rest of the anglers, black and white, unmolested."[145]

Dreaming

When I was in grade school we took one of those too rare field trips to the home of those believers, the Harmonists, in a town now named after a company. It's a National Historic Landmark. White picket fences and pictures of kids rolling hoops with a stick is all I remember. It bored me. They never mentioned labor strikes or anything Chinese.

Like others, Asians came to the Steel City to dream: "I am going to show them that a Chinese is capable of doing more than washing clothes, selling merchandise or serving Chinese dishes to the American public. I am going to buy myself the most beautiful home I can get in Pittsburgh. I prefer it in the Squirrel Hill locality. Then I shall invest in a retinue of servants, buy a good high-power motor car and take things easy while these young Chinese whom I shall train conduct my business."[146] Lee Ah Jing, a Chinatown merchant and real estate investor, and many other Asians never saw their plans realized, but one hundred years later Squirrel Hill looks much like what he envisioned. The football-loving Japanese who visited Pittsburgh never saw their visions come to life, but the game did eventually capture the attention of millions in Asia, thanks to a mixed-race Korean player who would later star on the gridiron back in the Steel City. His story comes later in this narrative of race, labor, and play: of my hometown's persistent nostalgia for blue-collar heroes wrapped in black and gold who harken back to a time and place that is now harder and harder to invoke in a shiny city of tech startups, scenic riverways, and emerging communities of people we have never known.

CORNER KICKS AND COAL

Soccer, Community, and Recalling a Coal Mining Past

Whenever I am in Pittsburgh, "The Burgh" to natives, I make a pilgrimage to a small bell-on-the-door bakery shop in Millvale: a working-class community just miles from downtown. From here you can see the old US Steel Building, now occupied by the area's current largest employer, University of Pittsburgh Medical Center, a big UPMC on its dull side. Millvale is perhaps best known, however, not for its views, but for the spectacular murals of the Croatian artist Maksimilijian (Maxo) Vanka: a bug-eyed Mary grabbing the guns of soldiers, an idyllic bright Croatian countryside, and workers, mothers' sons torn up by the machinery of local industry. Inside Saint Nicholas Croatian Catholic Church are stunning works of cutting social critique like "The Immigrant Mother Raises Her Sons for American Industry." But I come here for croissants.

When I moved back home to help my mom care for my dad, the early morning drives down Route 28, cut through the steep shale cliffsides, with the green Allegheny on the left and the brick triple-decker houses bunched up like bulldogs below, were a respite from the slow decay I witnessed in his body. The croissants were an offering to my mother. She had grown up across the East River from the Manhattan skyline, traveled in Europe with her German parents, and suffered a cultural withdrawal the day my dad announced in an attempt at cheeriness, "We're moving to Pittsburgh!"

Pittsburgh with its stolid black soot-coated buildings and grocery stores where the only lettuce you could buy was destined to be hacked into a wedge. He assured her it was temporary. For fifty years she remained in that same house on a wooded hillside where I was raised. Jean Marc's croissants and palmier were a Madeleine-like transport to Lugano where she vacationed as a young woman, to a time before the grind of food trays, bedpans, a life closing.

The longtime Pittsburgh newspaper columnist Bill O'Neill described his relationship to Pittsburgh as familial, as with a brother, one he loves but who also "drives him nuts."[1] For me, too, Pittsburgh is like one whom I love, will defend to nearly any end, but who similarly, painfully disappoints. To be a Burgher is to have a chip on your shoulder, to fiercely defend the innumerable "jagoffs" who, as a colleague of mine did, use it as the bottom of the plumb line when assessing places one would least desire to visit, let alone live. This view of our home explains, in part, our passion for our sports teams and for places like Jean Marc's modest shop, with its unpretentious Old World cultural offerings. I walk in the door and am asked, "What can I get you, hon?"

When I first began coming here, in the late nineties, the walls were adorned with a few laudatory newspaper clippings, confined to the entrance, but dominated by artifacts memorializing the French national soccer team, Les Bleus, then recent winners not only of the coveted European Cup Championship but also of the greatest prize in all sports, the World Cup. I had admired the French side since the 1982 World Cup: the opportunistic Michel Platini and, most of all, the fearless runs of their left outside, Dominique Rocheteau. He crashed down the wings with elbows swinging and a French version of bad eighties hair, mullet-like: a style that still retains its hold on the heads of many of my fellow Burghers.

The French lost a heartbreaking semifinal to my team, Germany, Die Mannschaft, and Les Bleus would meet a similar fate in 1986. But in the late 1990s they would finally cross the threshold, winning the World Cup in 1998 and the European Cup Championship in 2000, and ostensibly relieve the French psyche of years of self-doubt. Or, as Geoff Hare summates, "Through football, the French have discovered they are not eternal losers."[2]

In the shop were banners, photographs, and posters of these saviors of French identity, including the brilliant midfielder Zinedine Zidane ("Zizou"), whose rise from Marseille ghetto to international soccer Valhalla was part of the mythos that surrounded the 1998 World Cup team. What was most remarkable about watching this side—and what brought both controversy and celebration—was what the team looked like. Unlike the earlier sides of even the 1980s, the French national team was filled with nonwhite players, a kind of athletic Benetton ad that reflected the history of French colonialism and the increasingly liberal view of who constitutes a citizen when it comes to soccer talent. Players like Youri Djorkaeff, Lilian Thuram, Patrick Vieira, Thierry Henry, Claude Makélélé, David Trezeguet and the ethnic Algerian Zinedine Zidane all played crucial roles in the success of Les Bleus. Their triumph was touted by the French and international media as healing the often ugly ethnic divides in French society, with its insistence upon a national identity that ignores the pull of ethnic tribalism and cultural affiliation, and instead a commitment to *lieux de mémoire*, repositories of a collective national memory.[3] Not surprisingly, despite their success in the uniform of the Tricolors—really because of it—they incited the vocal xenophobes of the French Right, notably Jean-Marie Le Pen, leader of the National Front. He famously accused players of not knowing the words to the French national anthem, "La Marseillaise," and noted that France "cannot recognize itself in the national side," and that "maybe the coach exaggerated the proportion of players of color and should have been a bit more careful."[4]

Le Pen's anxiety was not unique in French soccer history. French sporting authorities had banned foreign players from 1955 through 1966, with only a brief two-year period of opportunity in the early sixties. The striker Raymond Kopa, was the first Frenchman to win the European Cup, and he was the star of their third-place 1958 World Cup team. Originally named Raymond Kopaszewski, Kopa was the son of an immigrant miner, and changing his name was a gesture to denote his French allegiance. Although he was voted Best Young Player of the 1954 Cup tournament, fans spewed their displeasure with the team's dismal showing by chanting, "Kopa, retourne à la mine!" (Kopa, go back to the mine!).[5] As with their food and wine, the French desire a distinctly French form of football, a tradition tied to French soil, the nation's identifiable terroir. It is an increasingly difficult challenge in a world of rapidly dissolving borders of all kinds: cultural, economic, and sporting. Even the iconic French boulangerie is disappearing across France.[6]

The gilded legacy of the French national team of the 1990s soon dissolved, sometimes from self-inflicted wounds. In the 2006 World Cup, France again reached the final but lost in an unsatisfying penalty shootout after two periods of tense extra-time left the teams knotted at one-all. Worse, after a brilliant swan song tournament, the beloved Zinedine Zidane was thrown out of the final during overtime when he inexplicably and viciously headbutted an Italian defender who was marking him. Zidane later claimed that the Italian centerback had insulted him, his family. Media labored to decipher the mystery of what set Zizou off, leading him to compromise his team's, his nation's destiny.

The BBC hired a lip-reader who decoded the Italian fullback's retort as "you're the son of a terrorist whore."[7] True or not, it was the kind of anti-Algerian slander that had rained down on the brilliant midfielder his entire career. Unfortunately, for my favorite purveyor of baked treats and others, the World Cup in 2010 offered no redemption, only further disgrace. The French were knocked out in the initial round-robin part of the tournament, losing two of their three matches and playing listless, uninspired soccer. Their own fans booed them at home, and opposition politicians claimed that the players demonstrated the personal hubris of the ruling party. A French sports historian deemed the team's behavior "a social injury."[8]

Though Les Bleus later restored French pride with an impressive conquest at home in the 2018 World Cup, banners and photographs of the national team no longer dominate the decor of Jean Marc's bakery, only one photo of its former captain, Zidane, and a small banner from FC Nantes remain. Teams like Nantes from Europe's top soccer divisions now play in glitzy domes before international television audiences, but the roots of many European soccer clubs are in working-class towns similar to Millvale and to the industries that defined these towns, teams like Racing Club de Lens. Though the team is now known for its red-and-gold jerseys, "the blood and gold," its original colors were green and black, a symbol of the coal-mining region from which it drew its fans and players. The ascent of the French national soccer team to a symbol of cosmopolitan French identity belied this history of French soccer: its roots in working-class life and its long lack of national exposure and appeal, especially in comparison to countries like Germany and England, home of the original Racing Club. Jean Marc's store now broadcasts with posters, banners, and other sports swag the recent dynastic success of another sports team, the Pittsburgh Penguins. The bakery glows in black and gold, the official color scheme of all true Pittsburghers.

Soccer in Suburbia

I started playing soccer in the seventies—something my older brothers did and so inherently cool, something a little brother would aspire to. But it was also au courant. Soccer was in another chrysalis moment when its supporters were announcing the game had arrived. "Look out, baseball!"

Phil Woosnam, commissioner of the North American Soccer League, proclaimed: "Soccer will not only be the number one sport in the U.S., but also the major soccer center of the world. America will win the World Cup. More people will watch and play soccer here than in any other country."[9] While Woosnam's hyperbole was worthy of a Homer Simpson treatment years later, the Welshman did have reason to be optimistic. Not only were the star-studded New York Cosmos filling Giants Stadium, attracting a record-breaking 62,000 soccer fans in June 1977, but the game had found its way into the driveways and backyards of suburbia. There were 350,000 kids dropping their mitts and bats and learning to head, trap, tackle, and volley in official youth leagues. I first began playing in such a venue: orange slices, station wagons, and parents who yelled for their kids to check an opposing player. On lucky days it also meant a ride in Mrs. Ratnavale's Volvo, with the sunroof down and Bob Marley playing on the tape player—she was Dutch. To me soccer was freedom, for soccer is about space—recognizing, creating, attacking, imagining, and dreaming of space. Running diagonally across the field onto a ball played into open green space—just you, the keeper, possibility at your feet.

Today soccer continues to mushroom at the youth level and, as the former University of Pittsburgh soccer coach Joe Luxbacher put it to me, there are more and more "kids playing soccer, but not many soccer players."[10] Not only did the dream of a truly major professional league die, the North American Soccer League folded in the 1980s and the current Major League Soccer has remained a steadily growing but comparatively middling league compared to the likes of the National Football League (NFL) or National Basketball Association (NBA), but the quality of play at the professional level has been limited by a cap on the influx of foreign talent. Soccer is uniquely maligned in the American press. Some submit that using your head, feet, and chest and not just your hands in a game is akin to pissing on Old Glory.

In his popular book *How Soccer Explains the World*, the journalist Franklin Foer argues that soccer's relative obscurity and lightning rod status in the culture are due to its being a sport of the elite, the Yuppie, left-leaning, Chardonnay sippers of the coastal republic. He notes Jack Kemp's famous pillory of the game in a speech before Congress regarding the US bid to host the World Cup, when Kemp compared football to soccer—a speech that the former NFL quarterback later pointed out was meant to be humorous.[11] In 2006, however, Kemp penned a piece further defining his views on his beloved sport: "I've always likened football to entrepreneurial capitalism, because the quarterback is the risk taker who organizes the factors of production, (the offense) in such a way as to score touchdowns, (profits) and thus win games, (increase profits) and hopefully make windfall profits (with a championship)."[12] Later, a conservative commentator used the 2010 World Cup as an opportunity to extend Kemp's line of thought: "Soccer is a socialist sport. Think about it. Soccer is the only sport in the world where you cannot use the tool that distinguishes man from beast: opposable thumbs. 'No hands' is a rule only a European statist could love."[13]

A focus on the body is a bizarrely common emphasis in these debates, as in Sam Whitsitt's *Raritan* piece from 1994 in which he takes on the question of why soccer has failed in America. To Whitsitt it is because the very essence of the game's play, as a bodily activity, is counter to the WASP roots of American cultural identity: "The hands can grasp and possess, but the foot can at most control the ball; it can never 'have' it. American football, however, while it certainly relies on the foot, is finally antifoot, even opposed to the lower body—as is, correspondingly, WASP culture in general. Watch a WASP walk and you realize he or she doesn't know what to do with the lower half of his or her body."[14] Despite their entertaining theorization, what Kemp, soccer haters, and even other less-partisan individuals fail to note is just how deeply soccer has been tied to its WASP and, more importantly, capitalist roots in America: the rolling, tumbling, awesome, and ugly industrial boom that made western Pennsylvania wealthy, scarred, and divided. Soccer was a workingman's game and local players were our original lunch-bucket-lugging tough guy champions. But I, too, was blind to this history even when it was literally underneath my feet as I ran across lawns of play looking for space, a through ball.

The Workingman's Game

Soccer, like much of early American sporting life, was introduced to western Pennsylvania by British and especially Scottish immigrants, who, along with Germans, made up the bulk of the early waves of immigration into the area during the nineteenth century. Between 1860 and 1880, the local population jumped from 78,000 to 235,000.[15] Along with foxhunting, rowing, and rugby, these immigrants brought soccer to the region. And, as in England, its growth was first fostered by its appeal to the ruling class that attempted to organize local play.[16] Soccer's early roots in England included sometimes riotous games that were popular in the British Isles and involved mobs of players moving a ball over large distances in public places and with few rules directing their play. Not surprisingly the sport was banned or restricted by numerous English rulers, and these practices declined during England's modernization as sport became increasingly organized and a defining aspect of upper-class English life. Muscular Christianity's tenets of physical fitness and moral conduct infiltrated elite institutions, especially England's public schools. It was in these schools and among their alumni that the formalized rules governing the modern game of soccer were developed in the late 1800s and, given the cultural power of those institutions, these Englishmen became the putative creators of the beautiful game. Though pivotal in the establishment of a standard of play and in spreading soccer's popularity, the prominence of soccer in England was obviously more than top-down cultural diffusion, as scholars have increasingly made clear.[17]

Ball games based on kicking existed across the globe centuries before these events, including in China and Japan and among Indigenous peoples in the Americas.[18] The game that became the basis for modern soccer was at first still not wholly distinct from its relative, rugby, with many of the rules governing the contemporary game still unsettled, such as catching and carrying the ball and the degree of physical contact allowed. Wide variations in the game led to the establishment in England of the Football Association, the sport's governing body, and to the eventual codification of universal rules that defined the kicking game. A professional league was founded in the late nineteenth century and the game—this modern sport Americans dub soccer—spread to other lands in the kingdom, particularly Scotland, and across Europe, to Asia and beyond, supplanting natal kicking games. The beautiful game became a product of and defining aspect of modern English society, extending across classes and regions so that today those three lions ride on all English international players' jerseys, and England is home to the world's finest league and famously rabid, sometimes dangerous fans.

As the Pittsburgh region's industry continued to grow, its factories and steel mills demanded a bigger workforce: workers to dig the coal, load the fuel cars, feed the blast furnaces, keep the mills and factories along these valleys glowing into the night. When the city's industrial base transitioned to larger-scale steel production, the area experienced a massive immigration from southern and eastern Europe of mainly unskilled workers who threatened to change the tidy cultural milieu. Industrial barons desired means by which they could not only efficiently make their products but also placate and control an increasingly heterogeneous workforce. As did their predecessors in England, these men turned to sport, including soccer, as a tool in their management kit. At the Homestead Works, famous for its deadly 1892 strike, one superintendent noted how "a sane and moderate program of recreation that aims to give everybody something to do in his leisure time is one way the employer can insure his workers coming to work refreshed and alert and in a happy frame of mind."[19] The region's impressive, if largely forgotten soccer history was spawned and fed by the industry that still defines southwestern Pennsylvania and its people. The soccer historian Dave Litterer notes, "Unlike many other early hotbeds of American soccer, the soccer teams around Pittsburgh were primarily sponsored by commercial businesses rather than ethnic social clubs."[20]

Sports historians have claimed that immigrants, in general, did little to alter the nature of urban American sporting life, and added few popular games to the mix, instead assimilating by means of games like baseball, the national pastime. These "new immigrants from eastern and southern Europe came to American cities without a sporting legacy, and they did not become sports-minded. Their sons, however, who wanted to become Americanized, became active in sports."[21] Such comments are undoubtedly accurate to some degree—these later migrants to western Pennsylvania did not establish long-term sporting traditions of wide regional influence, and there were great pressures on them and their progeny to adopt the norms of the dominant class. The historian Frank Couvares has pointed out that the increased mechanization of the region's industrial base catalyzed a cultural shift from a "plebeian" society, one in which working-class identity was both public and influential, to a society marked by increasing class distinctions and the rise of the bourgeois elite.[22]

In his recent book addressing the stubborn refusal of American society to embrace the beautiful game, Andrei Markovits writes, "Elsewhere in the world, soccer maintains its aura (or stigma, depending on one's point of view) of being an exclusively male, working-class, vulgar, rough, and occasionally even violent sport."[23] But in towns like Homestead, Beadling, and Harmarville, soccer was and remains much like that. In the green hill valleys of western Pennsylvania, soccer was the miners' game. Though it was a site of ethnic affiliation, the organization, players, and fans more commonly connected via workplace and community ties, rather than blood or clan.

The first soccer match in the area is alleged to have occurred in 1885, but European immigrants were certainly playing the game informally on their arrival in the Steel City.[24] One of the beauties of soccer, after all, is its simplicity, the absence of mounds of equipment, or elaborate, and thus exclusive facilities. A game can occur in an alley with a ball of rags. Early teams in the Pittsburgh area included sides from East Liberty, Homestead, and Braddock. Though their specific sponsorship is now hard to trace, it is apparent that teams like Clairton Steelworks, Donora Steelworks, National Tube (later to merge with US Steel), and Homestead were directly tied to their communities' major industries. The Beadling Club, established in 1898, was first sponsored by the local coal company. In the early 1900s, Homestead was an especially strong side, stocked with top talent, players who had been weaned on the game in Europe, especially Scotland, then the home of soccer's cutting edge, where a style of play that emphasized movement and passing had become the apex of the game. One such player was Bill Morrison, described in a local paper as "the cleverest halfback in the country," who was both a junior international and professional in Scotland before joining the steel mill's team.[25] Not only did Homestead players arrive with European professional experience, but more than one player later sailed back to Europe to play. Harry Taylor, a striker for a few seasons with Homestead, joined West Bromwich Albion in 1920, the year after that team won the league championship.[26] While the Homestead eleven never attained national prominence, they garnered local honors: winning the regional championship in several years. At that time, the best team in the country was across the state, working and training on the grounds of Bethlehem Steel. From 1916 to 1926, the company's soccer team garnered the nation's top honors, winning the American Cup six times, as well as the US Open Cup five times. The latter was considered the de facto national championship, supplanting the American Cup, as it was the one tournament that brought together teams from across the country of all different levels—amateur to professional. Since the 1913–1914 season, American amateur, semi-amateur, and professional teams have vied for the hardware, which was fittingly donated by a Scotsman, Sir Thomas Dewar. Dewar was not only a great slinger of Scotch but also a supporter of soccer.

Like the Homestead team, Bethlehem's squad was dominated by Scotsmen, men who enjoyed "good positions in the mammoth steel plant and (were) allowed a great deal of time off in order to practice and make long trips."[27] This travel even included a tour of Europe in 1919, a first for any American soccer team.[28] Bethlehem's owner, Charles Schwab, invested significant resources in athletics, spending $125,000 in facilities for his employees, which included playing fields, tennis courts, a gymnasium, and field house.[29] His team would disband by 1930, but along with its rivals from Fall River, Massachusetts—the Rangers and Rovers—they once ruled American soccer. The players from New England worked not in the coal mines or steel mills, but in the area's once signature textile factories.[30] Given this history of industry support for soccer, it is only fitting that, unlike today, Labor Day would be a ceremony with not only picnics but also union soccer matches, as was the case at the 1915 annual gathering of the United Labor League of Western Pennsylvania, for it was "a sport that (had) taken with working men."[31]

When I was a soccer-breathing kid in the seventies, finding opportunities to see topflight play were akin to wandering in the desert in search of chilled Perrier. It was impossible to watch World Cup soccer on television at home, despite all those soccer balls sitting in suburban garages near the Schwinn ten-speeds. The World Cup was shown in a few places on closed-circuit TV. Later, I was thrilled when our public TV station began showing condensed English First Division games. But the sliced-up games filtered out the ebb and flow of a match's organic dance, which makes soccer so distinct and dramatic. And the typical English style of the period—defensively minded, with long balls to the wings, who then pounded crosses into the box—was, well, boring.

There must have been lightning outside the day our coach took us inside for practice and we sat down to watch a filmed game on one of those old projectors, the kind that made a tick-tick-tick sound as the film looped through, used by substitute teachers in need of a microwaveable lesson plan. It was the 1974 World Cup, and watching it felt like stepping out of dense forest for the first time to truly see: Der Kaiser. I sat stunned watching Franz Beckenbauer winning a ball in his own end and, without pause, immediately moving upfield to initiate the attack—moving through defenders as if on skates and always, always seeing all the field. Beckenbauer played libero, a single player behind the backline, who not only closes on any threatening attackers and through balls but sometimes initiates and at times finishes the attack.

Given these rare glimpses available to even a soccer-obsessed kid, it is hard to believe that a few decades earlier in Pittsburgh, the local media, especially the *Pittsburgh Press*, not only covered soccer but also actively promoted it. The *Press* founded a soccer league in 1909, and was followed by the *Pittsburgh Dispatch* as well as the *Johnstown Tribune* in 1911. The three papers played a major role in promoting the game locally, and they worked to create an umbrella organization to structure and coordinate play. In 1913, one of the country's two competing organizations received recognition from the international governing soccer body, FIFA, and eventually became the ruling national body. During the early 1900s, regional governing bodies emerged, such as the Western Pennsylvania Football Association in 1913, an organization designed to mimic the structure of play in England and to "firmly establish association football in this part of the state."[32] Soccer had arrived.

A 1911 all-star match pitting teams from the *Pittsburgh Press* and *Pittsburgh Dispatch* leagues drew an estimated ten thousand fans for the New Year's Day game, and crowds of a few thousand spectators were common for marquee games in these early leagues. Not until 1910 did the Pittsburgh Pirates, ensconced in their new state-of-the-art ballpark, Forbes Field, begin to average that many fans, even though they had won the World Series in 1909 with a team that included the future Hall of Famer and local product Honus Wagner, the Flying Dutchman. Wagner was German. He would win eight batting titles during his career and be recognized by the inimitable Ty Cobb, as "maybe the greatest star ever to take the diamond."[33] Similar, if less expansive claims were made by the local media about its soccer elite, touting some as the best in the United States and the quality of play here on par with anywhere in the nation.

This kind of comparison not only to other regions but also to other American sports was prominently in the minds of soccer's local supporters. One of these was R. Stanley Burleigh, a member of the Pittsburgh public schools physical culture staff, who saw in soccer an alternative to the "dangerous element that is so prominent in the American game," by which, of course, he meant American football.[34] Along with the *Pittsburgh Press*, Burleigh and other school officials helped promote the game in the early 1900s by organizing exhibition matches that were part showcase and teach-in, and he introduced the game into several of the local schools as "an opening wedge" for the eventual blossoming of the game. The *Press* used the front page of its September 9, 1913, edition to promote one such "Big Day for School Boys," but it also noted, "And school girls, you too, are invited."

To many current detractors, haters of the beautiful game, that invitation would seem redundant. Among the reasons now given for soccer's minor status versus baseball, football, and basketball is that it is something less than manly. American sports shock jocks like Jim Rome call out soccer players for their theatrical performances on the pitch: rolling in death throes after a foul, only to hop up after some spritzes from that magic spray can trainers always have at hand. I admit I cringe every time I see this, knowing how it feeds the soccer-hating-wired minds of the American media and public.

Before the US game with Ghana in the 2010 World Cup, the *Washington Post* columnist Tony Kornheiser opined to his cohost, "People take dives like divas all the time. When somebody comes within three feet of them they fall down and hold their ankles for years and years and years . . . it's a Julia Roberts kind of situation."[35] And while the *Pittsburgh Press* touted local players in the early 1900s for "the luster of their deeds in the strenuous and sensational contests" and claimed that "soccer spreads like wildfire or poplar sprouts wherever introduced," the paper, too, felt the need to counter the view that soccer was a "mollycoddle game."[36] The end of that October 1914 article addressing soccer's effete image was adjacent to a brief news item covering a local quarterback, Michael Kennedy, whose team was now disbanding on account of his death on the real men's playing field. In 1920, the first soccer fatality in the nation was reported: Robert Patton of Quincy, Massachusetts, died almost immediately after falling and breaking his neck.[37]

Despite the potential stigma of training effeminate young men, Burleigh, and others like him, such as H. B. Burns, the director of the Department of Hygiene of the city's Board of Education, were successful in introducing soccer into the public schools. By the end of 1913, soccer balls had been furnished to all schools, and the first league, made up of eight teams, had been established. Commenting on the Department of Hygiene's budget the following year, the *Press* noted, "One thing is certain, soccer football is going to be fostered."[38] By 1916, the first high school soccer matches in the city were played, and at local private schools such as Shadyside Academy, soccer matches were soon "developing a spirit of friendly rivalry between the various groups."[39] Within a few years, by 1920, one hundred local schools were playing organized soccer in the Steel City.

Outside of the school grounds, soccer was growing, too. And I wish I could transport Tony Kornheiser, in stiff leather boots and wool shorts, to a snow-covered frozen patch of gravel on a windy December day to play with the local actresses. Watch him take a both-feet-up tackle from behind or lunge to head the waterlogged and partially frozen, mud-covered leather ball against Jack Robson, a former professional player in England and later the star keeper of the Beadling side, a man "over six feet tall . . . built from the ground up, a gigantic mass of iron muscle and steel nerves, with never a superfluous ounce of flesh on his well-knit frame."[40] Pittsburgh soccer was notoriously physical.

The former Castle Shannon fullback Peter Merovich recounted his "baptism" at the time when he first began playing at the adult level: "It's a rough sport. It was . . . I was playing halfback and I just cleared the ball; the ball was on the other side of the field. The guy came down with his shoe, over on my left leg. . . . He just dug into that . . . he was a big guy. Started up here and he just went down the leg! . . . So he just stood there and kept looking at me. I guess he was waiting for me to say something. I woulda gotten clobbered!" During his playing days, Merovich's injuries included a dislocated shoulder and fractured instep, the latter injury never diagnosed until he entered the army.[41] Violence included fans as well. During a home game against rival Beadling, a Cecil supporter struck the opposing side's keeper in the mouth, opening a gash in his jaw that led to Cecil being barred from playing at home for the rest of the season.[42] A 1913 news article noted that rivalries had become so heated that some "near riots were engendered." The writer recalled another anecdote from that season: a supporter of the visiting team "was approached by several female natives of the town in which the game was being played, and firmly told that unless she wished to feel the sting of a dozen hairpins she would vamoose while the going was good."[43]

Every player has been in a match where the rules have become rough guidelines, only suggestions. Games with elbow blows and nasty-looking tackles, more and more shoving, swearing. When the referee has lost control. Given the passion of fans in these towns and the inherent physical play, it is not surprising that games would become akin to the felonious conduct the Crown imagined when it outlawed play. In fact, some players did end up in jail, as in 1934, when Riehl played a cup match in Cleveland and an onfield fight spilled into the sidelines. Twenty people were arrested. Early accounts of the local league record the struggle of the organizers to inculcate and enforce the rules of the game to ensure the safety of players, to prevent "actions . . . that might permanently injure an opponent."[44] Referees not only had to educate and discipline unruly players but also risk the wrath of local fans. In Gallatin, unpopular decisions were met with a christening in the cold waters of the Allegheny. No wonder one referee quickly absconded to a rowboat after blowing the final whistle.[45] As the journalist Eduardo Galeano writes, "In soccer's ritual sublimation of war, eleven men in shorts are the sword of the neighborhood, the city or the nation. These warriors without weapons or armor exorcize the demons of the crowd and reaffirm its faith."[46]

While the United States and western Pennsylvania—its soccer, too— remained shielded from real war, from World War I, Europe was ablaze in the latter part of the decade. Its young men were now warriors marching off to slaughter. Eventually, as more men in Britain left to join the front, gate receipts there plummeted, and public criticism of the game's frivolity at a time of war grew. To address the outrage of some in the public and to demonstrate "Dulce et decorum est pro patria mori," a battalion of English soccer players was organized. The *Pittsburgh Press* reported, "These fine leaders on the football field will make equally splendid leaders on the battlefield and with the fine material these soccer players are made of, the battalion will certainly give a good account of itself."[47] In England, the pro league shut down after the 1914–1915 season, but the game was spreading to new players. Soccer's institutionalization and embrace by the English elite had cleaned up its image so it was now proper for not only English public school boys to play—as amateurs—but even women munitions plant workers were reported to be playing during their breaks, with no less than an actual "regulation ball."[48]

At first, the US game seemed immune to the conflict, "European War Not to Affect Soccer" proclaimed a local September 1914 newspaper article.[49] But as the war dragged on it changed soccer not only in Europe but eventually in the coal towns and mill valleys of western Pennsylvania. By 1917, the *Pittsburgh Press* noted that the game had "felt the blow of turbulent wartimes" and "will suffer materially by the loss of good players."[50] These included men such as the Beadling keeper, John Barrett, who in December 1918 was reported to be in a hospital in France, recovering from having been gassed.[51] The same article noting Barrett's injury, however, also argued for the importance of keeping the game alive, as it was fine training for combat.[52] The military, along with the YMCA, devoted extensive resources in soccer equipment and training for the troops, believing the game was not only wholesome recreation but fit training for combat. And as the soccer historian Brian Bunk notes, "Such investments introduced the game to hundreds of thousands of men and provided a new cohort of potential players and spectators who fortified the leagues and other competitions that had emerged over the past decade or more."[53] The role of soccer as a training ground for war would be echoed later during World War II by a local editorial writer, Joe Williams, who bemoaned the army's deemphasis of "will-to-win" team sports like soccer, those "fighting games" that "make fighting men." He noted in an especially alliterative flurry, "Fighting quality was forged in the fires of fierce competition." Williams lambasted the "professional physical culturists" who had embraced and disseminated fitness programs founded in "the fascist countries, notably Germany and Italy," and warned that "this is truly a dangerous situation and a challenge to a vital part of American life."[54]

After World War I, soccer's growth in western Pennsylvania continued, and in July 1919, the *Pittsburgh Press* noted, "Predictions of greater patronage for soccer football as a result of the almost universal adoption of the sport as part of the training of allied armies during the war seem reasonably sure of being borne out."[55] It is unlikely that the writer could have imagined just how successful local teams would be, for the region was on the cusp of its golden age. From the 1920s to the 1950s, local teams would distinguish themselves as among the best in the nation. A sustained professional game would struggle here, however, as it would in much of the country, but for reasons other than its innate un-Americanness: infighting among its ranks, the financial upheaval of the Great Depression, the world wars, the draw of other major sports, soccer's evolution in style of play, and media neglect. But at the amateur and semiprofessional level, the run in western Pennsylvania was long and illustrious.

By 1922, the *Press* league boasted more than thirty teams and had founded a junior league, which promoted the development of youth players, who fed the adult league with fresh talent.[56] While the *Press* League would fold by the 1930s, the Keystone League, founded in 1921, would continue to provide an excellent training ground for local teams. In 1926 Heidelberg reached the finals of the National Amateur Cup, falling to the New Bedford Defenders 1–0, but in 1927 they brought home the hardware and repeated their success in 1929 by blowing out Newark First German 9–0, with Aldo "Buff" Donelli tallying a remarkable five goals. Donelli had starred for another local team from his hometown, Morgan, before signing with Heidelberg and was not only the area's greatest player but also a unique multisport talent. He played college football at Duquesne University and coached football at both the college and professional level— including for the city's then woeful team, the Pittsburgh Steelers. Like Jack Robson he was an imposing physical presence, and in a heated game with Castle Shannon that deteriorated into a donnybrook between spectators and fans, he and his brother challenged all comers. No one took up the offer.[57] As the *Pittsburgh Press* columnist Ralph David noted, "Americans were prone to look upon soccer as a sport for mollycoddles, but this was simply because they did not understand it."[58]

Though only an amateur, Donelli is legendary for scoring a record four goals in a World Cup qualifying match in 1934 and saving America's face by tallying the nation's lone goal in a 7–1 blowout by the eventual champion, Italy, in a game witnessed by Il Duce himself. Mussolini used the stage of the 1934 World Cup and sports in general to showcase his fascist regime and his vision of Italian identity. He is alleged to have sent the Italian team a message before the 1938 final, "Win or die."[59] Buff Donelli and many other local men of the era were inducted into the National Soccer Hall of Fame. Among them was Harry Fairfield, a referee, administrator, and writer for the *Pittsburgh Press*, whose columns demonstrated a passionate enthusiasm for the game, combined with a witty intelligence. Today, the World Cup is covered by the local Pittsburgh papers only through wire stories, and more than one local sports journalist is among the Jim Romes of the world.

The success of Heidelberg, the winner again in 1955 of the Amateur Cup, was matched by other local teams such as Morgan (1940, 1943), Castle Shannon (1935), and Beadling (1954). Teams from western Pennsylvania were also runners up a remarkable thirteen times. Even more impressive is the accomplishment of local teams in the tournament that crowned a national champion, the US Open Cup. From the 1940s and through the 1950s, local teams would win the tourney four times and come up short in the finals on an equal number of occasions.

King Coal

When I first began playing soccer in those promising youth leagues of the seventies, we regularly drove down Route 28 to play matches on a dirt, rock-strewn pitch under the shadow of the Pennsylvania Turnpike. During lulls, when my focus briefly moved outside the orb of that black-and-white patched ball to hear something beyond the pitch, I would notice the swish of semis and the rumbling of the bridge supports as the trucks raced across the Allegheny. Harmarville was a working-class town of rough-playing kids whose parents lined the field in their four-door cars, honking horns and flashing their headlights when a twelve-year-old scored, and screaming with a passion that startled me, accustomed to the restrained composure of our mostly suburban, maternal crowd—the original soccer moms. Sometimes the ref was a local guy you would see exchanging chummy greetings with the coach and parents before kickoff, never a good sign. I remember one game: a summer storm and a sudden swirl of wind blew the dry dirt toward us in a mini sirocco. We turned, covered our faces, and waited for the burst to break up, to see. When we could, the ball was in our net. One–nil. The horns honked and lights flashed in the darkening park lined by cinders.

We knew whenever we, the rich kids from Fox Chapel—the little fox on the right breast of our deep blue, long-sleeved jerseys—played here that we were in for a banging. After one game and the obligatory handshakes and exchanges of "Good game," a player on my team, bored or mischievous—I will never know—tossed a flat lighter-sized rock close, too close to some Harmarville fans. A woman charged us screaming, eyes beetle-like and arms like straight steles at her sides. Somehow our coach cut her off, calmed her down, said whatever, and mothers gathered players and slowly retreated to their cars, still yelling at us to "get the fuck out!" I now know the instinctive quick strike in protection of your child, but not the something more in her eyes. It had to do with more than soccer. It was about coal.

Teams such as Beadling and later Harmarville were founded on coal, the black gold fueling the furnaces to make the iron, the steel, and the glass that made Pittsburgh famous—both for its industry and choking skies. Black soot covered all the buildings and statues and gave the city its grimy grandeur, like the black-smeared statue of Beethoven seated before the Carnegie Museum, the iconic Pittsburgh institution donated by its namesake "to the people of the city of Pittsburgh." The large deposit of bituminous coal that cuts a wide path across western Pennsylvania, running roughly along the Appalachian Mountains—the bituminous region—employed over 33,000 miners in 1880, and these numbers skyrocketed in the following decades to approximately 200,000 by 1910.[60] Between 1880 and 1930, Pennsylvania had more coal miners than any state in the country.[61] The majority of these men were immigrants, and the early miners were among the first soccer players, northern Europeans: Irish, Welsh, and British. But as in the mills and factories, the mining companies soon filled their workplaces with men from eastern and southern Europe, placing them in the dirtiest, most dangerous jobs, with limited chance for advancement. Soccer was one avenue, if not for upward mobility, then to a better place for the men who dug on their knees with picks, loaded the tons of coal, and suffered the accidents endemic to the industry: suffocation from poisonous gas, crushing by wayward coal cars, or the dreaded collapse of a tunnel, envisioned by one of the Commonwealth's contemporary poets:

> Often in veins of coal
> I have imagined sighs of the dying
> cut off and at the last
> eating wood and leather belts,
> sulphur water turning their eyes ashen
> with dreams of angels.[62]

Among the scenes in the spectacular murals of Maxo Vanka in Millvale is a group of women mourning before the outstretched, Pietà-like body of a man. In the background, descending a hill is a group of men—coal picks and lunch pails in hand. One is looking over his shoulder waving a farewell, his pose mirroring the stricken woman kneeling before the body. Covering her face with her other hand, she appears too aware to suffer

2.1 *Immigrant Mother Raises Her Sons for American Industry* (Maxo Vanka, 1937). Reproduced by permission from Pawsburgh Photography.

another good-bye. Fatalities in the mining industry averaged over 2,000 annually and federal legislation to address the obvious disregard for safety was slow in coming. The first federal law governing mining mandated minimal change, measures such as barring children under the age of twelve from working in the mines. Not until 1941 was the federal Bureau of Mines authorized to inspect mines and it was not until 1952, with the passage of the Federal Coal Mine Safety Act, that mines received regular inspections from the federal government and monetary sanctions for violations. In the meantime, mining companies held control over the lives and often the deaths of their workers. Between 1901 and 1925 there were a reported 305 coal-mining disasters, a "disaster" defined as an incident in which 5 or more people died.[63] Individual deaths were apparently minor tragedies, such as that of the crack Beadling midfielder John Robson, who was electrocuted in the mine shortly after the birth of his second son, Tim.[64] From 1877 to 1940, roughly 18,000 men and boys died working in the mines of the bituminous region.[65]

In Beadling, where Robson had starred, and in many other towns, the local teams were first sponsored by the coal companies. Harmarville's first side, established by the town's coal company, began play in 1921, and the *Press* League was commonly known as the "Miners League." Like the steel mills, the coal operators recruited talent and offered the chosen footballing few more favorable work conditions: less demanding or more profitable employment and a half day off on Saturday gamedays. Most of these workers, at first wielding pickaxes and shovels to dig and load the coal, were paid by how much coal they extracted from the mine. The average worker at the beginning of the century loaded fourteen tons during one of his six workdays.[66] Despite this massive amount of work, the average coal miner made a paltry $300 in 1900 and pay rates remained frozen for years.[67] Moreover, coal companies were notorious for cheating workers out of pay by underestimating tonnage and diggers were penalized for loading coal mixed with waste, such as the slate common to the southwestern part of the Commonwealth. One former miner recalled how the Harmar mine's clerk used to "brag that every seventh barge that went out was a free one."[68] A talented player was often rewarded by working in parts of the mine where he could cut and load more coal. Having spent hours in all kinds of pregame rituals—cautious about taxing my energies, eating the wrong food—it freezes my mind to think of crawling on my knees, hacking a pick axe for hours in a rat-infested mine, breathing in choking coal dust, eating a quick cold lunch with only the water from the bottom of my pail, amid the smell of mule and human waste, to then emerge hours later into the light and play a hated rival on a muddy, partially frozen field in December. That was cross-training.

The influence of the coal operators in these communities was pervasive. They ran little fiefdoms that manifested the worst abuses of the era. The industry's geographic expansion into the narrow hollows of Pittsburgh's surrounding valleys provided ideal conditions for companies to control their workers' lives. As coal mines spread out into the area, beyond the reach of public transportation, businesses, and, most of all, housing, the lives of coal miners became increasingly controlled by their employers. Coal companies created separate communities where miners were forced to buy work supplies and equipment maintenance from them at inflated prices, and often their food, as well. Most significant was housing, for it bound workers to the company in ways that enabled managers to punish them, evicting at whim those deemed troublemakers. A study by the federal government succinctly stated, "A housed labor supply is a controlled labor supply."[69] By 1917 over 61 percent of the miners in the bituminous fields lived in company housing.[70] Homes were often substandard, with cost the dominant concern guiding their construction and not, for instance, federal housing standards that required bathing and toilet facilities. As most of these miners were married, the coal company's threat of eviction was a particularly powerful tool of control. Companies were required, at the least, to give ten days' notice for eviction; though, state law stipulated thirty days for all tenants. Miners also lacked written leases. One Harmarville resident, Helen Babich Sabol, recalled that shortly after her father was killed in the mine, the company forced her family out of their home: "Mother wasn't well the day they came to put us out she was sick, along with my brothers, Bill, Lanny, and sisters Daneen, and Mitzi.... When I got home from school I didn't have a home; they padlocked the doors! I was fourteen years old."[71] In oral histories, neighbors recall the family's belongings sitting out in the rain. Helen's mother had tried to stay in their home, offering to pay rent until they could relocate, but the company clerk refused. A few years earlier he had picked young Helen up on her way from school and attempted to assault her. She was eleven.

Helen's family was evicted because they no longer had a father contributing to the mine's productivity. Many families were also thrown out of their homes for fighting for rights, in towns devoid of the civil liberties that allegedly defined American life. Federal authorities investigated labor conditions in the region's coal communities, and the Committee of Inquiry on Coal and Civil Liberties was formed in response to the widely reported abuses during the coal strike of 1922. It investigated an astounding 713 company towns in Pennsylvania's bituminous coal fields and was led by Zechariah Chaffee, a Harvard professor and well-known advocate for civil rights. Though often sympathetic to workers' complaints, the US Coal Commission chairman's thinking was at times characterized by an ethnocentric bent. He noted elsewhere that such punitive practices were of concern because they violated the "Anglo-Saxon tradition that a man's house is his castle, whether or not the Poles and Italians may rightfully be denied the benefit of that tradition."[72] As in the steel mills, the mines were full of non–Anglo-Saxons, and the workplace was segregated based on bias against them. As another Harmarville resident noted, "The foreign class didn't have better jobs; those went to the English-sounding names, not to anyone with a 'ski' name."[73] A Black face was worse than a Hunkie-sounding name.

Coal towns such as Harmarville were segregated not only by white ethnicity but also by race, with Black residents occupying the least desirable ground. In Harmarville they lived near the bony dump, where coal marred by impurities was discarded. During the entire operation of the Harmar mine, from 1915 to 1980, only one African American worked there as a miner, Levi Twyman. In a perverse example of the mine's hiring practices, an immigrant man was denied work because of his dark complexion until a local woman "convinced them that Misho was a white Yugoslav from the southern region."[74]

At times the ruling class in Harmarville flaunted its status as a kind of cruel divertissement. The local soccer star and Hall of Famer Ray Bernabei, who defined the workers as "free slaves," recalled how as a small boy he watched the mine superintendent throw pennies on the ground for the miners' kids to scramble for while he laughed in smug amusement. "It was a form of ridicule which I sensed after the first time I saw this, when I was about six years old. After noticing what the bosses had in mind, I stayed away from that: no boss was going to treat me like a dog."[75] Bernabei's anecdote demonstrates the petty cruelties that mine owners inflicted on their workers' children. Even more chilling was the violence they rained down on those kids' communities and how the Commonwealth endowed them with absolute power.

Miners called them Cossacks. It was a moniker reflecting the Eastern European roots of many of the local miners, who recalled the role of this group in their homelands, as violent strongmen for the Russian Empire. Pennsylvania's Coal and Iron Police played a similar part for the industrial empires of the Commonwealth: the railroad, steel, and coal companies that, beginning in 1865 with the railroads, were granted the right to organize their own private police forces. In the hundreds of coal towns like Harmarville this meant that a band of sometimes violent amoral men, chosen and paid by the company, ran the town at the behest of their bosses.

Armed with a badge and a commission from the state, the Coal and Iron Police could commit any act of violence—terrorism at whim. Harmarville residents bitterly recount the acts of the hated Cossacks: "We were afraid to go in the little house because police on horses would gallop through. Another time, at the dance hall when people were inside, we kids were outside and saw a Dodge truck come up with blinds pulled down on the backsides. It backed up where the people were, and when the blinds were pulled up, what we saw was a mounted shotgun. . . . Everyone started running. One young mother ran across the field. She dropped her baby, and a horse ran over the baby and killed it."[76]

In 1930, the local union hall in Harmarville was bombed, and during periods of labor unrest, as during the 1927 strike, the police enforced a ban against more than two people congregating. Striking miners were evicted from their homes and spent months, including the winter, living in makeshift barracks in nearby Acmetonia. In neighboring Cheswick, where as a kid I used to go to see the latest blockbuster summer movies, the clubbing of local men and women by the police was publicly denounced by the former governor Gifford Pinchot. Cut off from the company store and without income, miners relied on aid societies and the goodwill of more fortunate neighbors like the Liebermans, a Jewish family that owned a grocery store and gave miners food on credit.

Because of widespread reports of the notorious Cossacks, along with the general poor working and living conditions in the bituminous patches, the federal government again sent officials to investigate in 1928. The region was at the time enduring a protracted battle between miners and the Pittsburgh Coal Company. The committee described the climate in these communities as a "reign of terror," one fomented by five hundred to six hundred Coal and Iron Police, complemented by deputy sheriffs who were also strongmen of the coal operators.[77] Joe Ludbresky recounted to the committee how he and his wife, though sick, had been evicted from their home and forced to live in the union encampment's unheated barracks. She died six days later.[78] Others repeated charges that the Coal and Iron Police had sexually assaulted girls. One sixteen-year-old testified to being kidnapped by a policeman who hid her for three weeks, along with several other girls, where they were visited by several other members of the Coal and Iron Police.[79]

Despite expressing sympathy to miners, lauding them for "the courage and determination . . . to stand up for what they believed was their due, an American wage, making possible an American standard of living," committee members were patronizing of miners and hostile to some of their supporters. Alluding to the relief societies that provided strikers with food and other necessary supplies during the long strike, the commission noted, "Everywhere your committee visited in the Pittsburgh district they found the slimy trail of an organization known as the Ohio and Pennsylvania Relief Society," a group it actually deemed "the most dangerous organization this country has ever known."[80] The committee was likely referring to the Workers International Relief, a domestic offshoot of International Red Aid that commissioners feared was pushing its subversive message in the Allegheny Valley.

Battles of the American Left with industry and more established labor unions like the United Mine Workers of America (UMWA) were often fought in these local coal towns, where the Left was able to organize more effectively than in the anthracite mining region across the state. This was, in part, due to the ethnic makeup of the region, as the membership of the communist National Miners Union was heavily eastern and southern European immigrants.[81] In fact, the union was founded in Pittsburgh and support for the Communist Party was strong enough in the area that the party's Workers' Soccer Association fielded six local teams during its brief existence from 1927 to 1935.[82] The Communist Party also realized the organizing power of sport, articulating in its sports manifesto the desire to counter the "exploitive system of paternalist athletics, ideologies of the YWCA and YMCA, the moneyed athletic clubs, the AAU [Amateur Athletic Union]; and college sports" and to produce "proletarian fighting units against militarism and fascism."[83] The National Miners Union (NMU) disavowed the revolutionary aims of the national Communist Party and focused instead on the material needs of laborers and social justice, including racial equality. Ending racial segregation in the coal industry was part of the NMU platform and helped it garner support from African American workers.[84] This agenda contrasted with that of UMWA leaders, who, "when they were not portraying black miners as country-bred, careless workers . . . were describing them in lurid racist terms as sex-driven, drug-soaked interlopers."[85] During the first national convention of the National Miners Union in 1928, the UMWA attacked the NMU delegates, leaving one man with a serious brain injury, his "memory destroyed," and local police arrested 125 NMU members. A representative of the International Labor Defense who was there recounted that "the police were definitely fighting on behalf of the Lewis gangsters," referring to John L. Lewis, the legendary UMWA president.[86] In the Harmarville area, the NMU was particularly active, and organized a 1931 march of 175 miners to the Harwick mine just outside Harmarville, the site of one of the industry's most horrendous "disasters," in which 179 men perished.[87]

Local Italians also made public demonstrations of support for the Italian immigrant anarchists Nicola Sacco and Bartolomeo Vanzetti, charged with and later executed for the murder of two men during a robbery. Michael Musmanno, the son of an Italian immigrant, worked in the local coal mines with his father, and then in steel mills, as he pursued a college degree and legal training. While attending law school, he volunteered his services to the Sacco and Vanzetti legal team as they worked on the pair's appeal, showing up unannounced and willing to sleep on the office floor. Musmanno became a successful attorney and later a member of the state legislature, where he penned legislation to drive a stake into the heart of the Coal and Iron Police. In February 1929, three of its officers bludgeoned to death a part-time miner, John Barkoski, a murder that catalyzed public opinion against the force. Musmanno represented Barkoski's widow during the trials of the officers, employed then by the Pittsburgh Coal Company, which paid Mrs. Barkoski $13,500, as money to cover funeral expenses and in compensation for her husband's death. She said of the money that it "didn't mean anything. . . . We'd have been all right if John was living."[88] In their first trial for murder, the men were acquitted but the state later charged them with involuntary manslaughter. Musmanno assisted the Allegheny County district attorney in the case. Eventually, two of the men were found guilty, with Walter Lyster sentenced to one year in the county workhouse and Harold Watts to ten months. After the trials Musmanno leveraged the publicity the case had garnered, and wrote a play about the murder that later became the basis for an overwrought Hollywood film of good conquers evil, *Black Fury*.[89] More importantly, Barkoski's murder was used by the young lawyer to rally support for his bill. Its legislative history underscores how difficult it is to realize justice outside the world of cinema.

Representative Musmanno crafted a bill that would do away with the Coal and Iron Police and replace them with security guards with limited powers enforceable only on company property. The following month Musmanno's bill, supported by numerous religious leaders and the American Civil Liberties Union, was marked up by the state attorney general at the request of Governor Fisher and left to languish in committee. An alternative bill, sponsored by State Senator William D. Mansfield of McKeesport, was introduced as well, one essentially maintaining the status quo. Though Musmanno's bill had overwhelming support, it was eventually vetoed by the governor, who endorsed Mansfield's legislation. Fisher would make some minor administrative rules governing the Coal and Iron Police, but the force, deemed a "throwback to feudalism which has no place in modern phases of police work," remained.[90] Supporters placed their hopes in the former and then incumbent governor, Gifford Pinchot, who on the campaign stump had vowed to end the Coal and Iron Police.

The representative reintroduced his bill in 1931, and it again garnered overwhelming support, with the vote 153–25 in the House of Representatives, even after Pinchot's administration attempted to quash it. As with his prior bill, the delegation from Allegheny County strongly backed Musmanno's legislation. Meanwhile, the governor vowed not to renew the police commission, which would expire on June 30. The Senate then sat on its hands, and again Senator Mansfield floated alternative legislation. A proposal from the administration to consider both bills was also soundly beaten in the House. Later in the spring the State Senate marked up Musmanno's bill, adding language that effectively erased its crucial provision limiting the police's jurisdiction to company property. Musmanno was scathing in his censure of his colleagues: "They mangled it in the same manner as the Coal and Iron Police mangled the body of John Barkoski. . . .

They have condoned the acts of gorillas who killed Barkoski; they have condoned the acts of those monsters who shot into a schoolhouse in Bruceton while children were attending classes: they have condoned all the acts of the thugs, gangsters, and plug-uglies that bore the name of the Coal and Iron Police."[91] Ultimately, the legislature would pass no legislation, and the governor's failure to recommission the force would lead to the end of the Coal and Iron Police and to the development of a professional police force, the Pennsylvania State Police. Enforcement of the law in towns like Harmarville was then left to local officials, including deputy sheriffs and others who had long sided with the lords of coal.

Remembering Soccer under the Tipple

When I was growing up, coal mining to me was something foreign, something out of a Hazel Dickens song, happening in "the green rolling hills of West Virginia." Western Pennsylvanians have always had our neighbors down I-79 to help us feel superior, the Hoopies who lived up in them hollers and represented the backwardness of Appalachia. They made us seem urbane in comparison. After all, in the Backyard Brawl of Pitt versus West Virginia, our noble panther was up against a man in buckskin with a coonskin cap and armed with a musket like some lost Davy Crockett. That was where coal mining, the basis for good bluegrass would be, not in the concrete world of the industrial and later postindustrial city of my childhood.

Yet when we descended from suburbia in our station wagon flotilla to drive along the Allegheny to play soccer upriver, there were markings of King Coal right outside the window. Before the Hulton Bridge were oddly uniform dark brick houses, smack against Freeport Road. I wondered who lived there, so close to the road and railroad in what I now know was housing for the Harmar mine. The tipple was still standing then, just down the road on the left: an odd-looking structure, with its chute and a shape that reminded me of the hulking dinosaur skeletons in Andrew Carnegie's civic cabinet of curiosities. It seemed out of place above the road with Laura Lanes, Choo Choo Pancakes, and the Pennsylvania Turnpike looming overhead. Yet back up in Fox Chapel, even on our home field, hundreds of feet below, men from the Harmar mine were digging that old black gold. Soccer and coal were entwined, on the ground and in the minds, in the play of twelve-year-old kids with mothers of fierce love.

The game grew out of these communities' hard mining histories, these towns where, as the Hall of Famer Peter Merovich noted, "Soccer was played early in life in most of the mining towns.... You started knee-high, even."[92] While the original Harmarville team had been sponsored by the local coal company, as in other towns such as Beadling, the team eventually became independent of the company. In Beadling the soccer team's current clubhouse was the mine's old machine shop, which included the main entrance to the mine, sealed for over ninety years. In Harmarville, the local team played in the Allegheny Valley League during the sport's heyday, holding their own against a lot of top teams, but eclipsed early on by the national success of local sides such as Heidelberg and Morgan. However, by 1936 Harmarville was the three-time defending district champion, and the significant number of Italians on the squad caused the *Pittsburgh Press* soccer journalist to exclaim, "Whether Il Duce knows it or not, there's going to be a skirmish on the Italian front when Harmarville invades Dunleavy territory." Dunleavy, then with sixteen players of Italian ancestry, "a roster of which reads like the history of the Renaissance" had beaten Harmarville at home earlier in the season, and Harry Fairfield exclaimed, "That's a casus belli of some consequence."[93] After World War II and the demise of Il Duce, Harmarville soccer reached extraordinary heights that I knew nothing of, despite regularly reading the daily newspaper that had played such a key role in growing the local game.

In 1947, the Harmarville businessman and soccer devotee Johnny Mojack began building a team, merging the existing Harmarville side with neighboring Indianola's and tossing in some of the area's most gifted booters. Soon afterward the Harmarville Hurricanes began to dominate local soccer and—like Gallatin and Morgan before them—prove themselves against the country's best sides. They played on a rocky field owned by the Harmar Coal Company, and they lined the field with coal dust when it snowed. Practices were hard to arrange, and they owned only two balls: one for practice, one for games. After matches many of the players showered in the mine's washroom. Mojack gave his players a small stipend, plus "all the beer they could drink" after matches, but unlike many of the teams they met in cup play, they were amateurs. Most of the men were workers in the local industries, such as coal or steel, and one former player credits this work for their success: "Most of our guys worked in coal mines or factories. When you worked in a mine or factory, you didn't sit around getting fat. We were all in good shape. People talk about the guys who have abs now. Well, we had the abs back then. We could run for miles and miles. We were tough."[94] The Hurricane player John Prucnal missed work at the mine one Monday while at a tournament in Fall River and he was given a choice—work or soccer. "Both," was his reply.[95]

That notion of toughness built and expressed through hard physical labor is still the wellspring of local identity—in the psyche of Pittsburghers and the way we talk about the athletes who represent us. It is also true that teams here, like the Hurricanes, have had highly skilled players. Bob Craddock, whose father was also inducted into the National Soccer Hall of Fame, was a member of the 1950 World Cup team that stunned England by beating them 1–0. Saint George could not save the strongly favored and dominant English from a late decisive goal by Joe Gaetjens, a Haitian immigrant who was playing that day because Craddock's bad back kept him on the sideline. It would be another forty years before the United States would even qualify again for the World Cup finals. Craddock was joined on the 1950 World Cup team by his Hurricane teammate Nick DiOrio, a defender from the coal-mining town of Morgan, who had played on other top local teams and with whom he had won the US Open Cup. In 1974, DiOrio was also inducted into the National Soccer Hall of Fame. Lou "Sonny" Yakopec was another defender on the Hurricanes during its glory years and he earned two caps playing on the US National Team. Because he was also a star football player at Aspinwall High, which would later become my grade school, he was posthumously inducted into my high school's sports hall of fame. An extraordinary athlete, Yakopec not only started at fullback on the football team at the University of Pittsburgh in his freshman year, but while a teenager he was offered professional baseball contracts by the hometown Pirates and the Boston Red Sox.

Like that American side of 1950, which beat a much more skilled team of professionals, the Hurricanes, as the longtime team captain Ray Bernabei recalled, "competed with grit and guts. Our opponents always outfinessed us."[96] The Hurricanes played consistently solid defense, complemented by excellent goal keeping, and looked to score with quick counterattacks: playing long balls forward to skilled strikers capable of creating and finishing scoring chances, players like Skip Yakopec and Steve Grivnow, another Harmarville player who made appearances at the international level. My favorite? Don "Pug" Malinowski, a draftsman from Harmarville who manned the nets for the Hurricanes for several seasons and for the US National squad in its three qualifying matches for the 1954 World Cup. With the profile of a boxer, ergo, the name "Pug," he played with a confident casualness and arguably a looniness not atypical of keepers. In a 1956 article profiling Malinowski and another local player who had been selected for the national team, Ed Zimbicki, Pug is described as "the most nonchalant young man ever to don cleats," noting his habit of leaving the goal to chat with nearby fans. "Why worry?" he stated, "as long as the ball is down at the other end of the field they can't score here."[97]

The Harmarville side was also tactically innovative, relying on an unusual 1-2-5-2 formation, with two center forwards and a sweeper, the team captain and Hall of Famer Ray Bernabei, whose style of play in the 1950s anticipated Franz Beckenbauer, Der Kaiser. With grit, talent, and inventiveness, the Harmarville team swept through the local leagues, and from 1947 to 1963 compiled an impressive record of 360 wins, 60 losses, and 46 ties. They won five West Penn Cup championships, and in both 1951 and 1952 lost in the finals of the US Amateur Cup, with the 1951 loss an especially gut-wrenching match in which they outplayed their opponent, the three-time American Soccer League champion Philadelphia Nationals during two periods of overtime, but gave up the winning goal in the last four minutes. Most impressive was their appearance three times, in 1952, 1953, and 1956, in the final of the US Open Cup. In the 1952 two-day home and away series, the Hurricanes built an early two-goal lead in the first game, but despite four outstanding saves by Malinowski, they gave up four unanswered goals. The Hurricanes battled back to within a goal on a score by Yakopec, but a tying goal by DiOrio in the second half was disallowed. They lost.

But in the second match, played at home, the team blasted the professionals 4–1. And this side from a coal-mining town of a few thousand people in southwestern Pennsylvania was national champion. The Hurricanes would return to the finals the next season but fall to the Chicago Falcons, never tallying a goal in the two matches. In 1956, the Hurricanes again reached the finals of the US Open Cup, matched against a semipro team from the Windy City's ethnic soccer mix, the Chicago Schwaben. The first match had been a tough 1–0 loss. Playing the final deciding game at home before five thousand fans, the team fell behind but battled back, and a late goal by Tom Craddock, who had been working at the Heppenstall Steel Company until shortly before game time, forced overtime. With only eight minutes left in the second overtime, after nearly two and a half hours of grueling play, Harmarville's Buddy Uchtel crossed the ball from the right midfield toward the Chicago team's goal. George Resavage, standing at the top of the penalty area one-timed a volley into the upper-right-hand corner of the net as the goalie stood and watched, a paralyzed witness. After the match, the teams' players gathered at the Harmarville Athletic Association, drinking up their free beer with their opponents, who sang German songs accompanied by a Black Dutchman who had played soccer in their native Deutschland.[98] In 2003, that dusty field I played on as a teenager was dedicated in honor of these men and named the Harmarville

2.2 Harmarville Hurricanes versus German Hungarians, June 3, 1951. Reproduced by permission from Gerry Adair Collection, Thomas and Katherine Detre Archives.

Hurricanes Soccer Field. One local woman recounted, "Going to the soccer games was the highlight of my life back then."[99]

However, between that commemoration in 2003 and the glory years of Harmarville soccer—even since the heady days of my youth league career, when the *New York Times* touted soccer "chic" and with a "new audience . . . clean cut, affluent, 'upscale'"—the sport has suffered a local decline.[100] Professional leagues have come and gone. In Pittsburgh, professional teams such as the Pittsburgh Canons, Pittsburgh Miners, Pittsburgh Strassers, Pittsburgh Indians, Pittsburgh Phantoms, Pittsburgh Stingers, and Pittsburgh Spirit have generally enjoyed only brief runs. The sole local team now is the Pittsburgh Riverhounds, part of the United Soccer League's second division. The Riverhounds first played home games at local high schools and featured several players from the region. They are now an affiliate of a Major League Soccer team and play in a new riverside stadium with a side of increasingly worldly and talented players. The Riverhounds have also finally settled, I hope, on black and gold as team colors. Though their fan club is called the Steel Army, it's a modest unit compared to the tens of thousands of locals who consider themselves part of the local pro football team's Steeler Nation. Despite burgeoning participation at the youth level, professional soccer has yet to gain a secure place deep in contemporary culture. Why, as one local columnist put it, are soccer and even its local history still "for everybody except Americans"?[101]

Soccer is dull. Anyone watching that double overtime game in which Harmarville captured its second US Open Cup witnessed undeniable athleticism, grit, physical play, and simmering tension finally uncapped by that beautiful and conclusive goal by Resavage. The Pittsburgh sports radio personality Mark Madden, while addressing the "wrinkled old newspaper columnists who complain how boring soccer is when a World Cup comes around every four years," noted, "Soccer is the beautiful game. Always has been, always will be . . . You don't like soccer. We get it. You ran out of fresh ideas twenty years ago."[102] Mercifully, during the 2010 World Cup, gone were the television breaks and scrolling ads, the woefully ill-informed baseball announcers whom the American networks had insisted on to call World Cup games. Some 24.4 million Americans watched the final match between the magical Spanish side, filled with players from Barcelona who passed the ball in some telepathic miracle, and the disappointingly thuggish Dutch who had abandoned "total football" for total assault. The massive uptick in television ratings for the 2010 World Cup, 41 percent over the 2006 tournament, demonstrates that when Americans can watch quality soccer presented faithfully and intelligently, they do.[103] The success of the United States team catalyzed interest here; 19.4 million viewers watched its Round of 16 match versus Ghana—equal to the average TV audience for the prior year's World Series games—and fans did not turn off the set when the Stars and Stripes bowed out. This was a World Cup six television-producer-acid-reflux-inducing hours ahead of the East Coast, which meant games were being televised during the daytime hours of summer, far from primetime land. Yet ESPN reported an impressive 38 percent increase in viewership among men ages eighteen to forty-nine.[104] And these men were not, as some have suggested, only Spanish-speaking immigrants huddling around the television watching Univision and marveling at Andres Cantor's aerobic-capacity-challenging "Goooooool!"

This growth in American viewership continued during FIFA's 2014 World Cup, won by an impressive German side, with whom I celebrated my mongrel American existence by drinking Hefeweizen in a German soccer-ball-shaped beer glass and singing "Deutschland, Über Alles"—badly. Twenty-six and a half million viewers in the US watched Germany's final nervy overtime match versus its frequent dance partner Argentina, a record for a soccer match and larger than the audiences for the prior final games of the World Series and NBA Finals.[105] That figure was topped soon after in 2015, however, when the US Women's National Team thumped Japan. This fact points to another reason for soccer's less lofty place in American culture. Spectator sports have increasingly become "the great cultural unifiers" of American society, as more traditional institutions like the church or school have waned in influence, and sporting institutions tack conservative. It is hard to imagine Americans not splashing up on the media marquee American men's success in something the rest of the whole globe worships. The world's grandest tournament. But because women are, well, women—long defined as the antithesis of athletic prowess—their athletic accomplishments are by habit overlooked. The United States Soccer Federation's long unequal treatment and compensation of its more successful women players, four-time World Cup Champions, is one example of this larger bias that infects the sporting world and warps historical perspective.[106] The debate over soccer's putative effeminate nature points to the way that unstated cultural biases related to gender shape the world of sport and how we narrate the games we play and watch.

The increased investment that ESPN has made in soccer demonstrates a generally overlooked reason for soccer's alleged death upon import, the role of the American sports media. Soccer's popularity in the Pittsburgh area in the early and mid-twentieth century was spurred by the support of local journalists like Harry Fairfield from the *Pittsburgh Press* and later Jimmy Jordan of the *Pittsburgh Post-Gazette* and even the local sports broadcasting legend Myron Cope, inventor of the Steelers' talismanic Terrible Towel, who wrote a *Sports Illustrated* article on the Harmarville team in 1956. As Ray Bernabei noted, "The writers today are worse than in my day. They write very little about soccer. Why, I don't know."[107] In fact, Jordan's own former paper, when it does cover soccer, suffers from amnesia, as in a lengthy—for soccer—2003 article about the champions from Harmarville. The article noted, "Soccer usually was relegated to the back pages of the sports section. The day after the Hurricanes won the cup, the *Pittsburgh Press* ran six paragraphs on an inside page of the sports section."[108] Not only does the writer seem unaware of the former prominence soccer once enjoyed in the local media but also unaware that the crowning of the Hurricanes in 1956 was heralded on the front page of the Monday *Pittsburgh Post-Gazette*, with the headline "Harmarville Goes Wild."[109]

There are no local soccer-specific journalists penning pieces on the teams, the tactics, and promoting the sport, as was the case decades ago. Many Americans are ignorant of the game, befuddled and unaccustomed to soccer's nonstop ebb and flow—horrible for TV timeouts. The lack of discrete plays and one-on-one matchups lack the narrative drama American sports media feeds its viewers. Like the newbie to baseball who watches a 1–0 brilliantly played baseball game and thinks it numbingly dull, such viewers describe watching soccer as akin to attending a worm race. But like all sports, including football, soccer has evolved: its rules, tactics, technology, and athletes. Soccer has grown from ancient ball games, provincial mob donnybrooks over lawns, to a muddled cousin of rugby, and most recently into a fast-paced, attacking style of play defined at the highest level by the global transfer of talent for a world audience. Today's diehard NFL fan, weaned on elaborate blitz packages, five-wide-receiver sets, and streams of pass patterns and rule changes that push the ball farther and faster downfield, might prefer invertebrate races, or even soccer, to a game of football circa 1930, with its emphasis on slugging out run after run after run. And she might think she was watching a hybrid soccer match if she could watch a YouTube clip of that first legendary pigskin match in 1869 pitting Princeton against Rutgers.

The violent nature of football, others argue, was better suited than soccer to the land of cowboys, gangsters, and drive-bys: "The use of violence was both more common and, at least within certain limits and within certain contexts—one of which was sport—more acceptable. Given this situation it is perhaps not surprising that it was rugby rather than soccer which was taken up in America."[110] Soccer in no way compared to the physical contact inherent to rugby or its offshoot, football—with a battle line of smashing arms, heads, and elbows simply to initiate play. But which sport was in total more violent? The violence on these local soccer fields was apparent and included not just participants but spectators.

In Harmarville and other towns like Fall River, soccer's roots remained. Though after the 1956 championship, the local Harmarville team would not advance beyond the state level until 1968 and never move beyond the semifinals in any national tournament after 1961, the legacy of the town's Hurricanes has fed the game here. Springdale High School, later the high school for Harmarville's children, became the dominant soccer team in the Western Pennsylvania Interscholastic Athletic League (WPIAL) and was the bitterest rival of my high school. Dressed in their ugly and intimidating orange and black, the Dynamos ruled local high school soccer during the 1960s and into the 1970s, winning nine WPIAL championships under the guidance of a former Hurricane, their coach Dave Meloni. These players also developed their talent playing on the local youth team, whose coach later noted that some sixty of his players had received full or partial college scholarships. One local player was Lou "Skip" Yakopec, the son of Lou "Sonny" Yakopec, the star player from the Hurricanes of the fifties. The younger Yakopec was a high school All-American, one of four from Springdale High School during Meloni's coaching career. The younger Yakopec's WPIAL season and career scoring records still stand. From 1968 to 1972, the Dynamos won a mind-boggling seventy-two games, long a national record. The former player Mike Fogle recounted a mindset for success that echoed the Hurricanes before him, "Just about everybody in that little community was a coal miner or steel worker. They gave the players a work ethic a lot of us carried. No one was ever going to outwork us; no one would play the game harder."[111] Most recently, the girls' high school team was in the limelight. Since 1997 it has reached the state championship two times, including a heartbreaking 1–0 loss in 2009.

Another factor in soccer's second-rate status is the nature of those who play. American football's development was driven by a desire among the eastern elite to retain control of their game from the poor huddled masses cracking the lineups, making All-American—those hulks with last names ending in "ski."[112] Soccer then was relegated to table scraps, a game for the immigrant: the dweller of the ghetto, the barrio, the coal patch. But this story overlooks the broader history of soccer's development, how very American that game was in Harmarville and other towns in western Pennsylvania, not a dead-end cultural relic of the immigrant. It was from the soil. And its growth was entwined in the rapid industrialization that radically remade this area's physical and social landscapes.

Even supporters have offered similarly limited narratives of American soccer to explain its relative obscurity in relation to the triumvirate: football, baseball, and basketball. Opining about the poor attendance at closed-circuit broadcasts of the 1974 World Cup at the Syria Mosque, a former burlesque theater, an organizer explained, "We would have done better in

Pittsburgh if the Italians had gone farther than the Polish."[113] The owner of the former Pittsburgh indoor soccer team, the Spirit, optimistically noted of his potential market that it was not "ethnic kolbassi anymore."[114] Of course, they still eat kolbassi in Pittsburgh. Lots of it. I like mine with sauerkraut, German sauerkraut.

It is true that in the region, soccer possessed some of the ethnic flavor often associated with the game. In the early part of the twentieth century, the Pittsburgh Celtic team competed in the area. Like most teams of the period its side was filled with Scotsmen, who borrowed the name of one of their homeland's most famous, at times notorious teams: a flashpoint for the sectarian violence of Catholic versus Protestant. Today, the Celtic faithful still chant:

> Hullo, Hullo
> We are the Billy Boys
> Hullo, Hullo
> You'll know us by our noise
> We're up to our knees in Fenian blood
> Surrender or you'll die.

Before a game between local all-stars—Brits and a team of Scottish players—a parade led by a bagpipe band made its way to the pitch through the town of Rankin.[115] Though Rankin was not a Highlands' battlefield, this past was likely invoked in the minds of some locals, especially since the original Scottish teams had been founded in that partisan climate. As in other parts of the country, that history was often on display in the Pittsburgh area, such as when the Orangemen of Western Pennsylvania in 1920 held a two-day celebration on the 230th anniversary of the Battle of the Boyne, the clash that deposed the Catholic King James and established Protestant rule in Ireland. The festive two days included not only Irish and Scottish dancing but also a soccer match of British Canadian war veterans and local all-stars.[116]

Soccer was a vehicle for others to define ethnicity too. In an enthusiastic and lengthy article recounting a West Penn Cup semifinal match between the Rovers and German Sport, the *Press* journalist noted, "The whole German machine was a collection of cool, heady players."[117] Such stereotypes of German identity, as a methodical, machinelike, dispassionate collective have defined the German player; and the nature of Germany's recent World Cup sides—creative, attacking, and multiethnic—are therefore apparently un-German. In the 1960s, when the Pittsburgh Steelers owner Art Rooney founded the Philadelphia Spartans, a team in the outlaw National Professional Soccer League, management consciously crafted a multiethnic team: "In assembling the Spartans, the Rooneys aimed for a nationality mixture—Spaniards, Portuguese, Basques, Argentinians, Brazilians, and Europeans. The theory is that warm-weather players will be used on the attack while stronger, more durable Northern Europeans will play on defense."[118] Rooney's motley lineup for his cross-state team, though troublingly reasoned, was a fitting model for the local soccer clubs, which unlike in many other parts of the country, were not typically defined by ethnicity, but by a community, by talent as with the Hurricanes, who "favored no ethnic group."[119]

In the Spartans article, the writer claimed that soccer would be "making its debut," a claim based on the difference between "soccer on the World Cup level and what we have been looking at here."[120] This awareness of American identity, of natives having to prove their mettle against those from elsewhere, is also a theme that runs through the game's early history. In an article from 1913 covering an impending match between British and local players, the writer commented, "There has been some feeling lately in the various soccer camps on the question of whether the old country players are still masters of the game, and instructors of the American players. Some excitement therefore attaches to the big event."[121] The need to establish an American tradition included defining a style of play. In a 1918 article titled "Native Born Stars Developing," D. C. Adamson defined what he believed was an emergent American soccer, with "the spirit of aggressiveness and the general 'pep' which American born players inject into their plays" that "almost, now, overcomes the great dribbling prowess of Scottish players." Adamson noted, however, the general lack of great midfielders—the field generals—players who possess and distribute the ball. He argued that only international trials against European teams could answer the question, "Which is the greatest soccer nation in the world?"[122]

It is not surprising that the emphasis on establishing American credibility on the pitch was such a focus in the media, given the patriotic fervor in the aftermath of World War I and western Pennsylvania's history. Locals could not help but notice the Miner's League crowds of "several thousand spectators, most of them . . . shouting in languages we couldn't understand."[123] The 1920s was a period of increasingly restrictive immigration policies at the national level, which closed the spigot on the migration that brought the miners to these valleys. The soccer world stage was a place to tout the presence of "full citizens of the United States," as in the case of the Olympic Soccer team headed for Antwerp.[124] In 1918, the United States Football Association, the sport's governing organization in America, "went

100 percent patriotic" at its national meeting in Pittsburgh and banned noncitizens from holding office in the institution.[125] The 1950s Hurricanes team was noted for its all native-born lineup when facing teams such as the New York Americans, a pro team stocked with foreigner players.[126] This historical pull of American exceptionalism was another driving force in the establishment of the American sports hierarchy, illustrating how the current order was due to more than a simple embrace of football as suitably American; it was also a corresponding proscription on soccer to become American.

Key to soccer's transformation was the recent erasure of the roots of the game in America, so that the "exclusively blue-collar identification that soccer has had in many parts of the world has been supplemented in the United States . . . by a chic suburban profile."[127] In 1958, the city of Pittsburgh celebrated its bicentennial with a Pitt track meet against Penn State and a soccer match of local all-stars, including Pug Malinowski, Sonny Yakopec, and Ray Bernabei from the Hurricanes, against a German professional team. The program for the celebration included cheery ads from Pittsburgh Coke and Chemical and Consolidation Coal Company. The connected rise and fall of soccer and coal made the brochure a collage of the region's history that may now seem a bizarre, if fitting artifact. Teams like the Harmarville Hurricanes and their story represent an economic and social history, one less simple than that found in stereotypically suburban scenes of youth soccer and less cinematic and redeeming than sports tales staged in an Iowa cornfield at sunset. It is about struggle in blood and coal.

Scholars have noted that the working and living conditions in coal towns of southwestern Pennsylvania created uniquely tight bonds.[128] Despite ethnic divides, sometimes reinforced by housing patterns that fractured communities and provided barriers to organizing labor, institutions like soccer teams were vehicles for community pride that promoted a collective identity. Nathan Abrams, looking at the history of British soccer, notes that "the soccer team contributed to the intensity of local consciousness by evincing a sense of local belonging."[129] And the game played on these crude pitches was the vehicle for an identity that was less Scottish, Italian, or Hungarian, and more miner. A collective identity was especially prevalent among recent Eastern European immigrants, who were not only more geographically isolated from each other in the bituminous coal region, but faced even more powerful challenges to organization—by the coal operators and their army of Cossacks—than miners in eastern Pennsylvania: "One cannot isolate workers' labor experience from the other parts of their lives.... Ethnic particularism, while certainly present, was not a bar to cooperation evidenced not only by the union or church ... miners battled for their ideas of democratic community based upon an order of reciprocal obligations and relational justice."[130] For George Resavage, the winning-goal scorer in that dramatic match in the 1956 US Open final, it was the death of King Coal that doomed soccer: "When the mines shut down it just dwindled away. Soccer sort of died. It really died."[131]

Those weekend matches decades ago on the stony frozen grounds in towns like Harmarville and Beadling were expressions of desires well beyond the pitch. Soccer was a child's game, a tradition, a path to a better job, a day off, a parent culture, a community. Maybe contemporary critics who see the beautiful game as a threat apprehend part of its utility for those who do the dirty, dangerous work we depend on and deny. As a former English player in 1909 noted in the *Pittsburgh Press*, "Soccer is a thinking game.... There is no quarterback to give you the best play. A player has to think it out for himself."[132] In another one of those early instructional articles about soccer, titled "Head Work is Necessary in Soccer Football," William Meredith, deemed "the best outside wingman in Great Britain," claimed: "It is the man with ideas and observation who makes a good footballer."[133] It is the player who can imagine the space behind a defense to run through, who can anticipate the movement of a teammate who excels—one with vision.

The Man in Coal

It was a hot summer day. I parked behind the fire station before a chain-link fence by the park, where a young mother was wheeling her children about. I thought about my youngest, born just two months before. The state was tearing down the old turnpike bridge that loomed over the field I used to play on, where the parents honked their horns and yelled for the play of twelve-year-olds. A train trundled by, temporarily drowning out the concussive pulse of jackhammers. I wondered if the bar across the street was open.

Before me was a black life-sized miner, pick above his head, and standing on a mountain of coal. Tan brick walls with the names of miners flanked the figure: Mike Yakopec, in whose bar those '56 champions showered and drank free; Frank Dallas, killed on December 17, 1971; the Scotch Miners; and the Survivors of the 1927 Strike. Here, in Acmetonia, the neighborhood where families were forced to live after their eviction during that strike in 1927, the stories of the local men who imagined better lives for themselves, their families, and their community have been memorialized. The plaque reads, "Our communities were built / And this Proud legacy Began / As Industry Developed in these Valleys, / Fueled by Coal and Human Grit."

The miner stands on a mountain that includes a woman putting out laundry, a church of no clear denomination, a tipple, and emerging from the black metal, a small figure of a soccer player, his left arm and leg still stuck in the mountain. But, at his foot is the ball, his foot angled as if to pass to a teammate streaking forward. His right hand an oversized fist.

POACHED TROUT

Fishing and Hunting in Penn's Woods

When I was fifteen I fell in love—with a fish. Of course, I held other more emotionally charged affinities for my fellow species, but none would last as long as my love for the fabled noble game fish that I read about in Ray Bergman's *Trout*, a classic tome of fly-fishing. I imagined the languorous glide of an enormous, kype-jawed brown trout, *Salmo trutta*, as it moved to sip a dry fly in some rocky river. But for me, such a vision remained just that. The local stream where I could fish, Squaw Run, is a small tributary of the Allegheny River, allegedly named in remembrance of a brave "squaw" who defied her father, Guyasuta, to marry the man she loved.[1] But the stream where the two lovers of dubious legend hid in a cave was in my childhood a shallow shale-bottomed creek, far too warm and likely too polluted as well to hold any lunker brown trout. I contented myself with catching carp in the few pools I could find. Dough balls crimped on a barbed hook would have to substitute for a gaudy Royal Coachman dry fly drifted just so. The only trout within walking distance that I knew of were swimming on the grounds of the Pittsburgh Field Club, in a fenced-off pond below the club's green skeet tower, barely visible from the wooded road that snaked by the mansions of a Steelers star running back and the CEO of that most emblematic of Pittsburgh institutions, Heinz.

The Field Club was founded in 1882 as the Pittsburgh Cricket Club, and relocated to then rural Fox Chapel in 1915, where open land for a golf course was available; and it became an exclusive and "most gracious club," where on muggy summer evenings I attended dances in pursuit of the equally mysterious other sources of my teenage dreams.[2] But, unless one were a member of the club, its trout remained even more out of reach than the Fox Chapel girls in sundresses dancing to Earth, Wind & Fire. So I contented myself with reading about trout, taking a fly-tying class along the banks of Squaw Run, and learning from my teacher just what all those sudsy bubbles in the creek, or "crick" in the local parlance, were and why I wouldn't be seeing much more than minnows and crayfish scurry in it.

That anything would be swimming in the waters near Pittsburgh in the 1970s would strike many people as miraculous given the city's persistent image as Nature's Golgotha. Local rivers—the Monongahela and Allegheny—once provided rich harvests of species such as bass, catfish, and drum to the assorted Indigenous peoples who lived in and passed through the region and used weirs to harvest them.[3] After Native dispossession and European settlement, renaming of the land, local merchants sold fish from surrounding waters to the city's expanding settler population. But the waters flowing out of these hill valleys, including the rivulets that flowed out from the hills surrounding towns like Harmarville, carried an increasingly lethal legacy.

As early as the beginning of the nineteenth century, observers noted the noxious nature of the region's water due to the runoff from the coal-rich hills, a natural phenomenon logarithmically exacerbated once King Coal set down in the area. The release of large quantities of soluble acids was a by-product of coal mining, which exposed rocks rich with sulfides to contact with water, producing sulfuric acid. The pumping of accumulated water from within mines added to this acid load and would forever challenge the ability of species such as trout, which require water of more neutral pH, to survive. In 1910 an official from the US Army Corps of Engineers commented about the Monongahela: "The salmon and bass, which formerly abounded in its waters and in those of its large tributaries, have become practically extinct."[4] The acidic nature of the region's water not only destroyed aquatic environments but also seriously damaged the manufacturing equipment of the region's industries. To combat this damage, the manufacturers and railroad companies were forced to treat the massive quantities of water needed to operate their businesses, water they then dumped back into the rivers.

Mixed with this industrial waste from the region's mines, steel mills, and glass factories, was an increasingly large load of human waste that depleted water oxygen levels and exposed fish and humans to disease. Unfortunately, city officials in the late 1800s, aware of the increasing need for a citywide sewage system, decided to build a sewage infrastructure that combined rainwater runoff with the untreated waste from the city's burgeoning population. Eventually, by the turn of the twentieth century, the human waste of some 350,000 people was dumped untreated into the Allegheny upstream from Pittsburgh.[5] Residents drank the very water they and their upriver neighbors dumped their bodily waste into and, not surprisingly, the city long had, by far, the highest death rate from typhoid fever in the nation. The region's poorest communities, populated by immigrants and African Americans, were especially vulnerable, and had mortality rates double that of native-born white residents.[6] The region's scenic rivers were sewers. In response, Pittsburgh and other outlying municipalities finally began treating the drinking water supply. Disease rates quickly dropped. However, the large-scale pollution of the region's waterways continued for decades, and it did not help matters that the Commonwealth essentially defined the region's rivers as open sewers. In 1923 a state agency classified state waterways into three categories, with the Allegheny, Monongahela, and Ohio all deemed non-potable and unfit for recreation. This meant one was legally free to dump untreated waste right into them.[7] Not surprisingly, fish populations continued to decline well into the twentieth century. Although the city finally began segregating human sewage and rainwater, by the 1930s only one-fifth of the city's waste was treated, and in the early twenty-first century Pittsburgh still had the highest percentage of combined sewer systems in the United States.[8]

Although the region's waterways had been channelized, dredged, cordoned off, dumped in and on, they remained sites of play. In the early and mid-twentieth century, Harmarville residents swam amid the imposing barges on the Allegheny, and played in the orange-colored water of the local creek that was filled with mine waste and broken glass. On the Fourth of July, one especially fearless young man would celebrate his independence by climbing to the elegant, riveted steel truss of the Hulton Bridge, from which he would dive outward to the green waters of the Allegheny below. Kids played ice hockey under the tipple in winter, and residents fished in the mine canal for bass, sunfish, and catfish.

Fishing has long been a popular sport in the area, part of the rich history of Pennsylvania angling that includes American Indian fishing weirs and colonial sportswomen. The founder William Penn's daughter Margaret, writing in 1737 to her brother in England, asked that he purchase her new fishing equipment, as her "chief amusement this summer has been fishing."⁹ Just a few years earlier, a group of prominent citizens founded the country's first fishing and hunting club, The Colony in Schuylkill, later known as The State in Schuylkill. The club was founded by prominent Quakers who allegedly received the consent of local Lenni-Lenape leaders to use the site. However, in the early 1800s, "the encroachments of manufacturers on the banks of the river drove the club to seek new quarters." Members tore down their clubhouse and rebuilt it along the banks of the Delaware River, where they and their esteemed guests—presidents, ambassadors, and the like—could enjoy their regular repasts, washed down with the club's legendary Fish House Punch, and, abiding their 1790 resolution, toast General Washington, "the patriot, the soldier, and the statesman."¹⁰ In the 1940s, further industrial development would force the club to relocate again.

Across the state, including in the Pittsburgh region, men of means established similarly exclusive fishing clubs, as the waters became increasingly polluted and depleted of game fish. Local fishing clubs had been established by the 1830s and, with the region's growing industrial development, more such organizations, like the Argonaut Club, were created "for the purpose of recreation and pleasure."¹¹ However, members of clubs like the Argonaut or Duquesne Fishing Club, made up of men "prominent in the politics of this country," were not dependent on the game fish offered by area waters. They were wetting lines well outside the Commonwealth.¹² The Argonaut Club owned property on a lake in Michigan, with a steam yacht, cottages, and a "large fine club house," complete with a piano and a view of the club's beach, "one expanse of golden sand, stretching out over two miles."¹³ And members of the Duquesne, "glad to get away from politics as business," spent leisurely holidays on houseboats, attended to by African American cooks who ensured that "the wants of the inner man [were] provided for on an elaborate scale."¹⁴

Perhaps the most exclusive of such local clubs, certainly the best-remembered, was the South Fork Fishing and Hunting Club, whose membership roll included the city's A-list of businessmen: men such as Andrew Carnegie and his longtime business partner, Henry Phipps Jr.; the coke manufacturer Henry Clay Frick; the powerful banker Andrew Mellon; and the owner of the city's major department store, Durbin Horne. These were the men who built the Steel City into industrial might and founded the institutions that defined it, their names a lingua franca to all Burghers. The historian and Pittsburgh native David McCullough has described these men as "an early-rising, healthy, hard-working, no-nonsense lot, Scotch-Irish most of them, Freemasons, tough, canny, and, without question, ex-

3.1 Johnstown Flood, 1889. Reproduced by permission from Archives of Industrial Society Photograph Collection, University of Pittsburgh.

tremely fortunate to have been in Pittsburgh at that particular moment in history."[15]

These lucky few had purchased a rundown property, consisting of 160 acres and a shallow lake formed by an earthen dam, which loomed over the surrounding hillsides of a scenic river valley above Johnstown, a mill town east of Pittsburgh. Members rebuilt the property's dam, originally constructed by the state to create a water supply for its new canal system, and stocked the now restored lake with one thousand bass to challenge their angling prowess. They planted flowers and fruit trees and built cottages. On breezy summer afternoons members and their families cruised on the lake in sailboats, and later in the evening men shot billiards in the massive clubhouse. A stock certificate from the club, now archived in a folder inside the Senator John Heinz History Center, depicts a scene of tranquil sporting life: an angler stands in the bow of a canoe casting a fly rod, while another launches his craft into calm Lake Conemaugh, surrounded by gentle mountains. On the shore, a man accompanied by a spaniel aims his gun skyward to birds on the wing.[16]

Looking at that scene now, it is hard not to see those cumulous clouds above the far mountains as portending something less than idyllic, for in May 1889, less than ten years after the club's founding, several days of heavy rain threatened to overwhelm the amateurishly rebuilt dam. The club had never replaced the original drainage system, which a previous owner removed, and only a spillway, now jammed by a screen to keep fish in, was left to release water from the rapidly rising lake. Immigrant Italian laborers from the area were hired by the club in a frantic and futile attempt to shore up the dam. Late in the afternoon on May 31, 1889, an estimated 20 million gallons of water suddenly rolled down the valley at a rate recently estimated at three times the flow over Niagara Falls: 8,500 cubic meters per second. The flow gained speed as it raced into Johnstown, crashing into the town as a wave of water, trees, houses, and other debris that swept away everything in its fierce path.[17] Worse yet, a massive blaze, started by debris, incinerated many who had survived the floodwaters. Over 2,200 people perished. Walt Whitman quickly penned an homage, in which he called on readers to

> . . . mourn the old, the young untimely
>   drawn to thee,
>
> The fair, the strong, the good, the capable,
>
> The household wreck'd, the husband and
>   the wife, the engulf'd forger
> in his forge.

And the bard of Democracy also reminded us of Death's inevitability, a manifestation of the universe's power:

> Thou! thou! the vital, universal, giant force
>   resistless, sleepless, calm,
> Holding humanity as in thy open hand,
>   as some ephemeral toy.
>
> How ill to e'er forget thee![18]

Unlike Whitman, many Americans, including newspaper writers, saw something other than the divine operation of the cosmos. Humans were to blame, specifically the wealthy big shots of the South Fork Fishing and Hunting Club. One local described this view in less fluid prosody:

> Many thousand human lives—
> Butchered husbands, slaughtered wives,
>   Mangled daughters, bleeding sons,
>   Hosts of martyred little ones,
> (Worse than Herod's awful crime)

Sent to heaven before their time;
> Lovers burnt and sweethearts drowned,
> Darlings lost but never found!

All the horrors that hell could wish,
Such was the price that was paid for—fish![19]

The comparison of South Fork Fishing and Hunting Club members' acts to the uxoricide, filicide, and genocide of Herod may have been a bit of over-the-top poetic practice by this local bard, but he did record a realistic antipathy among the area's working class toward the modern kings of industry. Though their names remain etched in the monuments, museums, and parks of my hometown, it is less acknowledged that their influence spread across the terra firma and open waters of the Commonwealth.

The excursions of these anglers and, in the case of the Argonaut Club, their families, too, were part of a larger cultural shift in Americans' attitudes toward the outdoors. It was now a place of play. During the late 1800s, Americans established scores of game clubs, the number tripling from 308 in 1878 to 968 in 1891.[20] As the historian Daniel Herman has noted: "Hunting and angling had become by the Gilded Age the most popular middle-class participatory sports in America, far exceeding baseball, football, and boxing in popularity." The problem was, however, as Herman notes, "to celebrate Americanness through hunting, Americans had to have game, something that the popularity of hunting was making problematic."[21] It would become the mission of these elite sportsmen to address this threat to game and fish via an increasingly intertwined set of ideals: American patriotism, rational conservation, and prejudice against those deemed outside American identity. They would help establish a bureaucratic system to manage the Commonwealth's natural resources, and the success of that effort created a mixed legacy of commendable restoration of natural resources and ignoble alienation of those whom these men deemed unworthy to access the resources that they enjoyed in such luxury.

Chief Silver Tip and Friends

Any Pittsburgher who ever took a school field trip to Andrew Carnegie's impressive eponymous museum has witnessed part of this legacy. Over the wide marble staircase looms "The Crowning of Labor," a mural featuring an armor-clad Carnegie, complete with long sword, ascending through pinkish swirls of smoke above his mills and bug-eyed demons to receive a golden wreath from bare-breasted angels. But another artifact of local industrialists' largesse is also there from one of Pennsylvania's most influential sportsmen. Inside the museum's Hall of North American Wildlife, formerly Mammal Hall, are the stuffed bodies of massive elk in combat, a camel-riding courier in a death match with lions, a family of jaguars, and a grizzly bear. I liked the grizzly: all teeth and menace, encased inside glass. The family of jaguars and the grizzly were donated to the Carnegie by John M. Phillips, Pennsylvania's "Father of Conservation."

Phillips was born in Pittsburgh, the son of a cofounder of the Oliver Iron & Steel Company, and he followed his family into industry. An avid hunter in his youth, he provided an especially romantic origin story for the Pennsylvania Game Commission. Later in his life Phillips recounted to a convention of game management professionals a tale of hunting with a friend in the Allegheny Mountains in the 1890s. The woods were mostly devoid of signs of any deer, but the pair had managed to find the tracks of a lone buck. They tracked it for two days. On the second day, Phillips recollected: "We took up the trail again and succeeded in jumping and killing the buck. During that long chase, we didn't cross another deer track. I said to my friend, 'I am done—I think I have killed the last deer in Pennsylvania.'"[22] Though Phillips had not, in fact, taken the last stag in the Commonwealth, it was true that game populations were being decimated by overhunting and environmental degradation from large-scale logging, mining, and industrial development. Phillips vowed to do something.

Phillips, an accomplished big game hunter, made a gift to the Carnegie of a grizzly he had shot while on a two-month-long trip to British Columbia with his friend William Hornaday, a renowned conservationist, influential zoologist, and accomplished taxidermist. Hornaday helped establish both the National Zoo and the kind of naturalistic museum displays, complete with faux vegetation and painted naturalistic backgrounds that wowed elementary school kids during those much-anticipated trips to the Carnegie. At the time of their adventure in 1901, Hornaday was director of the New York Zoological Park, and he recorded his Canadian trip with Phillips in his book *Camp-Fires in the Canadian Rockies*. It sold well. Hornaday marveled at the athletic prowess and courage of his companion, who had been hunting in this "wonderland of Nature no sportsman has yet set foot without Mr. Phillip's consent and cooperation . . . carefully preserved from ruin," as it was. First Nations peoples had no claim. He described his host as a "true sportsman, game-protector, mountaineer, photographer and genial gentleman, all in one."[23] And in his sometimes hyper-enthusiastic prose, he described the fishing and hunting, mainly the latter, they enjoyed in this pure wilderness free from man's taint. Of special note were encounters with *Ursus arctos horribilis*.

Grizzly bear hunting in the United States, Hornaday bemoaned, was essentially over, "now so very rare that it is almost impossible for a sportsman to go out and kill one, no matter where he hunts, and no matter how much money he spends."²⁴ Unfortunately for Hornaday, he would not bag a grizzly on their trip, and he comes across as a rather effete progeny of the Pennsylvania native Daniel Boone, given his golf shoes and Lemaire opera glasses, a gift from Mrs. Hornaday's last trip to Paris. But he delighted in recounting the yarns told by the "well-seasoned and nimble-footed" Phillips and his dialect-inflected guides about the memorable bears they had observed, stalked, and shot.²⁵

Despite the narrative's focus on these manly, action-packed moments, as well as less emotive digressions on zoological topics, such as bear behavior, Hornaday's book is replete with the regretful pathos of a man peering over a relic—the world of the smokestack and skyscraper looming over the horizon. The author notes in his preface, "We dread the day of the ranch, the road, the railway and the coal-mine—anywhere near the Elk and the Bull Rivers."²⁶ He speaks of that unique American desire to find salvation in the wild, after we have sullied God's green earth. When on one outing they came across some bear tracks, he recalled "to Mr. Phillips it seemed morally wrong to let that bear go unscotched."²⁷ Yet his caption of Phillips standing over his freshly killed Pittsburgh-bound bear reads: "Mr. Phillips Regrets the Impending Extinction of the Grizzly Bear."²⁸ To men like Phillips and Hornaday, the grizzly was an idea, a manifestation of the romance of the wild that hunting could tap into, some mythical restorative spring: "Eliminate the bears from the Canadian Rockies, and a considerable percentage of the romance and wild charm which now surrounds them like a halo, will be gone. So long as grizzlies remain . . . just so long will brain-weary men take the long trail to find them . . . and whether they kill grizzlies or not, they will return like new men."²⁹

These men, and only men, came back not only restored urbanites, but as Nature's proselytes. Like Hornaday, Phillips was an avid supporter of the Boy Scouts and founded the nation's second Boy Scout troop. The scouts established a conservation award that was named in Hornaday's honor after his death.³⁰ The program for the awards was long sponsored by the giant chemical company DuPont. The Boy Scouts affectionately dubbed Hornaday's hunting pal Phillips, "Chief Silver Tip," and his conservation efforts extended well beyond the scouts. Phillips introduced his employees to the sport, founded the Lewis and Clark Club of Pittsburgh in 1904, another cadre of big game-loving power brokers, and, most important, worked to establish a system of public hunting grounds to make this noble blood sport accessible to all Pennsylvanians. His work on the latter began soon after that epiphanic deer hunt. He and other like-minded men were asked by the owner of a manufacturer of clay targets and traps to discuss a means to address the state's declining game. Phillips was chosen as a lobbyist for the group, the Pennsylvania State Sportsmen's Association, and their work led to the establishment of the Board of Game Commissioners in 1895, on which he served for thirty years, including as president.

Before the establishment of the Board, Pennsylvania's game regulations mainly existed at the local level, with limited enforcement and, therefore, no effective, centralized system existed to conserve game populations. Phillips and others, driven by no small amount of self-interest, wanted an independent state agency, funded by a licensing system, that also had policing powers.[31] Eventually, they would win political battles against legislators and farmers and establish an agency with both the financial power and personnel to enact their ambitious vision. The Commonwealth commissioned game protectors, outlawed practices such as using dogs and salt licks for deer hunting, and implemented other measures to check market hunters. The commission's efforts were aided by the growing influence of Progressive politicians, such as the two-term governor Gifford Pinchot (1923–1927, 1931–1935), who ended the reign of the Coal and Iron Police during his second term. As chief of the United States Forest Service from 1905 to 1910, Pinchot was the architect of a national forestry policy emphasizing the wise use of natural resources, a worldview in tune with the needs of Pennsylvania's sportsmen.

During his years in the nation's center of power, Washington, DC, Pinchot had someone in the Oval Office who shared his conservation ethos and with whom he could swap hunting yarns, Teddy Roosevelt, the founder and fellow member, along with John Phillips, of the Boone and Crocket Club, established "to promote manly sport with the rifle" as well as conservation of "large game."[32] It was a cadre of some of the nation's wealthiest and most politically powerful men, and thus, an especially effective conservation lobby.[33] Roosevelt believed American men's virile and resourceful nature was a direct by-product of our past as hunters on the land, so protecting access to that experience was banking the coals of democracy. He is well known for helping to preserve millions of acres of forestlands, but he also influenced conservation efforts in my home state. While Pinchot often had political squabbles with the Board of Game Commissioners—Phillips eventually left as a result—the board and the governor shared a common goal of science-based conservation, and in the early days, Roosevelt proved an especially useful PR man for the game commission's lobbying on behalf of a resident licensing law. He penned a letter to Phillips "recommending this idea to the sportsmen of moderate means who hadn't the time or money to go far afield in search of game."[34] The astute Phillips then blanketed the state with copies of The Colonel's missive. He attributed the measure's successful passage by the legislature in 1912 to this effort. With its own revenue stream, the Game Commission was then able to institute more ambitious programs. When 300,000 state residents plunked down their $1 fee for access to Penn's Woods, the agency enjoyed a sudden influx of monies that far exceeded its paltry initial $400 budget in 1897. In 1920, the state purchased its first game lands, property set aside for public hunting, through a $0.75 increase in license fees. State game lands currently total an impressive 1.5 million acres.[35]

The state, which also instituted a fish licensing law in 1919, gained additional income to bolster an increasingly ambitious project of managing wild game populations, raising and releasing both native and nonnative species to restock the woods and waters—sometimes successfully and sometimes less so. Planting Pacific salmon in the Susquehanna River was one of its less thoughtful conservation efforts. These measures were all part of a system of control: regulating who could hunt or fish and for what, where they could, when they could, how and with what equipment, for what purpose, and if and how much they could harvest of their captured quarry. And how much that privilege would cost them. It is therefore not surprising that historians would later deem the state game commission's legacy as both a symbol of democracy and a manifestation of the accretion of state power in a marketplace of its own creation.[36]

The role of the Commonwealth in establishing and determining all these limits on access to fish and animals was immediately a source of anger, and it remains an irritant to those who embrace "the belief that hunting is a right."[37] In response to the state's proposed decrease in 2010's deer harvest, found on the National Rifle Association's website, one resident of the Commonwealth protested: "The Game Commission is stealing the money for their retirement funds as they do the insurance industries [sic] bidding." Another sportsman recently described the Game Commission's deer hunting policies as an "atrocity."[38] Though such retorts may seem easily dismissible, as the hyperbolic rants of late night, possibly paranoid, or inebriated Internet trollers, they touch on a historic tension between individuals' assumed rights and the state's power to grant privileges in Penn's Woods.

When William Penn founded the colony it was a haven not only for religious freedom but also for the right to shoot, trap, or fish. In his native England, the right to hunt was the sole domain of property owners and by Penn's time, less than 1 percent of England's population enjoyed such status.³⁹ Originally, hunting rights were granted to all Pennsylvania settlers on "the lands they hold and all other lands not enclosed."⁴⁰ Gradually, as in England, property owners would gain more expansive rights in the colony, such as enjoying exemption from trespassing laws when pursuing game if they owned fifty acres.⁴¹ This privilege was similar to English law, which, under the doctrine of ferae naturae, granted ownership of game to the hunter who harvested it and not the landowner—excluding commoners whom the law barred from possessing weapons on the lands of the gentry. When the state's legislature enacted the first licensing law, it exempted those hunting on their own property. The expansion of the state's game agencies incited class conflict as prosperous farmers and wealthy urban sportsmen rallied around the power of the state to promulgate and enforce laws that protected their interests, while denying those of others. William Hornaday's recollection of his days afield in the Canadian Rockies includes a minor anecdote that reveals the contrasting interests of these hunters. It demonstrates how the elite sportsman's view of hunting could be myopic—as limited as viewing the landscape through only the narrow field provided by a delicate pair of optics purchased on a Parisian holiday.

While out hunting with his guide, John Phillips spotted a marten and instinctively took aim. "Hold on, Mr. Phillips! Don't shoot! Don't shoot! That pelt will be worth twenty dollars next month!" his guide, Mack Norboe, cried. For Phillips, the marten was a challenge, a specimen—if not a trophy like that grizzly behind glass at the Carnegie. To his guide, it was income. It was money to buy some shells, a pair of boots. The contrast between those who relied on hunting and fishing for sustenance and income and those who deemed it noble recreation would be the source of sometimes bloody conflict in Pennsylvania. It is not surprising that back home in the Alleghenies or Poconos many would defy the agency Phillips shaped. As one historian of Pennsylvania's hunting tradition has noted, "One man's poaching was another man's livelihood."⁴²

In his influential conservation tract, *Our Vanishing Wildlife: Its Extermination and Preservation*, William Hornaday argued that only legal sanctions like those in England could rescue America's decimated wildlife. Neither the press, nor conservation efforts alone would suffice: "To-day the wild life of the world can be saved by law, but not by sentiment alone! You cannot 'educate' a poacher, a game-hog, a market-gunner, a milliner or a vain and foolish woman of fashion. All these must be controlled by law."⁴³ Hornaday argued for stiff fines that, if not paid, would mandate "imprisonment at hard labor at the rate of one-half day for each dollar of the fine imposed." Moreover, he exclaimed, "A sentence of hard labor should be the *first option of the court!*"[44]

During the rise of the state's wildlife agencies, Pittsburgh's media reported not only on the state's evolving fishing and hunting regulations but also on the evils of those who defied them: poachers. And in a report from the late 1890s, the Pennsylvania Commission of Fisheries noted the role of the Fourth Estate in promoting its work: "The newspaper is the educator of the people and the commissioners have found the press of Pennsylvania ever ready to spread the results of their endeavors before the public."[45] The papers published stories from America and Europe, where punishments meted out to contemporary self-styled Robin Hoods were especially harsh, including the option of being shipped off to one of the English Crown's notorious penal colonies.[46]

In an article from the *Pittsburgh Press* in 1911, the writer recounted George Washington's characteristic courage during his encounter with a poacher who made the mistake of prowling the grounds of Mount Vernon. There, America's founding father and icon of the Schuylkill membership, after crashing into the river on horseback, dragged the scofflaw's canoe to the shore, "disarmed the poacher and gave him a sound thrashing then and there."[47] Another article from 1917, cheekily titled "Saved His Wild Oats," narrated Emperor Maximillian of Austria's resourceful mind. Seemingly distraught over the weighty affairs of state while abroad, an attendant asked his majesty what troubled him. It was not politics, but the welfare of his prized ibex, which he feared would fall victim to a local poacher. His "astute" attendant suggested that Maximillian send this man's wife a letter "offering her the best silk dress that could be obtained" if her husband would refrain from hunting the emperor's prized game, an appeal to the kind of female vanity scorned by Hornaday. The ploy succeeded. The emperor's ibex was spared, and the author noted that "such, alas, is the influence of the sex that history hints the bribe was more effective than 'all the king's horses and all the king's men.'"[48]

This cultural prescription against gaining something in illegitimate fashion—and of policing women—was also deployed by writers to remind nice young ladies just what it meant to be a nice young lady. The *Pittsburgh Press* advice columnist, while acknowledging that "even the very nicest girls poach at times," warned women against using those influences of their sex to steal the amorous emotions of other girls' fiancées or near fiancées. While admitting that such girls might not be aware of their influence, "nevertheless, they make themselves electrical" and cannot help but garner "more scalps" as "an indication of their power over another of their own sex." The writer again reminded readers of women's inherent vanity, a trait that equated them with Indian baseness. The gentle writer thus implored young ladies to save their "sweetest smiles and prettiest frocks" for their own fiancées. To do otherwise was "not being a good sport."[49]

On American soil, the role of the male hunter as model citizen met an especially receptive audience. Hunting would keep "the rich citizen, the man of wealth and luxury . . . from drivelling down into a mere gluttonous sensualist, or yet worse, a mere effeminate man-milliner."[50] Manliness was ensured through the sport, especially via the pursuit of male deer. American sportsmen, like their English predecessors, have a long fascination, obsession, with the big buck. The Pennsylvania folk historian Henry Shoemaker, in his book *Pennsylvania Deer and Their Horns*, noted of the stag, "Legends have clustered about it and made it part of the national life. In Pennsylvania, where there was much diversity of race among the early settlers . . . the picturesque side of the chase became a topic of absorbing interest. The hunters became a class apart."[51] Though he claimed that "an entire chapter could be written about women as deer hunters in Pennsylvania," he did not bother to write it.[52] Hunters are men. They are men who proudly but casually sit on the pickup's tailgate holding up the gun stock or displaying the twelve-point rack of a buck lifeless in the truck bed. In Pennsylvania, as elsewhere, sportsmen and others decried the allegedly spineless shooting of does and the state has had a hard time convincing the public of the necessity of culling Bambi's mommy. Not until 1928, after farmers suffered massive crop damage and hundreds of deer died from starvation, would Pennsylvania legalize a doe season. The world in the field mirrored the world in the modern city as "urban sportsmen's idealization of female deer in the fields and forests expressed, in part, their notions of women's place—particularly upper-class women's place. . . . Doe and woman were both reified as mother, noncombatant and, by extension, noncompetitor in the male world."[53]

Protecting the proper decorum of hunting was part of a larger project of maintaining the social order: the gender, class, and racial hierarchies that benefited the men who directed the Commonwealth's outdoor life. Members of the South Fork Fishing and Hunting Club had not only placed fish screens along their doomed dam, but also fenced off the property's trout streams, placed a barrier to keep spawning fish from doing their business upriver, and posted the streams and grounds. Locals tore out the fences, pulled out the stream barriers, and helped themselves to the club's fat suckers and trout.[54] In one night's fishing alone, a few of the club's neighbors harvested 220 pounds of fish, and "as they cared little for fish," sold the catch in the town of South Fork.[55] In his book on the Johnstown Flood, David McCullough notes, "A classic undeclared war between poacher and country squire went on for years."[56]

F-O-O-D

She was like no one I knew, as far from the matronly, pleated-skirt-wearing women of my suburban life as the green hardwood hollows of Pittsburgh were from the swampy lowlands and crumbly red soils of the South Carolina Piedmont. She carried a gun and had a lakeside cabin set in a grove of white pine. It was there that we took our big summer vacation when I was eight. She called a loon, a dipply-doodler, slept outside on the porch with a piece of plywood beneath her mattress and listened to Janis Joplin. Her big brother, Doc, had won the Heisman Trophy. She spoke in a measured drawl full of rich phrases, "Well, the long and the short of it is . . ." And she fished—a lot.

Over the years I would come to know our Aunt Mary well, visiting her lakeside cabin with my friends after college, where we would spend our days drinking early morning beers, water skiing, and fishing for stubborn bass in the timber-choked waters of Lake Marion. Having become an increasingly passionate angler and conservationist, I sometimes raised an eyebrow at her rather casual disregard for things like slot and creel limits. Everything went in the cooler. One day, maybe it was the beer, I said something. She looked at me, and referring to her longtime help, declared, "Well, Robert . . . what you don't understand is that for Bertha, this is F-O-O-D!"

Such was the case for many people living in the communities near Pittsburgh like Harmarville, people viewed as poachers under mandates of state agencies and the assured men who established them. Joseph Kalbfus was one such institutional architect: a dentist who had ventured out West, fought American Indians, and later the Molly Maguires of the Anthracite Coal Region. He became the state's chief game protector and headed the game commission from 1898 to 1919. While Kalbfus, Hornaday, Phillips, and other conservationists of their era rightly decried the decimation wrought by unchecked market hunting, they sometimes seemed unable to grasp the notion expressed by Aunt Mary so pointedly, that some people relied on the fish and game of their environs not for profit or sport, but for survival. Hunting and fishing traditions in Penn's Woods had always been multifaceted and tied to the realities of class, race, privilege, and want, tensions often sifted out of ennobling histories of redemption and restoration.

Despite the expansive industrialization around them, Harmarville residents had access to heavily wooded areas in Fox Chapel and rural Indiana Township and, of course, to the Allegheny River and its tributaries. They had gardens, foraged the hillsides for blackberries, and fed on catfish from the local canal that one woman remembered as "delicious."[57] Helen Babich Sabol, whose family was forcibly evicted after the mine accident that killed her father, recalled their foraging excursions into the local woods, sometimes onto the property of their Fox Chapel neighbors: "Dad always kept hunting dogs so that he could hunt with them. No sooner he came home from work, washed up, and went into the woods to hunt rabbits. We filled berries into his lunch pail and mother made pies. We would go as far as Fox Chapel, there were trails where the wealthy people rode their horses. We were probably on their property and taking apples."[58]

Mr. Sabol's commitment to hunting also hints at something more than just putting protein in hand. The hunting and fishing of these men filled personal desires for recreation and were likely tied to larger cultural notions, including masculinity. While the film star Gene Kelly hailed from Pittsburgh and his repertoire included dancing in one film, *Living in a Big Way*, on a construction site after a quick game of football—young men in Harmarville were expected to pursue more manly roles: "You know, years ago I remember if you sang you were a sissy or—if you danced. They frowned on it; that wasn't macho . . . guys were supposed to go fishing, hunting, or get drunk."[59] Fishing and hunting seem to have been the exclusive domain of men and boys in the town and sometimes guns were mixed with that other defining male recreation: drinking: "Every New Year people with shotguns got them out at midnight. . . . They sometimes got drunk and shot the corners of the roofs. Mr. Howard one time hit the transformer and all the lights went out." Years later, Johnny Mojack, who founded the crack Harmarville Hurricanes, established a rod and gun club, whose members, one hopes, practiced more responsible gun handling.

Given the industry's low wages and the coal operators' control of their employees' access to resources, including food, such practices were a means to assert autonomy. As another resident noted of the local men who worked the mine, "Lots of them were hunters from Europe. . . . They supplemented the food with hunting, gardening, picking wild fruits in the woods."[60] During the violent labor strikes that the community endured, hunting, fishing, and foraging were essential measures, F-O-O-D. Yet the cultural hunting and fishing practices that defined these men's activities derived from their eastern and southern European homelands, made them, in the eyes of many, unfit outdoorsmen in Penn's Woods. For Joseph

Kalbfus and his ilk, the guns and rods of these coal-mining men were a problem.

The Slaughter of the Innocents

In 1866, a group of men met at the ornate, green-domed state capitol in Harrisburg to address the state's declining fisheries, a meeting that led to legislation establishing the state's fish commission. Thirty years later, the fish commissioners noted that my home region was an especially troublesome area due not only to the body blows of mine drainage, industrial pollution, and sewage, but the presence of immigrants: "There is a large foreign element here, and this element has exhibited deep hostility towards the work of the Commissioners, and open defiance against the fish laws. Efforts to bring these miscreants to justice are thwarted in every way."[61] They repeated this charge again in 1902, noting that the state's "most persistent law breakers seem to be" in areas such as "Allegheny and Armstrong counties."[62] What most concerned those sportsmen turned public officials was the ethnic nature of this immigration: the Hunkies who abused our notion of liberty by assuming they could "do as one might please with a gun . . . especially . . . those coming from southern Italy and Sicily, and those nations of eastern Europe commonly known as Slavs."[63] The former group was especially worrisome, what William Hornaday described as "to our songbirds . . . a 'pestilence that walketh at noonday'" and threat to the "native American."[64] His fear was only reaffirmed by the murder of Deputy Game Protector Seeley Houk in 1906 by an Italian immigrant.[65] When the state was unable to solve the murder, John Phillips helped raise funds to hire the Pinkerton Agency, whose investigation led to the arrest, conviction, and eventual hanging of the accused, Rocco Racco. The Pittsburgh conservationist also paid for Houk's funeral. Though Houk's murder was one of several reported confrontations between conservation officers and immigrants, the state's response to this threat was extreme and influenced by racist notions of "this foreign element." Recent discussions of Pennsylvania's hunting tradition note the illegal activity of such immigrants—for instance, the outdoor writer Mike Sajna observes that during the first decade of the twentieth century, arrest records indicate that "over half all violations were committed by unnaturalized, foreign residents," but it is important to point out that the law had placed them in the crosshairs of enforcers and defined them as lawbreakers.[66]

In 1903, Pennsylvania legislators passed Act 136, a law mandating that nonresidents purchase hunting licenses, a seemingly reasonable measure to curb out-of-state hunters from violating residents' property rights and to conserve game for the state's sportsmen. However, the act also stated that "each and every person who is an unnaturalized, foreign-born resident" must also purchase a license for $10. Essentially, such immigrants were made "nonresidents" by this act and subject to a fine or imprisonment if they could not pay the hefty financial penalty that the act stipulated. The legislation also stated that possession of a gun "in the fields or in the forests or on the waters of this Commonwealth . . . shall be prima facie evidence of a violation." The state had the right to seize offenders' firearms and sell them at public auction.[67]

After an initial failed attempt, the state legislature went further in May 1909, passing the nation's first law prohibiting "any unnaturalized foreign-born resident to hunt for or capture or kill . . . any wild bird or animal." Moreover, "to that end," it made it illegal for any such individual to "own or be possessed of a shotgun or rifle of any make."[68] At the Sixth Biennial Meeting of the National Association of Game Wardens and Commissioners in 1912, Joseph Kalbfus defended the act's sweeping application to a whole class of residents by noting not only the death of game officers at the hands of immigrants but also the challenge to a more narrowed application of law because "said men so resembled one another in general appearances that it was almost impossible for the ordinary man to distinguish one from the other, and we were helpless."[69] Kalbfus acknowledged the shaky legality of the measure but noted the opinion of the deputy attorney general that "this proposition may not be constitutional," but it was necessary for the common good and remarkably for "the well-being and happiness of these people themselves."[70] Not surprisingly, some of the "these people" did not agree, nor did the courts of the Commonwealth.

Shortly after the legislation was enacted George Cosick pleaded nolo contendere to violating the new act and later appealed his conviction to the Pennsylvania Superior Court.[71] The court ruled the law unconstitutional, finding it problematic that the mere possession of a shotgun or rifle was considered proof that the appellant was guilty of hunting, a determination that then mandated the confiscation of his personal property. Despite the claims of the state's conservation officials that such measures were necessitated due to foreign scofflaws hunting on Sundays (outlawed in 1873), slaughtering songbirds wholesale, and taking game out of season, the court stated: "It will scarcely be claimed that conditions are such in the state that measures so radical and arbitrary as proposed by this Act, are reasonable and necessary."[72] The court released Cosick.

Unfortunately for George Cosick—as well as unnaturalized residents for decades—another case testing the law was moving through the

Pennsylvania courts, that of Joseph Patsone, an Italian immigrant living in Noblestown, southeast of Pittsburgh. Patsone was arrested when one of the Commonwealth's game protectors entered his home and found he had a double-barreled shotgun. No one provided any evidence that Patsone had used the firearm to hunt. However, zealous application of these anti-immigrant measures was not unusual. In the Game Board Commission's 1911 report, the agency noted the receipt of such complaints, how specifically "some come to us regarding the manner which some of our officers have gained entrance to houses of aliens to search for guns."[73] It is also likely that some men enforcing these laws were less than objective in commissioning their duties. Since it had only a handful of game protectors, the state began appointing special deputy game protectors, who included sportsmen and former members of the notorious Coal and Iron Police—well-practiced in the abuse of the region's working-class immigrants. The Department of Fisheries also relied on a similar cadre of citizen enforcers, special wardens, who as the commissioners noted, "might be expected . . . not to deport themselves properly."[74] Moreover, these enforcers initially had a monetary incentive to make as many arrests as possible since half of any fine went into their pockets. Such laws, framed as conservation measures, were effective means of limiting the firearms available to a class viewed as subversive. They were men deemed likely to participate in labor struggles and radical politics, especially the immigrant population of southwestern Pennsylvania. When company men forcibly evicted Helen Babich Sabol's family after the death of her father, among the items tossed out onto the street in the rain were her father's beloved hunting guns. The company police later took them.[75]

Joseph Patsone could not speak English, was provided no legal counsel, and no interpreter. Not surprisingly, he was convicted, fined, and forced to hand over his gun.[76] Patsone's appeals, all the way to the United States Supreme Court, were less successful than those of Cosick. Though the state never provided any evidence to support its crucial claim that firearms possession by "aliens" created a unique threat to the state's natural resources, the highest court in the land took Pennsylvania's reasoning hook, line, and sinker. Patsone's lawyer, Marcel Viti, argued that the law violated the Fourteenth Amendment, denying a class of individuals both their property and due process of law and that it also violated his client's rights under the treaty between Italy and the United States, a crucial liability to the state's case, as suggested by the Cosick court's holding. Nevertheless, Justice Oliver Wendell Holmes delivered the court's ruling against Patsone, in which he reaffirmed the previously established doctrine that game and fish preservation by states were legitimate police powers. Fishing and hunting were privileges, not rights. Moreover, Holmes essentially accepted the state's claim that unnaturalized immigrants' possession of firearms represented a "peculiar source of evil that it desired to prevent" and pronounced, "it is enough that this court has no such knowledge of local conditions as to be able to say that it was manifestly wrong." The justice also noted that the measure did not threaten the security of this class of persons since it allowed them to own pistols.[77] In 1917, the state would amend the act, barring them from owning a "pistol or firearm of any kind" and this would be the law of the Commonwealth until 1967.

Sportsmen across the United States applauded the Court's upholding of Patsone's conviction. *Forest and Stream*, the nation's leading outdoors magazine, which had previously defended the South Fork Fishing and Hunting Club against public attacks, published an editorial praising the court's ruling.[78] William Hornaday viewed Pennsylvania's harsh measures as the pinnacle of forward-thinking conservation. Such laws would stem what he termed in *Our Vanishing Wild Life*, "the Italian Slaughter of the Innocents," all the more pressing since the Italians were like locusts or feral hogs, "spreading, spreading, spreading."[79] And he argued that even naturalized southern European immigrants be barred from gun ownership for ten years after they became citizens.[80] In his address to his fellow game professionals the year following the Supreme Court decision, Kalbfus exclaimed, "We have arrested thousands of aliens and have confiscated thousands of guns."[81]

It is impossible to verify Kalbfus's claim due to the destruction of many of the commission's early records, but what evidence does exist suggests a bit of hyperbole at play in the warnings of men like Kalbfus and Hornaday. In the Department of Fisheries report for fiscal year 1913–1914, the warden for the region that included Harmarville, J. E. Conklin, made only eight arrests and noted, "There are not nearly as many [violations] as I was impressed there would be."[82] And while one-fourth of game violations in the 1916–1917 season were for infractions of these "alien" laws, this proportion rapidly decreased, and by the 1933–1934 season only 4 percent of violations were related to such measures. Prosecutions for breaching similar fishing laws were even less common. Nevertheless, in 1915, the state enacted additional legislation that barred unnaturalized residents from owning dogs and from fishing for "any fish of any description."[83] The measure barring dog ownership would be repealed in 1957, but noncitizens would not be allowed to wet a line in the state's fabled waters like Big Spring Creek or the dirty Allegheny until 1960.

The battle between poachers, sportsmen, and the Commonwealth continues. In 2007, groundskeepers at the exclusive Rolling Rock Club in the Allegheny Mountains, founded by the Mellon family, discovered a dead buck with an arrow in its back. Two local men were arrested.[84] However, despite William Hornaday's early call for imprisonment, even the most egregious violators escaped confinement until 2010, when the lobbying efforts of hunters, such as Melody Zullinger, the executive director of the Federation of Sportsmen, convinced the state legislature to revise the game laws. The increasingly global market in animal parts has made Pennsylvania vulnerable to market hunters dealing in such commodities as bear gall bladders, used for medicinal purposes, especially in China. In November 2010, Wildlife Conservation Officer David Grove was killed by a poacher whom he had pulled over and was in the process of arresting.[85] Two years before his colleague's death, Rich Palmer of the Game Commission noted, "These aren't Robin Hoods. They're bad guys."[86] In January of 2011, Anthony Marasco of Cheswick, a thrice-convicted deer poacher, was arrested while bow hunting from his vehicle on a residential street in Fox Chapel that sits just above the creek formerly named a slur. Marasco became the first person in Pennsylvania imprisoned for a game violation when he received two consecutive ninety-day sentences of house arrest. The arresting officer commented to local media: "We're not swatting people on the wrist for this type of behavior anymore."[87]

Sportsman's Paradise

Marasco's arrest demonstrates an evolution not only within state game agencies but also within Pennsylvania hunting and fishing in general. The lenient sentences for game violations in recent times contrast with the calls for harsh sanctions argued for by the Game Commission's architects. This change may be the ironic result of early conservationists who far exceeded their goal of expanding the number of Keystone State sportsmen. After the early days of the state's game and fish agencies, the number of hunters and anglers tromping through the woods and wading rivers, anchoring boats, and, of course, buying licenses, mushroomed. Pennsylvania's residents, especially in southwest Pennsylvania, would become some of the nation's most avid anglers and hunters. By 1930 the state was selling over half a million resident hunting licenses and the number, despite a slight dip during the Depression, soared after World War II. During the 1930s more game animals were culled from Penn's Woods than any other state. Moreover, the class identity of the outdoor sports enthusiast changed; a state survey of hunters in 1940 revealed that 47 percent were unskilled workers, with only 1 percent women. By the mid-twentieth century, outdoorsmen were often ex-GIs, men from the local steel mills and factories, who had union jobs, vacation time, and guns they knew how to use. They were blue collar: Robert DeNiro's Michael in *The Deer Hunter*—scrambling over rocks to sight a massive stag through his scope.[88] We had survived the Italians. Or, rather, they had become us. Fishing and hunting had become trickle-down cultural praxes.

At the same time, on average, only a few nonresidents purchased licenses to hunt in Penn's Woods each year. During the 1940s, a brief summary of the commission's history by its chief of education—a unit that organized talks to Boy Scouts' summer camps and sportsmen's conventions—recalled the past troubles with "the foreign population, who did not understand our system, who often were fiery in temperament . . . one of the early sources of trouble in managing the game properly."[89] Although concern about immigrants fishing and hunting has mostly disappeared from public discourse regarding game management in Pennsylvania, access to the state's trout and deer remains a contentious issue. The most recent debate was about repealing the long ban on Sunday hunting, which was in effect until 2021. Opponents included the state's powerful Farm Bureau and the Humane Society, whose state director pointed out that hunters "already enjoy recreational opportunities disproportionate with their numbers."[90] Why give them more special rights?

On the other side, sportspeople echoed Evan Heusinkveld, a representative of the US Sportsmen's Alliance, who claimed, "At the end of the day, it all boils down to American freedom."[91] Other advocates of repealing the ban, including the National Rifle Association, which has a large membership in the Commonwealth, pointed to the economic benefits of added days in the field—more gasoline bought, hotels booked, pancakes eaten, and coffees ordered to go; and, of course, revenue for the Commonwealth in related taxes and licensing fees. The US Fish and Wildlife Service (USFWS) estimated in 2011 that hunters spent nearly $1 billion annually hunting in Pennsylvania.[92] Furthermore, a report by the state estimated that ending the ban could pump an added $630 million into the state economy.[93] Though opponents challenged the accuracy of such figures, none can contest that the sale of hunting licenses, which peaked at nearly 1.3 million in the mid-1990s, has been in decline here, part of a nationwide trend. Since most hunters are older, the steep decline in sales of junior resident licenses, more than 40 percent over the past decade, is especially alarming to the Game Commission and hunting advocates.[94] They argued that allowing Sunday hunting was one way to address this decline.

Sales of fishing licenses, first mandated for residents in 1922, have experienced a similar drop-off. From an initial 205,829, the number grew to over 740,000 by 1956, aided by the influx of returning servicemen—who enjoyed free licenses—a burgeoning middle class, and more access to open waters. After a dip during the early 1960s, sales numbers continued to grow, peaking in 1990 at 1,163,758, from where they have slipped nearly each year. The number of resident licenses sold is now roughly equal to what it was in the late 1960s. Allegheny County, despite having lost over 381,000 residents during that period, representing nearly one-quarter of its population, still leads all counties in the state in fishing license sales.[95] It traditionally leads all counties in hunting licenses as well.

The overall decline in these sports in southwestern Pennsylvania and beyond has fish and game officials, outdoors enthusiasts, conservationists, and others asking: Why? Is it those self-righteous people at the Humane Society, PETA, and their ilk sucking more joy from life, turning the public away from blood sports? Is it technology replacing the outdoors in the lives of increasingly sedentary adult Americans and their kids, who would rather thumb smartphone keys than cast a fly line or load a shell? Is it too much land posted or paved over for another Walmart? Too much water ruined? Whom can we get to hunt and fish?

Do Black People Hunt?

Joseph Kalbfus had imagined Pennsylvania as a sportsman's democracy, "a place in which our people of all classes can find pleasure."[96] The rapid growth of outdoor sports and popularity among the region's working class seemed to indicate that his imagined place became reality. However, the present state of American fishing and hunting suggests that something else has happened in our woods and on our waters. Finding an answer requires us to ask who, as in John White Alexander's murals at the Carnegie, has been left out of our imagined American scenes.

On a blog devoted to outdoorsmen, in 2004 a participant inquired, "Do black people hunt?" The assumptions are, of course, gaping, but, at the same time, the absence of Black people in the public realm of outdoor sports is real. Leaf through those worn hunting and fishing magazines at your next doctor's office visit and you too may wonder: Do Black people hunt?[97] So implicit is the association of whiteness with hunting, and fishing, too, that in the United States a Black hunter or fly fisher seems out of place—perhaps is out of place.

The paucity of African Americans in hunting and fishing is part of a more pervasive lack of visibility in outdoor recreation. A *Pittsburgh*

Tribune-Review article's headline succinctly stated, "Minorities Missing from the Outdoors."[98] Various outdoor recreation organizations and government agencies, including the National Park Service and the US Fish and Wildlife Service, have reached the same conclusion. A 1996 study of hunting and fishing among African Americans, Hispanics, and women conducted by the US Fish and Wildlife Service noted that only 2 percent of African Americans hunted, and while 10 percent participated in fishing, this share was still far less than that of the general population. And only 15 percent of those anglers resided in the Northeast.[99] Data from the US Fish and Wildlife Service's regular national survey of fishing and hunting, the nation's most comprehensive, were most recently completed in 2016. The survey reveals similar trends. Ninety-seven percent of hunters and 86 percent of anglers are white, and hunters are also predominantly male and aging.[100] Although Pennsylvania has not recently studied the racial and ethnic makeup of its anglers and hunters, it has studied the use of its state parks, and similar disparities emerge. In these parks, 97 percent of visitors are white. The Pennsylvania Outdoor Writers Association, with nearly two hundred members as recently as 2010, had only one Black member.[101] Such disparities have the National Park Service, state agencies such as the Pennsylvania Game and Fish and Boat Commissions, and the media seeking answers. It is vital that they do so given increasing local and global environmental threats and the nation's shifting demographics. Sportsmen's organizations have long been vocal lobbyists in Pennsylvania politics, and these groups contribute money to political campaigns and lobby legislators to address the environmental degradation threatening their hunting and fishing.[102] In recent times, the continued threat to the state's natural resources, especially from the rapid development of hydraulic fracturing, is alarming government agencies and environmental organizations that rely on outdoor recreationists to fund their agencies and support their agendas. In a 2006 survey of Pennsylvania sportsmen, 77 percent agreed that global warming is occurring and 70 percent agreed that it is "an urgent problem requiring immediate action." A majority also agreed that moving away from fossil fuels would not have a negative impact on the state's economy.[103]

In his book on the state's storied deer hunting legacy, the outdoor newspaper writer Mike Sajna opines that "women, blacks, and other minorities have never had the same strong hunting traditions and hunter role models—Daniel Boone, Davy Crockett, Hawkeye, Jim Bridger, and the rest—as the white male."[104] The US Fish and Wildlife Report of 1996 similarly concludes that the low participation rates of women and minorities are "primarily the result of cultural differences."[105] However, Henry Shoemaker's book of Pennsylvania deer hunting lore includes references to some of the state's "best known 'colored' hunters." Of course, men like "Black Sam" and "Prince" were likely the kind of meat hunters denigrated by those who shaped the state's game agency, even if another one of these hunters, "Black Headed Bill," was also a veteran of the legendary Bucktail Regiment, a unit of woodsmen from the rugged northern mountains who distinguished themselves in the War between the States.[106] Conservationists like Hornaday and Kalbfus had long associated hunting, not team sports like soccer, with military readiness, especially after World War I. In 1917, Kalbfus specifically noted the Bucktails as well as the Boer in South Africa as examples of how hunting prepared men for battle and "for this reason, if for no other: the State must supply young men with the incentive to this training."[107]

Shoemaker's discussion of these men from the rugged counties of northcentral Pennsylvania reveals what inquiries about Black participation in hunting and fishing simply overlook: African Americans do hunt and fish and have done so with great avidity—including back home in western Pennsylvania's cricks and hollers. And any narrative absent of these men and women is a partial vision of our shared space, what these sports mean to us, how to preserve their benefits and for whom.

Foxes and Groundhogs

The Pittsburgh region's uniquely strong fishing and hunting traditions were catalyzed by its growing industrial base, the waves of wealth and migrant populations that created a pool of recreational sportsmen and politically influential industrialists. The latter helped create unparalleled public access to Pennsylvania's woods and waters and a bureaucracy to manage the waters and keep the fields full of game. The opening of the Pennsylvania Turnpike in 1940, the first superhighway of its kind in the nation, further expanded the reach of outdoor enthusiasts. The region's postwar economic prosperity also put more dollars in workers' pockets to spend on the latest fishing tackle, shotguns, and rural hunting camps. And although the local hunting tradition became iconic enough to receive Hollywood treatment, no documentation apparently exists to quantify the popularity of these sports in the region's significant African American community.[108] Coverage of hunting and fishing in the local Black press, however, reveals a rich history left in the shadows of stock cinematic narratives.

Founded by the H. J. Heinz Company security guard and poet Edwin Harleston in 1910, the *Pittsburgh Courier* became one of the country's leading Black newspapers. Under the editorship of Robert Lee Vann, the paper's circulation grew to hundreds of thousands, publishing both local and national weekly editions. The paper was a passionate and effective advocate for African American rights in employment and housing, as well as in the sports world.[109] The *Courier* not only covered outdoor sports in its earliest years but beginning in the 1950s and through the 1970s it offered regular columns by its own outdoor writers—Walter Pettey, Claude Fisher, and Wellington Allen. Their articles provide an unparalleled window into the region's African American history, including the rise of Pittsburgh's Black upper and middle classes and their love of hunting and fishing. That African Americans were able to achieve such status in the region is a testament to their fortitude and faith, for blatant anti-Black sentiment is as much part of the cultural fiber of the Pittsburgh region as our curious dialect. *Nigger this* and *nigger that* was part of the painful public soundtrack of my childhood. The flip side of the heritage-conserving and, thus, charming ethnic neighborhoods we Burghers often tout to the outside is the estrangement of Black bodies that made them possible.

African Americans, enslaved and free, have lived in the city since its earliest days and made up more than 4 percent of the city's population by 1900. By 1920 their numbers had grown by nearly 50 percent due to the arrival of Black Southerners, especially those from Virginia, who invested their hopes in a move to the Northern industrial city.[110] The post–World War I expansion of local industry, coupled with new restrictive immigration laws that cut access to cheap labor from Europe, further catalyzed Black settlement. By 1930, 78,000 Black people were residing in the region. Although the rise of unions helped the white millworkers and carpenters of the Steel City gain a shorter workweek, more vacation days, and higher incomes, these organizations typically barred Black men from membership. Many employers would not hire African Americans; one steel plant manager in 1923 implored, "Don't send me any more niggers. I am sick and tired of them."[111] If they did hire African Americans, employers typically relegated them to the lowest-paying, least desirable jobs, where they were stuck. A state report in 1942 concluded that half of the city's firms practiced such patterns of discrimination.[112] The building trades were especially hostile to hiring Black employees. Despite a membership of over 1,400 workers, the city's electricians' union had but one African American on its rolls as late as the 1960s.[113]

The pages of the *Pittsburgh Courier*, however, at times portrayed views of the sporting life that would be familiar to the fine men and women of Fox Chapel, such as participants in the Pittsburgh Hunt, who, bedecked in top hats, worked their horses during the 1920s and 1930s near the group's elegant Fox Chapel clubhouse just down the hill from the exclusive Field Club. The clubhouse is now a private home, near the intersection of Squaw Run and Hunt Roads, overlooking McCahill Park, whose name recalls one of the club's families, the McCahills. They rode bedecked in the family plaid.[114] As early as 1912, the *Courier* reported on the hunting and fishing excursions of its readers and the activities of African American fishing and hunting clubs, such as the Professional Club of Western Pennsylvania and West Virginia. A June 1926 *Courier* article reported on the club's recent meeting, during which its members discussed plans to build a clubhouse in western Pennsylvania, complete with ballroom, reading room, indoor pool, and guest rooms, adjacent to a river where fishing and canoeing could be enjoyed. The club's hunting lodge was scheduled to be finished in September, complete with a "pack of thoroughbred pedigreed hounds." The business meeting of these professional men included talk of the upcoming Spring Fling, for which "neither time nor expense [would] be spared."[115] Reading the article reminded me of William Hornaday's remarks about John Phillips's generous supplies for their Canadian excursion, "a stock of provisions which fairly made me gasp at the luxuriance—and weight—of the array . . . John believes in living well."[116] After the adjournment of their meeting, the men of the Professional Club of Western Pennsylvania and West Virginia retired to the "palatial home of Dr. J. H. Boulware and spent the rest of the evening dancing and supping of the toothsome repast served by Dr. Boulware's charming wife."[117]

As was the case in other local newspapers, the *Courier* increasingly devoted space to outdoor sports, reflecting both their increased role in the larger culture and in local African American life. Of course, there was a crucial difference: race. While the Pittsburgh Hunt in the 1920s did admit, gradually and without voting rights, a Jewish member, Ralph Sunstein, one imagines that a Black member would have been unthinkable.[118] Since the late 1800s, recreational spaces had become increasingly segregated by race, so the rise of Black interest in recreation in the early twentieth century was supported by an attendant development of separate Black social clubs and recreational spaces such as Idlewild, Michigan.[119] Originally, a white-owned development targeting Black vacationers, the Midwestern resort became one of the better-known resort sites in the country that were owned and operated by African Americans. W. E. B. Du Bois, who in 1897 argued for the recognition of recreation's importance to Black Americans, later asked, "Can you imagine a more marvelous thing than Idlewild?"[120]

Du Bois's essay, originally published in the *Southern Workman*, touches on one of those "cultural differences" that may explain the paucity of Black participants in outdoor recreation: the Black church. His piece was mostly an appeal for the church to view recreation not as a temptation to idleness, but as a key component to "the development of Negro character to its highest and holiest possibilities."[121] He urged skeptical church leaders to use their influence to promote healthy recreation to meet those ends. In 1926 the *Pittsburgh Courier* recounted the results of a survey on recreation given to eighty clergymen, which was also reported in the *Southern Workman*. Not only were six of these men against the seemingly innocent endeavor of roller-skating, but an overwhelming seventy-one of these men condemned "'goin' a fishing.'" The writer was clearly flabbergasted. Assuming the preachers saw every moment of recreation as only an opportunity to wager, he exclaimed, "Surely there is no gamble in fishing, except to be against the intelligence of the fish. Poor fish!"[122]

Not only did the *Courier* continue to poke fun at such critiques but it also published articles and advertisements demonstrating how readers had become consumers of the outdoor life. Ads promoted Canadian excursions and beauty products, such as Madam C. J. Walker's Tan-Off, which allowed the beauty-conscious Black woman to enjoy "swimming, boating, fishing, motoring, golf, tennis, picnicking etc." and still "take no chance" with her complexion.[123] Writers sometimes satirized the very nature of such excursions: "This is the season you quit the comforts of home and pay an exorbitant rent for an ovenlike shack by a mosquito infested river, where the drinking water is warm and the fishing is rotten, and call it a vacation."[124] The paper also promoted Black resorts like Idlewild, the Black Eden, and noted benefits beyond the obvious salubrious lifestyle found in mosquito-ridden Mother Nature, such as simple relaxation or good fishing. In the late summer of 1929, the paper reprinted a letter from a vacationer, Grace Lowndes, detailing how visitors, who included Walker and Du Bois, were using the "Negro playground" to "an undreamed extent." She noted "the freedom of the girl on horseback, the freedom of the boy with his boat and fishing tackle . . . the absolute independence of the whole scheme."[125] Such recreational outings provided "an autonomous space in which to relax and socialize" that could not be found in the Jim Crow South, its Northern counterpart—cities like Pittsburgh.[126]

Most of the Black migrants who came to the Pittsburgh area after 1915 were young, rural, and male, and they came from farther south of the Mason–Dixon Line than their predecessors. The general characteristics of this group also define most of today's Black hunters and anglers.[127] Because they were generally denied access to open land and clean water, free time, or a market for selling game and fish, the hunting and fishing traditions they brought became less visible. A lack of disposable income certainly limited such opportunities, too. These men became part of the industrial workforce, "a reserve of unskilled, casual labor," while Black women, denied jobs in industry, were mostly consigned to work as domestics.[128] These later migrants' lack of industrial job skills and the racially biased business practices of employers and unions made them vulnerable to the antipathy of the white working class, labor unions, and local African Americans. The upward mobility enjoyed over time by many in the already established African American community was, in general, closed off to these new residents.[129] Used as strikebreakers, during the coal strikes of the late 1920s and the Great Steel Strike of 1919, they posed a threat to the established Black middle and professional classes. In *Making Their Own Way*, Peter Gottlieb writes of the period, "The migration forced an encounter between upper and lower levels in Pittsburgh's black community, and through this encounter the identities of both groups grew more separate and more sharply defined."[130] Therefore, it is not surprising that these migrants would be the target of critiques from other Black residents, as when the *Courier* chastised Black coal miners for crossing strike-lines to work in the coal mines and seek opportunities that the United Mine Workers seemed unwilling to secure for them.

In late 1923, John T. Clark, the secretary of the Urban League of Pittsburgh, the organization at the forefront of efforts to aid these newcomers, conducted a study of pawnshops located in the Hill District. Concerned that firearms displays promoted criminal behavior, he lobbied the City Council to adopt legislation banning such window displays. In March 1924 the council passed Bill Number 621, which banned the display of "pistols, dirks, bowie knives, jimmies, blackjacks, handy-billies and knucklers," and outlawed the sale of the last item entirely.[131] A press release from the Urban League noted a connection between the disproportionate number of Black people arrested for "gun toting" and the large number of guns for purchase in the shop windows of the city's major Black community. However, the league further noted, "it should also be remembered that there has been a great influx of Negroes, mostly from southern rural communities, characterized by poor schooling facilities if any at all and enforced periodic idleness.... Small wonder that people so environed are seriously handicapped in adjusting themselves socially and civicly to our urban center essentially industrial and complex!"[132] The institutions of the established African American elite and middle classes, such as the

Urban League and the *Pittsburgh Courier*, were voices that sought to aid, but also to distinguish themselves from these populations within the city's African American community. Fishing and hunting offered ways to do just that and to assert Black progress and integration into the larger social world of America.

On April 19, 1930, an article in the *Courier* began with a direct address to its readers, "Well, folks, much water has runneth under the bridge," and then updated readers on the current activities of the Sylvania Gun and Rod Club, so as "to awaken more interest among the people of our race for outdoor activities." Members of the club had "traveled extensively" in the surrounding four-state region and Canada, where they enjoyed "everywhere the courtesy of true sportsmanship . . . among all people." The writer, James Smith, noted that among the many benefits of hunting are "confidence in yourself" and "strong, hard muscles," while fishing "creates that old die-hard spirit." Smith asked his readers to note the number of "successful businessmen and great executives from the President of the United States down" who led such sporting lives, and he assured his readers that despite how surprisingly and quickly one could acquire gear, "you will not notice the cost, either."[133]

The homosocial world of hunting and fishing found in these African American sportsmen's clubs mirrored elite white institutions like the South Fork Fishing and Hunting Club and the Argonaut Club. Members even participated in that most elitist of hunting practices—fox hunts—though not on horseback or clad in Scotch plaid.[134] W. E. B. Du Bois's fear that church leaders would bar the development of Black recreation was clearly not realized, for later local Black clergy were also plodding across the fields in search of game. In May 1941, the Canonsburg Club, composed of "twenty-one . . . ardent hunters," held a banquet at the Payne A.M.E. dining room. The *Courier* noted that the African Methodist Episcopal church's pastor, Reverend Williams, was not only a member of the club, but owned one of the group's most impressive "array[s] of guns."[135] During his tenure with the paper, from the late 1950s to the mid-1960s, the outdoor writer Walter Pettey discussed on several occasions the link between guns and God.

Although Pettey's father would never hunt doves, since "Noah and company might still be floating around on flood waters" without their assistance, his son pointed out the many local men of God who fished and hunted and the Bible's many important hunters and fishers.[136] He noted that of the twelve disciples, a full one-quarter—Peter, Andrew, James, and John—were fishermen. And in one column from 1957, Pettey not only listed local clergy who were outdoorsmen and prominent ones from the Bible, like David whose slingshot skills certainly came in handy, but also argued for the role of outdoor recreation in helping one apprehend his or her maker: "More and more men and women are turning to the fields and streams, where they can be alone to commune with the One who leads them beside still waters and restoreth their souls."[137] Apparently, in some congregations, the divide between recreation and religion had wholly collapsed. In one Homewood church, the Episcopal Church of the Holy Cross, a special service was held in October 1967 for local hunters preparing for the upcoming season. Special seating was reserved for the huntsmen, who were asked to come adorned in their hunting gear—boots and all.

Hunting season is like that back home. Schools are closed or delayed on opening day in both the city and outlying townships; blaze-orange hunting clothes hang outside airing on porches; and roads are full of pickups pulled off to the side—their owners traipsing with anticipation through the leaves and shrubs. *Courier* writers captured the opening day excitement of hunters and anglers, offered tips about equipment and tactics, informed readers about changes in game and fish laws, and shared the news, including photographs, of trophy bucks and catfish. The goings-on at local Black hunting and fishing clubs were common topics. Though these organizations remained largely invisible to the readers of the major city papers, they were connected to the wider world of sportsmen and, thus, operated both as segregated Black social worlds and entry points into the larger social sphere.

By 1950 there were at least fifteen African American sportsmen's clubs in the region, although some would fall dormant and new ones would become established over the next few decades. Two of the more prominent of these included the Bucktails Hunting and Fishing Club and the Triphammer Gun Club. Several clubs owned hunting lodges in the state and Triphammer even had a lighted shooting facility. Clubs held shoots, sponsored hunting and fishing excursions, as well as social events such as the Triphammer club's annual banquet, where in 1957 the guests supped on a bellyache-inducing spread of "raccoon with stuffing, fried squirrel, roast leg of venison from the Pennsylvania forest, baked fish, roast wild turkey, golden fried chicken, stuffed rabbit, corn muffins, candied sweets, potato salad, hot rolls, and everything necessary for a perfect feast."[138] These organizations were part of a larger network of sportsmen's clubs that were especially popular in southwestern Pennsylvania, with its large population of outdoor enthusiasts. The *Courier* noted that in 1956, there were over 30,000 such club members in Allegheny County alone, and many were part of a

3.2 Hunters in Hill District, 1949. Reproduced by permission from Charles "Teenie" Harris, Carnegie Museum of Art.

larger umbrella organization, the Allegheny County Sportsmen's League. This organization claimed to be "the voice of 200,000 sportsmen," and it still exists.[139]

As members of this larger organization, clubs like the Bucktails, Triphammer, and the Dorie Rod and Gun Club helped promote fishing and hunting in the region, including helping officiate during the 1950s and 1960s at the Family Fishing Contest at North Park Lake, an event that drew tens of thousands of local anglers, who wet a line for the chance to win prizes such as a car, bicycle, TV, or fishing tackle. These organizations directly lobbied state fish and game agencies and legislators for policy changes to improve outdoor recreation, recalling the efforts of those nineteenth-century sportsmen who created the Pennsylvania State Sportsmen's Association. Members of the Bucktails were active in the Aero game-feeding program, which air-dropped feed to game animals during winter months in isolated regions of the state, a once common conservation practice in the mid-twentieth century. Triphammer offered local Boy Scouts shooting instruction and some clubs also had direct affiliations with the National Rifle Association (NRA), an organization now infrequently associated with Black urban life. Yet, the Centre Avenue YMCA in the Hill District, the city's Black Y, where Walter Pettey was employed, offered a gun safety course conducted by an NRA instructor.

Even more significant was the role these clubs and the *Courier* played as advocates for environmental causes. The *Courier* is best known for its role in advocating for civil rights, but its outdoor writers were also increasingly vocal during the 1950s and 1960s in decrying the environmental degradation so apparent in the Pittsburgh region and its African American communities. Reporting on the beginning of the city's long overdue sanitation system project in 1956, the paper proclaimed, "It is more than the sportsmen's battle for clean fishing streams, it is a movement which will benefit the entire population of all the states."[140] The foot-dragging of the state in addressing the endemic problems of mine drainage and industrial pollution caused the paper's writers to harshly criticize the Commonwealth's agencies and legislators.

The passage in 1905 of "An Act to Preserve the Purity of the Waters of the State for the Protection of the Public Health" might more aptly be dubbed "An Act Designed to Preserve the Profitability of Coal Companies at the Cost of Public Health." The legislation specifically exempted "waters pumped or flowing from coal mines."[141] It would be over three decades before the act was repealed, but the exemption of coal operators from enforcement would remain. Before this legislation, in an infamous state Supreme Court case involving a farming family whose water supply had been contaminated by the recent opening of a nearby mine, the justices offered a ruling that gave free reign to the state's business interests. This ruling and the 1905 act, along with subsequent legislation, demonstrated the influence of industrial and mining interests on the state's political landscape, influence that has long stymied efforts to conserve and protect the state's natural resources and punish its polluters.

The *Courier* frequently criticized the lack of action on the part of the state in addressing obvious violators, as when it pointed out a mine dumping acid waste into Pine Creek, just down the Allegheny from where I grew up. The small stream was part of a watershed studied in the 1920s by a local college student named Rachel Carson, who was attending the Pennsylvania College for Women. In 1957, Walter Pettey criticized the Sanitary Water Board for ignoring this case of pollution, "right under [its] nose."[142] When a depletion of oxygen in the Allegheny River, a common phenomenon during summer months, led to a massive fish kill that year, he argued in language echoing Hornaday, "Prison terms for those responsible would stop the wholesale slaughter."[143]

After fishing license sales began to decline in the 1950s, Pettey directly attributed the drop to pollution and claimed that this decline would continue "so long as companies which are responsible for these conditions can expect no more than a slap on the wrists."[144] The columnist continued his critique into the 1960s and when the state legislature shot down a bill curbing some of the well-known abuses of strip mining, he warned: "All sportsmen organizations have pledged the 'kiss of death' to these Representatives who seek political offices in the future. A list of those who voted against the bill will be given in this column next week."[145] Pettey's challenge to the state government to curtail such abuses was continued, if less stridently, by Claude Fisher who succeeded him at the *Courier*. It was, of course, during the mid-1960s that media, activists, and others drew widespread national attention to environmental degradation. These efforts included the writings of that former college student from a farm near Harmarville, Rachel Carson. Her groundbreaking book *Silent Spring* detailed the widespread environmental impact of chemicals like DDT, much of it produced by DuPont, the sponsor of the Boy Scout award long named after William Hornaday. Although another 1965 act did finally include mine drainage as an industrial waste to be regulated, serious measures to combat environmental degradation were slow to arrive. Success was realized ultimately in the massive decline of heavy industry in the region and the enactment of federal environmental legislation. Fishing improved, and by 1971 fishing license sales would reach their 1956 levels. However, the toxic legacy of the area's industrial past remains. Today the state advises the public to consume no more than one meal of fish per month from the local waters of the Ohio River drainage due to PCBs.[146] Although a 1998 study noted "water quality and pollution are serious sources of dissatisfaction for all anglers," people still fish, and for F-O-O-D.[147] The 2006 U.S Fish and Wildlife Survey found that African Americans are the most regular anglers and are more inclined to eat their catch. Thus, the region's poorest population, including its African American residents, suffer the most from eating the area's fish, another reason to avoid the sport.

Back to Black

Early reports of the Commonwealth's fish and game agencies often included references to and excerpts from popular literature of the day. The 1938 biennial report of the Pennsylvania Board of Fish Commissioners includes one such example, a poem from "The People's Poet," Edgar Guest crafted lighthearted, often schmaltzy poems that were cited in the *Pittsburgh Press* outdoors column, as well as in *Forest and Stream*, since some rhymes were explicitly about fishing. The poem found in that 1938 report, "The Sportsman," defined the traditional notion of the sporting life promoted by the men who helped found the agency.

> Said a six-inch trout as he scampered back,
> "not all of the human race is black.
> I've just met a sportsman in a boat
> A fearful man in a leather coat.
> I fought for my life, but his line was strong
> And I couldn't get loose of the hook's sharp prong.
> And I shivered with fright as I saw him grin
> With terrible glee as he drew me in.
> Then the hook came out and his line grew slack,
> And he patted my sides, and he threw me back.
> Then I heard him say as I dove down deep,
> 'Good luck to you, lad, you're too small to keep.'
> 'Yes," said the wise fish, "now and then
> The human family does breed men."

While Guest's use of "black" in the poem is arguably symbolic, the association of Black people as a group in opposition to sportsmen was long-established and disseminated in the print media read by outdoorsmen, in magazines like *Forest and Stream* or its competitor *Field and Stream*, with which it merged in 1930. As noted earlier, these publications espoused the true sportsmanship of elite white Southerners and took anti-immigrant stances. They also supported the slew of measures in the late 1800s that curtailed fishing and hunting by African American people, and included laws controlling guns, limiting access to hunting grounds, and mandating licensing fees.[148] Fishing and hunting by Black people in the postbellum South were subsistence practices more similar to those of the coal mining families in western Pennsylvania than to those of readers of such print media: "Hunting and fishing became forms of work that demonstrated not aristocratic pretension but the pressing need for food and income."[149] At times, they provided African Americans the chance to live partly free from the stranglehold of Jim Crow, to assert autonomy. Therefore, these practices were especially threatening to the social order of white dominance, and popular culture outlets such as Currier and Ives prints or *Field and Stream* promoted the unfitness of African American people to enjoy such privileges of American identity.

In the early part of the twentieth century, the editors of *Field and Stream* created a platform for print minstrelsy via a column titled "Uncle David's Filosofy," later "Unkel David's Letter," in which a former slave in Texas offered folksy advice to readers, such as "Don't ever argue with a ignorant man. Shoot him."[150] In 1911, Uncle David addressed the sportsman's anxiety about immigrants by assuring his readers, "As a gaim killer, I will bak Sambo aginst a duzzen Spagettys and Kazookowzkis."[151] John Phillips's hunting buddy, William Hornaday, and others would no doubt have nodded in agreement with Uncle David's boast of Black people's potential to be slaughterers of the innocents. In 1891, Joseph Kalbfus, at the time the secretary of the Board of Game Commissioners, penned an official report in which he noted: "Because negroes of the South and others know no better, are disposed to kill robins and flickers and other valuable birds, is no reason why we should either destroy, or permit the destruction of our best friends."[152] In this report, Kalbfus quoted Hornaday, who was even more direct in his views on African Americans. In *Our Vanishing Wild Life*, in a section titled "Destruction of Song Birds by Southern Negroes and Poor Whites," Hornaday dismissed those who would charge him of racial bias: "Whenever the people of a particular race make a specialty of some particular type of wrong-doing, anyone who pointedly rebukes the faulty members of that race is immediately accused of 'race prejudice.' Because of the facts that I am now setting forth about the doings of Italian and negro bird-killers, I expect to be accused along that line. If I am, I shall strenuously deny the charge. The facts speak for themselves."[153] In another section, "The Guerrillas of Destruction," in which he decried the damage inflicted by pothunters and included a picture of a Black duck hunter; a typo might have served him better. For in 1906, the very year that he would publish his account of his hunting escapades in the Canadian Rockies, Hornaday, as director of the New York Zoological Park (now the Bronx Zoo) became embroiled in a controversy involving the literal conflation of apes and Africans.

On September 8, visitors to the zoo were treated to a sensational sight: a small, Black, barefooted man with sharpened teeth, cavorting with an orangutan in the zoo's Monkey House. To jazz up the display for the next day, museum staff threw some bones on the ground and placed a target in the Monkey House for the small man, Ota Benga, a Congolese Pygmy, to shoot at with his bow and arrow and amuse the thousands of visitors now streaming to the Monkey House. The media was also abuzz by then with reports of a heated debate about the propriety of placing a human being on public exhibit. Though the *New York Times* reported that "few expressed audible objection to the sight of a human being in a cage with monkeys," Black religious leaders immediately expressed outrage.[154] Reverend James H. Gordon, the superintendent of the Howard Colored Orphan Asylum, demanded that Benga be released to his care, so that his physical and spiritual needs could be met: "We think we are worthy of being considered human beings, with souls."[155]

Benga had already experienced life as an anthropological curiosity for public display. After the slaughter of his family by the notorious Force Publique, a military force of Africans, Belgian soldiers, and mercenaries organized by the Belgians, Benga was enslaved. It was in a slave market that an American anthropologist, Samuel Phillips Verner, purchased him; he then brought Benga to the United States, where he was placed on exhibit at the Saint Louis World's Fair, held in conjunction with the 1904 Olympics. Benga was part of the ethnographic displays of primitive nonwhites, including Filipinos, that promoted ideas of scientific racism—the superiority of the white race.

After being exhibited in Saint Louis, Benga traveled back to Africa, where he struggled to adjust. He returned to New York in 1906 with Verner, who placed him and other African collectibles of his at the American Museum of Natural History. When that arrangement proved untenable, William Hornaday agreed to house parts of Verner's collection, including Benga, at the zoological park. There Benga was free to roam the zoo but began visiting the Monkey House, a practice the directors then used to create their infamous display, where an estimated forty thousand visitors came to see him on September 17. They "poked him in the ribs, others tripped him up, all laughed at him."[156] Within weeks of his arrival, his bizarre story created a public debate between these African American clergymen and the park, which eventually ended the display, and Benga moved to Gordon's asylum. In the meantime, an elderly French woman had written the *New York Times* offering to buy him.[157]

William Hornaday refused to see fault in his organization's exhibition of Benga and noted in a letter to the mayor that he and the park's secretary, Madison Grant, felt it "imperative that the society should not even seem to be dictated to by these clergymen." Grant has gained posthumous notoriety, for he was not only a leading conservationist, friend of Teddy Roosevelt, and beginning in 1893 a member of the influential Boone and Crockett Club, but one of the nation's most vocal promoters of scientific racism. He penned the widely read, 1916 eugenics tome, *The Passing of the Great Race*, an alarmist pseudoscientific book of race theory that warned of race suicide if whites did not mobilize to protect their borders and their bloodlines. He leveraged his public platform and connections to shape restrictive immigration policies and anti-miscegenation legislation. Despite the brouhaha, in his letter to Mayor George B. McClellan, Hornaday declared, "When the history of the Zoological Park is written, this incident will form its most amusing passage."

In 1910, Ota Benga moved south to Lynchburg, Virginia. He worked at various jobs and enjoyed visits from both Booker T. Washington and W. E. B. Du Bois; but on March 20, 1916, he shot himself in the heart. In a 2006 *New York Times* article recounting Benga's troubling tale, an official from the Wildlife Conservation Society, which now manages the zoo, was asked by the reporter how Benga should best be memorialized: "The way we memorialize the Ota Benga experience is by making sure that the place where Ota Benga came from remains a place where his people can continue to live."[158] It seems best we forget his legacy here.

Like the area's earlier immigrants, those Spagettys and Kazookowskis, Black Pittsburghers had reason to feel that the worlds of fishing and hunting, as defined by these elite whites and their institutions, were not meant for them. Yet they did not accept this assumption. They also appreciated the bounty of the lands and waters that William Penn had praised, and his daughter so enjoyed; and they wished to protect and access those natural resources. They protested.

An editorial piece from 1956 published in the *Courier*, titled "Vacation Blockade," features a well-dressed Black couple, a child between them, in a convertible stuffed with golf clubs and luggage, ascending a hill, at the crest of which is "White Palace Beach." Blocking their path is a gigantic white man with a Colonel Sanders string tie and upraised hand—signaling them to stop. The text of the editorial challenges the assumed "FREEDOM in the United States for colored citizens" by noting that "they are BARRED from many of all beaches, mountain resorts, hunting lodges, motels and summer hotels in this country." The piece argued such recreational outlets were of import to African Americans for "the urbanized Negro is far WORSE off than other citizens, and his NEED is as great or greater."[159]

The journalist Walter Pettey made his appeal even more specific, directly addressing the Commonwealth's agencies and encouraging his readers to join in the rebuke. He opened his June 29, 1957, column by asking, "Did you know that although thousands of Negroes support the Pennsylvania Fish Commission yearly through the purchase of fishing license[s], not one has ever been employed as a paid worker for the commission?" Therefore, he urged readers, "if you would like something done about this condition tell it to the State Fish Commission. If you talk loud enough they will bend an ear."[160] Five years later, he repeated this charge and noted that during his thirteen-year association with the Fish Commission's sister agency, the Game Commission, he had "never seen where a Negro had been cited for work in conservation in any state."[161] And, to his knowledge, neither agency had ever employed a Black worker.

What is intriguing about Pettey's claims in 1957 is that he quantified Black fishing participation, claiming that roughly 20 percent of licensing revenue was obtained from African Americans. Based on his numbers, and assuming they include all resident and nonresident license sales, perhaps as many as 170,000 African Americans purchased fishing licenses in the state during the prior year. There is no way to assess the accuracy of Pettey's claim, and the number he provides for total license sales does not match the license sales records of the Fish Commission. However, these numbers were sometimes reported based on licensing year or calendar year. What is significant is the likelihood that he obtained the data on the number of Black anglers from the Commonwealth—as this was the basis for further public reprimand.

Pennsylvania had long required individuals purchasing hunting and fishing licenses to indicate their race, and it is possible that the state maintained a similar accounting of the racial makeup of license holders. The destruction of these licensing records in a fire and the lack of any documentation addressing this question make it impossible to know. However, what is recorded is the African American community's response to being asked this question. The *Courier* reported in 1952 that "after considerable correspondence . . . between the Dorie Rod and Gun Club . . . and the Pennsylvania Game Commission and the State Department of Revenue," the club had received notice from these agencies "authorizing elimination of the designation."[162] It seemed Pettey was right; you could bend an ear.

Hoods in the Woods

"*Kap-plow. Crack. Boom. Pow-pow . . . Boom. Boom. Boom,*" so begins the celebrated Pittsburgh author and Homewood native John Edgar Wideman's disturbing short story, "Hunters." Following this concussive, auditory in medias res opening is a conversation between two unnamed persons, whose dialogue chillingly reveals the situation: they are two white men who have just shot a Black woman, whom they mistook for a man, and they are now contemplating the rape of this "bitch" with her "sure-nuff chocolate roundeye." Suddenly, after a line break, the narrator's voice intrudes and recounts "what white boys did to my baby," to the woman "born Jill Jones" who "curtsied and churched and niced her way into the light-skinned Jack and Jill social set."[163] In a few pages of lyrical monologue that slips into the present, the narrator recounts the larger social violence inflicted upon Jill and African American people writ large: her accomplishments as a swimmer, debater, scholar, musician as means to counter white expectation, but from which Jill "simply sank deeper into the miring clay of other people's perceptions in which she played the role of exception to the rule."[164] The narrator reveals how that day of the shooting was, however, to be a hopeful escape from the "deep self-destruct of race's grasp." He had imagined, "after escaping far from the ugly city on a bus," a sexual and chimerical merging, in which they could discover "what we might offer each other, do for one another once we'd molted, once we'd discarded if we could the silly skins of Jack and Jill and rebaptized ourselves in Zion's cool, clear, crisp waters, our spirits hungering, loving the chance for a new day." It was not to be. The story ends with the narrator pleading to hit reboot, to "start the scene again. All the players on their feet, whole, cleansed of crimson wounds and burns." And he appeals to Jill, "Forgive me. Forgive yourself. Let's start again. Let's begin. Let's run."[165]

In this brief story Wideman limns the borders of American life that answer to and interrogate that Internet inquirer, "Do black people hunt?" Wideman reveals the individual stories and practices lost in the "mixing into the larger life" and the violence that maintains social order. Given the constructed history of hunting in America, the sport remains "a badge of ethnic identity for white Americans, a badge that, though tarnished, is still worn."[166] Most troubling, this perspective not only perverts the historical record but it has also made the woods and waters racially demarcated zones, borders to be rightly defended, us against them.

The legacy of racially motivated violence inflicted on African Americans, recalled in Wideman's story via the imagery of black hair "set afire and left burning on her skull for centuries," reminds readers of some Americans' fear of being the hunted. Although the US Fish and Wildlife Service did not address this legacy as a factor influencing the participation of African Americans in hunting and fishing, and a recent *Pittsburgh Tribune-Review* article noted that FBI hate-crime statistics "show those fears to be largely unfounded," personal narratives and studies suggest otherwise.[167] Most hate crimes go unreported, and it is not necessarily the experience of such an event that dissuades minority outdoor participation, but the expectation of it.

Responsive Management is a leading public opinion research firm that focuses specifically on outdoor recreation. In 1998 they conducted a study similar to the one in 2016 conducted by USFWS but limited to fishing and boating. The research included focus groups, one conducted in York, Pennsylvania. An interviewee remarked, "That KKK mentality. I took my grandchildren, and it was awful the names my grandchildren were called.... My grandkids were scared.... If you're out there fishing, it's not worth it." The Responsive Management study noted the anecdotal versus quantitative evidence of its data, but also that "issues of racial intimidation and race-based issues ... probably indicate an underlying factor in participation among African Americans."[168] These suggestions are corroborated by subsequent studies, leading one scholar to profess, "Bad things happen to Black people in isolated, rural, pine needle-carpeted locations. African Americans have been and continue to be wary of bucolic landscapes. They view such spaces as places where Whiteness knows few bounds."[169] Local anglers experienced such intimidation. In 1964, seventy-five-year-old Mary Reid and her two friends attempted to spend a relaxing day fishing at one of her favorite spots north of Pittsburgh, near North Park. Some young white men approached and began harassing the group of friends. The anglers, as best they could, ignored them. But when they returned to their car, they found swastika-adorned signs plastering it: "Nigger haters unite ... join the American Nazi Party" and another "Kill all blacks." Mrs. Reid remarked, "It would indeed be foolish for me to go back"—even to a favorite fishing hole.[170]

As a counterpoint to the final words of Wideman's narrator, an essay from the February 1958 *Courier* by the author and famous Klan infiltrator Stetson Kennedy, begins with the call, "Don't Run ... Shoot!" In sardonic prose, Kennedy offered a mock field guide for African Americans who enjoy the sport of Klan hunting. The first rule is to "wait 'til they come after you" for "the minute they set foot on yours [your property], you can let em have it! That deed or last rent receipt is all the hunting license you need." Meant to be darkly comic, Kennedy's advice was legally sound, for American courts had long before adopted the basic legal principle from English law that deadly force is justified in the protection of one's home. Kennedy continued, "Don't shoot to kill—they aren't worth killing ... just cut their legs out from under them." He also enthusiastically noted that there was no bag limit, so "you can keep right on bowling them over." My favorite quip is at the end, however, when Kennedy offers an extended inquiry as to which shot is most appropriate for this quarry. He reasons like some warped Goldilocks that "buckshot is too good for Ku-Klux" and that number eights or sixes were not heavy enough, finally concluding that number fours were "just right." And, he offered, "ask the man for chilled shot, for maximum penetration."[171]

Downriver

By the time the *Courier* published Kennedy's mordant instructional piece, the paper was in decline, with its readership shrinking to less than a hundred thousand; and in 1965 the paper went bankrupt, eventually being sold to John Sengstacke, the owner and publisher of the *Chicago Defender*. Sengstacke would resurrect the paper in 1966 as the *New Pittsburgh Courier*, but it never again enjoyed the reach and influence it had in the past, nor would fishing and hunting in the city's African American media. The decline of the paper, this platform for Pittsburgh Black life, mirrored the increasing pressures on the community, as Black unemployment rates rose to sometimes twice or more the rates of the city's white residents.[172] The African American population became further concentrated into public housing and the city's most rundown and impoverished neighborhoods. The once robust Black fishing and hunting clubs would eventually fold, such as the Triphammer Club in the 1970s after ongoing problems with vandalism at the club's facility.[173] The gap between the city's upwardly mobile African Americans, those of the Jack and Jill set, and the increasingly large African American underclass widened.

In the summer of 1966, one young man, out of work and hungry, came across Harold Johns, who was testing out his new fishing tackle at the Allegheny Wharf. Without saying a word, he shoved Johns and his new tackle into the river, where the victim's shouting alerted police who dragged him from the water and his assailant off to jail. Johns's attacker had snapped. The *Courier* explained, "Striking out with flailing arms and legs in any direction because an American Negro is out of work, broke; hungry or disgusted with his lot . . . can take the form of envy not only against a white middle class shop owner but even against the affluence which permits a fellow Negro who has climbed up into the middle class high enough to afford snazzy fishing equipment."[174]

Like Johns's tackle, the legacy of the region's once robust Black outdoors life would sink out of sight, seeming to echo Frederick Douglass's words written in 1870, "Pictures come not with slavery and oppression and destitution, but with liberty, fair play, leisure, and refinement."[175] But pictures do exist. The photographs of the longtime *Pittsburgh Courier* photographer, Teenie Harris, show men in woolen, red-checked shirts, ankle-high leather boots, and broad smiles as deer carcasses hang behind them. Hunters posing in Harris's studio hold armfuls of fat raccoons. In flash-lit night shots, rabbits are splayed out like a poker hand across the hood of a Plymouth sedan.[176] A photo of the comfortable interior of the exclusive Loendi Club shows men standing before a wall adorned with Pieter Bruegel's classic painting, *The Hunters in the Snow*.[177] It is embarrassing now to admit that when I first saw these on exhibit at the Carnegie Museum, they startled me. Black hunters? But outdoor life in western Pennsylvania has always been more than the static image of a proper pipe-smoking, tweed-clad fly fisherman or working-class sons of the Spagettys and Kazookowskis testing their manhood against a noble stag silhouetted against a mountain scene. It has also been Black men in the industrial city vying for first place in the *Courier* Groundhog Derby; or great-grandmother Annie Steward, who moved north from the Palmetto State and in 1967 at age sixty-six, after two strokes, was still toting her shotgun out in the field to shoot squirrels, rabbits, grouse, fox, and deer. She also fished, and I'm guessing well.[178]

There was at least one all-female Black game club in the region, Club Deltier, established in 1947.[179] The *Courier* first noted women in the field in 1935, and the author commented that he "was surprised to see a member of the opposite sex out hitting the trail." When this hunter realized the writer's obvious doubt about her shooting skills, she assured him she had taken over two-dozen squirrels the prior season. He concluded, "I am of the opinion that since she lives in this section, some unlucky buck will fall victim to her marksmanship before the season is over."[180] Twenty years later Walter Pettey observed, "There was a time when the gals stayed home while hubby followed whatever sport was in season. Those days are in the past, now it is not unusual to see women hunting and fishing with their men folk and many hunt alone."[181] The writer welcomed women's participation, hoping only that they did not become too like their male counterparts, recounting how a friend of his had shot a deer, but when he went to tag the animal, a woman hunter attempted to tag his kill. Pettey quipped, "They are getting more like the men every day."[182]

In contrast, the state Fish Commission still felt the need then to segregate outdoor recreation by gender and for the benefit of men. When the commission opened a special "Ladies' Stream" section at its popular Fishing Project at famous Spring Creek in the 1950s, it argued, "When we succeed in selling fishing to our wives and sweethearts in a thorough manner, it will not be necessary in the future for us men folks to manufacture so many excuses and unbelievable stories as has been the rule when we were contemplating a fishing trip."[183] Reading the *Courier* reminds us that women were likely making their own excuses: women like Clara Smith, who belonged to the Deltier Club and was an active member of the Triphammer Club. She caught the first and greatest number of fish during a deep sea fishing excursion when most of the party was fighting seasickness that forced them all back to the pier three hours early.[184] The *Courier*

3.3 Angler with Carp, 1950. Reproduced by permission from Charles "Teenie" Harris, Carnegie Museum of Art.

reported that in 1957 one-third of the state's anglers were women.[185] Pettey even listed some local women who "can show the men a thing or two when it comes to fishing."[186] Today, the one bright spot, in fact, in the world of hunting is the steady increase of women's participation, a trend Pennsylvania's Game Commission seeks to foster through support of programs like Women in the Outdoors.[187] Despite an overall decline in hunter numbers in Pennsylvania and nationally, one in ten hunters is now female and at an all-time high in the state, having recently increased 44 percent in less than a decade.[188]

The pages of the *Pittsburgh Courier* remind us that casting a dough-ball into the muddy Allegheny or even a Royal Coachman dry fly near some mountain cabin among the hemlocks or tracking a ten-point buck edging along a dry cornfield has always been about more than sport. Sports are more than a singular image, especially for those who fall outside the borders of the frame, whether one holding an image created by a sixteenth-century Flemish painter or by a Black newspaper photographer from America's Steel City.

Poached Trout

Fishing was glue. During those teen years, when dialogue with my parents mainly consisted of questions followed by monosyllabic grunts, "What?" "Hunh?" it was one way to bridge the distance between my father and myself. So, on rare Saturdays we would wake up at 5:00 a.m., and, with the car loaded with waders, rods, and a cooler of soft drinks and tuna fish sandwiches, drive the Pennsylvania Turnpike into the Laurel Highlands. On the way to Dunbar Creek or Laurel Hill Creek, we often passed the entrance to Fallingwater, the famous Frank Lloyd Wright home owned by the Kaufmann family of Pittsburgh. But we did not talk architecture, or much of anything beyond sports: Willie Stargell's leadership of the 1970s Buccos, the Steelers training camp hopefuls. Only now do I understand that my anger was about what it cost Dad to make such a life for me: the Sundays spent in his office, business trips away half the year, the stresses and slights that aged him.

He learned fishing from his brothers on trips into the Sierras, where he once landed a five-pound rainbow when they left him, little half brother, alone to fish on a rock while they sought out the better waters. "Just a poor boy from Sacramento, trying to make a living," he always said. He had gone from there to Cal, to an American concentration camp, medical school, the army in Germany; and he scrambled all his life, sacrificed too much to sit atop the pinnacle of his profession. With a squash racquet in one hand, a Manhattan in the other, and always a Cheshire grin, my father ascended his own world of whiteness. But it was still one in which he was often reminded by even the most outwardly friendly that he did not belong. And when he bought me golf clubs, wanting to teach me the game he had learned in the army, he tried to enjoy the "most gracious" living of the Pittsburgh Field Club. But he was still too yellow to play a dogleg left there. They blackballed him.

My mother was visiting her parents in New Jersey that week, so it was just Dad and I, baching it. From my evening runs on the soft grass hills training for soccer—when the heat finally began to break during those muggy, hazy Pittsburgh summer evenings—I knew how to get there easily, without being seen. Park the car by the riding trails and slip down into the oak woods below the shooting tower. So, I got up at first light, grabbed my hand-me-down blue aluminum fly rod, a green canvas creel, and drove his car to the woods of Fox Chapel. There, I snuck into the Field Club's private trout pond and caught two fat fifteen-inch rainbows on a warm Easter morning: an offering. I gutted and grilled them for us for dinner. Poached in aluminum foil, with a little olive oil, herbs, thin slices of lemon . . . they were delicious.

BASKETBALLS, BUNK BEDS, AND BRIDGES

The Irene Kaufmann Settlement House and Its Neighbors

We call our town the City of Bridges, commemorating the steel and concrete spans that cross our rivers and contain our collective and personal memories: the Fort Pitt Bridge and its Dorothy-in-Munchkinland-like deliverance from beneath Mount Washington into the now gleaming downtown; the once lavender and rusted trusses of the Hulton Bridge from which young men in Harmarville arched out into the Allegheny to celebrate their independence. Or the Bridge to Nowhere, now one of the Three Sisters, the hulking identical downtown bridges, painted golden and named after our civic heroes: Carson, Clemente, and Warhol.

Spanning the Allegheny and connecting the city to the suburbs north of Pittsburgh, the Highland Park Bridge is another portal to the past. We crossed it on rare trips to the zoo, where I would blissfully ride the carousel and stare at the matted snow leopard in his concrete cage, or to Pitt games where we streamed uphill in revved-up hordes to see Tony Dorsett and to always, always boo Notre Dame. We rolled across it to buy hardware at the Sears in East Liberty for another home project. The view upriver from the bridge is home: the scrap metal yard and rusted barges, the river bending out of sight into the rolling hillsides on my right.

In recent years, that crossing is with two ponytailed kids who love carousels and French fries and a woman whom I realized I loved—and had to tell so—while crossing here over the flooded Allegheny one December night. Barring any further reminiscence, the kids enter some bawdy theatrical exhibition that causes me to playfully quip—and spy their mom's reaction at this claim to a legacy not mine—"Kids, stop it! You're nice Jewish girls."

Nice Jewish Girls

When local Jewish women founded the Columbian Council School in a Pittsburgh neighborhood, molding nice Jewish girls is what they too had in mind. The first Jewish woman known to have resided in the area, Zipporah Mordecai, helped her husband run a tavern in the 1770s. Mordecai's family later moved from the region: a pattern typical of many of the region's first Jewish residents.[1] The area's Jewish community remained small—and without a synagogue—until the mid-1800s. As was true in many other cities, most of these early Jewish migrants were German. By the time of the much larger influx of Eastern European Jews in the late 1800s, some of these earlier coreligionists had established lucrative business careers, men like the Kaufmann brothers of Viernheim. The oldest brothers first worked as peddlers before opening a small clothing store. In 1872 they were joined by the youngest brothers, Morris and Henry, and in 1887 opened a store that would become a Pittsburgh institution, Kaufmann's Department Store: known for its ornate street-side clock and Tic Toc Restaurant where hamburgers and fries rescued many a child's forced shopping trip. The Kaufmanns joined their countrymen in worship at Rodef Shalom, where services were conducted in German for most of the nineteenth century.[2]

In 1877, there were 2,000 Jews in Pittsburgh and by 1889 roughly 5,000, half of them Lithuanian, long the region's largest Jewish ethnic group.[3] They were soon followed by waves of Polish, Galician, Hungarian, and Romanian Jews fleeing the institution of the draft in Russia, economic hardship, and increased government support for violent antisemitic campaigns. For the more established Germans, these coreligionists posed a challenge: Jews like the Kaufmanns sought to maintain their social status in the predominantly genteel and staunchly Protestant social environs of Pittsburgh, but they also felt compelled to aid their fellow Jews despite or perhaps because of the cultural divide between them, just as they had helped the Jewish community of Johnstown after the devastating flood.[4] Women led the way.

On May 24, 1894, the Pittsburgh chapter of the Council of Jewish Women (CJW) was established at a meeting at Rodef Shalom and its members dubbed their group the Columbian Council.[5] The majority of recent Jewish immigrants had settled in Pittsburgh's Hill District, a gradually sloping plot of land directly adjacent to downtown, defined by cheap housing. The CJW volunteers committed to bringing their work directly to the Hill, and these women of means began visiting the homes of their charges, some "reeking in filth and vermin," and offering classes on manners, ethics, and sewing.[6] Soon a Sabbath School was established, located on the third floor of a house with a staircase "so dangerous that when school was dismissed" one of the volunteers "stood at the top to properly start each child down, and the other stood at the bottom to catch him if he fell."[7] Recalled during a 1950s commemoration, this scenario was an apt metaphor for the charitable work members of this organization imagined performing for their imperiled coreligionists.

In 1890 members of the Columbian Council convinced their husbands to purchase a former residence that became the Columbian Council School, with a charge to "guide the foreign born to American conditions . . . encourage self-improvement . . . stimulate healthy pleasures . . . broaden civic interest, and . . . create proper ideas of conduct." As noted by Mrs. A. Leo Weil in her President's Report of 1902, published in the city's *Jewish Criterion*, the institution would help keep young Jewish women "from the streets or from harmful surroundings, or if not actually harmful, from surroundings that would not be elevating." They would mold nice Jewish girls, or at least employable ones, a major concern of Jewish American philanthropic organizations, which sought to limit the dependence of immigrants on relief agencies.

The school established an employment bureau and offered classes in basketry, dressmaking, and cooking, skills that were useful in the home and in the city's growing industrial economy. In the same report, Weil noted: "We attempt to teach the brain, the body, the conscience," and, thus, a major emphasis of the institution at the outset was offering physical recreation. Weil pleaded potential donors to help realize the school's dream of housing a bathhouse and gymnasium. In the meantime, the school opened a modest playground for children, complete with a sandpile, where "little ones could play" and catch "a glimpse of paradise." Weil's plea would soon be answered. The issue of the local *Jewish Criterion* that included her report began with a front-page story announcing the donation of funds by Mr. A. R. Peacock for the building of such a facility. The writer also included a stinging rebuke of the school's critics, those who had initially expressed "the coldness, the utter lack of sympathy" for these women's efforts. Furthermore, the article revealed how men had taken control of the organization; an advisory committee would now "consult on all questions affecting the welfare of the school," a move that would aid in "bringing the male portion of the community into closer contact with the operation of the school and will without a doubt prove advantageous to the women and to the men."[8] The institution became independent of the Council of Jewish Women in 1905, but the council remained the nostalgic "mother of the Settlement."[9]

This restructuring provided the Columbian Council School with financial resources to significantly expand its work in the community. The institution became part of the nationwide settlement program, a reform movement defined by trained, professional social workers, mainly men, who resided or "settled" in buildings located in poor urban areas, where they offered a wide range of social services to residents. By the turn of the century, there were as many as four-hundred such institutions.[10] A good portion of these were founded by Jewish organizations, up to seventy-five by 1910.[11] In 1911, leaders of the movement, including Jane Addams of Chicago's influential Hull House, formed a national umbrella organization, the National Federation of Settlements, to promote settlement work outreach, aid settlements with programming, interface with private and public institutions, and advocate on issues affecting settlement communities. The dominant, often heroic image of Addams's Hull House and the settlement movement, in general, have until recently obscured the heterogeneity of settlement houses, how each institution "reflected local characteristics and, at each period of its development, the individual caprices and goals of its specific leader."[12] In their reports, the board and staff of the Columbian Council, and its later iteration, the Irene Kaufmann Settlement (IKS), often cited the organization's ability to evolve in tune with such local circumstances. These individuals were often unaware of or unwilling to examine how their own "caprices" directed their work, although such foibles would later surface during vexing interrogations over whom the organization served, who a neighbor was.

In the Playground and Gym

One thing that remained constant over the institution's evolution was its focus on recreation, and while the bathhouse immediately drew large numbers of people since many Hill residents lacked any other means of bathing, the gym was for moral cleansing. The young women and increasingly boys, too, were drawn together "under elevating and refining influences," a prophylaxis to the "evils of bad associations and from the temptations of the city."[13] These included its "seducing dancehalls."[14] In her 1904 report, the Columbians' head resident, Julia Schoenfeld, noted the wide appeal of the new gym, where the school's "most important work" was accomplished. By then, both boys and girls were receiving training in formal physical education classes conducted by a female staff member, with the younger boys' classes being conducted by two men. In addition, the boys enjoyed basketball games that "kept them interested in the regular drill work." At the time, physical education classes, shaped by men like Doc Hitchcock, the founder of Amherst College's influential physical education program, emphasized group exercises, often accompanied by music, that included light calisthenics and rhythmic movements with weights such as wooden clubs—exercise intended to offer muscle suppleness and overall health, not muscle mass. Not surprisingly, many young men were less than thrilled by such routines.

By 1907, Henry Kaufmann had donated new gym equipment to the settlement and the President's Report of that year noted the widely accepted "necessity of this work for the physical development of men and women" and the "discipline, self-control, fairness in judgment" that children developed in the Columbian School's gymnasium.[15] Henry Kaufmann would further contribute to the institution and help expand the reach of its mission when he and his wife, Theresa, donated both a new building on Centre Avenue and an endowment of $40,000. In memory of their daughter, the institution was renamed the Irene Kaufmann Settlement House in 1910, and Kaufmann, or "Uncle Henry" as he was known to the community, would continue generously supporting the IKS during much of his lifetime. In 1929, he donated a whopping $650,000, and ten years later added another $100,000 to the settlement's endowment: monies that supported major expansions of the organization's community work.[16]

Scholars have questioned the aims and methods of leaders of the settlement movement—arguing that settlements were forms of social control over mainly immigrant, working-class populations, and this critique extends to their often-expansive recreational programs. Writing specifically of the German Jewish philanthropists who founded and directed the well-known Educational Alliance in New York, one writer later stated:

> The Barons tried to check autonomous play because play provided a set of linkages that were in and of themselves threatening. . . . Play links the past and the present with the future; it connects the body with its background; and it helps to shape a participant's understanding of time, space and motion (relationships). At the same time play is an art form; a mode of physical expression; and a restatement of the social order or a transcen-

dence of the same. Play can point towards an entirely new definition of the situation, and in this capacity especially, it is a danger to the powers that be.[17]

None of these philanthropists or settlement workers could have predicted how Pittsburgh would transform, what new challenges would arise on the Hill and for the city's Jewish community—what dangers play would invoke in the Steel City and to its social order. Seemingly simple acts of recreation would take on new meanings that both conformed to and defied the planners' aims. IKS history reveals how the original intentions of the social engineers operating the settlements were often challenged by the desires of membership and the social conditions in which they lived, including the meaning of sport in America.

The IKS's mission during the first half of the twentieth century was "the advancement of the civic, intellectual and social welfare of the surrounding community," and its means to accomplish these goals was still: "(1) by guiding the foreign-born to American conditions; (2) encouraging self-improvement; (3) stimulating healthy pleasures; (4) broadening civic interests; (5) creating ideals of conduct."[18] In its earliest days, the IKS was clearly marked as a Jewish organization—with Jewish staff and volunteers serving a mainly Jewish clientele. The settlement was closed on the Sabbath; the house newspaper was the *Menorah*; members staged Yiddish plays; and a wide range of local Jewish groups used the IKS for meetings, including the Young People's Socialist Singing Club, the Stogie Makers' Union, and the leftist Bakers' Union. Friday evening services were "entirely Jewish ethical" and a Saturday morning ethical class for children enrolled six hundred kids before the time of World War I.[19] However, during the war the organization increasingly focused on Americanization efforts, one of many factors that made it more secular over time. The IKS became a United States Government Advisory Board to aid community members with draft registration; it staged patriotic displays, and in the gym staff prepared young men for their draft physical examination. The house was open every day of the year, and Friday nights typically included a musical performance, basketball games, and dancing. The showcasing of members' basketball skills—and on Sabbath nights—demonstrates how quickly sport had become significant to the IKS and its now 2,765 members.

Relying on recreation to accomplish such civic aims was consistent not only with settlement movement ideology but also with a larger societal emphasis on sport as an activity that ameliorated the negative influences of modern urban life. The most powerful proponents of this ideology were, of course, American Protestants, such as Luther Gulick, but Jewish organizations also embraced a similar focus on the connectedness of physical, mental, and spiritual selves. Their shared reformist agenda and belief in recreation as a mechanism for social reform allowed Jewish settlement houses like the IKS and Protestant organizations to embrace a similar ideology of sport as a social tool and to enjoy an often close association. As the director of physical training in the New York City public schools from 1903 to 1908, Gulick had a far-reaching impact on physical education in the US. During this period, he was also president of the American Physical Education Association, the national umbrella organization of physical education professionals and the first such organization in the field. Gulick later became the director of the Department of Child Hygiene at the Russell Sage Foundation and, along with Jane Addams, was a major figure in the playground movement. With his wife, he also founded the Camp Fire Girls. By 1913, only one year after its formal founding, a Camp Fire Girls club was meeting at the Irene Kaufmann Settlement. By the following year, the club was popular enough to include two groups of girls between eleven and thirteen years old.

Gulick's beliefs regarding physical recreation compelled him to charge his underling, James Naismith, with the task of developing an indoor game that would capture the waning attention of the YMCA's clients, many of whom, like boys at the IKS, had grown disinterested in its program of tiresome gymnastics. Naismith's assignment, of course, led to the development in Holyoke, Massachusetts, of the game that would quickly become wildly popular at the Jewish settlement in Pittsburgh: basketball. Sport and religion grew intertwined within a heterogeneous range of influential American institutions that increasingly blended scientific rationalism with, if sometimes veiled, religious impulses.

The social reformers of the era used methods of science-based inquiry in their work, closely cataloging and analyzing the social ills of the day that play could combat—if it were available. *Pittsburgh Survey* writers identified recreation as a critical area of reform: providing workers, their families, most of all their children, with someplace to play. In her report, Beulah Kennard, the president of the Pittsburgh Playground Association, bemoaned the city's emphasis on work: "Characteristically also the city which had forgotten the meaning and the uses of leisure had forgotten the value of recreation."[20] She noted that in 1896, Pittsburgh had only two parks and "of these[,] Highland Park was only a barren, almost treeless hill ... out of reach of the poor."[21] This left only the dirty streets, dangerous railyards, and dark alleyways as playgrounds. Kennard and like-minded women mobilized to compel city officials to expand play opportunities for the poor children of Pittsburgh. She claimed that the lack of play led boys to criminality, while the fate of girls was to surrender their childhood: "One pathological condition early observed among the little girls of Pittsburgh was their feverish, unchildlike desire for work—real work, not play activity. This was found to be most intense in the Hill District."[22] These women too set out to save local girls.

Legislation passed in 1895 authorized officials to use school property as playgrounds, as well as to obtain land for such purposes, and these civic-minded elites began to seek agreements with school officials to create play spaces on their grounds. The local Civic Club created a Playground Committee, and in 1895 the group received its first appropriation from the city, $1,500. However, the club still relied on private contributions and volunteers to perform this work, which expanded to establishing "city playgrounds": recreational centers to be owned and managed by the municipality. At the time, no such places existed in the city, but by the time of the *Pittsburgh Survey*, these reformers were successful in establishing five city playgrounds and committing the city to pay for their upkeep. The Civic Club later limited development of new playgrounds and instead expanded the programming at existing sites by combining playgrounds with vocational schools to reach older children, who were otherwise destined for the mill or clothing factory. Here they could find recreation as well as instruction in art, cooking, and other practical endeavors.

The women were shocked by how working-class children at first "did not know how to play." The mollifying effects of the sandpile and swing set, however, were soon evident in these "subnormal" boys and girls. Free from an early life of labor, "the child who was small and delicate for his age . . . ran and jumped and built 'pyramids' with other boys, playing with earnestness which expanded his lungs, straightened his back, and steadied his active little brain for another year of effective study. In some districts the gang has been tamed."[23] The role of play in rescuing city kids from the ills of industrialism and urbanism was articulated not only by Kennard, but by other *Survey* writers, who lobbied city schools and government to build on the work of the Pittsburgh Playground Association and its supporters. Lila Ver Planck North, a professor of Greek at Goucher College, writing about the city's parochial schools, argued that "lack of attention to the physical development of the children . . . was a conspicuous fault in their educational scheme."[24] She also broadly indicted the public schools for failing to provide the space, facilities, or equipment for proper physical training, especially in congested urban districts, warning that "schools could not without reckless waste ignore in the children the physical disabilities that threatened to make their costly instruction ineffective."[25]

In 1914, Julia Schoenfeld, previously the head resident at the Columbian Council, returned to assume that role at the IKS. She had spent the prior three years as secretary of the Playground and Recreation Association of America, the organization Gulick helped found. Schoenfeld noted in her initial report at the IKS: "Athletics have taken a large place in the Settlement.... Athletics accomplishes more for the individual than all the preaching that leaders can possibly do. It is a trite but true saying that a healthy body produces a healthy mind, and a healthy mind [e]nsures sound morals."[26] Luther Gulick would, no doubt, have nodded in consent. By August 1915, the roof garden at the settlement was functioning as a playground and its popularity demonstrated to staff the need to expand such opportunities for the Steel City's children. The IKS annual report of 1916–1917 noted that the resident director had given public addresses to promote playground building, and the organization had helped establish two local municipal playgrounds. In addition, the IKS later organized citizens' committees to develop additional playgrounds.

Less than two years later, Schoenfeld was replaced by Sidney Teller, who would remain the director at the IKS for twenty-five years. Teller's appointment signified both the increasing male control over the settlement, and its reliance on professional social workers steeped in the latest physical education methods. Teller later became a member of the National Association of Jewish Community Center Physical Directors, founded in 1929. The organization's 1930 conference was cochaired by the director of Physical Education at the renowned Springfield YMCA, and included an address by the president of the Playground and Recreation Association of America.[27] In 1916 Teller chaired a committee on recreation at the National Conference on Community Centers and Related Problems, an event organized by Luther Gulick and others, who hoped "a vital contact between workers, and a discussion focalized through reports carefully prepared in advance of the conference, will have the effect not only of enriching the experience of all those engaged in the movement, but of clarifying the philosophy and defining the ultimate program."[28] Nowhere in Schoenfeld's accounts, or in any of these early institutional records including Teller's many reports, do IKS staff or directors claim that sports are a means for promoting Jewish identity. Such claims would come much later when the IKS and other organizations grew anxious over the secularization of Jewish youth, a process they had helped inaugurate.

Hoop Dreams

The increasing popularity of Naismith's invention at the IKS was demonstrated in its 1913 Annual Report, which prominently featured photographs of house basketball teams. The director of Boys' and Men's Work, Bertram Benedict, noted the necessity of getting all the boys into the gym to release their steam-like energy, lest there be "an explosion." The need to offer recreation as a check against "social explosions" was especially dire following the Great War. "What is Pittsburgh going to do for the boy when he returns? . . . Recreation was not one hundred percent clean and wholesome here when he left." The answer, of course, was for "this City to outline a program of recreation for all of its people."[29] This battle for community morals became increasingly significant under Teller's leadership. He issued detailed sociological reports on the Hill's moral well-being, including analyses of the neighborhood's "negative forces," complete with maps detailing the saloons, pool halls, and movie houses that led one to ruin. The IKS staff did not stop there: the settlement reported "all violations of law," protested the granting of additional liquor licenses, and caused some establishments to be shut down by authorities. Teller's view on repairing the social fabric was never more succinctly stated than when he claimed: "The solution of a neighborhood's delinquency is wholesome recreation and an efficient police force."[30]

Basketball then was a means to achieve not only moral and physical well-being for the individual but also social comity, for "every hour spent in the 'gym' was an hour devoted to the doctrines of a strong body, of true sportsmanship, and the necessity of teamwork."[31] Basketball built better bodies, better minds, better morals, and also created bridges across the ethnic, national, class, and religious divides of the settlement's increasingly diverse neighborhood. This belief in the unifying power of team sports was a popular notion among Progressive Era reformers, who often bemoaned the individualistic nature of the burgeoning capitalist society.[32] The need to find common ground seemed especially pressing in the Hill District with its mixture of "Russian Jew, American Negro, American White, Italians, Roumanians, Austrians, Assyrians, Poles, Germans, Irish, Canadians, Portugese, Greeks, Armenians, French, Croatians, and Lithuanians."[33] According to the IKS, because "no one is denied membership," the IKS gymnasium seemed an especially promising space to realize such lofty goals.[34]

Even in its early years, though, the IKS staff was aware of the challenges inherent to controlling play. Sidney Teller noted in his 1918 Resident

Director's Report: "The plan of the gymnasium work was to get away from merely playing basketball, and to establish a beneficial system of physical education." Although the IKS staff worked to expand the range of recreational opportunities, there was no way to put the genie back in the bottle, or rather, the ball back in the closet. The game of hoops was drawing more and more players and bigger crowds to the gym on Centre Avenue. During 1918, the settlement's fourteen basketball games drew two thousand spectators, and even Teller commented on how, at the postgame dance the IKS team, "appearing in uniform and often winning over its competitor, made for a loyalty and House spirit."[35] Winning mattered.

And the IKS increasingly gave its members more and more opportunities to win: first, organizing intramural leagues in basketball, swimming, and volleyball—another new sport created in a Massachusetts YMCA in the service of God. IKS teams were soon playing other teams from the city and beyond. By 1924, the house had organized a swim team, and the 24 basketball games at the IKS attracted 7,870 players and spectators. Sidney Teller boasted, "Irene Kaufmann Settlement won more championships in competition in sports in 1924 than in any year in the history of this Institution."[36] Clearly, Teller's thinking had evolved from his claim in 1919 that the "physical instructor's work was judged, not so much by the number of games won, as by the small number of fouls, which were reported against the team."[37] By 1925 *Neighbors* noted not only that many youngsters found good health in the IKS gymnasium but also that "we hold our own in athletic competition. Our trophy case is crowded—we need a trophy room."[38]

The house began staging an annual Athletic Jubilee in 1927, a showcase for IKS athletes: boxers, wrestlers, but most of all ballers. The purpose of the event was "to celebrate the athletic triumphs of our basketball teams," and "the most attractive feature to the fans, undoubtedly will be the much-heralded basketball game between the IKS Varsity and the 'Old-Timers,'" a squad of former IKS players. The year had been the settlement's most successful basketball season, with three teams garnering Amateur Athletic Union (AAU) championships.[39] As was the case with soccer, the *Pittsburgh Press* sponsored area basketball leagues, including the AAU tourney. The achievements of IKS athletes led the paper to devote space to a large picture of these young men in its April 18, 1925, issue. The following evening was the house's annual basketball banquet, at which the teams would receive their trophies from the *Press*, adding to the thirty-six that the IKS had already garnered in the past decade. The *Press* writer began the piece with a series of short questions with obvious answers: "Is the Irene

Kaufmann Settlement active in athletics? Does it enjoy success, too?"[40] Oh, yes. Yes, indeed.

The Ones Who Don't Eat Ham

By the 1930s, the IKS's basketball league play was drawing over 1,600 participants and thousands of enthusiastic fans who cheered on the young men, the "Nat Holmans and Johnny Beckmans of the Settlement" as *Neighbors* called them.[41] This reference to two well-known Jewish basketball players of the era, members of the Original Celtics and eventual Hall of Famers, illustrates other consequences of IKS sports programs that ran counter to its planners' goals. Basketball made stars, individuals whose singular prominence could eclipse any putative lessons of self-sacrifice and team building the game allegedly transmitted. These individuals functioned as polestars of group identity for Jewish Americans, who were now the kings of the courts, prominently displaying their skills on teams across the country and on crack fives in Pittsburgh.

In the 1990s, the former Pittsburgh mayor, Sophie Masloff, enthusiastically recounted the cheer of a former secondary school that served the Lower Hill District, Fifth Avenue High School: "Izzy, Ikey, Jake and Sam / They're the boys that don't eat ham! / Go team!"[42] Along with the IKS and Fifth Avenue teams, other local squads featured Jewish athletes who instilled pride in Jewish identity, such as the Enoch Rauh Club, named after a graft-busting city councilman, whose wife had been a member of the IKS Board of Trustees. The Coffey Club, a top squad of local barnstormers, included Meyer Gefsky and Ziggy Kahn, later the longtime athletic director of the IKS. On the road, the team was sometimes approached by rabbis who wished to meet Rabbi Coffee of Pittsburgh's Tree of Life, not knowing the team was named after its founder, John D. Coffey, the circulation manager of the *Pittsburgh Press* and a Catholic.[43]

Local Jewish newspapers as well as IKS publications proudly covered the exploits of these young men and the athletic accomplishments of other coreligionists, often highlighting their identity as "Jewish boys." They, too, were once credited with being harbingers of soccer's imminent American reign. In his "Jewish Sports Notes" section of the *Jewish Criterion*, George Joel touted the arrival of Prague's Sparta Club in the United States: "The moguls of the professional soccer leagues must be pinching themselves and asking each other if they are not dreaming. Never before in the history of the sport has soccer received the attention that it is now getting and all because a group of Jewish boys from Vienna came to the country to play a few games."[44] Joel was referencing the recent exploits of Vienna's Hakoah club, which drew forty-six thousand fans to the Polo Grounds in New York in 1926, a record for an American soccer match that would stand until the 1970s. The Czech team was touring the United States and scheduled to play the Brooklyn Wanderers, who had recently vanquished the acclaimed squad from Bethlehem Steel. The year before, on August 15, 1925, the *Jewish Criterion* published a lengthy article titled "Jewish Athletes Win Spurs in World of Sports." The intense focus on the achievement of these athletes and their Jewishness is a practice that has continued. In 1965, the five-hundred-plus-page *Encyclopedia of Jews in Sports* was published, the jumping-off point for a score of books recounting the history of Jewish sports figures: *Great Jews in Sports*; *The Baseball Talmud: The Definitive Position-by-Position Ranking of Baseball's Chosen Players*; *The Big Book of Jewish Sports Heroes*; and a personal favorite, *Jew-Jitsu: The Hebrew Hands of Fury*.[45] Why this attention to Jews and their relation to sports?

Their Jewishness was often a salient aspect of their experiences as athletes, and increasingly as nationalism became a more salient aspect of modern sport. In one of his *Jewish Criterion* columns, Joseph Brainin imagined what a team of all-Jewish Olympic athletes, those "who were discriminated against and deprived of an opportunity to exhibit fully their prowess," could accomplish if they represented Palestine.[46] Leading up to and during the 1936 Berlin Olympics, Brainin's musings resonated profoundly due to the virulent antisemitism of the Nazi regime, which barred its Jewish athletes from competition. The challenges faced by Jewish American athletes were underscored by the US Olympic Committee's decision to attend the games, despite the lobbying efforts of groups and individuals, including Ziggy Kahn, who organized the Anti-German Olympic League. Kahn and a representative of the AAU even obtained an audience with President Roosevelt, with whom, according to Kahn, they "got into one heck of an argument."[47]

In his memoir, the acclaimed Pittsburgh poet Gerald Stern recounts the violent clashes between Jewish residents and their neighbors that were spurred, he notes, by the antisemitism brought by Eastern European immigrants to America, the economic struggles they faced here, and the "physiography—hills, rivers, and bridges" that demarcated ethnic boundaries.[48] In the 1940s, while leaving a pharmacy with his friend Bill Kahn, Ziggy's son, Stern was sucker-punched by a young man who called him a "fucking kike." After regaining his bearings, Stern chased down his antagonist, knocked him over, and began bashing his head against a car bumper until his assailant slumped over unconscious and was eventually dragged away by his buddies, onto a bus back to Homestead.[49] Sucker punches were also thrown on local basketball courts. Wyoming Paris, while playing an away game against a major rival, the Duquesne Lafayettes, a team of Polish steelworkers, unloaded on an opponent after suffering similar insults.[50] A melee ensued.

With its particularly strong Christian milieu, Pittsburgh made for a sometimes-toxic climate of intolerance. On October 9, 1936, the infamous Father Charles Coughlin spoke in Pittsburgh, and while many, including the *Pittsburgh Press* denounced the controversial priest, others, no doubt, embraced his platform, including its xenophobic and antisemitic vitriol. They listened at home by the radio and nodded in agreement with the world he portrayed, the threats he defined: plotting Communists and clannish Christ Killers. Pennsylvania in general, and western Pennsylvania, in particular, were hotbeds of radical Christian faith groups that espoused white supremacy and its attendant antisemitism; though, in the region anti-Catholicism was a uniquely toxic fuel for Klansmen, too. They love to hate. During the 1920s and 1930s, the Pittsburgh area was home to scores of what we now dub "hate groups" and during the Klan's apex, "the imperial heartland was to be found in the steel and coal regions of southwestern Pennsylvania," where ninety-nine Klan klaverns with some 60,000 members were organized.[51] Up the river in West Kittanning, over 25,000 Klansmen gathered one night in the 1920s for a rally.[52] On some nights above the hills overlooking Harmarville, where in high school we used to get high and drink barrels of beer, fiery crosses burned against the night sky.

Tough Jews

No wonder the Jewish American press and its readers espoused the physical prowess of these hoopsters and especially the impressive line of Jewish boxers like Max Elling, a kid from the Hill who fought with a Star of David on his trunks. Such symbolic representations were even more important given the stereotypes of Jews circulating in the public sphere, as physical degenerates, weaklings who used their brains, not their bodies, to meet their ends. When I was a kid, a Jew was something not to be. When divvying up gum or sharing a water bottle, we sometimes admonished peers who took more than their fair share. "Hey, don't be a Jew!" Such poisonous notions of Jewish identity emerged in the realm of sports, as in the prominent *New York Daily News* columnist Paul Gallico's often-quoted musing: "The reason, I suspect, that it [basketball] appeals to the Hebrew with his Oriental background is that the game places a premium on an alert, scheming mind and flashy trickiness, artful dodging, and general smart-aleckness."[53]

Overcoming such essentialist writing about Jewish identity and sports has been slow to come, and at times, Jewish Americans have helped sustain this myopia and the stereotypes it promotes. Some philanthropic German Jews who directed settlement houses relied on recreation to remake what they too perceived as the weak bodies of their brethren. The director of Boys' and Men's Work Bertram Benedict surmised: "It is claimed sometimes that Jews possess more brain than brawn, and perhaps a Jewish neighborhood needs opportunity for physical development more than other neighborhoods."[54] Although Benedict's comment is unique in IKS records, the Jewish press sometimes defined the prowess of Jewish athletes as manifestations of essential Jewish qualities. Joseph Brainin, in a section "Not American Product," explained the success of Jewish boxers like Benny Leonard, who were a conspicuous presence in the realm of title holders between 1910 and 1940. Brainin asserted that these boxers were part of a Jewish legacy established in Europe that had transformed this infamous blood sport into the "sweet science." He stated of the Jewish pugilist: "He is a scientific boxer and overcomes his adversary by a quick thinking brain and a perfect coordination of mind and muscle."[55]

As the renowned sports historian George Eisen pointedly notes: "What should be understood is that when Jews ponder sport, like all people, they create an image of themselves as they wish the public to see it."[56] Or as they wish to remember it. Another consequence of this attention to men like Leonard as counterpunches to the negative depictions of Jewish male identity is the long failure to investigate the sporting lives of Jewish women. Women like Julia Grossman, an eighteen-year-old from the Bronx who in 1926 unsuccessfully appealed to the New York State Boxing Commission for a boxing license to fight in the ring—against men. George Joel had met Grossman and claimed she appeared able to "slaughter any number of men fighters," yet he could not also help but note she was "nice and buxom."[57]

Nice Jewish Girls Revisited

Although the board of the IKS would certainly have frowned on a similar request, offering recreational opportunities to young women remained a primary goal of the institution. The "elevating and refining influences" of the gymnasium were enjoyed by "large numbers of young people," but by 1904 only one gym class of twenty-five girls was running and basketball was limited to boys. However, as the settlement facilities grew, including the addition of a new swimming pool, opportunities expanded.[58] Although recreation was confined by the strict gender mores of the staff, who desired that the girls "learn lady-like ways . . . and, above all, respect for the work that true ladies are not ashamed to perform," as with the young men, sporting practices for women and girls evolved in ways that these careful planners had not imagined.[59]

By 1913, the IKS not only offered four separate gym classes for girls, followed by swimming instruction but also touted a "very good basketball team" of girls.[60] And girls' increased use of the pool, encouraged by IKS staff, was such that in the house's 1916–1917 report, Director Teller noted the need for a larger facility. By the following year, there were 185 classes in swimming, which drew 3,073 female swimmers to the pool. And by 1919, over 5,000 girls "had realized the benefits and pleasures to be obtained by exercise" in the pool. Nearly 400 had participated in basketball classes. It seemed these young women had chosen the pool and court over the sewing table, as the number of participants in swimming alone exceeded combined attendance at the classes offered in cooking and hand sewing. At this time, the gymnasium was used to teach classes in traditional gym exercises, as well as dancing, an activity strongly encouraged by the Playground Association of America. The total attendance at these programs was 6,313. The roof-top playground was even more popular: holding 135 sessions for 8,573 children, who glimpsed Paradise from its roof.[61]

Although girls' competitions would never receive the kind of notoriety as boys' games, these were unique opportunities in a society that greatly restricted such athletic opportunities, including swimming. In 1941 the *Jewish Criterion* observed that "little, if anything, has been written about the Jewish women who have also reached championship heights. . . . This radical change in a race that was accustomed to see its women clad in sheitels rather than in shorts is really revolutionary in ideas as well as in practice." The author then went on to sketch the lives of some of these women, notably Charlotte Epstein, who "did more for women swimmers in this country than anyone else."[62] It was not hyperbole. Epstein had been a key member of the National Women's Life Saving League and later founded and managed the Women's Swimming Association, which produced some of the world's finest female swimmers: Olympic champions and world record holders.[63] She successfully lobbied to have women included in Olympic competition and helped train the era's most renowned female swimmer, Gertrude (Trudy) Ederle, the first woman to swim across the English Channel. Ederle shattered the men's record in the process and

4.1 Irene Kaufmann Settlement Swimmers, 1931. Reproduced by permission from Jewish Sports Hall of Fame Photographs, Thomas and Katherine Detre Library and Archives.

became the inspiration for a Hollywood film and popular song. Epstein was also a vocal suffragist and succeeded in opening AAU competition for women, allowing them to toss their silly mandated stockings and don formfitting swimsuits, more suitable as well as more attractive. The *Jewish Criterion* advertised the new "Trudy" swimming suit, "noted for its formfitting [style]" and on sale downtown at Kaufmann's Department Store.

Along with providing girls the opportunity to compete in basketball, the IKS organized a swim team for boys and girls in 1924.

The impulse to frame sporting activities, including those at the IKS, solely through the lens of Jewishness, however, glosses over the complex reality of American sport—specifically its inherent connection to larger societal and historical forces.[64] As the Hill District changed, the IKS evolved to include and serve non-Jews, while Jewish membership simultaneously waned. Children at one time were given Easter eggs for Passover, and the Sabbath was observed with a basketball game and dance. As George Eisen rightfully points out, "the most burdensome yet fundamental question is how an individual's involvement and accomplishments in sport can be tied to his/her ethnic identity—especially in light of a rapidly transforming community."[65]

The tendency to recollect these practices as solely Jewish also elides the sentiments of those who at the time viewed such activities as decidedly non-Jewish. Even icons of Jewish athletic success, like the wildly popular Hakoah soccer team, were both embraced and derided for their Jewishness—the perceived lack thereof. The *Jewish Criterion* closely followed the team's tours of the United States in the 1920s, touting their triumphs and the hopeful impact of their play on the growth of soccer stateside. The *Criterion* proclaimed: "If soccer continues to enjoy the popularity it has recently tasted, credit must be given to the most colorful team of them all—'Hakoah.'"[66] After their initial tour, some of the Viennese team's members decided to stay in the United States, and joined the Brooklyn Wanderers.

Some in the Jewish community perceived the soccer players' decisions to leave Hakoah as traitorous. Others, including columnists at the *Criterion*, expressed more tempered regret about their actions, how they had "succumbed to the lure of the American dollar," effectively breaking up "the pride of European Jewry." The Wanderer owner Nathan Agar assured critics that his intent was "transforming the Wanderers into an ALL JEWISH team. I am a Jew and would be the happiest man if it were given to me to build up the strongest Jewish football club of the World."[67] While Agar never realized his goal, some of the players he signed eventually formed a solid all-Jewish side, the New York Hakoah, which won the National Challenge Cup in 1929, the same tourney the men from Harmarville would star in during the 1950s. Six months later, New York Hakoah merged with an American Soccer League team called Brooklyn Hakoah, forming a new side, the Hakoah All-Stars. These were only the earliest of many Hakoah soccer teams in the history of US soccer, a tradition that continues today with the Sport Club Hakoah, an amateur club in New Jersey. One of its sponsors is El Al, the Israeli airline.

At the time of their exploits, these soccer stars were a focal point of growing concern within the evolving American Jewish community. One of the first public gestures of the newly formed Synagogue Council of America, an umbrella organization of rabbis representing the major branches of Judaism, was to denounce Hakoah for playing matches on the Sabbath. The organization issued a statement in which the rabbis voiced that they "unanimously protest against this desecration," a practice also followed at times by the IKS, which invited similar rebuke from the observant in Pittsburgh.[68] The prominent role of sports in Jewish organizations like the IKS was a consistent source of concern among Jewish religious leaders who felt that recreation, especially competitive sports, pulled Jews further into the secular world of modern America and away from the religious tenets of Judaism. Some rabbis, such as Cleveland's Armand E. Cohen, railed against Jewish organizations sponsoring such decidedly un-Jewish practices. Cohen even suggested that these organizations shed their Jewish affiliation and come clean by opening themselves to "all citizens regardless of race, color or creed."[69] This battle of "shul versus pool," as the historian Jeffrey Gurock phrases it, continues, if sometimes only within the inner lives of Jewish Americans, such as Shalom Auslander's self-laceratingly humorous account of his struggle to rationalize viewing his beloved, long-snakebitten Rangers in the National Hockey League playoffs during Sabbath. "I had decided to switch on the television Friday afternoon—before Sabbath began, at sundown—and just leave it on until Sabbath ended, twenty-five hours later, on Saturday night. This wasn't technically, 'being in the spirit of Sabbath,' but it wasn't technically a sin, and the Rangers were very likely nine victories from winning the Stanley Cup for the first time in fifty-four years."[70]

What ultimately did participation in these sports at the IKS mean to participants and observers—the heterogeneous mix of immigrant and native born? German and Lithuanian? Socialist and capitalist? Orthodox and Reform? Male and female? Those who directed the house's programs had their notions of building better citizens by building better bodies, but sports inculcated or gave expression to notions of individuality and notoriety that fell outside this vision. The success of group endeavors also instilled pride that could easily devolve into ugly tribalism, as when games between the Coffey Club and Black Loendi Club "soared to such a pitch that contests at the Labor Temple are unsafe from a spectator's standpoint, to say the least."[71] It is likely that some immigrants saw bouncing a basketball as dangerously asserting Americanism. To sometimes rowdy and listless young men, like those who inspired Naismith to invent basketball, a day in the IKS gym may have been no more than what sports continue to be for many: pleasure. Some were driven by an individual desire to win, to challenge the self, or just to experience the ecstasy of the body attaining that fleeting perfect moment: watching the ball's arc and just knowing its destiny; or to feel the satisfying aches that come after training one's muscles. To a young, working-class woman it may have been the chance for better health, for an experience different from what her community prescribed for her—including the chance to encounter others she rarely met.

Please Won't You Be?

Pittsburghers who grew up in the city during the 1960s and 1970s recall fondly how Fred Rogers, with his monochrome cardigans and canvas slip-ons, spoke to us through the ubiquitous box whose pull Auslander fretted over. In his hushed, slow voice, Rogers assured us that we, too, were . . . special. He liked us just the way we were. We were . . . all of us, neighbors.

I can still hear the tinny "clink clink!" of Trolley as it rounds the bend to appear magically from inside the wall of Mr. Rogers's studio home, see the blinking stoplight that was part of its décor. It may be that what appealed to me so much about *Mister Rogers' Neighborhood* was that message of belonging. And why not, for Fred Rogers did, in fact, live nearby—just across the river. And as I grew older, I became increasingly aware of the way we were not part of our neighborhood. My parents did their impossible best to shield us: not reveal how, when we moved to Pittsburgh, a real estate agent in the southern suburbs laid it out to Mom and Dad, "There are no houses available for couples like you, nor will there be." How while browsing in a neighbor's store, this woman carped to another patron in a volume just loud enough for Mom to hear, "What is she doing in here with those children?!" Those mongrels. And we made a family joke of the neighbor four doors down who dutifully warned new neighbors of the threat in their midst, "They're Korean, ya know!?" But after a goofy redheaded kid in my sister's class rushed up to me in the marble-floored bathroom in second grade, fingers holding up his eyes, grinning, and shouting like a mad scarecrow, "Asoo! Asoo!" nothing was as before. Not even games. Not when you're the darkening tip of spaces stubbornly white. Years later, he and I would continue this dance on a basketball court at our local park that commemorated the Native American girl who defied her father out of love. Other boys pulled us apart.

Pittsburgh's suburbs, in general, remain stubbornly white. Meanwhile, parts of the city proper underwent dramatic shifts in ethnic and racial composition during the twentieth century. In an October 1925 issue of *Neighbors*, under the title "Do You Know?" there appeared a list of paragraph-long tidbits about the settlement intended for the Hill's newest residents. In response to the query, do you know? the *Neighbors* writer observed that "the Morgan Community House at 73 Fullerton Street; the Young Women's Christian Association, Wylie Avenue Branch at 2044 Center Avenue; and the Young Men's Christian Association, Center Avenue, provide for the recreational and social activities of the Colored boys and girls, young men and women of the neighborhood, and will gladly be of any service to a Colored person?"[72]

What inspired this cheery advice was the recent wave of Black migration into Pittsburgh, a "great swarm" as noted in the house's 1918 Year Book. By 1920 African Americans made up one-third of the Upper Hill's residents and one-fifth of those residing in the Lower Hill district.[73] The influx of these more Southern and rural Black neighbors tested both the tolerance of the established Black community and the benevolence of the IKS. The Great Migration challenged the larger settlement movement in general, which was now confronted with serving urban neighborhoods with a burgeoning mix of native whites, immigrants, and Black migrants. Sidney Lindenburg and Ruth Ellen Zittel of Philadelphia's Neighborhood Centre implored their settlement coworkers across the country to respond to this changing landscape. They noted how "the density of the Negro population in these areas, which are the areas where Settlements are located, has greatly attenuated the terrific problems of recreation, education, social welfare, sanitation, and health which already existed." The authors were pointed in their critique of how settlement houses had responded to this "constantly growing problem." They asked rhetorically what settlements were doing and stated, "In most instances absolutely nothing."[74] They cited the IKS as an example of a settlement that did attend to the health concerns of Black neighbors, but closed its doors to any other opportunities, including recreation. Lindenburg and Zittel countered the common response, articulated in the 1925 *Neighbors* piece, that Black people had their own institutions that could adequately provide for them. The authors noted that, while such self-reliance may in fact be the preference of some in the Black community, historical employment discrimination and the relatively small numbers of economically successful African Americans meant that their communities lacked the resources to provide the facilities now being denied them. Who could be Black Pittsburgh's Uncle Henry?

In a prescient commentary, the Philadelphia workers further noted that settlements would have to address the partisanship of "sectarian federations or individuals" who wished "to cater to particular groups to the exclusion of others." They provided examples of institutions that were integrating their houses, such as Pittsburgh's Soho Community House. And they concluded with a question that countered the IKS's assumption that providing for African Americans was not their mission: "What Is The Settlement, the 'Champion of the Underprivileged,' the 'Committee of Welcome' to the Immigrant, Going to Do to Meet the Crying Needs of its Newest Neighbor—The Negro?"[75] Like much of the history of the settlement movement, writers and historians have obscured the IKS's historical segregation by defining the IKS only by its final years when it was a multiracial organization. Its struggle to extend full membership to African Americans is a revealing story of the challenges marginalized groups have faced in the larger American sphere: the entwined history of good intentions and self-interest by those in power. Recreation for local Jews was not just about one's Jewishness, but about Jewishness in relation to another's Blackness.

Camps and Ball for All

Like the reformist-minded conservationists of the era, such as John Phillips, IKS leadership and others early on had come to see that "a bit of country outing is now recognized as a real necessity of life for the modern city dweller."[76] In 1908, Henry Kaufmann's brothers, Isaac and Morris, purchased a farm up the Allegheny River in Harmarville, home of the Hurricanes, and named it Camp Emma in memory of Isaac's wife, who had died in 1894. The Kaufmanns established the Emma Farm Association, which used the property as a working farm for wayward boys and as a recreation site for city children and adults, including those referred by the IKS.[77] Earlier attempts by the Columbian School and Settlement to offer summer respites, using private facilities, had met resistance since they did not adhere to kashrut, but the bylaws and Constitution of the Emma Farm Association mandated that these Jewish dietary laws be observed.

By 1914, the IKS was sending 400 children and over 70 adults, mothers, to the farm, all of whom were first visited by IKS staff in their homes to assess their deservedness, since demand far exceeded capacity. By 1916, the settlement house had taken over management of the association, and in 1921 the Harmarville property was sold, and a new site was found to construct a state-of-the-art facility north of Pittsburgh in Harmony, the former home of the German utopians, along the banks of Connoquenessing

Creek. Facilities included a swimming pool, baseball diamonds, basketball courts, a volleyball court, and a playground. The camp motto was "Health and Happiness." Director Sidney Teller, along with his wife, was intimately involved in the camp's management and a vocal proponent of camps, viewing them as crucial sites of physical and spiritual renewal. In an address to the Pennsylvania Public Health Association in 1923, he noted that twenty-five summer camps were then in operation, serving the health of some 15,000 campers, but that was just a starting point: "There will be camps not only for babies and mothers and smaller children, but there will also be camps for fathers, as well as family camps.... The doctors will more often write prescriptions for factory workers as well as bankers, laborers as well as capitalists, to go out to camp to recuperate."[78] Between 1922 and 1942, the IKS offered a series of two, two-week trips for boys and girls during the summer, but eventually dropped its trip for mothers in 1942 due to the war. By observing dietary laws, the IKS demonstrated its desire to be inclusive of the broader Jewish community, and in these summer camps—sheltered from outside influences—the IKS would establish the kind of definitively Jewish site that its house in the Hill District struggled to maintain.

When Sidney Teller announced his departure after twenty-five years at the helm of the Irene Kaufmann Settlement, the *Pittsburgh Courier* published a lengthy article in which the director expressed consternation that Black neighbors charged him with discrimination, an accusation "frequently... laid at Mr. Teller's door."[79] He attributed the all-white membership of the IKS to the establishment of the Morgan Community Center, which met the needs of the community's Black population, and he noted the fourteen Black staff members working at the IKS. Teller had been criticized before in the *Courier* due to his zealous morality campaigns. In 1926, the paper criticized Teller for focusing his approbation on Black-owned businesses and individuals, while ignoring Jewish bootleggers and gambling establishments.[80]

Of course, the IKS was not alone in denying African Americans the opportunities for recreation it espoused as essential to a healthy existence. At the time and for much of the twentieth century, professional baseball was the dominant sport in the nation, and Pittsburgh had a team, the Pirates, with a history of success and a palace of baseball. The city's first professional hockey team and the Steelers, too, were once dubbed the Pirates. Baseball was a putative microcosm of American identity, including racial segregation.

The city's African American literary production reminds us of the reality of the national pastime's ugly history. In the Pittsburgher August Wilson's searing play *Fences*, the lead character Troy is a former Negro League ballplayer, embittered about what might have been. Troy works as a city garbage man, and at the play's opening has just questioned his boss as to why he and other Black employees can't drive the garbage trucks. He rails over the closed doors that have defined his life, including in baseball, and he sabotages his son's chance at a college scholarship playing football because he is convinced it will not get him anywhere. In one scene, he angrily spits out, "I saw Josh Gibson's daughter yesterday. She walking around with raggedy shoes on her feet!"[81] I had never even heard of Gibson—one of the greatest baseball players ever and from my hometown—until long after I moved away from Pittsburgh. It embarrassed me, pissed me off. When I mentioned this to my brother, he asked, "And how many times did you read the sports page?" Every day.

The African American community in Pittsburgh had its own set of diamond heroes, like Josh Gibson, a 6-foot-1-inch, 215-pound slugger from the city who hit some of the longest homeruns in history and was called "the greatest hitter who ever lived" by the legendary pitcher Satchel Paige.[82] Who better than the greatest pitcher in history to judge? During his career Gibson played for both the Crawfords and Homestead Grays, two local powerhouse teams that dominated the Negro Leagues in the 1930s and 1940s and were loaded with scores of future Hall of Famers, including Paige. The Crawfords were financed by their owner Gus Greenlee's numbers business and sometimes help from his friend Art Rooney. In the 1930s, Greenlee built the country's first Negro League ballpark in the Hill District and during that decade drew as many as 200,000 paying fans a year.[83] The mayor and other local politicians were there for opening day on April 29, 1932. Meanwhile, Major League Baseball (MLB) faithfully maintained its wall of racial isolation. As the Pittsburgh sports historian Rob Ruck succinctly notes of Black Pittsburgh at the time, "Sport helped bring forth black Pittsburgh's potential for self-organization, creativity, and expression. . . . It played a supportive role in the coalescence of a black community both during and after the migrations of the early twentieth century. Through identification with teams and players, sport fostered a sense of pride in black Pittsburgh."[84]

The Homestead Grays first began as a sandlot team of players, many of whom worked in the Homestead Mill, and they regularly played at the Pirates' Forbes Field. And when Barney Dreyfuss was asked by the prominent *Courier* journalist Bill Nunn Sr. about the most versatile team he had ever seen, Dreyfuss replied: "The Homestead Grays. They're truly baseball's miracle team."[85] Yet, the miraculous Grays had to dress at the Centre YMCA, the city's Black Y, before home games at Dreyfuss's magnificent but segregated ballpark. Given the success of the city's Negro League teams and major league baseball's long segregationist stance, the Pirates were of limited appeal to Black Pittsburghers. They had their own teams, playing legends, and media that proudly chronicled Black excellence, while MLB remained committed to its exclusion of nonwhites.

Barney Dreyfuss of course did not need the newspapers to recognize the Black talent within his reach. Upon Dreyfuss's death in 1932, the Grays owner Cumberland Posey recalled how "he seldom missed a game" and how "the favors he did the Homestead Grays are too numerous to mention."[86] As the remaining male in the family, Dreyfuss's son-in-law, William Benswanger, assumed ownership of the club after Dreyfuss's death. He, too, was aware of the remarkable talent nearby, players "of high caliber and worthy of the highest in baseball."[87] Moreover, he seemed willing to give them a chance. In a 1938 *Courier* article titled "Pirates Owner Would Favor Sepia Players in Organized Baseball; Lauds Gibson, Satchell," Benswanger remarked that he "watched almost every game involving colored teams at Forbes Field for many years" and that several of these men "appear to be as good as many of our men in organized baseball."[88] What Benswanger probably did not realize when speaking to the *Courier*, was how much the paper would hold him—and baseball—accountable for giving Black players a chance to make it to "The Show."

Not only did the *Courier* at times question the entertainment value of the sometimes-hapless Pirates, compared to the skill and success of their local Negro League counterparts, as in a piece titled "Why We Would Pick the Grays over the Pirates," but the paper began an aggressive campaign to integrate the national pastime.[89] The *Courier*'s campaign was joined by other Black papers and the Communist Party's *Daily Worker* as well.[90] In the 1940s Benswanger promised tryouts for Black ballplayers, a commitment Cum Posey accepted. The paper arranged for four players, including Gibson, to work out for the team, but the tryout never happened. It soured the paper's view of the Pirates. Thousands of Black ball fans boycotted the Buccos. Even after Benswanger left in 1946 and the Pirates were managed by Branch Rickey, the team never signed a Black player. Rickey had been the president and general manager of the Brooklyn Dodgers when they signed Jackie Robinson, who broke baseball's color line, which had been in place since 1889. He had even given tryouts to Japanese Americans held in our nation's concentration camps. None were signed.

During his initial season in MLB, Robinson's Dodgers came to play the

Pirates for a weekend series in May. Robinson was trailed that year by the *Pittsburgh Courier* writer Wendell Smith, and the paper, while supportive of Robinson, was critical of Rickey's position that Negro League players were free agents, ripe for MLB's picking. MLB teams could sign Negro League players like Robinson without any compensation to their teams, which were soon raided of their top talent, precipitating the league's decline and eventual demise. Meanwhile, some local fans were so appreciative of the Dodgers' push to integrate, that they organized a group trip to Forbes in 1946 to root for the Dodgers after they signed Robinson and four other Black players. They were going to cheer "a double victory over Pittsburgh." The organizer of the trip, the local businessman Sam Jackson, proclaimed that they had a message for Benswanger, the Pirates owner: "When he sees us out there at the park, he may realize how much money he is missing by refusing to sign Negro players to the Pirates."[91]

When Robinson's Dodgers came to town for that series in May 1947, the Pirates bench shouted slurs at him from the dugout. He responded by banging out six hits in thirteen at bats. One of these was a bunt, during which the Pirates first baseman, Hank Greenberg, the Hebrew Hammer, was pulled off the bag by the pitcher's throw. Robinson, racing down the baseline, collided with Greenberg's arm, fell, and continued safely to second base. It was a common play, but given the circumstances, the *Courier* commented, "that particular play was the type that prejudiced writers and players and big league owners used to say would cause a riot." As the paper and Robinson acknowledged, any confrontation was avoided due to the response of Greenberg, who later in the game asked if Robinson was all right and encouraged him to persevere, "I know it's plenty tough. . . . Just stay in there and fight back, and always remember to keep your head up." The *Courier* and other papers commented favorably on the two players' encounter, noting that Greenberg's experiences with antisemitism on the field gave him insight into Robinson's challenges. Greenberg was in his final year of a brilliant career that had made him an icon to American Jews, including those from Squirrel Hill who cheered on the Hebrew Hammer from their seats in Forbes Field's Greenberg Gardens. Seven years later Jackie, now chairman of the National Conference of Christians and Jews, would return to the city for Brotherhood Week, during which he attended a lunch with Jewish and African American athletes, toured the United Steelworkers of America's office, and visited with teens at the Irene Kaufmann Settlement.

The region's entrenched segregation and the virulent anticommunism of the time likely instilled a sense of caution in the Pirates' management.

The active role of American communists, many of whom were Jewish, in fighting segregation fed the nation's paranoid and nativist minds. After the Black Sox scandal, the industrialist Henry Ford who decried the Jewish influence on sports in general, including the number of Jewish owners like Dreyfuss, wrote, "Better no baseball than every park an afternoon midway filled with the alien and Red elements of the country. . . . If baseball is to be saved, and there are those who seriously doubt it ever can be restored, the remedy is plain. The disease is caused by the Jewish characteristic which spoils everything by ruthless commercial exploitation."[92] The irony of arguably the most influential architect of consumer capitalism blaming the capitalist impulses of Jewish owners for baseball's imperiled state was apparently lost on Ford, and likely the locals as well. But I can't get over what might have been—Josh Gibson in black and gold.

Though it was slow to address the needs of African Americans, the National Federation of Settlements, like many American organizations, changed course in the 1940s and encouraged houses to integrate. Individual settlements like the IKS responded in various ways.[93] Pittsburgh's Kingsley House, for instance, relocated in 1918 and its former facility was converted into a Black settlement operated by the American Baptist Society.[94] The Irene Kaufmann Settlement House would chart a different course, one that would lead to an increasing distance between Jews and their Black neighbors. This history echoes a *Courier* writer's earlier encapsulation of the relation between Jews and Black people. Although expressing admiration for the impressive philanthropic record of the city's Jewish community, a record worthy of emulation by its Black readership, the writer ultimately concluded, "The Jew is for the Jew."[95]

Hello Muddah, Hello Faddah

Dad used to listen to comedy records—Bill Cosby and Allan Sherman—the latter's humorous take on a child's summer camp experience, complete with alligators and disgruntled staff, loaded into my jukebox. What I didn't realize at the time was how much Sherman's send-up described a cultural practice that had been as much a part of childhood for many Americans as Frank Sinatra hits and Allan Sherman schticks were to mine. The first summer camps in the nation catered to the children of elite Northeasterners, the same genteel class that founded the early fishing and hunting clubs of the Commonwealth. Camping was also embraced by Muscular Christians like the Gulicks who sought physical and spiritual rejuvenation in God's green outdoors. During the early twentieth century several groups promoting camping—the Camp Fire Girls, the Boy Scouts, and the Girl

Scouts—were founded, and settlement workers like Sidney Teller looked to the outdoors to perform similar uplift for their urban charges. Participation in summer camps soared to an estimated two million children by the end of the 1930s.[96] Each of these organizations, as well as the private camps that were increasingly dotting the Adirondacks, Alleghenies, and Catskills, served a specific constituency and promoted the goals of their directors. As a result, these spaces were in general—white. "Camps were deeply segregated spaces," as one historian notes, "far more effectively segregated than the urban constituencies that sponsored them."[97]

For the nation's Black children, all that "swimming, sailing, playing baseball" that Sherman's narrator realizes is part of camp life—and reason for telling his parents to disregard his ominous missive—was generally not available. Despite the explosive growth of summer camps in the early twentieth century, a study conducted by Pittsburgh's African American community revealed that of the 12,000 local children attending summer camps in 1938, only 47 were Black kids. That fall the local Urban League, headed by Mrs. David Alter, organized a meeting with representatives of agencies catering to the city's African American community including the YMCA, YWCA, and the Soho Community House. The Urban League board member Wister I. Lynch was tapped to head a committee to raise funds for a camp for the city's Black youth. The league's first executive director, the *Courier* editor and publisher Robert L. Vann, endowed the initial $60, and he used his newspaper to lobby for further community support. The league signed a lease for a 150-acre parcel of land in Raccoon State Park and the camp opened in 1939.[98] It offered 397 children fishing, hiking, swimming, or the chance to "just sit on the porch railing in the bright light of the moon."[99] The camp was named Camp James Weldon Johnson in honor of the writer and longtime secretary of the National Association for the Advancement of Colored People (NAACP). Cabins were named after Booker T. Washington and George Washington Carver, and the camp featured a Negro History Contest. The James Weldon Johnson Camp Association proclaimed its goal of providing "adequate camping available to the Negro of Allegheny County."

After its successful first year of operation, the camp secured funding from the Community Chest, which greatly relieved pressure on the local African American community to raise funds. Despite Sidney Teller's claim that Hill residents had sufficient recreational opportunities, Black members of the community desired more camping, and for years, "as would be expected, the great preponderance of the campers" were from the Hill.[100] As was true of Camp Emma, demand for Camp James Weldon Johnson far

4.2 Camp Johnson, 1948. Reproduced by permission from Camp Johnson Photographs, Thomas and Katherine Detre Library and Archives.

exceeded the available slots. Unlike Camp Emma, however, the new camp west of Pittsburgh intended for its campers to establish cross-racial connections with other youth.

For the most part, American camping organizations demonstrated little willingness to integrate, despite the rhetoric they espoused. The most telling exceptions were those camps most questioning of American ideals, those operated by the American Left, some associated with leftist Jewish working-class communities. These camps were sites of radical politics and racial plurality.[101] The association of progressive racial views with leftist politics, unfortunately, caused critics to view the two as equivalent: anyone operating a camp designed for racial tolerance was a potential Red, an internal enemy. New York State even investigated its leftist camps during the 1950s. Camps promoting such an overtly inclusive racial perspective were therefore especially troubling to residents of the Commonwealth, which after World War II was "the scene of some of the fiercest anti-Red activism to be found anywhere in the country."[102]

As early as 1942, Camp James Weldon Johnson was coordinating activities with two other nearby camps: a Jewish camp and a Baptist-faith camp from Rankin whose parent organization had begun integrating as early as 1930.[103] The 1943 camp report proclaimed: "Prejudices were broken down through friendly associations. Stereotypes of the Jew; the American white man and the Negro were cast aside as those children came to know and enjoy one another—*each for what he was worth*.... This was Americanization, Democracy at work."[104] These "friendly associations" included relationships with both individuals and organizations that supported the camp. Many camp facilities had been built and were maintained early on by the National Park Service (NPS), and camp reports lauded NPS staff for their cooperation. The camp's grocer, Morris Schwartz, provided food to the camp at cost, supplied trucks, and donated money.[105] The descriptions of his generosity call to mind the recollections of Abe Lieberman, the grocery owner in Harmarville, who, during the lean times and especially the coal strikes, provided food on credit to miners and their families, even providing bail money for those arrested by the hated Coal and Iron Police. His daughter later recalled the oft-repeated commentary of her parents: "They have children; we can't let them go hungry."[106]

Such inclusive and expansive notions of community were encouraged during World War II and after by mainstream organizations, such as the Girl Scouts and the YMCA, that embraced camping as a democratic practice open to all when "our soldiers of all backgrounds are dying for the same cause."[107] In 1942 the American Camping Association (ACA) published a report containing a set of guiding principles for the future, *Camping a Wartime Asset*. The ACA was the national umbrella organization for camps, and its parent organization was established in 1910. By the 1940s, the ACA functioned as the accreditation and educational organization for camp owners and professionals. The organization's wartime dicta included developing "an understanding, acceptance, and appreciation of other nationalities, races, economic groups and religious faiths."[108] This reorientation of groups like the ACA and later the Girl Scouts led to the design and implementation of camps that were interracial, as opposed to the system of separate camps for Black campers and for white campers, which was the established practice. In 1945, the ACA published in its magazine a report, "Establishing Racial Good Will through Camping," in which the organization offered advice on operating an interracial camp, a uniquely "favorable and controlled situation in which to further" the goal of racial harmony. The ACA maintained that camps receiving public support via funding sources such as a Community Chest "have a moral obligation to provide service to all elements among the contributing public who need camping service."[109] In the Steel City, some camps complied with ACA's philosophy, some only after pressure, and others remained segregated.

In 1944, Camp James Weldon Johnson's Board of Governors announced that the camp would accept white children, though no agency eventually referred any white boys or girls. Nonetheless, the camp did hire a white counselor that year. Earlier in 1939, the Centre Street YMCA had asked that Black youth be admitted to the regional YMCA camp, Camp Kon-O-Kwee. A few decades later my brothers would return home from there wearing T-shirts with a brave donning a feather headdress on the front. For three years, the Y leadership discussed the request and finally, in 1942, eight African American kids attended one of the camp's sessions. By 1944, the Y's board voted to open the camp's whole summer program to all races. A local African American Girl Scout leader similarly challenged her organization's leadership when in 1942 she questioned why her girls could not attend the Girl Scout camp, Camp Redwing. Her advocacy led to a meeting of Girl Scout officials, the Urban League, and others who developed a study committee and a detailed outreach effort to parents announcing the Girl Scouts' plan to offer integrated camping.[110] In addition to these local community organizations, camp organizers enlisted the help of the American Service Institute (ASI).

The records of ASI's consulting work demonstrate the major challenges that staff faced. One was the general racial climate, the common fears of those who associated racial tolerance with a threat to democracy. As one settlement worker at Soho Community House observed, "interracial and social action programs are identified by many as Communistic programs which should be disapproved and shunned."[111] Not surprisingly, camp directors had to address and defuse the concerns of troubled white parents. When YMCA staff queried Kon-O-Kwee parents in 1941 about the proposal to integrate the camp, some parents either threatened not to send their children or they expressed support—for separate camping facilities. The ASI reports contain several accounts of parents and campers expressing apprehension at the prospect of intimate contact with Black children—for example, when children complained of bunking with Black kids or two girls expressed their desire not to shower at the same time as Black girls. Long-established fears of the Black body—a site of moral decay and physical danger—made these intimate spaces threatening to this young generation of white Pittsburghers. ASI reports, however, also document numerous examples of children rejecting racist ideals once they came to know others as bunkmates and teammates. And some parents were aware of the need to overcome such unexamined fears. One man acknowledged the benefit of interracial camping by admitting that he "had an unconquerable fear of the Japanese." And because of this handicap he stated that he "would consider it a real opportunity to have my boy live intimately with boys of other races."[112] Adults were still often wary of the way in camp settings that "bodies became tangible, active and exposed; interaction was intimate and unscripted."[113]

Camp staff reached out to religious and educational institutions in the community to explain their goals and build support. One ASI report noted that parish priests in Pittsburgh directed their flocks to specific YMCAs.[114] Black children were carefully selected for participation since their conspicuous presence in mostly white camps meant that every individual act was subject to communicating the nature of African American identity writ large. When a counselor at the Brashear camp told children that the source of the song they had been singing was "in the cotton fields with the slaves," all the campers immediately turned to the one African American girl in the group. She replied, "Don't look at me; I'm no slave." Although this girl disarmed the situation with aplomb, another young girl's challenging behavior "supported many stereotyped ideas on Negroes."[115]

The issue of Black representation in the camps was most acute in relation to staff. Traditionally white camps had trouble recruiting Black staff and those whom they did hire sometimes were impossibly burdened by low expectations of their abilities and a demand that they be exemplary in behavior. In an article touting Camp Kon-O-Kwee's efforts at interracial camping, the author recounted how its sole Black counselor overcame the prejudice of one camper, as well as fellow staff who "never before had . . . known there were Negroes of education and breeding," let alone "a fine-looking, athletic and intelligent young man" like this, who "represented the finest type of Negro."[116] The Jack and Jill set.

At James Weldon Johnson, conversely, the challenge was the recruiting of white staff, and by 1949, the camp still employed only one white staff member. Agencies, including the Brashear Association, remained slow to refer campers, and not until 1948 was there more than one white camper at a time. Recruiting white girls was especially difficult. In 1952, only three white campers enrolled, but by the late 1950s, mainly through word-of-mouth referrals, the camp population was sometimes as much as one-quarter white. Campers created interracial organizations such as the female Greenwood Society, whose programming included dialogues about issues like race prejudice. Camp staff reported, "The experience was highly successful and enriching for both campers and staff. It is important to note that nearly all the white campers expressed definitely and enthusiastically their wish to return to Camp Johnson next year."[117]

The ASI worked not only with summer camps such as Camp Redwing but also with settlements like the Brashear Association on the South Side, which operated four separate settlement houses, including one specifically for Black people, Carver House. The organization had begun interracial camping in 1940, drawing most of its campers from the Hill, which was not surprising given the demand. In 1949 alone, Camp James Weldon Johnson had to turn away four hundred kids. The Brashear Association was founded in 1917 by Mrs. Harriet Phillips, the wife of John M. Phillips, the donor of those stuffed carnivores to Carnegie's eponymous museum, and our Father of Conservation.

ASI reports on its work with Brashear during the late 1940s and into 1950 demonstrate that community sentiment and the blind spots of staff often crippled integration. In one report, a counselor expressed his strong belief that children were not prejudiced, and thus interracial programming would only "make issues of everything" and teach children to be biased.[118] The presence of Black staff also created tension, such as when another white colleague questioned the qualifications of a Black counselor. Still, at other times, white staff expressed overcoming some of their biases because of having worked with African American staff—as colleagues.

As was true at Brashear's Camp Claudine Virginia Trees, the staff and campers at Camp Redwing were overwhelmingly white and the camp had trouble hiring Black counselors. This situation troubled one of the camp's senior staff who felt it imperative for Black campers to have "Negroes their own age or somewhat older and to be able to discuss what it feels like to be a Negro in an almost all white setting."[119] African American campers entered an established culture—a unique social space with defining traditions and practices. And the culture of most American summer camps assumed a white racial identity, an unexamined if consistently influential historical perspective reinforced by rituals that included masquerading as nonwhite—most notably playing American Indian.[120] When these camp communities began to include more than those like themselves, white people were soon confronted with how differently nonwhite campers and staff experienced the culture of their camps. They discovered that by simply living their lives and doing the things they did, even playing the games they played, they could insult and alienate others, even those they sought to welcome.

ASI reports chronicle the expected incidents of name-calling that Black children were subjected to by other campers. More revealing, however, are the numerous discussions around practices that had never been questioned before integration. One of the most challenging issues was the soundscape, the songs that campers sang in dining halls and around campfires, many of them minstrelsy songs like "Old Black Joe," "In the Evening by the Moonlight," or "Swanee River," the actual title of which is "Old Folks at Home," by Pittsburgh's own minstrel machine, Stephen Foster. The consultant to Camp Redwing recounted how a camper had insisted on singing "In the Evening by the Moonlight," with its opening line of the chorus: "In de ebening by de moonlight, you could hear us darkies singing."[121] She recorded the ensuing conversation during which she stressed how one can "slip very easily into accustomed patterns without realizing that we may be hurting someone in the group."[122] On another occasion, in 1949, campers in an integrated cabin at Redwing decided to attend a campfire as a group. One camper suggested that they attend as a plantation family since "there was always a white family and a Negro family."[123] Consultants also reported confrontations that arose when white children wanted to play "Nigger baby" or "Tar baby" and were incredulous as to why this game that they played at home with pleasure now needed modification. Such practices cultivated a shared sense of history and identity among white campers and "insisted on the distinction between white performers and the objects of their attention."[124] The consultants had much to undo.

Staff at these camps also realized the need to educate children about religious difference, and some saw this issue as more pressing than promoting racial tolerance. Staff designed programming to educate children about various religious practices and worked to provide campers access to their respective religious observances, which was primarily a concern for Catholic children who wished to attend Mass. The predominantly Protestant character of these summer camps required that they adjust practices to accommodate the region's mix of Eastern Orthodox, Roman Catholic, and Jewish families. As at Camp James Weldon Johnson, kids at the Brashear camp interacted with youth from other camps: Camp Kon-O-

Kwee and Camp Emma, where mothers enjoying a summer outing exchanged information about Jewish customs and culture with mothers from the Brashear camp. Since Claudine Virginia Trees was also located along Connoquenessing Creek near Harmony, its Jewish youth were able to visit Camp Emma for Friday night Shabbat services.

This contrast in Jewish campers' routines due to their faith was part of a larger separation of Jews from the heavily Protestant social patterns of the Commonwealth. In addition to lobbying for the establishment of playgrounds, IKS staff also worked to open access to them on Sundays, the one weekend day when recreation was most available for those who did not associate spring with fish sandwiches and dyed eggs. Like anyone wishing to buy bourbon or bag a buck on Sunday, Jewish kids in the early twentieth century hoping to visit a public playground were prohibited by the Commonwealth's blue laws, and at times public officials zealously enforced these laws restricting private conduct. *Pittsburgh Survey* investigators noted of Pittsburgh: "There is no city in the country, and probably none in the world, where strict Sabbath and liquor legislation is more strenuously enforced."[125]

William Penn first established such measures in the 1600s to preserve the sanctity of the Sabbath as a day of rest free of immoral behavior, including sport since it might "excite people to rudeness, cruelty, looseness, and irreligion."[126] The laws have had an impact on recreational opportunities well beyond fishing and hunting in Pennsylvania, even after statehood and massive immigration altered the population and the hold of Quaker doctrine. Legislators modified the laws over time, notably permitting genteel activities such as polo, tennis, and golf, while still continuing to restrict other public conduct on Sundays, at times promulgating laws even more severe than those of their Quaker predecessors. An 1878 law stated: "There shall be no hunting or shooting or fishing" on Sunday.[127]

In the 1920s the struggling Philadelphia Athletics professional baseball team appealed its case involving the prohibition against hosting Sunday ball games to the State Supreme Court. In a 7–2 decision the court affirmed the Commonwealth's right to ban business activity on Sunday, noting: "Christianity is part of the common law of Pennsylvania and its people are Christian people. Sunday is the holy day among Christians. No one we think would contend that professional baseball partakes in any way of the nature of holiness."[128] Finally, in the 1930s, state legislators, led by the local maverick Michael Musmanno, introduced legislation that would offer the first serious challenge to the blue laws. Although initial attempts failed in the State Senate, in 1933 the Progressive governor Gifford Pinchot signed legislation allowing local communities to decide in the upcoming

November elections if they wished to have Sunday football and baseball. The measure passed in many larger towns and cities, making the Commonwealth the last state to end its banning of America's game on Sundays.

Pennsylvania courts have continued to loosen restrictions on private conduct but measures limiting business activity on Sundays remain more fixed. These laws have been of particular concern to observant Jewish business owners who risk losing an entire weekend's business. The latitude held by local authorities regarding adoption and enforcement has made Pennsylvania's blue laws especially problematic for these proprietors and others in the Commonwealth who could be subject to violations, which at times have included a jail sentence. State and local laws assumed—and at times mandated—a Christian identity, and private organizations like the Pittsburgh Council of Churches once actively sought to convert Jewish residents. Given the Christianizing mission of most social service agencies in the city, such as the YMCA, and the sometimes-violent antisemitism of residents, it was reasonable and necessary that the Jewish community create its own organizations to meet its needs, whether that was to find language instruction or a place to swim under the trees. But once they had done so, major demographic changes in their community and economic forces complicated their commitment to the democratic tenor of the age. Sidney Teller was never more correct than when he noted: "To be a NEIGHBOR—most people are just little neighbors—is the simplest and yet hardest task in the world!"[129]

Leaving The Hill

Like other agencies in the region and across the nation, the IKS was confronted with the issue of racial integration in the 1940s. Irwin Wolf, the vice president of Kaufmann's Department Store and president of the IKS, was, along with Mrs. David Alter, an early supporter of Camp James Weldon Johnson, and he helped initiate the gradual process of integrating the IKS. The Board of Trustees of the settlement commissioned a self-study in 1942 that produced two major objectives: developing a plan for an interracial policy and undertaking extension into the areas of wealthier East Pittsburgh, to which many of the Hill's Jewish residents had moved. The two findings pointed to the tension now inherent in the institution's mission: simultaneously serving a socially and geographically mobile Jewish community and a multiethnic, multiracial working-class neighborhood to build "better understanding, attitudes and relationships between all peoples and groups in the Hill."[130]

The IKS enacted a gradual process of integration at its Centre Avenue home, beginning with children's programs. The original plan adopted by its board was to conclude with the full inclusion in 1951 of Black adults. The organization's own Community Cooperation Committee protested the proposal, arguing that it might further "accentuate feelings of segregation."[131] Staff members worked to inform members and the community of their intentions and to combat ill-feelings from the "restrictive membership policy in the Hill District" that had "made many resentful."[132] The IKS's first step was to open the rooftop playground, a move met with "hostility on the part of some neighbors."[133] Next, the nursery school was also desegregated and operated with the stated mission "of developing interracial and intercultural understanding."[134] Later, Black elementary school children were offered membership. After staff lobbied the board to admit teenagers and adults as members, the house was fully integrated in 1948 when all interested adults were allowed membership. However, studies of the IKS at the time revealed that, even after the board's change of heart, "the past policy of Irene Kaufmann Settlement regarding Negro membership still act[ed] as a damper to Negro participation and membership."[135] The former IKS president Nathaniel Spear's 1911 warning in the settlement's first annual report now seemed especially resonant: "A house divided cannot stand."[136]

When the settlement did open the gym doors to its African American neighbors, they came. The agency's report of 1948 indicated a "notable spurt of interest and enthusiasm for the IKS program" after the settlement "adopted a full equality membership policy."[137] By 1949, the IKS membership was half Black, 28 percent Jewish, and the rest non-Jewish white. But there was an immediate decline in Jewish members after the change in policy, and by 1951 they made up less than a quarter of the membership. As a group, Jewish members were the least involved in the limited number of truly mixed-race groups at the settlement. Most of the Jewish members were elderly longtime residents of the Hill or men who participated mainly in the IKS sports program but lived off the Hill. Most non-Jewish white and Black members were Hill residents, although these white members too were mainly male. Black members were evenly split among men and women, but the settlement was now overwhelmingly male in membership, a phenomenon some attributed to the emphasis on "active sports."[138] Youth membership was now overwhelmingly African American, especially in the youngest groups, and these newer members made more extensive use of the IKS's programs than Jewish peers did.

The IKS had also begun to hire Black professional staff who worked alongside longtime IKS Jewish colleagues like Ziggy Kahn, who was still directing the physical education program. Even before the policy change, Kahn had offered use of the IKS gym to a local Black team that lacked a home court, an act the *Courier* considered a "fine gesture toward better racial relations on the Hill."[139] As more institutions began offering Black neighbors the opportunity to compete in athletics, Black media like the *Courier* encouraged and took note of the accomplishments of "sepia" players, just as the local Jewish press had earlier trumpeted the accomplishments of Jewish jocks. In November 1950, the *Courier* detailed the recent exploits of some of these athletes and noted that the IKS's now integrated basketball team was the tallest local team ever to come out of Pittsburgh.

The settlement's recreation program was at that point still robust, with members making extensive use of the house's gym and pool, where a trained lifeguard was available to offer swim lessons. In 1953, the IKS staff noted increased interest in its swimming instruction program among young children and, responding to demand, Ziggy Kahn arranged a regular gym time for nine- to eleven-year-old girls, whose "consistent attendance" demonstrated "their real need and interest in gym activities."[140] By 1948 the majority of adult members participated only in the IKS's physical education program, a trend that worried some staff who felt that the IKS was now perceived as only a recreational organization. The focus on athletics was most pronounced among the majority male membership as indicated by the schedule for the settlement's gym, which provided designated hours for several men's and boys' groups, including team practices, but none solely for women. This trend was, as some suggested, the result of increased focus on competitive athletics, since the House "desir[ed] group quality in recreational activity ... with the fine results that the majority of participants have had an active part in the formation of champions."[141] It is also clear that, despite the staff's efforts, robust interracial interaction was difficult to realize, and the integration of the IKS likely influenced the low white female participation in the athletics programs.

In 1948 the house sponsored two swim meets, AAU tournaments in boxing and basketball, as well as intramural basketball leagues and an all-Jewish basketball tournament in which the IKS hoopsters prevailed. One IKS member, Herb Douglass, garnered an Olympic medal in the long jump at the London games that year and was the first African American to receive an AAU award honoring the best athlete in the tristate region. In 1954, the nation's icon of integration, Jackie Robinson, revisited the IKS and was given a lifetime membership.

Nearly a decade before Number 42's visit, the IKS opened its first extension into East Pittsburgh, to Squirrel Hill. Shortly afterward the

Recreational-Educational Council of the Federation of Jewish Philanthropies (FJP) commissioned a study of the facilities available to Jewish youth in the city's East End. Local Orthodox rabbis believed educational needs were more pressing, and the YM-YWHA leadership maintained that the area was overserved. Others felt "the necessity of a specific Jewish recreation as a means of strengthening the Jewish content and giving the children an opportunity of development in a Jewish group." The IKS unsuccessfully applied for Community Chest funds to support this extension work, which it then financed on its own as a pilot program in 1948. The Community Chest initially disagreed with the IKS and the FJP that there was a lack of recreational opportunities for Jewish youth in East Pittsburgh. However, a subsequent study commissioned by the Community Chest to revisit the question of financial support to the IKS's extension and other more general questions about its future supported the use of these public funds, despite concerns of board members that the Community Chest should not support programs "essentially sectarian in nature."[142] Critics argued that other more pressing needs should be addressed with these limited community funds.

Unknown at the time to IKS members and even some staff was that its main benefactor, Henry Kaufmann, was already setting the future course of the organization. The settlement had requested funding from the Henry Kaufmann Trust to expand the Squirrel Hill site, which along with the East End project was taking up 20 percent of the IKS's budget by 1948. In February 1949, the trust responded, stipulating that the Community Chest first agree to distribute all funds from its endowment "together with any donations which the Henry Kaufmann Foundation might make in the future to the Settlement or to the Jewish Federation only for the Squirrel Hill and East End Extension Centers."[143] This request meant that the original Centre Avenue IKS would be wholly dependent on Community Chest support.

By 1952 the IKS had developed a separate board for the Centre Avenue site, one composed of Jewish, Protestant, Catholic, and Black members, and in 1956 incorporated as a new and independent organization, the Anna B. Heldman Center, named in honor of the settlement house's longtime nurse. The IKS offered the new agency use of the facility via a five-year lease costing $1.00 annually. That same year the Henry Kaufmann Foundation committed up to $350,000 for the building of a new facility in Squirrel Hill.

In June 1967, a community group, the Organizing Committee against Community Exploitation, wrote to a bank official associated with the

Kaufmann Trust about the old Centre Avenue IKS. The writer noted that due to "financial difficulties" the once "beautiful and resourceful establishment" was "now abandoned and a haven for alcoholics, prostitutes, dope addicts and illegal sexual activities."[144] Only a few decades after the moral crusades of Sidney Teller, the building he viewed as a fortress of moral uplift had instead become a nesting site for the ills he so stridently fought to vanquish.

More and Better Jews

Consolidation of the IKS's programming and its evolving coordination with the local YM-YWHA were part of a national trend among Jewish social agencies in the postwar years. By 1951, the two agencies were meeting to coordinate programming and eventually they merged, forming the Y-IKC in 1961. The Y-IKC would be renamed the Jewish Community Center, signaling the organization's focus on preserving and promoting Jewish life and providing for the development of Jewish youth. As stated earlier, the continued emphasis on recreation at such organizations had made them targets of significant criticism from Jewish religious leaders, one of whom pointedly remarked: "A community that accepts the philosophy that a gymnasium is as essential to Jewish life as a synagogue and that a Jewish basketball team is as conducive to Jewish survival as a Talmud Torah, is on the way to extinction."[145] However, one component of recreation seemed palpable to a range of American Jews, from the avowedly secular to the most observant: camping.

Jewish-run settlement houses like the IKS, Zionist groups, community centers, and other Jewish organizations had all begun to operate camps in the early part of the 1900s. As one writer noted, camping "engaged the collective imagination of the left and the right, the working class and the newly affluent, the Yiddishists and the Hebraists, the Zionists and the cultural nationalists."[146] Whereas the basketball court of a settlement might now serve a mixed-race clientele, a summer campfire circle provided organizers an opportunity to create a truly Jewish-bound space—a site where Jewish children were surrounded by exclusively Jewish cultural ideas, values, practices, and people. Amid the increasing threats to American Jewry posed by social mobility, suburbanization, and integration, Jewish leaders increasingly relied on the potential of Jewish camping to sustain Jewish identity. The Jewish Welfare Board (JWB) claimed in 1959, "The camp experience presents a matchless setting for restoring or growing community 'soul.' . . . For many Jewish children, a consciously Jewish camp may be the best or only means of providing the psychological security that can come from an experience where, for once, he is no longer a minority person, but lives joyously and specifically as a Jew." Sidney Lindenberg cited this JWB report when discussing the future role of the Pittsburgh YM-YWHA's Laurel Camp, then closing due to the merger of the two organizations. Lindenberg noted the recent "dramatic growth" of camping services provided by Jewish organizations and declared, "The potential for the camping experience . . . is so great that this trend was inevitable."[147] After the IKS clarified its intent to focus on the area's Jewish community in East Pittsburgh, its camp evolved to do the same. No longer designed to offer the physical and emotional benefits of the outdoors to a neighborhood's needy children, Camp Emma was intended to "serve the needs in conformance with the Jewish customs and traditions of the boys and girls of the Jewish faith."[148]

After the merger, Camp Emma maintained much of its character in terms of programming, offering its range of impressive outdoor activities including coed swims and swimming lessons, nature hikes, and group sings. While other camps in the region worked to diversify their campers and staff, Camp Emma's mandates narrowed the campers' opportunities to engage with non-Jews. Intergroup programming was limited to visits to outside camps, such as James Weldon Johnson, and the camp's intake policy also transformed its class composition. Whereas the Emma Farm Association had once asked those who could afford it to pay a nominal $2.00 fee, in 1948 the association mandated a minimum $8.00 fee and set up a sliding-scale pay system. As the Y-IKC noted, the Community Chest at the time was trying to "get out of subsidizing camping as much as possible." The camp board established an actual-cost fee of $58.50 and from 1950 to 1960 the proportion of campers paying the full fee rose from 26 percent to over 95 percent. This change "cleared the Camp of the stigma of being a 'poor' children's camp."[149] As Sidney Lindenberg noted, this satisfied the middle- and upper-middle-class Jewish parents of the community who desired and were "willing to pay high fees to buy both for themselves and their children such things as private camping, cabana clubs, sailing camps, European youth trips, fraternities, sororities, and things of this nature."[150]

As a result of the merger, the Y-IKC closed and sold the former Y camp, Camp Laurel, in 1961, and Emma Kaufmann Camp relocated to a new site in West Virginia, where it remains today. The property had once been a farm that was part of the Underground Railroad. However, few Black people or any residents from the Hill found sanctuary there. In 1961 not a single Hill resident attended Camp Emma or Camp Laurel. Of course, this fact did not mean that these campers were wholly isolated from African Americans or to ideas about them. The camps often employed Black workers, mainly as cooks and grounds workers, and Camp Emma and Camp Laurel attendees sang "plantation songs" like "Shortnin' Bread" and "Pick a Bale of Cotton." But, unlike at Redwing or other camps, there was no one in their cabin to tell white kids what it felt like to be portrayed so in song.

When the IKS finally did attempt to serve its African American neighbors, one staff member observed, "The feeling of the Jewish members was not merely insecurity but a feeling of being left out, of having lost something they once had."[151] The efforts of the IKS toward inclusion also might have fueled ill-will, not tempered it. As one staff member noted, "when Negroes came in[,] the understanding that they are people went down the waste basket. They [staff] did not have the feeling for helping people."[152] During this period the IKS enlisted the help of the ASI to work through "cultural and interracial factors" that had caused tensions among the staff. The consultant reports from these meetings in 1951 reveal how the muddled mission of the house, the mixed staff, and feelings from the past hampered the IKS's efforts to operate a successful multiracial organization. Eventually, the ASI informed the settlement that it could provide no further help since "the problems presented indicate a need for greater clarification and agreement within the agency about group work principles as they apply in this particular setting."[153] Jewish philanthropic organizations' choice to focus on the specific needs of Jewish youth, coupled with the community's move to more affluent, segregated neighborhoods, shrank the social world available to Jewish youth into one that mostly excluded Black people and prevented children, including nice girls from Squirrel Hill, from knowing these neighbors.

The ASI consultant Eleanor Ryder recounted the words of Lauree, a counselor in training at Camp Redwing in the late 1940s, to her fellow trainees during the opening campfire. Ryder noted, "Lauree said that most of her activities, both in school and out, were with other Jewish people and that she had chosen to come to Camp Redwing because she was anxious to have a living, working camp experience with people who were non-Jewish."[154] Lauree's desire to encounter non-Jews was not only supported by the work of camps such as Redwing, but later by the National Conference of Christians and Jews, which ran its own camps, specifically designed to inculcate notions of tolerance and understanding. Decades later, Phyllis Palmer, a sociologist, interviewed many of these campers, women who had been very much like Lauree, young white girls of means, to investigate how these camps altered their views on race. Palmer found that those summer days and nights, including dances with nonwhite boys, had profoundly shaped these women. One recalled, "Those people were now a part of me. I wasn't just who I was when I went there. I actually now encompassed also the experiences that they shared with me and who I became when I was with them."[155]

In Pittsburgh, those opportunities became increasingly limited. Housing segregation, enabled by social practice, law, and geography, kept girls like Lauree in white worlds. Palmer found that women in her study who had developed relationships outside their race soon found that their relationships "could not easily survive the segregated realities of daily life for young people."[156] The widespread practice of redlining, denying bank loans to those living in neighborhoods of mixed racial and ethnic composition, was widely employed by local banks and real estate agencies—effectively barring African Americans from purchasing homes in most neighborhoods and spurring white flight. From 1947 to 1953, 7,000 new homes were built in the region with FHA insurance; only 130 of these were available to African Americans.[157] As early as 1930, half of the county's residents lived outside the city, a proportion second only to that of Los Angeles.[158] Where class had once been the defining organizer of geographic and social space, race now became a dominant driver of who got to live where and what opportunities a child might get. What games she might play and with whom.

Even after the passage of federal antidiscrimination housing laws, local housing covenants and the outright racial discrimination of real estate agencies persisted and denied nonwhite people, like my family, the chance to live where they desired. African Americans became increasingly concentrated in a few urban neighborhoods with cheap, often substandard housing; for example, the once multiethnic Hill District went from a 40 percent Black population in 1940 to nearly 100 percent by 1960.[159] Homeownership rates among Black people still lags behind that of white owners, and due to the impact of redlining on real estate values, the equity in many African American–owned homes will never realize the growth experienced by those fortunate enough to have settled in the city's outlying suburbs. Neighborhoods once defined by their immigrant working class have become poorer, darker, and more stigmatized—another legacy of race's sclerotic choke on American life. By the time I graduated in 1981, only two African Americans were part of my Fox Chapel High School class of over six hundred.

Even progressive white people were sometimes placed at odds with those they wished to help when acting as agents of the institutions to which they belonged. Irwin Wolf, who worked to open the IKS's doors to its Black neighbors and contributed to the United Negro College Fund, and who claimed to "hold liberal views in respect to the hiring of Negroes" was forced to negotiate with angry African Americans picketing Kaufmann's Department store due to its policy of not hiring them as store clerks.[160] The social milieu of the region, including its racism and anti-Red fervor, made social activism, especially in support of racial justice, potentially costly—even if all one wanted to do was take a swim in a city pool on a muggy July afternoon.

Highland Park

In the initial 1949 report concerning the IKS extension program, Sanford Solender observed that the public facilities available to Jews in the East End included Highland Park, with its lavish pool, which was "used only by whites."[161] The facility had been the scene of an unsuccessful battle for integration after it opened in 1931; local white residents violently barred Black swimmers as did other white people across the nation. These events during the 1930s demonstrated "that white swimmers, police officers, local magistrates and even top city officials all sought to exclude black Americans from Highland Park Pool."[162] During the 1940s and continuing into the 1960s, groups including the NAACP, the Urban League, and the Progressive Party battled segregation at Highland Park Pool and other public swimming facilities that remained off-limits to the city's nonwhite residents. The need to open these facilities was especially pressing since some YMCAs, and even settlement houses like Pittsburgh's Kingsley House did not allow Black people in their pools, even after they let them onto their gym floors. The *Courier* reminded its readers what was at stake, with storylines like "While Pool Problems Rage, Three Drown in Rivers."[163] Today, the drowning rate of African American children in our nation's pools is five and a half times higher than that of white children.[164]

Using lawsuits, organized swims, and the media, the multiracial coalition of activists eventually integrated municipal pools after numerous violent clashes that sometimes spilled into city streets. Their efforts at reform also targeted private businesses, including iconic Kennywood Park and its pool. After being pressured by the group and others to integrate, management paved over it. The coalition of pool activists included members of the Jewish community, like the activist and socialite Florence Reizenstein, who served on the local NAACP's Swimming Pool Committee and the union activist and Progressive Party radical Nathan Albert. When the NAACP committee reached out to local community service groups to enlist their help with integrating neighborhood pools, the IKS declined, responding that the settlement "had no occasion to use the facilities."[165]

In early 1948, Albert and other activists first attempted to swim at Highland Park pool. He was arrested after a battle ensued, provoked by white youths from the area. Four people, including members of a local Black church, were injured and sixteen arrested. Albert was tried on charges of inciting a riot, based mainly on the testimony of a police officer who claimed Albert had coordinated the attack via hand signals, like some seditious baseball manager calling a bunt. Local media described Albert as a "Wallaceite" and "Communist," and his defense was kneecapped by the surprise testimony of Matt Cvetic, a local undercover mole for the FBI—whose dime-store-novel-like tales of Reds secretly plotting to destroy Pittsburgh were later proved to be just that—fiction. The tales were so good, in fact, that a really bad movie was made about Cvetic's escapades, *I Was a Communist for the FBI*. Cvetic claimed he had witnessed Albert inciting Black locals to stir up trouble at the pool. Unfortunately for Albert, he appeared before Judge Harry Montgomery, a member of Americans Battling Communism (ABC), a cohort of local well-connected politicians, judges, and business leaders determined to quash the threat of communism.[166] Montgomery gave Albert a twenty-three-month sentence and denied him bail.

Chief among ABC's leaders was the former Sacco and Vanzetti supporter and now red-baiter extraordinaire, Michael Musmanno, a McCarthy acolyte and architect of the Commonwealth's law banning communism. With zeal and recklessness Musmanno later attacked Hymen Schlesinger, Albert's lawyer during his Highland Park case. During another case involving trespassing by one of Schlesinger's clients, Musmanno emptied the courtroom of all but lawyers and the press and directly confronted Schlesinger, demanding that he answer the judge's query as to whether he was a member of the Communist Party. When Schlesinger refused to answer, Musmanno found him in contempt of court. The lawyer later had his case overturned by the State Supreme Court, which chastised Musmanno for adopting a "detestable method employed by communists themselves in arbitrary and unjudicial proceedings contrary to all our cherished traditions of law and legal procedure."[167]

The investigators, artists, and funders of the *Pittsburgh Survey* hoped to sway public sentiment and inspire legislation that would better the lives of the city's industrial underclass. By offering a comprehensive, scientific study of the city, including its opportunities for recreation, they hoped to inspire the American public and its institutions to save them:

BASKETBALLS, BUNK BEDS, AND BRIDGES

Pick your way through the narrow alleys between the houses, look into the closets and shacks that fill the courtyards, grope your way through living rooms, go up the narrow, black stairways, note the ceilings patched with papers where the leaking roof has sent the plaster to the floor, feel the wintry wind as it drives its way through rattling windows and flimsily constructed doors, look at the worn, tired bodies and faces of the mothers, at the little children huddled about the stove; go out on the street and scan closely the faces of the boys and girls who are growing into manhood and womanhood and see what kind of men and women these environments are producing, and then, as you sit in your own comfortable home that evening, ask yourself squarely the question what chance you would have had under such conditions, ask yourself the question if you are not in part responsible for them and if you are doing all in your power to relieve them.[168]

Local organizations, such as the IKS, and individuals, such as girls like Lauree and some of her coreligionists in Pittsburgh, tried to answer, yes. But in Pittsburgh a range of forces have supported Sidney Teller's claim that a neighbor, a true neighbor, is the hardest thing in the world to be.

Chicken on the Hill

As I head over the purple Hulton Bridge, machines are driving pylons into the water below me. It's coming down, to be replaced by an ugly four-lane concrete span. Mom now lives up the hill. The names on the doorway in her hall are new each time I visit. She recedes into the narrative bits of her youth that she retains: the wunderkind boy from childhood who is now The Famous Poet. Have I seen the book he signed for her? How she was tennis champion at Camp O-Peachey. She no longer uses my name.

I pass over the Hulton and by the old redbrick houses of Harmar Coal Company, some now sprouting AC units and satellite dishes. Racing up the highway, I crest the hill and glide by clumps of office buildings: an industrial park that was a prison farm where we used to buy apples. As a boy, I could see from my front porch across the valley the farm horses in a field and an American flag like a stock scene from picture books at school.

Under the Highland Park Bridge, someone I cannot see is fishing the deep pool below. Light rain gives the lights looming on the other side a fuzzy glow. The pool that so many battled over is closed for the season.

There is an LA Fitness in the old Nabisco factory building where my hotel is and the stairway has a constant, sharp smell of sweat, even in the cold. The Google employees next door and other busy residents of East

Pittsburgh keep fit here on the treadmills, cycles, and rowing machines. The neighborhood I once knew is captured in historical murals lining the streets. It's hard to find a parking space. When I pull into one, a new silver SUV sits beside me with a sticker for Camp Emma: "We Are Family."

I smile as I think of the Sister Sledge song of that title, the rallying call for the 1979 Pirates, led by Willie "Pops" Stargell, who captained the city's professional baseball team during their dramatic comeback World Series win. I learned to tolerate disco since this was the Pirates theme song that memorable year, capturing a feel-good sense of community that was easy to indulge, like too salty snacks late at night. During our neighborhood games, I wore my yellow plastic Pirates batting helmet and mimicked the windmill windup of Willie's batting routine.

He had a chicken store in the Hill District and it was said that whenever he hit a home run, it was Chicken on the Hill with Will! They gave out free chicken to folks in celebration of his long ball.

I tried to imagine it. But no one I knew, no one from my neighborhood ever accepted the offer. We might love him, but we lived on the other side of the river.

TERRIBLE TOWELS AND SIXTY-MINUTE MEN

The Pittsburgh Steelers and Forgetting a Black (and Yellow) Past

I like beer. OK, since people I know well are going to read this, I like beer a lot. And on any Wednesday that I can, I drive fifty miles roundtrip to stock up on delicious hoppy IPAs at a little brewery surrounded by farmland and those stone walls that are ubiquitous in New England. Cars swarm in from Connecticut, New York, Rhode Island, and beyond from which beer geeks, beer dudes, and beer dads, some strapped to small children, emerge like locusts. "Hops! Hops!" they all seem to mouth as they rush to queue up and wait to score cult status beers that they can post pictures of on Instagram from exotic locales: Tahiti, Norway, Cancun.

On my way home during one of those Wednesday pilgrimages, I pass through a small town with a smattering of holiday decorations but also something so unpleasantly dissonant that I nearly drive into a pond. First, an iconic and comforting symbol of Pittsburgh Steelers fandom, a large and badly sun-faded banner spanning a garage door: "Steelers Country." It transports me to frigid Sundays in the ugly gray dome of Three Rivers Stadium. I think, a comrade, here in heathen New England, where my wife says I've only become a more brazenly obnoxious Steelers fan? But, then along the garage corner is another smaller banner with one word in blue, "Patriots." In Steelers Country?!

Professional sports are increasingly the knots of our social fabric. They bind and remind us, become a mirror into our imagined, more favored past notion of ourselves. Pittsburgh, we like to note, is a shot-and-a-beer town, a place where the waitresses call you "Honey" and bring extra straws for your kids; where Polish grandmothers make pierogies in the basements of churches built by the hard-earned dollars of their grandparents; and where seemingly everyone in town dons black and gold on Sundays to cheer for the local football team in untroubled communion. The city's NFL franchise, the Pittsburgh Steelers, or Stillers in the vernacular, is the city's most beloved institution, with a storied history and rabid fanbase. In a 2002 ESPN fan poll, over 90 percent of Pittsburghers followed the NFL, and half admitted to missing work or school because of their fandom.[1] When the team held a press conference in January 2007 to introduce its new head coach, local TV stations interrupted their regular programming to broadcast live from the team headquarters. The new coach would only be the team's third in the past thirty years, an exceptional record of stability in the NFL, where coaches' tenures have recently averaged less than three years.[2] Dressed in a black suit and gold tie, thirty-four-year-old Mike Tomlin, a surprise, and somewhat controversial pick, faced the media and thousands of fans watching at home. Many in the city had been pulling for one of the in-house candidates, including the former University of Pittsburgh and NFL star, Russ Grimm. Tomlin's first comments were perhaps a comforting introduction to those who questioned his hiring. He stated, "It's a great honor to be a part of one of the most storied franchises in professional sports.... We intend to make no bold predictions about what we are going to do. What we are going to do is promise to have a first-class blue collar work ethic in how we approach our business."[3]

In a few sentences, Tomlin not only acknowledged the responsibility of leading a professional franchise by then accustomed to unprecedented success, but he also invoked the image of the region so steadfastly held by its residents, manifested by its beloved Steelers and touted by multiple Monday Night Football announcers: a blue-collar town wedded to values forged in the mills and mines of its industrial past. But it was not always so, especially the winning part. In fact, until the 1970s the Steelers were more commonly associated with three letters that emitted a less attractive legacy, SOS, for Same Old Steelers, a team defined by fecklessness, having played in only one playoff game in its first thirty-eight years. They lost, 17–0. During their first three-dozen seasons, they had only eight winning records and even played home games in other cities like Johnstown and Latrobe to boost attendance. The Steelers were also known for being physical. It is a characteristic perhaps best illustrated by the famous 1964 *Life* photograph of the Hall of Fame quarterback Y. A. Tittle kneeling in the Pitt Stadium end zone: eyes blankly staring at some unknown truth in the grass and his bald head streaked in blood. He appears like a battle-worn Shakespearean warrior before the final soliloquy. Asked years later about the iconic photo, Tittle responded, "I really don't remember the ballgame because I was knocked out. I didn't really regain consciousness until the end of the game. I missed a lot of the events."[4] The majority of Pittsburghers also would have had scant recollection of the game, absent the photo. In the image, front rows of seats are empty, and the game was not televised in town, as was the case for years because of the NFL's mandated TV blackouts in local markets that lasted until 1973.

At this time and for much of the twentieth century, professional football in the city, as in the rest of the country, was eclipsed by the popularity of baseball. And Pittsburgh had a team, the Pirates, with a long history of success, including a dramatic seventh-game victory over the New York Yankees in the 1960 World Series that has forever immortalized the Pirates second baseman, Bill Mazeroski, who probably never again had to worry about paying for a beer in Pittsburgh. In the bottom of the ninth inning of a tied game, Maz, the son of a coal miner, hit a homerun to left-center field over the redbrick wall of Forbes Field that sent the heavily favored Yankees home as stunned losers. Pittsburgh was now a championship city at the onset of the era of televised professional sports.

It is that image of white, working-class male identity that has come to dominate representations of the city: the Poles, Croats, Italians, and Lithuanians who streamed here at the turn of the nineteenth and early twentieth centuries, providing the brawn for its burgeoning industrial base. They suffered nobly and endured enough even to win, at times. Movies like Michael Cimino's *The Deer Hunter* reflect how the city's once marginalized and heterogeneous white working class melded into a mythic local identity: the immigrant steelworker and his male progeny.[5] It is an identity that seems unfit for the impossibly green baseball diamond, its crisp uniforms and roots in America's pasturelands, on plantation lawns. As in Cimino's film, Pittsburgh was defined by the mills—by Joe Magarac.

Millhunk to Middle Linebacker

"Know why America has the best steel mills in the world? It's because a fellow named Joe Magarac jumped into a bath of metal."[6] These opening lines from a 1952 Ohio newspaper article introduce readers to the folklore character who came to encapsulate the Pittsburgh region's workforce and civic identity in mid-twentieth-century America. The writer, Owen

Francis, sketches out the basic narrative of Joe's tale: how he suddenly appeared at a contest for the hand of Steve Mestrovich's beautiful daughter, Mary, where he bested all the locals in a contest of lifting steel bars. He revealed, upon lifting his shirt that he was in fact made of steel, having been born in an iron ore mountain. Much to everyone's surprise—and Mary's relief—he turned down his trophy: "What you think, I catch time for sit around house with womans? No, by Gods, not me. I joost catch time for workit dats all." And work he did—too well. In the popular renderings of Joe's story, including the one first published by Francis in *Scribner's Magazine* in 1931, the mighty Joe squeezes out steel rails between his massive fingers and, working all day and every day, forces a shutdown of the mill. Realizing what he has wrought, Joe sacrifices himself into the mill's molten steel. When the workers and managers arrive to resume work the following day, they find Joe and plead with him to get out. Joe reassures them, "Dats fine. Dats good business, dats joost what I want it. By Gods, I be sick dis time of mill what shut down." Having heard the boss say they planned to build a new mill, Joe decided he would offer his steel body to make "best mills in the whole Monongahela valley, what gonna be best mills in whole world."[7]

This *Toledo Blade* article noted the Magarac tale's ongoing life in the mill communities of Pittsburgh and encouraged readers to "saunter into a tavern in Braddock or Homestead or drop into the home of any steelman," where one might hear the story. It also announced an ambitious plan to literally make Magarac part of the city's built environment. Frank Vittor, an acclaimed local sculptor, had proposed a massive 100- to 120-foot-tall stainless-steel rendering of Joe that would sit at the city's triangular Point, the meeting place of the Allegheny and Monongahela. In Vittor's clay model, Joe stands erect, his sculpted bare chest bowed outward. His massive arms lead to two furnaces pouring forth streams of molten steel that meet at his feet and mimic the confluence of the rivers, where the city was planning to erect a water fountain. Vittor had produced busts not only of Mark Twain and the acclaimed hunter and conservationist Teddy Roosevelt but also of the Irene Kaufmann Settlement House's patron, Henry Kaufmann, whose bronze likeness was relocated to Squirrel Hill when the settlement moved to East Pittsburgh. Vittor created many of the city's markers of public history: war memorials, historic panels, Schenley Park's imposing Christopher Columbus monument, and a bronze statue of Honus Wagner, The Flying Dutchman, for Forbes Field.

The sculptor claimed, "In Pittsburgh, we're proud of our steel industry. We are known throughout the world first for our steel. Our people want our industries and the city's background shown."[8] During the 1950s, the local landscape was dominated by the hulking mills: their smokestacks incessantly bellowing dark soot that coated city buildings and homes, families' laundry. As a kid I never considered that the massive stone façade of Carnegie Library was something other than black stone until steel's legacy was scrubbed away after I left. At night, the mills blew puffs of steam and smoke and glowed an eerie light that bounced off the surface of the dirty rivers.

The development of modern American football coincides not only with the rise of industrial society in Pittsburgh, but also with its increasing ethnic diversity. Football's roots are in English rugby, an influence that also explains its early incubation at upper-crust schools in the Northeast among that class of young men whose first names sound like last names—Ward, Spencer, Chase. Football was a British import refashioned in the evolving climates of prep schools and elite universities like Harvard, Yale, and Columbia, where it soon attracted media attention and a wider range of participants and spectators in the late nineteenth century. These were individuals whose "attitude towards upper-class sportsmanship was much more ambivalent . . . and they were unwilling to subordinate themselves to a collegiate aristocracy who would thereby have been held to norms of correctness."[9] The game became increasingly violent. The eighteen deaths that occurred on gridirons in 1906—and at places like Princeton, Harvard, and Trinity—called into question the correctness of the popular game.[10] The dean of University of Chicago's Divinity School remarked, "Football today is a social obsession—a boy killing, education prostituting, gladiatorial sport. . . . I do not know what should take its place, but the new games should not require the services of a physician, the maintenance of a hospital, and the celebration of funerals."[11]

After lobbying by President Roosevelt, whose son's football injury had tempered his enthusiasm for the game, modifications, including legalizing the forward pass, were adopted. And the game, which the commentator George Will has claimed is definitively American due to its bureaucratic and bloody nature, "violence punctuated by committee meetings," continues to evolve.[12] Perhaps, more accurately it has developed to complement the industrial workplace, a recreational replication of the glassworks or steel mill. As Jack Kemp noted, the discrete division of labor in football, the rigid scheduling, reliance on teamwork, and emphasis on planning and execution are logical extensions of the modern workplace environment, with its focus on efficiency, productivity, specialization, and most of all—profit. The modern steel mill came to epitomize scientific management, and it was where corporate managers first implemented such practices on a massive scale. The increasing formalization of rules in football reflects the need to accommodate similar societal shifts, including pressures over time to minimize the collateral damage that consumers' desires inflict on the bodies of these gridiron workers. That risk is also the game's appeal.

The region's immigrant working-class world paralleled football, and "the hard-fought style of the game . . . appealed to the laborers in the mines, mills, and factories."[13] As early as 1907, over half of the labor force at US Steel's famous Homestead Steel Works was made up of immigrant Slavs.[14] Such workers were generally less skilled and thus exposed to the greatest hazards, accustomed to physically demanding and dangerous work. At the time of the *Pittsburgh Survey*, it was common for laborers to work twelve-hour days, with a twenty-four hour shift every fortnight. Accidents were frequent: "An investigation at the Carnegie South Works between 1907 and 1916 discovered that twenty-five percent of the recent immigrants employed there had been injured or killed."[15] As part of the *Pittsburgh Survey*, researchers studied industrial accidents in the region from 1906 to 1907, and found that of the 526 deaths recorded that year, 195 were in the region's steel mills and more than half of those workers were foreigners.[16] At the time, employers were not mandated to record these figures and official state tallies were deemed "worthless" by the researchers.[17] Survey authors decried the human toll of industrialization, how the "Slavs" with "brawn for sale," were also the "greatest sufferers from accidents . . . for to their lot falls the heaviest and most dangerous work."[18] Employers' legal responsibilities to protect workers and compensate them when hurt were limited and their concern often lacking. Commenting on an accident in which a molten steel load killed four immigrant workers, a plant superintendent observed, "Americans would know enough to keep out from under those loads."[19] The sight of men crippled from accidents was "so common as to excite no comment."[20] Worse, these immigrant laborers were deemed a threat to their coworkers' economic security. Considered by many employers as lacking intelligence but with the "willingness to work long hours and overtime without a murmur," the Slav was gaining "his foothold in the Pittsburgh industries, and while gaining it he undermines the income of the next higher industrial group and incurs the enmity of the Americans."[21]

Despite its alleged ubiquity, the legend of Joe Magarac turned out to be more likely fakelore than folklore. That the word "magarac" means donkey in Croatian and Serbian, and more specifically, "a stupid, unintelligent person, a foolish idiot," had always been a puzzling element of the yarn.[22]

Owen Francis recounted two Hunkies exchanging the label and how they "laughed and spoke in their mother tongue, which I did not understand."[23] It seems the jackass may have been him, for "Joe may be a symbol of strength and endurance, but indeed he is a 'magarac' for cheerfully sacrificing his life to the company."[24] Anyone willing to give up an idealized partner, social status, and his life to improve the profitability of a callous employer is, well, a *magarac*.

National media and the steel industry itself promoted stories of Joe, as US Steel did in a 1950 comic book, *Joe the Genie of Steel*. He is the model American worker. He does not join unions or go on strike as did many steelworkers during the famous 1898 Homestead Rebellion or the massive Great Steel Strike of 1919, which involved over 350,000 workers, many of them immigrants pitted against native-born workers who crossed the picket lines, including African Americans. While writers and city leaders fashioned this usable image of Joe Magarac, he became something different for the real Joe Magaracs of the region and their descendants—another symbol of masculine power, sacrifice, and ethnic identification—tied to the steel communities of the region. And he was therefore destined to play football.

Like basketball in the city neighborhoods, football offered not only individual and collective pride and greater social acceptance but also a chance for the immigrant laborers' descendants to escape the dangerous jobs and limited opportunities that defined local working lives. Echoing George Resavage's comments on soccer and coal mining, the NFL Hall of Fame member "Iron" Mike Ditka has said of the region's football tradition: "I think a lot of it's heritage. . . . It's the way they grew up, what they were instilled with from their parents and grandparents."[25]

In his poem "Autumn Begins in Martin's Ferry, Ohio," James Wright could be describing the steel towns along the Mon Valley:

> In the Shreve High football stadium,
> I think of Polacks nursing long beers in Tiltonsville,
> And gray faces of Negroes in the blast furnace at Benwood,
> And the ruptured night watchman of Wheeling Steel,
> Dreaming of heroes.
>
> . . . Therefore,
> Their sons grow suicidally beautiful
> At the beginning of October,
> And gallop terribly against each other's bodies.[26]

In the Western Pennsylvania Sports Museum in downtown Pittsburgh, there is a map with the names of local gridiron heroes, names well known not just in the hills of western Pennsylvania, but across the country and beyond: Blanda, Namath, Montana, Ditka, Dorsett, and Marino. I grew up watching the latter two in the old Pitt Stadium, with its splintered wooden benches and smashed college students, who sometimes got carried out when the whiskey kicked in. All these NFL Hall of Famers first starred at high schools in the region, and western Pennsylvania was once the mother lode of high school football talent. Recruiters from the major college programs flocked to the stands of its playing fields on weekend evenings to find their future stars whose exploits you could tune into on crackly AM radio.

During the 1920s alone, the high school student population increased more than eightfold in the region, the area's rapid suburbanization providing fertile ground for the expansion of local scholastic football.[27] Games began attracting not just hundreds, but thousands of fans. In local school districts, broader allegiances based on high school football further challenged the influence of traditional urban ethnic institutions like the Polish Falcons, Turners, and Sokols that promoted ethnic affiliation through sport. High school and later professional sport emerged as platforms to communicate a regional affiliation and identity: the parish kid became everyone's local schoolboy hero. Ethnic groups, too, rallied behind such local football stars not solely as representatives of Aliquippa or Beaver Falls, but as exemplary Poles, Italians, or Jews whose ascent into the spotlight of fandom made them worthy representatives. For players, football was a literal and figurative field of opportunity that seemed to many egalitarian in retrospect: "Football gave acceptance . . . acceptance into the democratic fraternity of the entertainment world where performance counts and ethnic origin is hardly a handicap."[28]

The Pittsburgh region was once a proving ground for young men like Mike Ditka—who used football to attend the University of Pittsburgh, then play and coach in the NFL—but the two markers of the area's history, high school football and steel, suffered a decline in the latter half of the twentieth century. School districts once dominant in football experienced large population losses as people moved to outlying suburbs or were part of the general exodus following the collapse of the region's industrial base in the 1970s and 1980s. During that period, the area lost over 90,000 manufacturing jobs, many of them well-paying ones in the steel industry. The Pittsburgh metropolitan region bled nearly 300,000 residents between 1970 and 1990. Some local high schools, such as Aliquippa, have

5.1 Joe Magarac, Edgar Thomson Works, 2018. Photograph by the author.

continued to produce successful teams and players, but the heyday is past. Moved south. Participation in high school football programs has dropped significantly and the area no longer produces such a bumper crop of crème de la crème college recruits. The once elite University of Pittsburgh football program, national champions in 1976, has struggled over the past few decades to reclaim its place among the elite. Gone, too, is most of the industry that defined the region and its character. Though US Steel had twenty-five blast furnaces in the Mon Valley alone in 1950, only two remain. Both are at the Edgar Thomson Steel Works in Braddock, the site of the company's original mill, and during the Whiskey Rebellion of the 1790s, the site of a rally of thousands of armed protestors unhappy with the young republic's taxes.

Outside the mill now stands a massive fiberglass Joe Magarac bending an iron rail. He was rescued from Kennywood Amusement Park, where for decades it was part of its Olde Kennywood Railroad ride. Joe got a makeover: his blond hair now black, work jeans a bright orange, cinched tight with a wide belt. With his chest sporting a thick metal chain tied to a US Steel medallion, he looks ready to hop into a 1970 Chevy Nova with its eight-track blaring Styx. He only lacks a mullet.

With nearly 40 percent of its population living below the poverty level, Braddock is struggling to find a way to rebuild its economic base after emerging from bankruptcy. Its story garnered national attention in a Levi's ad campaign that placed Braddock's evolution within our national mythology of the frontier. Accompanied by soaring music, a young girl's voice assures us over images of strangely beautiful urban ruin, peopled by Levi's-wearing residents: "A long time ago things got broken here . . . Maybe the world gets broken on purpose, so we have work to do." People are trying. They have built urban gardens, started small businesses, and constructed a playground—something the community lacked. The acclaimed Pittsburgh chef Kevin Sousa opened a new restaurant here, Superior Motors; he had first considered the name Magarac. Looming over the brick and glass eatery is the hulking blue-gray Braddock Works. Down the street a trendy spot for craft beers has opened. It's got big glass windows and lighters you can buy with the brewery's logo. I sat there sipping seven-dollar drafts while locals queued up for gyros from a food truck.

Like many local communities, Braddock is wrestling with the ravages of deindustrialization, a hard blow to the psyche that has left Pittsburghers often looking backward to what we once were. Allegheny County, in which Pittsburgh resides, has in recent years had one of the oldest populations of the country's urban centers. The past one hundred years have seen the region transform from one of the nation's most heavily immigrant communities—where 25 percent of locals were immigrant—to one of its smallest immigrant populations. As recently as 2014, only 5 percent of Allegheny County's residents were immigrant.[29] The region's white ethnic working-class identity is increasingly a memory, like Forbes Field and now even Three Rivers Stadium. And residents of the city and the diaspora of former residents now spread across the country increasingly invoke this collective memory through the town's professional football team, the Pittsburgh Steelers.

Here We Go, Steelers! Here We Go!

When I see someone in a Steelers T-shirt or cap, I have to say something. "Hey, nice shirt! Go, Steelers!" Gas station, shopping mall, airport terminal, it does not matter. I have joined group cheers in public spaces at the least encouragement. I guess what I most hope to hear in reply is, "Where'd yinz live at?" And I feel a little betrayed, even annoyed otherwise. Please, don't ever tell me you just liked the look of the shirt! Professional teams provide fans with a collective set of symbols around which we unite and signify community: "In rallying around the home team, people identify more closely with a broader civic framework in the spatially, socially, and politically fragmented metropolis."[30] NFL broadcasters typically note the presence of Steelers fans at contests across the country, "How well Steelers fans travel." I have been to games in Green Bay and Atlanta where thousands and thousands of men and women dressed in black and gold have filled the seats. Cities across the US and even overseas—Zurich, Bangkok, Rio—have bars where Steeler fans gather to watch the games, cheer, suffer, and reminisce.[31] What the TV talking heads fail to acknowledge is how many of these fans at away games are part of that exodus of workers and families who left the city when industry crashed. The Steeler Nation is a diaspora.

The early years of pro football and of the Steelers certainly did not suggest that the team would function as any collective symbol. Professional football was a relatively minor sport in the first part of the twentieth century, college football being much more popular; and it was not until the mid-twentieth century that pro football began to attract mass audiences, especially with the rise of television, its sports-specific programming, and the clever marketing of the NFL. The dramatic NFL Films, accompanied by a propulsive soundtrack, slow motion shots, and John Facenda's godlike narration made a simple screen pass appear a distillation of epic tragedy. As noted earlier, the Steelers were perennial losers for decades. Their role in conveying local identity was due to more than their turnaround on the field—dramatic as it was—or to the growth of professional football and the mass media that has catalyzed its explosive growth. A combination of social, cultural, and economic forces during the 1970s coincided with the Steelers' rise to become the most dominant team in the history of the NFL and provided Pittsburghers with a powerful impulse to paint their faces black and gold.

It is impossible to discuss the Steelers organization without analyzing the influence of the team's majority owners, the Rooney family of Pittsburgh. As Dave Anderson observed, writing in the *New York Times*, "In any sport, a team's character usually reflects, for better or for worse, the franchise's dominant personality."[32] Although many NFL teams have experienced a slew of owners, the Steelers have remained a family business, controlled and defined by the Rooneys. The patriarch, Art Rooney, who died in 1988, was the son of Irish Catholic immigrants and grew up on the city's North Side district, where he lived all his life. The neighborhood had once been an independent town, Allegheny City, which Pittsburgh annexed and reconfigured.

Rooney's father had emigrated from Wales and worked in both the mills and coal mines of western Pennsylvania, later moving to the North Side where he ran a saloon in a predominantly Irish working-class, rough-and-tumble neighborhood. Rooney and his five brothers were enthusiastic sportsmen, especially as boxers, and Art qualified for the Olympics in 1920 but opted to fight professionally instead. He later worked as a boxing promoter, played semipro baseball and then college football at Duquesne University, where he received a business degree in 1924. He began his career in professional football during the 1920s as a player, owner, and manager of a semiprofessional team based in his neighborhood, which later became the NFL team known as the Pittsburgh Steelers. For many years the Steelers were, at best, a break-even proposition that suffered from Rooney's focus on other endeavors, notably horse racing. Rooney owned both a horse farm and racetracks and earned his fortune at the racetrack, in a huge payday during one now-legendary weekend in 1936. Rooney's hot hand, however, did not extend to his football team. The Steelers suffered from horrible luck—or decision making—when it came to personnel. They let the future Hall of Famers Johnny Unitas, Jack Kemp, Len Dawson, and others slip through their hands. Although during his years at the helm, Rooney's Steelers were often the basement dwellers of the NFL, Rooney was widely respected around the league. A Saint Louis reporter commented, "If sentiment and the law of averages were considered in the determination of NFL titles, The Pittsburgh Steelers would surely be lopsided favorites."[33] Not until his son Dan took over the helm in the 1960s would the Steelers begin the tradition of winning that is now synonymous with the organization. Between just 1974 and 1979, the Steelers won a then unprecedented four Super Bowls and fielded scores of Future Hall of

Fame players. They dominated and intimated. And Art Rooney, "The Chief," always remained the personality, the ethos behind the organization: a successful, yet unpretentious man who never moved away from his childhood neighborhood, even as it became increasingly Black and impoverished; who attended Mass nearly every day and went to countless wakes of strangers; and who gave generously to local organizations and individuals. His social contacts were wide, and included Cum Posey, owner of the legendary Homestead Grays. As previously mentioned, Rooney helped fund Posey's team, and he served as a pallbearer at Posey's funeral. The local sports historian Rob Ruck summarizes well the legendary status and influence of Art Rooney: "In the somewhat mythic but still essentially accurate saga Pittsburghers have woven out of the strands of Art Rooney's life, sport is a product of hardworking people and tight-knit communities."[34] Art's son Dan continued this legacy, even moving into his father's former home on the North Side. Like his dad, Dan Rooney's community was also the touchstone of his character, as he described, "I know this sounds impossible but in those days growing up on the North Side, we didn't think about your skin color, or your accent, or what church you went to. What mattered was that you lived up to your word, pulled your own weight, and looked out for your friends."[35]

One of Dan Rooney's most important decisions upon assuming operational control of the organization was the hiring of a new head coach, a young assistant coach of the Miami Dolphins and former high school star from a working-class Cleveland family. Chuck Noll immediately instilled an attitude of professionalism and commitment that echoed across the roster. The longtime kicker Gary Anderson recalls, "I really responded to a guy like that. . . . If you showed up for work in the morning, he assumed you were professional enough to get the job done."[36] The Steelers also displayed the toughness embodied in Art Rooney, who is famously quoted as saying, "Don't ever let anyone mistake kindness for weakness." The former Steeler middle linebacker Jack Lambert, a Steeler legend for his violent play and missing front teeth, which commonly elicited comparisons to Dracula, defined the Steelers' style as a "culture of hard-hitting, hard-drinking, blue collar masculinity."[37] And it sold as well as Big Irons—the sixteen-ounce version of the local brew, Iron City. Opponents may have expected to win against Pittsburgh, but victory would come with its lumps. The former NFL quarterback Len Dawson recalled, "They intimidated. It began with their defense."[38] With Noll at the helm and a new group of exceptionally talented players, the team reached legendary prominence, just as the town's defining economic base collapsed. Yet the Steelers, through their name, their symbols, and physical style of play, keep the memory of those hulking mills, smokestacks, and once thriving towns like Braddock alive on Sundays.

Not only did the team's name derive from the region's defining industry, but its logo as well—a strange set of geometric shapes that adorns each player's helmet on one side and countless T-shirts, playing cards, beer mugs, blankets, coasters, pens, paper plates, pillows, beer coolers, pajamas, socks, bottle openers, luggage tags, sweatshirts, license plates, key chains, and baby bibs. I've owned them all. The Steelers, who had earlier worn uniforms adorned with the city crest, adopted the symbol of the three hypocycloids in 1963. If you can find something in your basement or attic made of steel, you will find this symbol of three geometric shapes in gold, red, and blue. The symbol was originally developed by the marketing division of United States Steel Corporation and was meant to convey the lightness, smartness, and versatility of steel. It is probably the second shape my kids learned to draw, right after the circle.

Fans not only embraced these official symbols of Steelermania but also developed a cadre of others that echo the town's industrial past, which seems harder to find every time I return to a scene of more new glass office buildings, artisanal coffee shops, and hipsters who look like they got lost on their way to Brooklyn. Some fans called themselves "Steelheads" and wore plastic I-beam cross-sections on their heads. More common in the 1970s and through the 1980s—but noticeably rare now—were simple hard hats of black and gold with the team logo. The most recognizable of the Steeler symbols was conjured up in 1975 by the longtime Steeler color commentator Myron Cope: an erudite, excitable and wholly original radio personality with a heavily Pittsburgh-inflected, nasally voice once described as a "yawping, squawking instrument . . . that sounds as if his larynx had been dragged through chopped-up blocks of cement."[39] Dan Rooney said, "Myron Cope *is* the Pittsburgh Steelers."[40] As a gimmick for his employer, WTAE, Cope, who passed away in 2008, invented the Terrible Towel, a simple dyed dish towel with allegedly magical powers that Steelers fans now buy by the thousands every year and wave like battle-axes. At her first game, my wife feared losing an eye amid the gyrating gold talismans. I have lots of those, too. My favorite is a solid black one picked up off a dirty concrete ramp in Three Rivers amid the streaming hordes of fans, cheering, "Here We Go, Steelers! Here We Go!" after we crushed the Houston Oilers, now the Tennessee Titans, on a sleet-covered field in the AFC Championship. The Oilers ran for twenty-four yards.

In a town whose football team is understood to "embody the town traits of hard work, no glitz," a simple towel—something you use to wipe your hands or, after working up a sweat, your face—was the ideal icon to convey one's allegiance.[41] The local writer and theologian Michael Novak stated, "People of Western Pennsylvania share a long historic sense of suffering, of poverty, of lower status immemorially from the time of serfdom in eastern Europe. . . . The work they could find, for which they were enormously grateful, was hard and dirty and violent. Football dramatized the immigrant experience, the underdog experience."[42] The Steelers in the 1970s, too, had gone from underdog to Uber Men. Long the butt of jokes for our ugly city, we were now world champions.

No player better symbolized the team's transition from tough loser to dominating winner than Joe Greene, the team's number one draft pick in 1969. Greene was a tenacious defensive lineman blessed with freakish speed and bullish power that he used to blow up opponents' plays. At times he turned the course of a game through his singular effort. He was from an obscure school, the University of North Texas, and welcomed by the media with encouraging articles such as "Steelers Draft Joe Who?" Greene anchored the Steelers' dominant defensive line, "The Steel Curtain" during the Super Bowl years of the 1970s and was nicknamed "Mean Joe" for his intimidating and sometimes explosive demeanor. I remember being in the car with my dad, driving somewhere, probably to Sears and listening to the Steelers on the radio. We heard the announcer's suddenly incredulous tone as Greene hurled his helmet into the stands in frustration. I tried to picture the headgear spinning out over the seats like a satellite. Greene's intimidating persona was later the basis of an iconic TV commercial for Coke, where the fearsome warrior, limping off to the locker room bequeaths his jersey to a sheepish young boy who has just offered him the cold refreshment. Greene's style of play was perfect for the Steelers, whose fans cheer a touchdown, but get up out of their seats in a bloodlust to scream DEE-FENSE! DEE-FENSE! The sense of defending your ground, having your back to the wall but ready to strike back—and hard—is an apropos symbol for people who did dirty and dangerous jobs and endured an often-combative relationship with their employers and city leaders, the powers that be.

After economic forces decimated a way of life that won't come back, the Steelers were an anchor to moor local pride: "We were the industrial center of the universe. Now we're in the dumps. The Steelers show we're alive, a major city, still a force."[43] The team's ascendance was not only a manifestation of a region's self-image, but a tonic for the anxiety and anger people felt watching the security of good-paying jobs slip away, their children, too. As Cope later recounted, "This has always been great football territory. High school football was so big around here. Football became even more important here when the steel industry went down the tubes, and so many people were out of work, when the mills were closing down for good. The Steelers gave them something to be happy about, something to cheer. You could look forward to the games on Sunday and it helped you get started on Monday. It was a psychological shot in the arm."[44] It was also for some a way to claim whiteness.

Good Things Will Come to Those Who Work and Wait

In 1971, a group of Pittsburgh-area men sat watching the announcement of the Steelers' second-round draft pick, Jack Ham, out of Penn State. One of them spontaneously announced a toast to "Dobre Shunka," or the "good ham" in Slovak.[45] Jack Ham was a freakishly athletic kid from nearby Johnstown, site of the disastrous 1889 flood. Major colleges had ignored him coming out of high school due to his small size and his school's lack of gridiron reputation. But, after making the roster at Penn State, he blossomed into an All-American and was a perfect fit for Chuck Noll's plan to rebuild the Steelers roster with young athletic players. In the 1960s the team had traded away its top draft picks and built a team of castoff veterans that enjoyed some minor success but never reached the playoffs. Noll wanted to develop players characterized by athleticism, intelligence, and self-motivation. Ham possessed all these. His uncanny ability to diagnose plays, combined with his speed, made it seem that he had been in the offense's huddle when he destroyed their plays from the outset: stepping in front of a receiver to intercept a pass or shooting a gap in the line to drag down a running back. He was a crucial piece of their championship teams, a Hall of Fame inductee immediately upon eligibility, and one of the greatest linebackers in NFL history.

However, it was his Polish heritage and local working-class roots that first made him a symbol of pride to these local men and the larger Slavic community, and that draft day toast was the genesis of a fan club, the Dobre Shunka. The club joined local Poles and other Slavs together in a celebration of football success and ethnic pride. The expression of Polish identity and, more generally, of white ethnic identity became a major part of the culture surrounding the Steelers of the 1970s. Myron Cope, a member of the Western Pennsylvania Jewish Sports Hall of Fame, often quipped about things on the field not being "kosher" and yelped "mazel tov" for a job well done. The Steelers tight end during the team's four Super Bowls, Randy Grossman, was embraced by Pittsburgh's local Jewish community, though he had been raised in a nonreligious home. He, too, was inducted into the Western Pennsylvania Jewish Sports Hall of Fame, which was founded in 1982 with Ziggy Kahn, the longtime IKS staff member, as the first inductee. The hall is in the Squirrel Hill Jewish Community Center, and every year there is a banquet to honor inductees with proceeds funding local athletes' travel to the Maccabi Games. Grossman was dubbed by his prankster teammate Ernie Holmes, the Rabbi.[46] What else for a Jewish kid from Philly?

Among his zany stunts, Cope recorded a takeoff of Barry Manilow's "Copacabana," the "Cope Cabana," during which he screams, "What is Ukrainian for you're having Steelermania?!" I don't know, but there is probably a T-shirt with it. Several years ago, two local brothers sold shirts allowing a fan to proclaim love for the Steelers and her Italian, Ukrainian, German, Irish, Chinese, Russian, or Lithuanian heritage. I got a Jewish one for my wife. They had no Japanese ones. On game days, she now joins other Steeler fans in Pittsburgh and throughout the country with a traditional meal of spicy kielbasa. I drive twenty minutes one-way to a local hill town to buy ours from the grandson of a Polish sausage maker. He is a Cowboys fan. If it's a big game, the playoffs, I may put on my Joe Greene jersey and blast the team's most famous fight song from back in the day: a polka written and sung by Jimmy Pol, originally Jimmy Psihoulis, a Greek immigrant with a thick accent who sang Pittsburgh as "Peesberg." His signature song, to the familiar tune of "The Pennsylvania Polka," ends with the exhortation, "Good things will come to those who work and wait!"

The Steelers' rise in the 1970s coincided not only with widespread anxiety about the region's economic future, but with a larger cultural anxiety about the future of white ethnic identity that at times echoed earlier claims of race suicide from men like Hornaday and Grant. The difference at the time was that the Italians and other once marginalized ethnic groups were on the other side of that boundary line, now fully white. The Dobre Shunka was one example of the return to ethnicity among white Americans later referred to as the "white ethnic revival," and this symbolic display of ethnicity has been described as also working class.[47] Michael Novak was among its chief architects.[48]

Behind this renewed sense of ethnic self-identification, this return to roots, were various social and historical forces. These included both white working-class frustration with economic and social conditions, and renewed pride and nostalgia for southern and eastern European cultural roots that many individuals felt were lost or devalued through their ancestors' forced assimilation to Waspish norms. In Pittsburgh, the Steelers became a vehicle for individuals and groups to express these roots with gusto, especially by associating themselves with players like Jack Ham who could so well represent their identity as ethnic Pittsburghers—and as men. Even "Mean" Joe Greene, a young Black man from Texas, had his cadre of fans who called themselves Joe Greene's Polish Armed Forces. A more dramatic example of this phenomenon involved a young Afro-sporting mixed-race running back from New Jersey, Franco Harris.

Like Ham, Harris had been a star at Penn State University, where so many locals like those from my high school went for their degrees, and he was a sensation from his first game. During his rookie season in 1972, a group of local Italian Americans, aware that Harris's mother was Italian, began to claim Harris as one of their own, a paisano. Harris's mother was a World War II war bride, who moved to America with Harris's father, a Black GI. Pittsburgh had been a major destination for Italian immigrants in the early twentieth century and by 1930, 15 percent of Allegheny County's entire immigrant population was Italian.[49] They established themselves in specific Pittsburgh neighborhoods, like East Liberty, where one family, the Ventos, operated grocery stores. Al Vento met Harris through one of his customers, another Steelers player. Like many second-generation Italians, Vento was somewhat distanced from his cultural roots, but fiercely proud of them. He recalled that his family had been forced to conceal their heritage: "It seemed that everybody had to be Americans, instead of Italian. In fact, they try to talk English, try to eliminate the Italian heritage, which they found was a mistake. And I think that the Italian heritage should live on forever and ever and ever."[50]

Justice Michael Musmanno could not have agreed more. In 1936 he had issued a court holiday in observance of Columbus Day, and he was a regular speaker, both in person and on radio, on Columbus Day over the years. In 1965, when Yale University published a book claiming the discovery of a map, the *Vinland Map*, that established Norse exploration of America well before Columbus's journey, the judge went on the offensive, penning a bitter critique of the work, *Columbus Was First*.[51] He was the keynote speaker in 1958 at the dedication of the impressive Frank Vittor statue of Christopher Columbus in Schenley Park, now wrapped in plastic as the city and the Italian Sons and Daughters of America fight in court over its future. After dramatically recounting spending a night on the beach at the site of Columbus's first landing in San Salvador, the justice summarized, "He taught man that no matter what be the opposition or antagonism, if his cause is just, he will achieve the port of his ambition."[52] Michael Musmanno died on October 12, 1968—Columbus Day.

As one of the founding members of Harris's fan club, Franco's Italian Army, Vento would help create a means by which he and thousands of other local Italian Americans could symbolically participate in and enact their Italian heritage as Musmanno and others have through Columbus. Of course, what was most ironic about this display of ethnicity was that its vehicle of expression, a professional football player, was African American. Harris's identity as a Pittsburgh Steeler helped eclipse his obvious racial identity and its powerful negative associations, as it collapsed him into the larger working-class identity the team had long represented. Harris even defined himself in such terms, "Pittsburgh came from steel mill and coal mines, and its teams were the working man's teams. We're the working-class athlete. We come to work every day. Nothing flashy, just tough football all the time."[53] Although Harris was respected as a hardworking player, his running style was widely criticized by fans and the media during his playing days. His tendency to scamper out of bounds to avoid contact was seen as soft and antithetical to the hard-nosed physical style of play associated with the Steelers and their fans. It could be, however, that once wrapped up in the red, green, and white of the Italian flag, Harris's play was less damaging to his reputation, more a sign of clever Italian self-preservation than of Black cowardice.

Franco's Italian Army was no minor unit; its ranks swelled into the thousands, with members spread across the country, including the nation's most famous son of Italy, Frank Sinatra, who was inducted into the army in a special ceremony in 1972 when the Steelers were in California. They toasted with Riunite. During its five-year span, Franco's Italian Army received widespread media attention and became a major part of Steelers culture. My dad had one of their T-shirts as he seemed endlessly amused by the crew. They were a bizarre sight: members in old army fatigues, complete with helmets bearing hand-painted stripes of the Italian flag. Their ranks even included a canine unit and a chaplain, who helped sneak bottles of Italian wine into the game. One familiar banner read, "Run, Paisano, Run." Through one of the members, John Danzilli Jr., a colonel in the army reserves, they brought a Jeep and a two-and-a-half-ton truck with a 105-millimeter Howitzer mounted on it to Three Rivers Stadium. The army members waved Italian flags, ate Italian food, and even employed Italian folklore to vanquish the Steelers' opponents. Members carried *cornito*, small crooked horns believed to ward off evil spirits. Some hexed the opposing team with the *malocchio*, or "evil eye." Before one home game, Danzilli arranged a military aircraft to drop posters calling for the hated Oakland Raiders' surrender. However, the airdrop missed and most of the posters landed in the Hill District, an ironic message to its mostly Black, impoverished residents.

A few years before the Italian army's air campaign, riots broke out on the Hill after the assassination of Martin Luther King Jr. The governor called in the National Guard to police its streets, which had been decimated by ambitious urban renewal projects promoted by Pittsburgh's civic and corporate leaders, including the financier Richard King Mellon, who formed the Allegheny Conference on Community Development in 1944. These civic leaders sought to address Pittsburgh's horrible air pollution, endemic flooding, and urban blight, by using new federal laws, public funding, and eminent domain to rebuild the city with a focus on commercial development. While the pollution abatement programs and construction of a series of locks and dams addressed environmental issues that afflicted all local residents, the city's new Urban Redevelopment Authority's renewal projects eviscerated the predominantly Black and politically weak Hill District, where local businesses and over 1,500 families were pushed out to clear space for a highway and a sports and entertainment venue, the Civic Arena, further exacerbating the city's segregation.[54] Greenlee Field, home of the Pittsburgh Crawfords, once the pride of the Hill, had already been leveled to build public housing projects since the Negro Leagues died after integration of the majors. With insufficient housing available to them, many Hill residents moved to substandard overpriced housing in the city's other poor, Black neighborhoods. It was part of Pittsburgh's rebirth, its Renaissance.

Franco Harris not only had an army at his back, but a team with a less acknowledged tradition: providing African Americans unique opportunities in the racially segregated world of professional sports. It is a franchise of notable firsts. When Art Rooney was organizing his first team in the early 1930s, he approached a graduating senior at Duquesne University's athletic banquet about joining. Ray Kemp took up the offer and would become one of only two Black players in the league in 1933. The following year Kemp took a job as a college football coach, a decision unrelated to the gentlemen's agreement among NFL owners to bar Black players from the league beginning in 1934, a ban that lasted until 1946.[55] Franco Harris would not only go on to the Hall of Fame, he also became the first African American MVP of a Super Bowl, when he helped lead the team to the franchise's initial Lombardi Trophy in Super Bowl IX.

The Steelers' hiring of Black players was a major reason for their meteoric rise in the 1970s; the team's rosters filled with star Black players, many from historically Black colleges and universities (HBCUs) in the

5.2 Downtown Pittsburgh with Civic Arena and Three Rivers Stadium Construction, 1969. Reproduced by permission from Melvin Seidenberg, Thomas and Katherine Detre Library and Archives.

South that other teams simply ignored. In the early 1960s, only roughly 13 percent of the NFL's players were African American.[56] Key to the Steelers' success in drafting these players, who included men such as John Stallworth, Ernie Holmes, and Mel Blount, was the former Pittsburgh *Courier* sports and managing editor, Bill Nunn Jr. At the *Courier*, Nunn succeeded his father as managing editor and in selecting an annual Black college All-American team. Each year he hosted a banquet in the Steel City for players that Rooney helped to fund. On the insistence of Art Rooney, he joined the Steelers scouting department in 1967, later becoming a full-time scout for the team during Noll's tenure. "You cannot write the history of the Pittsburgh Steelers without Bill Nunn. When you look at the Steelers of the 1970s, none of that would have happened without Bill Nunn," commented the legendary Hall of Fame cornerback Mel Blount.[57] Bill Nunn remained with the organization until his death in 2014 at the age of eighty-nine, and in 2020 he was selected for the NFL Hall of Fame.

In the 1972 draft Nunn helped the team select Joe Gilliam, a rifle-armed, poised quarterback from another HBCU, Tennessee State. No other position in football is as vexed as that of the Black quarterback: first, argued too dumb to play the position; then, too athletic to play it right; and finally, too cocky or loudmouthed once he proved all the former charges undeniably wrong. Due to the 1974 strike, Gilliam finally got a chance to start and led the team to a 4-1-1 record before being replaced by Terry Bradshaw, the first pick in the 1970 draft. Gilliam was an extraordinarily gifted player but never got another chance to start for the Steelers, who would win two Super Bowl rings with him as Bradshaw's backup.

The Steelers' willingness to hire African Americans also extended to coaching opportunities. In 1956, the team drafted a dynamic All-American wide receiver from Michigan who began the year in spectacular fashion, as both a receiver and kick returner, scoring two touchdowns in only a handful of games. Unfortunately, Lowell Perry was grievously injured, suffering a fractured hip and pelvis in his sixth pro game and spending months in the hospital recuperating. Art Rooney visited Perry in the hospital and told him, "Lowell, as long as I own the Pittsburgh Steelers, you have a job in my organization."[58] The following season Perry was on the sidelines as a wide receivers coach, the first Black assistant coach in any professional sport during the modern era. Rooney later paid for Perry's law school education, and he would go on to be a trailblazer in other arenas: the first Black manager of an American auto plant and the first Black television football broadcaster. In 1975 he was tapped by President Ford to head the Equal Employment Opportunity Commission.

By the 1980s, the once mighty Steelers began to slip, missing the playoffs for several years during the decade. Joe Greene and other key players were gone and Chuck Noll, the Emperor Chaz as Cope dubbed him, without any prodding from the Rooney family, walked away. His replacement was, like Noll, a young, promising NFL assistant coach, but also a local boy who made good. Bill Cowher had grown up in Crafton, a middle-class community outside of Pittsburgh and his thick Pittsburgh accent, a sign of local working-class roots—of being a Yinzer—as well as his physical intensity made him an instant hit with local fans. Unlike Noll, Cowher was a fiery personality: a volatile coach who stalked the sidelines with a jaw that looked both chiseled out of rock and ready to spit a rock out—in pieces. He showered anyone near him with waves of spittle as he yelled, which he often did. Within a few years, he had the Steelers back in the Super Bowl, although they lost to the hated Dallas Cowboys. I read no newspapers and watched no TV for a week. I still can't utter a certain quarterback's name. During his tenure, Cowher would guide the Steelers to six AFC Championship games and finally win another Super Bowl in 2006, the "one for the thumb" that the fans, the Steeler Nation, had long awaited. In my little Wisconsin town, I ran outside and lit off a massive firework that woke up my neighbor who told me the next morning, "Quite a celebration last night! It's okay. We were rooting for them, too."

Cowher's teams were marked by the same physical style of play as earlier incarnations of the Steelers and had potent defensive units manned by several All-Pro and future Hall of Fame players. Addressing his team before their Super Bowl clash with the Seattle Seahawks in February 2006, Cowher implored his men, "You play smart; you play hard. But, most of all, you play physical!" Fans hung banners in Three Rivers Stadium welcoming opposing teams to "The Blast Furnace," the only one left downtown in the city they dubbed Blitzburgh. In the mid-1990s the team's nearly all-Black defensive unit adopted the name, "Sixty-Minute Men," a suggestive testament to their blue-collar, hypermasculine image, something constantly espoused by Cowher, who noted that the team was "an extension of this city and of the fan who watches us play."[59] That year's team made an incredible run through the playoffs as underdogs, winning three games away from their home field, driven by the collective desire to win the game for their beloved teammate, the running back Jerome Bettis. Bettis had been the face of the franchise in previous years, embraced for his personable nature, charitable work, and commitment to excellence. His jersey remains a common sight in the city and at games. His nickname, "The Bus," spoke of his overpowering style of running in which he commonly ran through opponents as well as his lunch-pail identity. He was no European luxury sedan driving casually around Fox Chapel's winding wooded lanes, but a clunky public transport trundling downtown for the common man and woman. In 2004, Bettis took a $2.6 million cut in pay to stay on with the team, gaining even more respect, if less money.

With the increasingly higher salaries of NFL players, it is remarkable that fans seem able to maintain any sense of identification with young men driving fully loaded, late model luxury vehicles, sporting one-carat diamond studs, and living in homes fit for the cover of *Architectural Digest*. In the 1970s football was far from a lucrative profession, so that many players did have blue-collar jobs in the off-season. They shared beers in local taverns amid the fans and lived among them like their truly blue-collar predecessors, the soccer players of the Miner's League. It is only the most recent generation of players that enjoys substantial compensation; in 1980, the average player's annual salary was still only $78,657.[60] When the perennial All-Pro Jack Lambert signed his new five-year contract in 1976, he was the league's highest-paid defensive player. His deal was worth a total of $1.25 million. NFL players now have achieved a median salary of over $1 million per year, although the rookie minimum as recently as 2000 was under $200,000. Long-term financial security still eludes most of these players.[61] The average NFL career is just shy of four years, the length of a player's rookie contract. Unlike other professional sports, player contracts are not guaranteed in the NFL, meaning a player can be released or laid off at will, and the owner is not obliged to honor the remainder of his contract. Despite its now super-sized status—the megastadiums with colossal scoreboards, popular online fantasy leagues, and its own TV channel—the NFL still echoes earlier, less glamorized workplaces. As an economics professor observed in the *New York Times*, "It brings to mind the high-risk jobs of the earlier industrial period."[62] A player's career can end in an instant due to serious injury. However lucrative or celebrated he is, his work will be done in pain. Retirement is often marred by the physical disabilities incurred by injuries sustained in a highly dangerous and physically demanding profession whose full risks the industry's leaders resist acknowledging. Like those wounded workers noted by the *Pittsburgh Survey*, crippled NFL players are too common to be noteworthy.

Media and fans are now more aware of the game's grave toll on its workers, such as Mike Webster, Iron Mike. Webster was the perennial All-Pro center on the Steelers great teams of the 1970s and played sixteen years in the league. I was amazed at his arms: massive and bare regardless of the weather. When I moved to Wisconsin, his home state, I realized this was a cultural thing: big tough people who seem impervious to cold, and walk around in twenty-degree weather in shorts and flip-flops. Webster once said, "I've found that the human body and mind are capable of doing much more than people expect. No matter what you're up against, the number one ingredient in life is that you continue to fight with everything you have."[63] Mike Webster, because of the numerous blows he suffered during his playing days, entered a hellish battle with his own mind after he retired. He suffered crippling depression; his marriage ended, and he was homeless at times—living out of his car. He would ask a friend to Taser him so that he could find some relief in sleep. After he died, his family continued his battle against the NFL and players' union for disability compensation. His family fought the NFL all the way through the federal courts, and a 2006 appeals court decision finally settled the matter by ruling in favor of Webster's estate. It was a watershed moment, the first time the NFL had lost a disability case. Webster's son commented, "I think the NFL and the Player's Association are a joke.... It's the players' union and the NFL against the players."[64] That history of battles between and among the players, their union, and the owners, including labor strikes is another way in which locals may see themselves, their histories in these young men, or in the horrendous costs of their fandom on these workers' bodies.

Since Webster's death, researchers have proved the link between football and the degenerative brain disease CTE (chronic traumatic encephalopathy), despite the NFL's repugnant campaign to discredit them; and former Steelers—Mike Webster, Terry Long, Justin Strzelczyk—provided crucial evidence of that sad legacy: their damaged brains. The writer Steve Almond offers the consumer of football a troubling self-inquiry, "What does it mean that the most popular and unifying form of entertainment in America . . . features giant muscled men, mostly African American, engaged in a sport that causes many of them to suffer brain damage?"[65] The recent lawsuit by two former Steelers players, Kevin Henry and Najeh Davenport, offered further cause for reflection. Henry played all eight years of his NFL career in Pittsburgh; he is now unable to work and "increasingly unable to perform the activities of daily living." In response to a class action suit by thousands of former players, the NFL finally agreed in 2014 to a settlement compensating its brain-injured ex-athletes. Many have criticized the agreement for letting the NFL off too easily and rewarding players too little. Davenport and Henry argued that the plan was also racist because it assumed a Black player's cognitive functioning was inherently lower than that of his white peers. The NFL adjusted an individual player's cognitive assessment scores based on his race by using its own statistical model. As a result former Black players needed worse scores to be eligible for compensation. The players' suit notes, "The NFL's scheme—executed through the League-sponsored Settlement Agreement—is particularly insidious because it presumes Black retirees to be less intelligent than their non-Black fellow retirees."[66]

Despite this horrible legacy, and increasing media critiques of the NFL, the Steelers organization is viewed by many as a model of commitment and charity to the community, as a good employer to its workers. Many of the city's other major corporations have abandoned the city and broken the social contract that we once believed sacrosanct, companies such as Rockwell International and Gulf Oil Corporation. The Steelers have thrived and remained in the city. While other NFL franchises like the Baltimore Colts and hated Cleveland Browns relocated their franchises and abandoned their hometown fans, the Rooneys kept the team in Pittsburgh and offered constancy in a town where more and more of its landmark businesses, such as US Steel, disappeared from the cityscape. As Dan Rooney says, "It's the people that matter most, the people in our organization, the fans, and it will always be that way in Pittsburgh. . . . We're here for the game. We're not here for Nike. We're not here for Coke."[67] Dan Rooney's father, Art, lobbied his fellow owners to recognize the players' union and even expressed the right of his veteran players to strike during the 1974 players' walkout. Rocky Bleier, whom the Rooneys had kept on the roster and payroll while he recovered from wounds suffered in combat in Vietnam, recalls Rooney telephoning him during the strike. Rooney heard that Bleier had been badmouthed in the press and called to reassure him, "I just want you to know that what I did for you, I would have done for any of my boys. And you paid us back, on and off the field, more than we could ever have asked. So if you believe in the strike, I want you guys to be out there tomorrow. Hopefully, we can get it settled and go on to play some football."[68] Joe Greene refused to join the strike out of respect for Rooney, The Chief. In 2010, his son Dan was awarded Citizen of the Year from the state's AFL-CIO, and as a national union official noted, "It isn't every day that union men and women get together to honor someone in the business world."[69] The sympathetic treatment of its unionized workforce by the organization is especially resonant in Pittsburgh, birthplace of the American Federation of Labor and a city with a long history of union participation and activism, another legacy fading into the past as fewer and fewer workers hold union cards.

For Pittsburghers and the city's former residents across the country, the Steelers are a touchstone to the imagined community of Pittsburgh's past.[70] As one longtime fan explained, "They are the team for all the ones who like the old things. For all of us who don't want fast food, who don't want to live in a new bedroom community and pay association fees, who don't want progress forced upon us. Pittsburgh is an old place. It feels just right."[71] This nostalgia includes a connection to the European immigrant roots that Pittsburghers treasure and have found increasingly hard to keep

5.3 Frank Sinatra, Myron Cope, and Franco Harris, 1972. Reproduced by permission from Thomas and Katherine Detre Library and Archives.

in place, but is also one that often elides Black deprivation and its ongoing legacy.

The Super Bowl media machine was stoked even higher than usual in 2007 because of another NFL first involving the Steelers. Two Black head coaches were leading their teams into the clash: Lovie Smith and Tony Dungy. Dungy's coaching career had begun in Pittsburgh, where he worked under Chuck Noll. He became the NFL's youngest assistant coach, and later its first African American coordinator when Noll promoted him to defensive coordinator in 1984, a common launching pad to a head-coaching gig. Lowell Perry's widow, Maxine, commenting on the impending Super Bowl, said, "I'd like to think that Lowell and Art Rooney are looking down slapping hands up there right now."[72] The achievement of coaches such as Dungy, the eventual winning coach of the 2007 Super Bowl, are markers of change, but their successes don't outweigh uncomfortable truths about race in the NFL workplace. It was not until 1989 that a Black man, Art Shell, was chosen to be head coach by any NFL team, the Raiders, who had also hired Tom Flores, the son of Mexican field workers, before him. At the onset of the 2016 season, there were only six nonwhite head coaches in the NFL, a league in which 70 percent of players are African American. Half of those coaches were men whose careers Dungy advanced. If one takes away the coaching legacies of the Raiders and the Steelers organizations, the base of the NFL's nonwhite coaching tree disappears: Tom Flores, Art Shell, Tony Dungy, Mike Caldwell, Herman Edwards, Marvin Lewis, and Mike Tomlin.

On the amateur and semipro playing fields of Pittsburgh on which the Rooney boys played, white and Black players developed bonds that defied the historical divisions defining much of life here and in sport. NFL teams, too, are places where the unquestionable skill of African Americans has been sought after, recognized, and rewarded; and where individuals, especially players, have built relationships that transcend barriers of ethnicity, race, religion. It was this ethos that players like Randy Grossman note defined the 1970s Steelers. But, within the industry of football, equity has been slow to be realized, pushed forward primarily by a few organizations and mandated measures of limited reach.

When Steelers fans seem most accepting of Black men, as in the case of Franco's Italian Army, what we can also display is blindness to the historical and ongoing costs of that identity. We embrace them as some of our own but we leave that identification with Black men in the stands, amid the empty beer cups and hot dog wrappers. The Steelers can be a bridge across divides in a city literally defined by bridges, but not if its symbolism obscures. As a writer from the *New Pittsburgh Courier* aptly summarized after the Steelers' fifth Super Bowl win:

> Few other issues seem to galvanize the populace like the Steelers winning. Few subjects break down geographical, cultural, racial, and class barriers like a good old-fashioned Steelers butt-kicking. . . . I don't know if Pittsburgh is the most racist city in America, as some pundits have claimed. . . . Suffice to say, it's bad here. . . . Here's to the notion that the euphoria surrounding this Super Bowl win will last, and that friendly conversations between the races can even extend beyond the Steelers. Maybe, we can even talk about the weather, or the schools, or politics or even the police, without running into the racial wall.[73]

Forgetting a Black Past

Franco's Italian Army was the assertion of Italian ethnicity via a Black body, the public embrace of a racialized man that at the same time erased his Blackness, with only whiteness remaining, a paisano. There was nothing Black about the group, either in membership, or in practice. For members it was part of building a new ethnic identity, one "based on a variety of factors, including pride in their Italian immigrant past, nostalgia for the Italian neighborhoods of their youth, and, perhaps, most importantly, love of their city's NFL football team, the Pittsburgh Steelers."[74] It is an example of what the sociologist Mary Waters has defined as the "symbolic, costless, and voluntary" options available to whites in American society.[75] These individuals of Italian ancestry chose this particular symbol, a Black football player, to use as an occasion for public displays of Italian heritage that they defined: Italian foodways, ornaments, and practices, "Ethnic symbols are frequently individual cultural practices that are taken from the older ethnic culture; they are 'abstracted' from that culture and pulled out of its original moorings, so to speak, to become stand-ins for it."[76] Such practices allow white Americans a greater social space, but without the awareness of that greater latitude. Yet, when white Americans, including Pittsburgh's white laboring class, began to see opportunities foreclose as economic forces gutted communities here, they sometimes saw themselves as society's disposables, the aggrieved.

In a 1999 interview, Al Vento Jr. expressed his sentiment that the government was unfairly favoring minority groups. "But see, what the government [does].... They're giving the jobs to not the qualified people, but to whoever they feel [is] the minority. Then Blacks take that as a thing."[77] While Vento was, at the same time, sympathetic and admiring of Black people, he seemed unable to comprehend the valid need for affirmative action programs. As Waters further notes, the way in which contemporary white ethnics "think about their own ethnicity—the voluntary, enjoyable aspects of it—makes it difficult to understand the contemporary position of nonwhites."[78] At one point during his interview, Vento bemoaned the lack of character in young individuals and pointed out how, in his day, kids learned values by working at one of Pittsburgh's famous institutions: Isaly's. The local ice cream shop once had stores throughout the region and is famous for creating that frozen caloric delicacy, the Klondike Bar. Pittsburghers also fed on the alliteratively named local lunch meat sold there, chipped-chopped ham, a staple of my school cafeteria, slathered in barbeque sauce. Isaly's was, along with Kaufmann's and other businesses, a local landmark picketed by protestors in the 1940s due to its refusal to hire African Americans to work at its counters. An even more telling example of the region's widespread job discrimination was the steel industry, the one so many Pittsburghers recall as a part of themselves, and one now bound up in black and gold.

Although African Americans shared, with the region's Poles, Italians, and Slovaks, a history of working-class struggle that pitted them against the city's more established earlier immigrants—the management class of English, Germans, and Irish—their life in the mills was defined mostly by their racial identity. Unions had helped improve working conditions by fighting for changes such as higher pay and the abolishment of the ten-hour workday and six-day workweek, but organized labor's focus was not on broad social justice. As in other local sectors, Black experience in the region's steel industry was one of constant struggle against institutionalized racism that limited economic advancement and placed African Americans in conflict with their white coworkers. The first major influx of African Americans was to replace striking whites, as in other industries like coal mining. Black workers took these jobs in the dirty steel towns of western Pennsylvania to achieve greater economic opportunity outside the oppressive Jim Crow South. At first, some of this promise seemed realized, as workers found not only better-paying jobs but also opportunities for advancement into skilled positions. However, the waves of new immigrants from Eastern and Southern Europe soon provided the steel industry with an alternative source of inexpensive labor and created an even more rigid color line in the workplace. While Black workers continued to enter the mills, constituting 13 percent of the total workforce by 1918, the practices of both management and labor unions kept them on the bottom rung.[79]

After restrictive legislation cut off major immigration in the 1920s, companies were forced to rely more on Black workers, whose low wages and relative lack of union activism made them appealing to management.[80] Steel mills operated with several distinct departments and Black employees were consigned to the most menial, dangerous, and dirtiest ones—those referred to specifically as the "black departments." An investigation by the state legislature in 1942 reported that half of the industrial companies in Pittsburgh and Philadelphia discriminated against Black people.[81] Because advancement in the mills was based on seniority in a mill's separate departments, Black workers could only hope to be promoted within these less desirable units. If a man could transfer out of his line, and managers often made sure he could not, it meant losing what seniority he had accrued. African American steel workers "reached the ceiling for promotions faster, with fewer opportunities, than whites."[82] Such tactics were motivated by white workers' desires to protect their own interests and by the common racist views about these men. A 1918 report questioned the fitness of Black men for the industry: "From our survey of the situation it must be evident that the southern migrants are not as well established in the Pittsburgh industries as is the white laborer. They are as yet unadapted to the heavy and pace-set labor in our steel mills. Accustomed to the comparatively easy-going plantation and farm work of the South, it will take some time until these migrants have found themselves."[83] African American workers' relegation to these jobs also meant they suffered a higher rate of accidents in the workplace than their white counterparts. Despite these conditions, Black workers from the South continued to move to the region in the early part of the twentieth century: the *Pittsburgh Survey* observed, "With the increasing influx a class of idle, shiftless Negroes is coming."[84]

The violent putdown of the Homestead Strike effectively curtailed union organizing for decades, but the post–World War II era marked a resurgence of union activity in the steel industry. Unfortunately for Black steel workers, unions continued to overlook their specific concerns. Within the unions, Black members had little voice. During the 1960s, a period of dramatic activity by the steelworkers' union, the United Steel Workers of America had over eight hundred officials. Although Black workers made up over one-fourth of the union's rolls, only twenty were union officials.[85] And when national union leaders did seek to address the rights of all their workers, local representatives often blocked those efforts. Some local union officials also ignored the complaints of Black workers and sabotaged efforts at addressing employment discrimination. In the latter part of the century, when shutdowns and layoffs became common, Black workers suffered a disproportionate burden of those work stoppages. Unions participated in this practice by retaining white workers at the expense of Black ones. As one worker noted, "the union was like the establishment."[86] And though some did manage to move up into higher-paying skilled positions, the pace was slow. In 1968, Black workers constituted 7.5 percent of the total workforce in the industry, but still only 4.4 percent of all white-collar and skilled positions.

This disparity led African American workers to create separate labor organizations and increasingly turn to the federal government and courts to affect change in the mills. US Steel took out ads in the *Pittsburgh Courier* espousing its affirmation of equal rights: "On the production line, in our mills, or in offices, or in transportation, quality people, for a quality product, are our first consideration. Numbered among these people are more than 32,000 Negroes willing and able to perform vital functions as members of a great team dedicated to the service of the nation."[87] The reality was that only the iron hand of the federal government could bring this industry to act in accordance with this ethos. In 1970 a Justice Department lawsuit led to a settlement with companies such as US Steel and Jones and

Laughlin that finally terminated the discriminatory seniority system so that workers were no longer trapped within specific departments. And in 1974 the major steel companies and the United Steelworkers of America agreed to sign a consent decree issued by the federal government, acknowledging that racial minorities and women were "systematically assigned to lower-paying jobs with little opportunity for advancement, denied training opportunities, and judged by more stringent standards than were White males." The decree mandated the payment of restitution to aggrieved parties, the establishment of hiring goals with specific timetables, and the abolishment of the seniority system in all hiring and layoff decisions.[88] Immediately, Black workers began to move upward in the industry, occupying a greater range of jobs and finally enjoying the social and economic benefits industry had promised others, but denied them. Although some white workers had fought hard for their Black coworkers, others resented what they saw as an undeserved handout, especially when the agreement shielded Black workers from layoffs as the industry began to collapse. They had arrived just as the end came. Unemployment in the region surged and the towns dominated by steel like Aliquippa, Homestead, and Braddock suffered horribly, and are still trying to recover. The damage was especially great in the city's African American working community, which had an unemployment rate of 17.4 percent in 1980, over twice that of local white residents.[89]

In a review of books detailing the history of the region's steel industry, some based on oral histories of former workers, the scholar John Hinshaw notes the striking contrast between the recollections of white workers and those of Black workers: "White workers also experienced racism, although they did not directly suffer from its petty humiliations and profound injustices; not surprisingly[,] racial identities were more assumed than articulated in their oral histories. In talking to historians, white workers were far more likely to emphasize class and ethnic experiences. The different ways that white and black men remembered their experiences suggest that selective memory helps to shape contemporary communities among working-class people."[90] Given the distinct working experiences and contrasting collective memories in Pittsburgh, the identification of the Pittsburgh Steelers with only the white working class is always about forgetting: forgetting the human costs of industrial labor, the historical marginalization of the region's Black community, the contrast between their lives and those of their coworkers, and how race has demarcated opportunity in workplaces and playing fields. As C. Richard King and Charles Fruehling Springwood have commented in relation to college football,

"Celebratory sporting discourses, whether exhibits playing tribute to greatness, stories of social progress, or accounts of individual achievement, erase race. They literally white it out."[91] The long association in America of the Black male body with violence, sexual promiscuity, and savagery lent a strange aura to Steelers home games, one magnified when flowing out of Three Rivers in mobs that marched through an impoverished, mostly Black North Side. Pittsburghers cheered and reveled in the boastful, physical display of powerful young Black men, seeing them as extensions of themselves. How we loved these young men—their violence.

Though anger, protest, and aggression have characteristically been what Pittsburghers least accepted or understood from the Black community, these players ironically have spoken to white fans' rage. Commenting on the harsh working and social conditions experienced by the region's working class, Michael Novak explained, "There can't help but be a degree of rage, resentment, hostility, and anger. And I think that's why people of Western Pennsylvania have often so loved football and felt rejuvenated by it. The beautiful thing about football is that it channels anger. It ritualizes all that. It supplies it with formal rules. It helps bring that out and express it and in a way purify it."[92]

Pittsburgh Steelers fandom performs a kind of racial alchemy, whereby the bodies of young men of color become symbols not of their own historical struggles but those of white people, specifically the burdens of the white working class in industrial and now postindustrial America. Football may better enable this process as players are in uniforms that cover most of their bodies, unlike the NBA players who have troubling tats and cornrows on open display: "The football helmet creates a certain facelessness that prevents fans from seeing players' emotional expressions and reactions; it also allows for an effacing of race and face."[93] Some suggest that this is the reason fans often tolerate off-the-field misbehavior of NFL players, in contrast to the antics of the NBA's workforce. They see the latter as Black, and "it's easier to embrace felons—of all colors—hidden under helmets than tatted-up black men in plain view."[94] In that case, the NFL's restrictions on modes of behavior and, in general, increasingly mindful packaging is arguably an effort at limiting the league's Blackness, especially manifestations of Black political expression as made clear by the league's response to Black Lives Matter and Colin Kaepernick. At the same time, others worry that touchdown dances and boastful slang have become a new form of minstrelsy that has flattened Black identity to the exaggerated gestures and speech of select pro athletes.

Writing about the wide popularity of Michael Jordan, David L. Andrews states, "African Americans are tolerated, and even valued, if they abdicate their race and seem to successfully assimilate into the practices, value system, and hence identity, of white America."[95] As long as any Steeler player's behavior, especially on the field, fits within the blue-collar framework of the region's identity, it works. But, even on the field, identity is not erased. Sports are like any other industry in which African Americans not only recall the grievances and dislocation of their laboring lives but continue meeting barriers. Joe Gilliam intentionally ran a slow time for NFL scouts so that he would not be switched to another position in the pros, since conventional wisdom held that Black players could not play quarterback and other more intellectually challenging positions like center and middle linebacker: "All the veterans said that Joe was the most talented guy—he had the best arm, and the best knowledge of the game. But Joe always felt that he had to be so much better to keep his job. . . . He felt like he had to win games throwing. Like he had to throw five touchdowns every week to keep his job. To a man, they'll tell you, in terms of talent and what the quarterback had to do—knowing the game, knowing the reads, and throwing the ball—Joe Gilliam had it all."[96] When Tony Dungy, who offered this assessment of Gilliam, joined the Steelers in the late 1970s, he suffered the fate Gilliam had feared and was switched from quarterback to defensive back. During the 1974 season, Gilliam not only had to handle the X's and O's, but sometimes ugly public responses and a hostile local media. One of the major papers printed a readers' poll that asked who the starting quarterback should be. Gilliam received death threats from fans and told his father, "There's a guy down on the sidelines staking me out, because they say they're going to shoot me from the stands."[97]

Later in the 1990s, Kordell Stewart would become the team's second Black starting quarterback after starring as Slash, a dynamic multipurpose offensive weapon in his rookie year. He, too, feared he would be moved to another position in the pros. Stewart played eight seasons in Pittsburgh, led the team to two AFC Championship games as quarterback and even made the Pro Bowl. However, fans turned against Stewart as the team faltered and he was caught on TV weeping on the sideline after being benched. Stewart was torpedoed in the press for his unmanliness. An earlier rumor that he was caught having sex with a man in public sounded a death knell to his popularity and his stay in the Steel City. So poisoned was the atmosphere for Stewart that he had to address the locker room, mutter a defense to his teammates about being into "Adam and Eve, not Adam and Steve." Stewart's alleged outing by a Pittsburgh cop severed him from the hypermasculine identity that so many Steeler fans and the media seek to remember.[98] A Black gay Magarac? He was soon off the roster.

Franco Harris was always a Black man, and Italian Americans claiming him as one of their own was seen by some African Americans as disrespectful or traitorous, on Harris's part. What infuriated some was that the appropriation of their identity was so easily obtained and without appreciation for the way Blackness comes with a cost. The ethnic revival of the 1970s was a backlash against the social elite and their still dominant cultural values, but also a reaction against a system believed to favor nonwhite minorities at the expense of white people, the true underdogs.[99]

Three Rivers

The Steelers stadium, Three Rivers Stadium, was fittingly ugly for a city then coated in soot: a solid, gray cement bowl. The name, Three Rivers, placed it firmly in the region's history, but its generic design and lack of architectural detail seemed to state simply: industrial. The Pittsburgh-born writer John Wideman recounts driving across town to visit his brother Robbie, locked up in the city's stark North Side prison. As Wideman drives by the hulking rotunda, he recounts, "I still live and die with the Steelers," as do so many of us from these hard valleys.[100] On gamedays, we parked almost a mile away in a cheap lot by the river and melded into the growing packs of fans wrapped in black and gold and carrying seat cushions, binoculars, and wine skins. It smelled of open fires, cigar smoke. Guys walked against the flow out in the street, yelling, "Hey, hoagies here!" And, before halftime, you could go out onto the ramps and share a joint, watch homeless people in the now quiet parking lot filling shopping carts with the empty beer cans strewn across the asphalt. Now and then cheers would echo down as men inside the rotunda smashed one another with their elbows, arms, and heads.

In 1969 a group of local protestors, the Black Construction Coalition, made another stand on this spot and were arrested for blocking the entrance to the stadium construction site. They were protesting the region's construction industry and the failure of companies, unions, and city officials to respond to earlier pleas to open it up to African American labor. The Civil Rights Act of 1964 had outlawed job discrimination, but local Black workers had long been shut out of the area's construction industry and the largesse that proponents of the Renaissance argued it would bring to communities like the North Side. While the building unions provided training for some Black workers, their membership killed efforts to employ them. A 1966 federal study concluded that "neither the union or nonunion sector of the industry have afforded opportunities for Negroes in any meaningful degree of employment."[101] A leader of the protest, the Reverend James Robinson, warned that the refusal of unions and construction companies left the city's African Americans few options: "one, go down peacefully, or two, take up arms and begin to shoot."[102] When negotiators failed to reach a solution, another march was held a few weeks later on August 24, which ended up shutting down several building projects across the city. The following day white construction workers held a countermarch vocalizing their anger. As negotiations dragged on, the protestors organized another march of over 3,000 Black and white demonstrators that started in the Hill. The federal government increased its pressure on the city by threatening to pull funding for other major development projects in the region. Eventually an agreement was reached in January 1970 that stipulated training and hiring 1,250 Black workers in the next four years. It was only a partial victory and the struggle for equity in the construction industry continues.[103]

As he describes driving across the city years after these events, Wideman notes how the old mills are now troubling specters, for "steel... continues to color the city's image of itself. Steeltown, U.S.A... Too many layoffs and cutbacks and strikes. Too much greed and too little imagination in the managerial class, too much alienation among workers. Almost any adult male in Pittsburgh, black and white, can tell you a story about how those hulking, rusty skeletons lining the riverfront haunted his working life."[104] But, what these men would relate differs, for outside of that symbolic arena of community, Pittsburgh has been a place where Black men on the streets have shared unique challenges, a "blackness that incriminated."[105] That threat and its legacy both haunt the minds of some at that site of symbolic civic identity, Three Rivers Stadium.

Ray Seals was one of those stadium performers, a member of Pittsburgh's Super Bowl team in 1995, one of the "Sixty-Minute Men" of its dominant defense. Seals is now retired from the NFL and living back in his hometown, Syracuse. It was where he had grown up with his cousin Jonny Gammage, who helped Seals with his charity work. On October 12, 1995, Johnny was driving through suburban Pittsburgh in his cousin's Jaguar when he was stopped by police for driving erratically. The officer who pulled over Gammage would later testify in court that the driver was tapping his brake lights and the trunk was riding low. He called for backup. In a few minutes Jonny Gammage would lie dead on the street, asphyxiated by officers. Death by compression, stated the autopsy report. Three of the five officers at the scene would be tried for involuntary manslaughter after a judge dismissed third-degree murder charges. The first trial, involving two officers, was declared a mistrial after the jury forewoman revealed to the judge that the one juror against acquittal, the lone Black juror, feared reprisals if he voted for the officers. The final trial, of the officer deemed most responsible for Gammage's death, ended in acquittal by an all-white jury.

Gammage's killing was one of the factors that motivated the United States Department of Justice to investigate Pittsburgh's police department. Although he was killed by suburban police officers, his cousin's visibility as a Steeler placed further pressure on the city's controversial force. Pittsburgh was already being sued by dozens of residents who complained of abuse at the hands of officers. The feds stepped in and in April 1997 Pittsburgh's department was placed under a federal consent decree, the first metropolitan police force placed under such oversight. We beat Los Angeles. An investigation of department records, dating from 1988 to 1995, revealed a department in disarray, with no system of accountability for wayward officers. The Bureau of Police did not issue formal annual evaluations of its officers, did not keep track of incidents involving the use of force, and routinely ignored complaints against officers. The report revealed that "according to court files, officers who beat suspects were not disciplined. When suspects talked back, they were falsely arrested for public intoxication in retaliation, but the officers involved were never disciplined. . . . Over that seven-year period, not one officer was fired on the basis of a civilian's complaint of misconduct."[106] Many of these incidents involved African American residents. Under the consent decree, the police department was ordered to make major reforms that included increasing training, establishing a formal evaluation system, and documenting use of force incidents. In 2002, the order was lifted but the unit that investigates civilian complaints remained under the eye of the federal authorities because it had maintained a poor record of investigating these complaints, approximately half of which came from African Americans.

Johnny Gammage's death on a suburban street at the hands of men charged with protecting him fits into a larger evolving narrative that has made the names of once unknown men national icons of a movement, Black Lives Matter. But before being armed with the undeniable evidence from smart phones, such men often remained nameless, faceless. In his autobiography Jackie Robinson bitterly recounted his own encounter with police that nearly ended in deadly violence. Robinson was accosted by a white officer in the lobby of the Apollo Theater, "He grabbed me and spectators passing by told me later that he had pulled out his gun. I was so angry at his grabbing me and so busy telling him he'd better get his hands off me that I didn't remember seeing the gun. By this time people had started crowding around, excitedly telling him my name, and he backed off. Thinking over this incident, it horrifies me to realize what might have happened if I had been just another citizen of Harlem."[107]

After his cousin's death, Ray Seals spent the following year on injured reserve, living away from Pittsburgh, and he played one last season for the Carolina Panthers the following year. Not even the football field, with its familiar sights, was an escape, "I swear to you, before the games, I used to see him strapped to that stretcher."[108] Seals, the son of a police officer, had tried to offer a voice of reason during the trials but after the last verdict, his comments had a bitter sting that echoes local divides between Black and white memories of our city and even of its most cherished institution: "Black experience is a whole lot different than white experience. Probably no one sitting on that jury had ever been harassed by a cop, didn't have an idea of what that can mean. . . . I don't hold it against the Steelers, but let them have Pittsburgh."[109] Many players who followed Seals to the Steel City and its namesake organization seemed to take up his suggestion, but their stories still at times reveal the region's ongoing amnesia about race, work, and play that stifle equality as it once again is challenged with a new set of residents "from nations not known," while mired in a self-image of an imagined white past.

He's Korean, Ya Know?!

Hines Ward, a multiposition offensive threat out of Georgia, drawl and all, was drafted by the Pittsburgh Steelers in 1998 and enjoyed a celebrated fourteen-year career with the team, retiring as its all-time leading receiver. Ward's number 86 jersey remains a common fashion statement in the malls, grocery aisles, and high schools of Pittsburgh. His intensely physical style of play was perfectly suited for the tradition of Steelers' "smash-mouth" football. Ward explained, "I think fans cling to me because I'm a blue-collar guy in a blue-collar city."[110] Unlike Franco Harris, who was sometimes criticized for avoiding contact, Ward relished it. Although a wide receiver, he was one of the team's most physical players, known for delivering punishing blindside blocks that ended up as fodder for ESPN's once popular segment, "Jacked Up," where talking heads gleefully reviewed in super slo-mo the most vicious hits from the week's games. John Madden loved him. Though Ward was selected to the Pro Bowl four times and was MVP of Super Bowl 40 in 2006, it was his mixed Black and Korean heritage that brought him both local and global attention. The diverse responses to Hines Ward highlight how sports figures today increasingly inhabit "multiple, flexible, and oftentimes mutable identities," and serve an increasingly diverse fanbase with various and sometimes conflicting desires.¹¹¹ He was at once industrial, national, racial, and postindustrial, postnational, and postracial.

After his MVP performance, Ward became an overnight sensation in Korea, a cause célèbre for the mistreatment of 35,000 Korean "mixed-blood" (Honhyeolin) people. Though Koreans paid scant attention to American football, Ward's success in the media-saturated Super Bowl coincided with Korea's rise as an economic and cultural heavyweight on the global stage. Football was embraced as a symbol of modernity in the early twentieth century by Korean college students, who learned the game in Japan during Japanese colonial rule.¹¹² Though it never reached the popularity it enjoyed in Japan, which has long had the largest playing population outside the US and where the NFL until recently held games each season, Koreans' association of football with Korean national identity and masculinity fueled the "Ward syndrome."¹¹³ Koreans today pride themselves on their penetration of international markets not only with telegenic perfectly synced pop bands but also with athletes—starting strikers in the English Premier League and dominant golfers on the Ladies Professional Golf Association (LPGA) links. It is all part of the Korean Wave, or Hallyu that has white American college kids streaming Korean soaps and dancing to "Gangnam Style." But it has unnerved others, like LPGA officials, who considered an English-language proficiency policy in response to Korean women's sudden dominance on the tour.

Shortly after the big game, Hines Ward went on a ten-day whirlwind tour of South Korea with his mother, Kim Young-He. Their arrival was broadcast live on Korean television. Hines Ward met with the president, received a certificate of honorary citizenship from the mayor of Seoul, and the "Korean black Pearl" provoked a national conversation about Korea's fixation on pure blood, on "one people, one nation."¹¹⁴ Ward claimed during his visit to have reconciled his mixed-race heritage: "I used to be ashamed of my Korean heritage when I was a child. But now I am proud to be Korean."¹¹⁵ After the trip, he established a foundation to benefit mixed-race Korean children; the Korean government suspended its use of the pejorative term to define them; ended the ban on mixed-race individuals serving in the armed forces; and agreed to provide, for the first time, legal status to foreigners married to Koreans. Some of these individuals, like Ward, are the children of Korean mothers and US servicemen, but an increasing number are "Kosians," mainly the children of rural Korean men and their Southeast Asian wives.

Ward's role in nudging the conscience of South Korea was one of 2006's most prominent feel-good sports stories, receiving extensive coverage in both Pittsburgh and national media, including a slick segment on ESPN, accompanied by an Asian-inspired soundtrack. American media had never before portrayed Ward as Asian; yet his role as a bridge across the racial divide was a familiar narrative of mixed-race peoples in contemporary America. As one mixed-race writer quipped, "I'm a magic pill on legs. Doesn't matter if I never lift a finger in my life. . . . Like Haile Selassie or Frodo Baggins, I was born to a higher purpose: to end the racial problem by erasing it."[116] Lost in all the tenderly rendered accounts of Ward's life was any critical attention to the fact that, although he was born in Korea, he moved to the United States when he was one year old; and it was here, not in Korea, that he lived as a mixed-race person, where he caught shit from all sides: "I was teased for a lot of things when I was growing up . . . I was black, but I wasn't black. I was Korean, but I wasn't Korean."[117] His mother recalled how local Koreans once invited her son onto their hoop team, only to overlook inviting him to the team's celebration after the tournament. Ward pointedly noted that his claim to Koreanness was more legitimate than these Georgia Koreans. They were not born in Korea.

Hines Ward's ascent into the bright klieg lights of the American media world demonstrates the increasing, if still marginal, place of Asian Americans in the country's cultural lingua franca, including sports. Like Jewish Americans before them, Asian Americans are recuperating a sporting past, establishing a place for Asians in this influential space, including scholarly discussions of Asian American sports and their increasingly diverse communities.[118] The transnational reception of mixed-race athletes like Ward highlights the increasing plasticity of sports stars in our globally mediated world. Such figures remain an anchor to both a usable past—old traditions like Pittsburgh's white ethnic working-class identity and Korean filial piety—and an aspirational future: Pittsburgh as a multiracial global center of capitalism and seamless transnational life, and Korea as a racially tolerant nation. They operate as powerful collective symbols but uncertain, unsubstantial tethers to bind together a range of historical identities and perspectives. And as the living embodiment of forces that have profoundly reshaped the modern world—immigration, globalization, colonization, and capitalism—they incite anxieties in a range of people: the racist, the nativist, the sentimentalist, and the purist. Hines Ward's reception in the wider culture and in the local Pittsburgh community reveals his story as one with multiple meanings, including how often we ignore racial narratives, even when they are as visible as the Korean letters tattooed on Hines Ward's right arm.

Like other Asian American athletes, Ward was a focal point of pan-

Asian identification, something missed in mainstream media renderings of his cultural currency. Though commonly discussed in the realm of politics, panethnic identification among Asian Americans also occurs through pop culture figures, athletes like Ward, and later Jeremy Lin. They function as symbols of masculine physical prowess and power for Asian American men that counter the unflattering stereotype of feckless, sexless tech geeks—Long Duck Dong. Just as Jewish boxers, like Pittsburgh's Max Elling, helped Jewish men counter the narrow image of nice nebbish boys more suited for handling dental picks than hockey sticks. Such panethnic orientation is further enabled by the changing demographics within Asian America, the high outmarriage rates that have made groups like Japanese Americans increasingly multiethnic and multiracial.

Yet public responses to celebrated figures like Ward suggest that one be cautious about predictions of an impending and inevitable postethnic America.[119] The growing but still small percentage of Americans who self-identify as multiracial is not an implacable cultural force that will dissolve the guardrails of race. For one response to such mixing, as illustrated in both synagogues and on playing fields, is an expressed fear of obsolescence. Some Asian American sporting leagues have established blood quantum requirements to assure the purity of their participants. Athletes and other public figures, like Franco Harris and later Tiger Woods and Hines Ward, who have asserted multiple identities, faced sanction for being traitors of a tribe. The multiracial remain "unmapped . . . within the monoracial cultural logic . . . treated as suspect by all parties for not being monoracial enough."[120] Not Black, or yellow enough. Or too much one or the other.

In addition, by framing Ward's story as Korean, American media performed a geographic dislocation that caused Americans to view him and his trials as solely Korean, not American. Not only were Asians foreign to America, but to racism as well. The coverage implied a contrast between the backward thinking of Korean society and progressive, color-blind America. This common portrayal of contemporary American life informs the arguments against programs to remedy historical inequities, the kind of programs Al Vento of Franco's Italian Army resented. The former Supreme Court justice Antonin Scalia argued in a 1995 opinion, "To pursue the concept of racial entitlement—even for the most admirable and benign of purposes—is to reinforce and preserve for future mischief the way of thinking that produced race slavery, race privilege and race hatred. In the eyes of government, we are just one race here. It is American."[121] Ward's and his mother's ostracism from both transnational Korean and

American communities, remained obscured by collapsing them into a narrative that denied how race and advantage evolved in these conjoined societies and shaped individuals' and families' lives.

The presence of American military personnel in Korea since the 1950s, which included Ward's father, and the influence of the American government in Korean domestic affairs have spurned deep-seated resentment toward Americans. And this animosity erupts into the sports arena, as during the 2002 World Cup when the Korean soccer player Ahn Jung-Hwan, after scoring a tying goal against the US side, ran to the corner flag where he relished pantomiming an ice skater. What may have seemed another silly soccer antic to American viewers was an insult directed at them. The gesture was protesting the Japanese American skater Apolo Ohno's earlier Winter Olympics gold medal, awarded after disqualification of the winning Korean skater. The ESPN crew did not have a clue.

Amerasian offspring in Korea, like Ward, embody these historical animosities: their mothers tainted in the eyes of many Koreans due to the legacy of industrial-scale prostitution associated with American military instillations—the infamous camp towns. This shaming is especially harsh if the fathers are Black, for American occupation not only brought Black men to Korea but also transported American racist notions of them. In addition, due to a powerful cultural bias for light skin that is both class- and race-based, a "dark skinned foreigner brought additional misery to their Korean spouses."[122] The triumphant homecoming of Hines Ward, "the first time ever in Korean television that the black body was represented with honor and respect," underscores just how much Koreans had to disavow and forget in that embrace.[123] And it illustrates why many mixed-race Koreans were doubtful a new day had dawned with his jet's landing.

In the United States, Ward's mother lost custody of him, having been deemed an unfit mother due to her lack of language skills and job prospects, and only after working three jobs for several years was she reunited with her son. She was still working in a school cafeteria when they triumphantly returned to Korea. None of the American media commented on the obviously anxious, pained look on her face when she arrived in the Seoul airport. How could she forget being spat on during her last visit? The gratitude Ward expressed for his mother's hard work, humility, and self-sacrifice was widely circulated in Korean media, however, and redeemed Kim as an exemplary Korean mother. Ward's work ethic and that of his mother also reified the standard American view of Asians as a model minority: hardworking, family-oriented, and humble. It is a label that not only elides our historical struggles but also operates as a counterpoint to alleged Black self-destructiveness. Articles about Ward often contrasted him with the Dallas wide receiver Terrell Owens, long vilified in the media for his arrogance, selfishness, and bravado—his Blackness to some. The one public statement about Ward that alluded to the unique challenges of Korean African Americans was from Congresswoman Diane Watson of California, whose district includes LA's Koreatown, a site associated with the apparent irreconcilability of Koreanness with Blackness after the LA Riots—after Sa-I-Gu.[124]

Watson's plea on the House floor to recognize such individuals was a reminder of their historical erasure. Ward's complex identity is incompatible with the way that most Americans think of their nation and how most Pittsburghers remember their home and their neighbors. In his comedy routine, the Korean Irish comic Stephen Byrne, a native Pittsburgher, jokes that when people ask him where he is from and he answers, "Pittsburgh," they say, "No, seriously, where are you from?" I often get, "No, originally?" When the American Olympic skater Michelle Kwan lost to Tara Lipinski at the 1998 Olympics, the MSNBC website headline read "American Beats Kwan." During moments of international conflict, Asians have often been the usual suspects, like the Muslim men pulled from the crowd and interrogated by the FBI at a New York Giants game—for praying.[125]

Even as Hines Ward was embraced by many here and in Korea, he was also the subject of ugly media attacks from communities—Black, Korean, or football—that might claim him, deemed a "chigger," a "freak of nature," and berated online by one disappointed fantasy football owner who reminded him that football was "not a kimchee party for you and your family where you eat spicy noodles and beef bulgogi."[126] The inability of media and fans to fully acknowledge Ward as a mixed-race, Korean-born, Georgia-raised American wide receiver left unexamined the many ways that being Black, Korean, or both comes with costs that few walking around Pittsburgh with a Hines Ward jersey on their back will ever appreciate. They need not consider the homes they could not buy, the families they could not join, the games they could not play—the simple unexamined privilege of being unremarkable.

In contemporary Pittsburgh, the role of professional sports as communal vehicles for remembering an immigrant-rooted, working-class identity—whiteness—is waning. The Pittsburgh region continued to lose population into the twenty-first century—between 2000 and 2006 the only metropolitan region to suffer a greater drain was New Orleans. As noted previously, the area's immigrant population significantly declined over time, and from 1990 to 1999 the city had the smallest influx of immigrants of the nation's largest metropolitan centers.[127] But immigration to the region is now accelerating, with twice the number of immigrants settling in the area in the first six years of the twenty-first century than during the entire decade of the 1990s. The city needs these newcomers, many coming from Asia, to counter its long population and brain drain. The city's Asian population is ballooning, in Allegheny County by 63 percent between 1990 and 2000 alone. Many of the newcomers are recent immigrants from India, China, and Korea. The eventual liberalization of federal immigration policies after 1965 opened immigration from Asia and catalyzed an influx of immigrants from these countries. Unlike earlier Asian immigrants, these newcomers are scattered across the region, with over half settling in suburban communities like Scott Township and the exclusive Fox Chapel Borough. In language echoing the Harmonist Society elders, local leaders implore Pittsburghers to embrace these new immigrants. Mayor Bill Peduto hoped to encourage thousands of new immigrants to settle, "It is not just the welcoming heart of the city, it is the economic growth of the region that is the biggest beneficiary."[128] Pittsburgh's immigrant community is among the nation's most highly skilled and highest paid.[129] In the region's new postindustrial economy, they are the lab technicians, software engineers, anesthesiologists, and other highly educated women and men on whom the city is relying to fuel the region's prosperity. In the case of Karim Kassam, a Canadian of South Asian descent, and Ariko Iso, from Japan, they helped maintain the excellence of the city's most prized institution: the Pittsburgh Steelers. Iso was an athletic trainer for the Steelers for nine years, the first woman trainer in the history of the NFL. Kassam, a former Carnegie Mellon University professor, with the apt Twitter address @professormullet, was until recently crunching numbers at the Steelers facility on the Southside as the team's analytics and football research coordinator. The city is trying to attract not only such highly skilled individuals but also investment from Asian companies like the South-Korean-based Adcus, a data file transfer company that moved its American headquarters to Pittsburgh. Meanwhile, local institutions like the Jewish Family and Children's Services, Catholic Charities, and Vibrant Pittsburgh are funding projects that encourage immigrants to make Pittsburgh their home and to aid them on arrival.

Like their predecessors, the Germans, Jews, Italians, and Poles, these new migrants to the Steel City are transforming the cultural landscape, including its sports: playing games like cricket and training locals in Taekwondo. In several locations across the Pittsburgh region, the Young Brothers schools have trained thousands of Pittsburghers in the Korean martial arts form. They have taught not only Olympians but also Pittsburgh

Steelers like Franco Harris, Terry Long, and Greg Lloyd, once voted the most feared player in the NFL and now an accomplished Taekwondo black belt who attributes his lengthy and celebrated career to his martial arts training. In 2005, a group of mainly expatriate East Indians, Pakistanis, and Australians founded the Pittsburgh Cricket Association, a formally recognized league whose teams compete against each other and across the eastern United States. The league has over twenty teams, including the Yinzers, and in 2018 the first female player joined. These athletes are reintroducing Pittsburghers to a sport that leaves most of us perplexed. Googly? A Yorker? The first local match was played here back in 1850, when the sport was deemed "a very healthy and respectable amusement."[130]

As with the region's earlier immigrants, local sports, particularly the Pittsburgh Steelers, offer these new Pittsburghers a way to claim local identity, to be a Yinzer, like the Lees who for nearly two decades have been selling Steelers gear to local fans and tourists at their Strip District store. As for some local Jews, sports may become a means to maintain their sense of collectivity. During the Super Bowl in 2006, pitting the Steelers against the Seattle Seahawks, Pittsburgh Jewish organizations waged bets with their counterparts in Seattle and held Super Bowl–themed services. At one local temple, congregants came to Steeler Shabbat services decked out in their favorite players' jerseys and other black-and-gold wear, even singing prayers to the tunes of Steeler fight songs. The cantor remarked, "Why not, if it gets people into the synagogue. It can't be anything but good."[131]

Some, in fact, call these Asian immigrant Pittsburghers and their more established American counterparts the "new Jews," a term denoting both minority groups' celebrated achievement and ascent up the American social ladder, especially through education. But, like their predecessors, this new wave of Asians also includes refugees, such as the Bhutanese, who after years in Thai refugee camps are laboring to establish a firm footing in the Steel City. They are among the over 100,000 ethnic Nepalese stripped of citizenship and forced out of Bhutan when it instituted a "One Nation, One People" policy of ethnic cleansing in the 1980s. An estimated 5,000 now live in the Pittsburgh area. The region's rivers and steep green hills remind them of home.[132] Nepali is among the most common languages spoken by children enrolled in the Pittsburgh schools' ESL classes. Some of these youth, like earlier generations, are using athletics to build their futures and community. Soccer, which they played in refugee camps, has given the Bhutanese youth, both boys and girls, a gateway onto high school sides and college campuses. Local Bhutanese have organized soccer leagues and travel to play other communities in the East. The beautiful game is a platform for older second-generation Bhutanese to pass on life and educational skills to those who follow.[133] However, many of the older generation, with limited language and vocational skills, remain consigned to busing tables at the riverside casino, cleaning University of Pittsburgh Medical Center hospital rooms, and fetching packages at the local FedEx facility. Depression plagues many. Here they must adjust to a land of new laws and traditions and a common wariness of the foreign: "A lot of people are saying they were dumped here and are on welfare."[134] The Bhutanese immigrants have experienced misunderstandings, taunts, and violence.

Shortly before the Bhutanese arrived here, in the late afternoon of April 28, 2000, an emotionally disturbed man from Mount Lebanon went on a murderous spree: targeting synagogues, an Indian grocery, a Chinese restaurant and karate studio. He began by murdering his parents' longtime Jewish neighbor and then drove to her temple to riddle it with rounds. Police in the old company town of Ambridge finally ended his deadly twenty-mile trek. He killed five people. Later that week hundreds gathered in the parking lot of the restaurant he attacked, and listened solemnly as a mourner played "Amazing Grace" on his pan flute.[135]

The current national tenor over immigration alarms these new Pittsburghers. Even those Asians living the good life in wooded suburbs like Mount Lebanon and Fox Chapel and sending their children to its best schools can encounter the uglier side of Pittsburgh noted in that American Service Institute report from the 1940s. At Fox Chapel Area High School, my alma mater, a student in 2007 used a then-emerging social networking platform, Facebook, to create a site for current and former Fox Chapel students: Anti-Asians Anonymous.[136] The page included sophomoric jokes about eating dogs, claims that two atomic bombs were not enough, and blunt comments such as "I really do hate Asians . . . They all need to go back where they came from." National and local Asian American groups discovered the page and brought it to the attention of school district officials and Facebook. The creator, a Fox Chapel student and member of the football team—and of my family's church—took the page down and claimed it was only a joke. The school principal expressed his shock that the group included some of the high school's "best kids," some of whom perhaps proudly wear Hines Ward jerseys, cheer him on as one of their own.

Black and Yellow

When Mike Tomlin appeared before the Pittsburgh media, he seemed to offer an affirmative "yes, I'll take it!" to Ray Seals's offer to let others "have Pittsburgh." Although Tomlin had unexpectedly leapfrogged over the assumed frontrunners, the assistant coaches Grimm and Whisenhunt, his career in the NFL was already tied to the organization. It was under Tony Dungy, the former player, assistant coach, and coordinator, that Tomlin got his start in the league. And although at the time he was the youngest head coach in the NFL, he was the same age as Bill Cowher had been when he took the helm. Like Cowher and Noll before him, Tomlin was a young assistant defensive coach who barely registered a blip on the national sports media radar. However, unlike Cowher and Noll, Tomlin was Black; and he became the first Black head coach of the beloved franchise. That was news.

While the national press concentrated on the issue of race and the NFL as part of the Super Bowl media feeding frenzy, focusing on opposing coaches Lovie Smith and Tony Dungy, the Steelers head-coaching job was the hot take in football-drunk Pittsburgh. By the weekend of the 2007 Super Bowl, Assistant Coach Ken Whisenhunt was out of the picture, having taken a head-coaching job in Arizona. Over the weekend a Pittsburgh paper reported that Russ Grimm had the job. But the Rooneys had been "blown away" in their interviews with Tomlin. His record was impressive. He had helped turn a suspect defense into a dominant one against the run, the staple of Steelers teams, coached on a Super Bowl title team, and was mentored and personally recommended by a highly regarded former player and coach. In his first press conference after he was hired, Tomlin expressed his vision of the team's future. It sounded like a Steelers stew: "A fundamentalist football team that wins by attrition, that is mentally and physically tough . . . I promise that I am going to be blue-collared in how I go about this business, thoughtful in terms of the decisions that we make. We're going to work extremely hard. We're going to work smart."[137] Chuck Noll meets Bill Cowher. The executive director of the players' union hailed Dan Rooney's decision. Newspapers published an interview with Franco Harris titled "Franco Harris Says Tomlin Hiring Shows Racial Progress."[138] And local radio, blogs, and TV news branched out to take the pulse of the Steeler Nation.

In a gesture reminiscent of Joe Gilliam's days, a local newspaper did a fan vote in response to Tomlin's hiring. The results of the nearly 36,000 votes were 60–40 in his favor. Those reacting negatively to Tomlin's hiring expressed a range of reasons: some cited the failure to choose Grimm or Whisenhunt. Yet, the denial of the job to a popular assistant was not unprecedented. Joe Greene had been one of the finalists when the team hired Bill Cowher. Some fans felt Tomlin lacked experience, despite Cowher's similar youth when he took over the job. What most stuck out, though, was that some felt Tomlin had an improper advantage in the process—his race. One blogger on the local *Tribune Review* website opined that Tomlin should resign if this were true "because winning a job where the better man lost ONLY because he is white . . . Well. That pretty much makes everybody involved a racist doesn't it."[139]

In 2002 the NFL had installed the "Rooney Rule," named after the Steelers' owner Dan Rooney, who was chair of the league's diversity committee at the time. The rule mandated that each team interview one minority candidate for any available head-coaching position. It has since been expanded to apply to general manager and other front office positions in NFL teams. Tomlin was the second minority coach interviewed by the Rooneys and some were now complaining that the process was a fast track for Tomlin to grab the brass ring. A local sports journalist asked, "But, what if Mike Tomlin isn't necessarily the best choice? What if he got the job because Steelers owner Dan Rooney cares just a little more about his NFL legacy than about his franchise? What if Tomlin got the job, at least in part, because of the Rooney Rule?"[140] There were no such claims of race favoritism when Cowher was hired.

Tony Dungy had provided Rooney, upon his request, with a list of minority coaches whom he recommended, and Tomlin's name was included on this list. Without that measure, he might still be poring over film in Minnesota, waiting for his chance, and Steeler fans might have one less ring to brag about. Despite the article's title, that seemed the point Harris was making to the *Tribune Review* reporter. The Rooney Rule is a proactive measure to address a history of institutionalized racism that disadvantages minorities and continues to keep them from the sidelines and offices of the NFL and from sharing equitably in its billions of riches. As recently as 2020, although roughly 75 percent of the players were nonwhite, there were still only four nonwhite head coaches.[141] The Rooneys, unlike other teams, seemed interested in doing more than the bare minimum, in more than words.

The Rooney Rule is symptomatic of a wider problem in football. Among the nation's top Division 1 football programs, the main coaching talent pipelines to the NFL, the lack of Black coaches is startling. Although roughly half the players at these programs are Black men, during the 2018–2019 season only eighteen were head coaches, just over 7 percent.[142] The vast majority of offensive and defensive coordinators at these schools are white, and the disparities are only more dramatic in the smaller programs. Excluding the HBCUs, as recently as 2007, there were only eight colleges in all of Divisions 1-AA, 2, and 3 football that had a Black head coach.[143] The number of Black head coaches in all D3 sports is still outnumbered by the number of women coaching men's teams.[144] The Black Coaches Association considered a Title VII Civil Rights Act case to force colleges and the National Collegiate Athletic Association to address this disparity, but the organization later folded. Critics are lobbying now for a college football mandate like the NFL's Rooney Rule, although the measure has proved ineffective in significantly diversifying the NFL coaching ranks.

The NFL's hiring mandate is the corollary of earlier measures deemed necessary to push national and Pittsburgh institutions into offering non-white residents something equivalent to the treatment that white locals have long enjoyed and benefited from at its steel mills, mortgage lenders, and swimming pools—a level playing field. The Steelers organization has more faithfully applied the ethos behind these measures, but even celebrating this storied franchise goes only so far. The Steelers were part of the league during its gentlemen's agreement that barred Black players; have been complicit in ignoring the grievous health risks incurred by its players; and are only as civic-minded as any billion-dollar privately held business receiving millions of dollars of public money to build a new stadium can be. At least they first sold the naming rights to Heinz—to locals.

But the camaraderie and communal identification that cuts across the ordinary divides of class and race in the Steelers' new home too soon dissolves when we step outside those stadium walls. Hiring a Black coach should have been recognized as only consistent with Steelers tradition and a smart business decision. Two Super Bowl trips under Tomlin's leadership have proved that. His hiring is a symbol and its importance significant, but his treatment too rare. Like so many Black athletes and workers have done in recent decades, he excelled when an ethos of equity and excellence prevailed. His hiring and nonwhite athletes' successes have been embraced both by white fans and by minorities, who cannot always count on such conditions within their own American lives. But it's not proof of a world beyond race. And as a rallying cry it alone won't change the city. It remains a place where one-third of African Americans live below the poverty line and where Black youths are arrested at six times the rate of their white peers. It's a place where the unemployment rate among working-age African Americans in 2010 was nearly 40 percent.[145] It's a place where homicide is often the leading cause of preventable death among the county's African Americans, and where Black adults are fourteen times more likely to be murdered than white residents.[146] And it's a place where one in five African Americans has asthma and where Black infants die at a rate much higher than in most of the country.[147]

As the *New Pittsburgh Courier* writer Aubrey Bruce offered, in a piece he promised was his final word on Tomlin's hiring: "Sports are meant to entertain the masses. Sports are not designed to function as a societal masking agent or a placebo to cover and appease some of the negative aspects that exist within our society. Games are meant to be a diversion from our daily grind. Games are not meant to create and foster illusional and delusional expectations. Hiring someone, anyone to a position of power does not change the facts, it just profiles them."[148]

I wonder if, at times, the screams of a proud nation have deafened us to the pain, protest, and possibility of lives on both the playing fields and the streets of the Steel City. What if in the Steelers black and gold, we chose to see the black and the yellow in their truer, less symbolic meanings?

Here We Go, Steelers! Here We Go! . . . Again

We say goodbye underneath the old Bridge to Nowhere, now the 279 Expressway carrying the elated hordes home to the growing northern suburbs. My friends are headed back to Wisconsin; tomorrow I fly home to Hartford. Even home games are for the diaspora.

My buzz is wearing off but not the thrill of the last-second win against the hated Ravens, the former Browns organization to whom the Steeler Nation immediately transferred our collective ill will. A pro football team is weak glue for binding together a disparate city—its former and present residents—and its hold is slipping. People are not showing up when it's too cold or too rainy. The longtime sports broadcaster Stan Savran tells me the Penguins now own the hearts of young Pittsburghers, those who grew up always a winner in a most livable city.[149]

Sure, we hug strangers and high-five after a big sack or a touchdown during what we always hope, insist is our journey to another Super Bowl. The megascreen with megadecibels leads us to cheer, "ANOTHER STEELERS FIRST DOWN!" So, we scream. And dance badly to Wiz Khalifa. But I miss the sudden rise of tens of thousands screaming DEE-FENSE! DEE-FENSE! in a chorus arising from the mixed lull of vendor calls, organ tunes, and wind in a dull bowl filled with cigar smoke and hard hats.

The pumped up, drunk, and vacationing still pack the streets where Three Rivers once stood. They are lined with new bars and restaurants, a shiny hotel. At the old stadium's groundbreaking ceremony, Jesse Owens predicted, "As long as men of all color and creeds can play baseball and football together here, as long as they share the team spirit and understanding required of all athletes, this hallowed ground is worthwhile under the eyes of God." Nice words. But his comment that Three Rivers would be "where the thrill of the touchdown pass and the long home run will create legends" is the more realized hope.[150]

Given such hyperbole, it is not surprising that as the new home for the Pirates and Steelers was being planned in the 1960s, with a massive influx of public monies and a wrecking ball at the ready, the civic import of pro sports would be argued as rationale for the massive public funding of the ambitious project, part of the city's Renaissance. The City of Pittsburgh agreed to donate land on the North Side for the construction of a public stadium that would be leased to private interests, and it established the Stadium Authority of Pittsburgh, which eventually entered into a loan agreement with local banks to finance the project via the issuing of Authority Bonds. A local CPA, Robert Conrad, filed a lawsuit to block the plan, arguing that it violated the state constitution sections that limited the amount of debt a municipality could incur without voter approval. Conrad had earlier proposed an alternative site that he and others just happened to own, which was rejected, but he claimed he was "just a man who is tired of paying taxes."[151] The lawsuit was fast-tracked to the Commonwealth's Supreme Court to avoid potential construction delays. He lost. The complaint was dismissed, with prejudice. And Justice Michael Musmanno, who in 1951 was elected to the state's highest court, wrote a concurring opinion in which, after summarizing the specific legal arguments against the plaintiff, he reminded the court what was at stake, Pittsburgh's identity:

> The objective of a community is not merely to survive, but to progress, to go forward into an ever-increasing enjoyment of the blessings conferred by the rich resources of this nation under the benefaction of the Supreme Being for the benefit of all the people of that community.
>
> If a well governed city were to confine its governmental functions merely to the task of assuring survival, if it were to do nothing but provide "basic services" for an animal survival, it would be a city without parks, swimming pools, zoo, baseball diamonds, football gridirons and playgrounds for children. Such a city would be a dreary city indeed. As man cannot live by bread alone, a city cannot endure on cement, asphalt, and pipes alone. A city must have a municipal spirit beyond its physical properties, it must be alive with esprit de corps, its personality must be such that visitors both business and tourist are attracted to the city, pleased by it and wish to return to it. That personality must be one to which the population contributes by mass participation in activities identified with that city.
>
> Hardly anything in America symbolizes a large city more than its National or American League baseball team. To take the Pittsburgh baseball team out of Pittsburgh would be to deprive its people of the

opportunity for a spontaneous outburst of civic pride, for which there is no substitute. In fact, it is practically impossible to visualize Pittsburgh without its Pirates. To take the Pirates out of Pittsburgh would be like taking them out of the history of the Spanish Main, it would be like diverting the course of the Allegheny and Monongahela River[s] so that they would not form the Ohio at the immortally historical Fort Pitt, it would be like turning the Golden Triangle into a Tin Pan Alley.[152]

Despite the justice's passionate and, well, Tin Pan Alley rhetoric to the contrary, Conrad had a point, one only more relevant as sports venues become increasingly subsidized by public dollars in deals that enrich wealthy owners who tap whatever wells of revenue streams they can imagine—new "experiences" they can offer, including the virtual—to enrich themselves. When the stadium that Pittsburghers eventually helped finance, Three Rivers Stadium, was demolished in 2001, a big pile of debt was left amid the rubble, $23 million. Taxpayers were left owing more than it cost to build the stadium. One wonders how many playgrounds, swimming pools, schools for the "benefit of all" those monies might have supported. During the city's budget crisis of the 1980s, two-thirds of city pools were closed.

It's cold, 1:00 a.m., but people are taking selfies at the Maz statue, and along the river the building lights shine on the black water as bright colored lights spiral up the trusses of the Three Sisters. I pick up the pace as the homeless people burrow under their blankets.

I will get my voice back in a few days.

On the drive to the airport, there are signs for "Modern, Luxury Townhouses" and around the corner posters with photos of what East Liberty used to be—what I remember. Worker-bee-like Uber cars prowl the streets now filled with white millennials checking apps on the way from their hotel to the latest eatery. Pittsburgh has become in the eyes of the eating cognoscenti a "destination."

But if I see some dude with a wool hat, beard, and little dog strapped to his chest stepping into a Soul Cycle, I may have to run him down in my rental car. Call it historic preservation.

We hope that we are left with something, something concrete to purchase a grip on the landscapes we love, that nourish and mold us.

At the airport, I consider the inevitable question when I get home, "What did you bring me, Daddy?" and prowl the stores. I want to feed my kids' love for this city. So, I pick up the Steelers hat one wanted and bracelets for the other: black and yellow.

They are the new generation of this nation, living in a land unknown to those before them. May they remember.

ACKNOWLEDGMENTS

I first thank Joe Skerrett for his generous comment to a student many years ago; without your kind gesture this book would not be.

This work would also have been impossible without the individuals, organizations, artists, and scholars whose words and visions I have relied upon to write this story. For their time and generosity, I am grateful to Randy Grossman, Alan Mallinger, Balaram Gurung, Diwas Timsina, Joe Luxbacher, Stan Savran, and Houston Graves.

My thanks for the enormous help they provided to the staff at the University of Pittsburgh Archives and Research Center, Thomas and Katherine Detre Library and Archives, and the Pennsylvania State Archives. For permissions to reprint materials, my gratitude to the Carnegie Museum of Art, Wesleyan University Press, Adastra Press, and the Society to Preserve the Millvale Murals of Maxo Vanka.

I am grateful to the University of Wisconsin Institute on Race and Ethnicity and the former dean of Amherst College, Greg Call, for research support, and for the many current and especially former colleagues at Amherst College who welcomed me to the college. To Franklin Odo, mentor and friend, *mahalo nui loa*.

Thank you to Josh Shanholtzer and the University of Pittsburgh Press staff for embracing this work and making the process seamless, and to my thoughtful reviewers. Thanks, too, to Clark Dougan for first showing interest in this project.

I was blessed to have wonderful mentors at UMASS who supported me there and beyond: Judith Fryer Davidov, David Glassberg, Jules Chametzky, Ron Welburn, and Margo Culley. And from those days as well I am fortunate to have such wonderful friends in Albert Turner, Angelo Robinson, and Anna Creadick—whose whipsnap students helped spark the penultimate push to finish this book.

I also wish to thank the Amherst Fire Department and EMTs, Baystate Medical Center doctors and staff, and the amazing folks at Cooley Dickinson Hospital Cardiac Rehabilitation. I am only here today because of your dedication and compassion.

Finally, I thank family: my siblings, and children, Shayna and Naomi, who have grown so much during the course of this book and keep me afloat, move me forward, every day. You are my blessings. To Mom and Dad for never taking a book away and for loving the idea of raising a writer. I miss you.

And, most of all, to Wendy Bergoffen—for love, for life.

NOTES

1: FROM NATIONS YOU KNOW NOT

1. Pew Research Center, "Portrait of Jewish Americans."
2. CBS News Pittsburgh, "Increase in Asian Population."
3. Mallinger, interview.
4. McCart, "America's Next Great Chinatown."
5. Liu, *Accidental Asian*, 95.
6. See Rode, "Johann Georg Rapp."
7. Rhoads, "'White Labor' vs. 'Coolie Labor,'" 4.
8. *Reading Times*, June 5, 1874.
9. *Pittsburgh Daily Post*, August 20, 1870.
10. Albert Rhodes, quoted in Rhoads, "'White Labor' vs. 'Coolie Labor,'" 5.
11. Rhoads, "Asian Pioneers," 135.
12. *Pittsburgh Post*, August 17, 1872.
13. Rhoads, "'White Labor' vs. 'Coolie Labor,'" 11.
14. *Pittsburgh Weekly Gazette*, March 3, 1873.
15. Isaiah 55:5.
16. *Pittsburgh Weekly Gazette*, April 23, 1873.
17. Excerpt from the *American Manufacturer*, reprinted in *Pittsburgh Post*, January 25, 1873.
18. Wang, "Race, Gender, and Laundry Work," 60–65.

19. *Pittsburgh Daily Post*, January 5, 1874.
20. Wu, "Chinese in Pittsburgh," 75–76.
21. Wu, "Chinese in Pittsburgh," 80.
22. *Pittsburgh Post-Gazette*, January 17, 1888.
23. *Pittsburgh Dispatch*, September 6, 1889.
24. *Pittsburgh Daily Post*, December 1, 1899.
25. *Pittsburgh Daily Post*, December 10, 1887.
26. See United States v. Wong Kim Ark, 169 U.S. 649.
27. Kung, *Chinese in American Life*, 57.
28. *Pittsburgh Commercial*, July 1, 1876.
29. *Los Angeles Times*, November 23, 1908.
30. *Washington Post*, November 14, 1907.
31. See Lui, *Chinatown Trunk Mystery*.
32. *Los Angeles Times*, September 30, 1909.
33. See Chin and Ormonde, "War Against Chinese Restaurants."
34. *Pittsburgh Press*, September 12, 1910.
35. *Pittsburgh Daily Post*, September 13, 1910.
36. *Pittsburgh Post-Gazette*, January 10, 1911.
37. *Pittsburgh Press*, January 20, 1911.
38. *Pittsburgh Post-Gazette*, May 23, 1893.
39. *Pittsburgh Post-Gazette*, December 4, 1900.
40. *Pittsburgh Post-Gazette*, July 1, 1898.
41. *Pittsburgh Post-Gazette*, April 4, 1893.
42. *Pittsburgh Daily Post*, May 19, 1877.
43. Chin and Ormonde, "War Against Chinese Restaurants," 739.
44. *Logansport Pharos-Tribune*, April 8, 1893.
45. *Pittsburgh Daily Post*, November 7, 1909.
46. *Pittsburgh Dispatch*, February 15, 1890.
47. *Pittsburgh Daily Post*, April 26, 1913.
48. *San Francisco Chronicle*, June 1, 1920.
49. Gulick, "What the Red Triangle Stands For," 774.
50. See Guttmann and Thompson, *Japanese Sports*, 90–95, and Duke, *History of Modern Japanese Education*, 249–53.
51. Light, "Japan," 477.
52. *Pittsburgh Daily Post*, November 19, 1917.
53. *Chicago Tribune*, September 22, 1917.
54. *Chicago Tribune*, September 29, 1917.
55. Kawashima, "We Will Try Again," 122–23.
56. Jerome and Schwartz, "Chinatown, My Chinatown."
57. *Pittsburgh Daily Post*, October 28, 1880.

58. *Pittsburgh Press*, February 4, 1924.
59. *Pittsburgh Daily Post*, September 21, 1921.
60. *Pittsburgh Press*, April 6, 1934.
61. *Pittsburgh Press*, August 3, 1925.
62. *Pittsburgh Post-Gazette*, November 25, 1974.
63. Wu, "Chinese in Pittsburgh," 77.
64. *Pittsburgh Press*, July 8, 1957.
65. *Pittsburgh Press*, November 19, 1984.
66. *Pittsburgh Press*, October 13, 1989.
67. *Pittsburgh Daily Post*, September 27, 1921.
68. *Reading Times*, February 14, 1880.
69. Wu, "Chinese in Pittsburgh," 20.
70. *Pittsburgh Dispatch*, August 3, 1891.
71. *Pittsburgh Post-Gazette*, December 10, 1936.
72. Seymour, *Baseball*, 566.
73. Gems, *Sport and the American Occupation of the Philippines*, 6.
74. See Bieler, "Patriots or Traitors"? 1–89.
75. *Pittsburgh Press*, April 30, 1911.
76. *Honolulu Advertiser*, April 11, 1918.
77. *Philadelphia Inquirer*, October 21, 1921.
78. *Philadelphia Inquirer*, November 4, 1918.
79. *Bridgeport Telegram*, September 14, 1918.
80. *Bridgeport Telegram*, September 16, 1918.
81. *News-Herald*, September 20, 1918.
82. Guthrie-Smith, *Transpacific Field of Dreams*, 6.
83. Guthrie-Smith, *Transpacific Field of Dreams*, 34.
84. Nomura, "Beyond a Level Playing Field"; Mullan, "Ethnicity and Sport"; and Franks, "Asian American Baseball."
85. *Pittsburgh Daily Post*, May 31, 1911.
86. *Pittsburgh Press*, June 24, 1917.
87. *Pittsburgh Daily Post*, December 21, 1911.
88. See Franks, *Barnstorming Hawaiian Travelers*.
89. See Walker, *Waves of Resistance*, 14–41, and Laderman, *Empire in Waves*, 17–52.
90. Franks, *Barnstorming Hawaiian Travelers*, 35.
91. *Pittsburgh Daily Post*, March 17, 1912.
92. *Pittsburgh Post-Gazette*, May 12, 1912.
93. *Pittsburgh Press*, August 15, 1912.
94. *Pittsburgh Daily Post*, August 17, 1912.
95. *Pittsburgh Post-Gazette*, September 8, 1912.

96. *Pittsburgh Post-Gazette*, June 5, 1913; *Pittsburgh Press*, June 3, 1913.
97. *Pittsburgh Daily Post*, September 6, 1913.
98. *Pittsburgh Daily Post*, June 1, 1913.
99. "Yellow Peril," *Pittsburgh Press*, January 29, 1915; "clever fielder" and "crack batter," *Pittsburgh Press*, December 5, 1914.
100. *Spokesman Review*, December 27, 1914.
101. *Spokane Chronicle*, December 29, 1914.
102. *Los Angeles Times*, December 27, 1914.
103. *Pittsburgh Press*, July 29, 1918.
104. *Bridgeport Telegram*, July 29, 1918.
105. *Pittsburgh Press*, September 23, 1923. See Franks, *From Honolulu to Brooklyn*.
106. *Pittsburgh Press*, January 16, 1928.
107. *Pittsburgh Press*, April 8, 1914.
108. *Pittsburgh Post-Gazette*, October 12, 1913.
109. *Pittsburgh Post-Gazette*, February 16, 1932.
110. *Pittsburgh Press*, December 9, 1941.
111. *Pittsburgh Post-Gazette*, March 19, 1942.
112. *Pittsburgh Post-Gazette*, May 2, 1942.
113. *Pittsburgh Press*, December 19, 1940.
114. *Pittsburgh Post-Gazette*, December 21, 1940.
115. *Pittsburgh Post-Gazette*, December 21, 1932.
116. *Pittsburgh Daily Post*, February 6, 1888.
117. Page Act of 1875, 18 Stat. 477, 43rd Congress, Sess. II, Chap. 14.
118. Wu, "Chinese of Pittsburgh," 96.
119. *Pittsburgh Press*, January 18, 1903.
120. Wu, "Chinese of Pittsburgh," 100.
121. Wu, "Chinese of Pittsburgh," 30.
122. Untitled Report, Brashear Association Records, 1891–1978, AIS.1979.17, Board of Director Minutes, box 1, folder 14, University of Pittsburgh Library System, Archives Service Center, [UPLS, ASC].
123. The Chinese Children's Club, Brashear Association Records, 1891–1978, AIS.1979.17, Board of Director Minutes, box 1, folder 14, UPLS, ASC.
124. Gladys Taylor to Helen Green, June 24, 1943, Brashear Association Records, 1891–1978, AIS.1979.17, Board of Director Minutes, box 1, folder 12, UPLS, ASC.
125. Summer camp offers from the Salvation Army: Charles McNally to Helen Green, June 22, 1943, Brashear Association Records, 1891–1978, AIS.1979.17, Board of Director Minutes, box 1, folder 12, UPLS, ASC; and Offers from the YMCA: Untitled Report, Brashear Association Records.

126. Richards and Lee, "Bringing Children to Recreation," 232.

127. Summary-Analysis of the Downtown Project from October 17, 1944, through August 14, 1945, American Service Institute Records, AIS.1963.01, ASI Conferences, UPLS, ASC.

128. Summary-Analysis of the Downtown Project from October 17, 1944, through August 14, 1945.

129. Brashear Association, November 1943, University of Massachusetts Translation Center, Brashear Association Records, 1891–1978, AIS.1979.17, Board of Director Minutes, box 1, folder 12, UPLS, ASC.

130. Summary-Analysis of the Downtown Project from October 17, 1944, through August 14, 1945, 2.

131. "How to Tell Japs from the Chinese."

132. History of the Pittsburgh District Office of War Relocation Authority, American Service Institute Records, AIS.1963.01, Japanese Resettlement, box 5, folder 6, UPLS, ASC.

133. *Pittsburgh Sun-Telegraph*, April 7, 1943.

134. "Acute labor shortage": History of the Pittsburgh District Office, 15; "thousands of Japanese": *Pittsburgh Post-Gazette*, March 22, 1943.

135. History of the Pittsburgh District Office, 55.

136. History of the Pittsburgh District Office, 2.

137. History of the Pittsburgh District Office, 56.

138. History of the Pittsburgh District Office, 62.

139. History of the Pittsburgh District Office, 108.

140. History of the Pittsburgh District Office, 76.

141. Robert M. Cullum to Dr. Arthur B. Kingsolving II, October 31,1944, in History of the Pittsburgh District Office, 19.

142. Commission on Wartime Relocation and Internment of Civilians, *Personal Justice Denied*, 18.

143. Thomas, *They Came to . . . Pittsburgh*, 66.

144. Wu, "Pittsburgh Chinese," 110–11.

145. Wu, "Pittsburgh Chinese," 114–15.

146. *Pittsburgh Daily Post*, November 13, 1913.

2: CORNER KICKS AND COAL

1. O'Neill, *Paris of Appalachia*, 109.
2. Hare, *Football in France*, 3.
3. Nora, *Realms of Memory*.
4. *Guardian*, June 29, 2006.
5. Marks, "French National Team," 49.
6. *New York Times*, July 11, 2017.

7. BBC, "I'm Sorry But No Regrets—Zidane."
8. Philippe Tétart in *New York Times*, June 23, 2010.
9. *New York Times*, August 28, 1977.
10. Luxbacher, interview.
11. Foer, *How Soccer Explains the World*.
12. *New York Sun*, June 21, 2006.
13. Thiessen, "Soccer Is a Socialist Sport."
14. Whitsitt, "Game America Refuses to Play," 58.
15. Couvares, *Remaking of Pittsburgh*, 32.
16. Bunk, *From Football to Soccer*, 75–98.
17. See Curry, "Origins of Football Debate," and Goldblatt, *Ball Is Round*, 1–82.
18. See Bunk, *From Football to Soccer*, 11–30, and Goldblatt, *Ball Is Round*, 4–15.
19. L. C. Gardner, quoted in Ruck, *Sandlot Seasons*, 25. See also Gems, "Welfare Capitalism."
20. Litterer, "History of Soccer in Pittsburgh," and Bunk, *From Football to Soccer*, 11–30.
21. Riess, *Sport in Industrial America*, 8.
22. Couvares, *Remaking of Pittsburgh*, and Martin, *Killing Time*.
23. Markovits, *Offside*, 28.
24. Bunk, *From Football to Soccer*, 78.
25. *Pittsburgh Press*, March 3, 1915.
26. *Pittsburgh Press*, October 26, 1920.
27. *Pittsburgh Press*, July 2, 1916.
28. Allaway, Jose, and Litterer, *Encyclopedia of American Soccer*, 29.
29. *Pittsburgh Press*, July 2, 1916.
30. See Allaway, *Rangers, Rovers and Spindles*.
31. *Pittsburgh Press*, August 13, 1915.
32. *Pittsburgh Press*, August 10, 1913.
33. Cobb, *My Life in Baseball*, 123.
34. *Pittsburgh Press*, October 15, 1913.
35. *Pardon the Interruption*, ESPN, June 25, 2010.
36. *Pittsburgh Press*, September 28, 1913; and *Pittsburgh Press*, October 25, 1914.
37. *Pittsburgh Press*, October 24, 1920.
38. *Pittsburgh Press*, October 25, 1914.
39. *Pittsburgh Press*, October 25, 1917.
40. *Pittsburgh Press*, February 19, 1913.
41. Merovich, interview, 41–44, Peter Merovich Papers and Photographs,

MSS #0729, Thomas and Katherine Detre Library and Archives, Senator John Heinz History Center.

42. *Pittsburgh Press*, November 12, 1914.
43. *Pittsburgh Press*, February 19, 1913.
44. *Pittsburgh Press*, August 23, 1914.
45. *Pittsburgh Press*, May 28, 1967.
46. Galeano, *Soccer in Sun and Shadow*, 17.
47. *Pittsburgh Press*, January 1, 1915.
48. *Pittsburgh Press*, December 12, 1916.
49. *Pittsburgh Press*, November 20, 1914.
50. *Pittsburgh Press*, September 9, 1917.
51. *Pittsburgh Press*, December 1, 1918.
52. Pope, "Army of Athletes."
53. Bunk, *From Football to Soccer*, 167.
54. *Pittsburgh Press*, April 8, 1943.
55. *Pittsburgh Press*, July 25, 1919.
56. Litterer, "History of Soccer in Pittsburgh."
57. *Pittsburgh Press*, May 28, 1967.
58. *Pittsburgh Press*, February 19, 1913.
59. Galeano, *Soccer in Sun and Shadow*, 70.
60. Slavishak, *Bodies of Work*, 25.
61. Mulrooney, *Legacy of Coal*, 12.
62. Humes, *Robbing the Pillars*.
63. Mine Safety and Health Administration, "History of Mine Safety."
64. "Carry on Beadling."
65. Pennsylvania Historical and Museum Commission, "King Coal."
66. Slavishak, *Bodies of Work*, 47.
67. Beers, *Pennsylvania Politics*, 19.
68. John Lofink, quoted in Cecil, *Our Coal-Mining Community Heritage*, 21.
69. Magnusson, "Employers' Housing," 45.
70. Mulrooney, *Legacy of Coal*, 14.
71. Helen Babich Sabol, quoted in Cecil, *Our Coal-Mining Community Heritage*, 64.
72. Chaffee, "Company Towns," 102–3.
73. Phil Marchese, quoted in Cecil, *Our Coal-Mining Community Heritage*, 137.
74. Diane Sever Mihalich, quoted in Cecil, *Our Coal-Mining Community Heritage*, 13.
75. Ray Bernabei, quoted in Cecil, *Our Coal-Mining Community Heritage*, 171, 175.

76. John Begovich, quoted in Cecil, *Our Coal-Mining Community Heritage*, 37–38.
77. *Los Angeles Times*, March 12, 1928.
78. *New York Times*, March 12, 1928.
79. Norwood, *Strikebreaking and Intimidation*, 126–27.
80. *New York Times*, March 12, 1928.
81. Howard, "National Miners Union," 92.
82. Logan, "C'mon, You Reds."
83. Logan, "C'mon, You Reds," 387.
84. Howard, "National Miners Union," 93.
85. Gottlieb, "Black Miners," 235.
86. Abern, "Attack on the National Miners' Union Convention," 551.
87. *Pittsburgh Press*, June 13, 1931.
88. *New York Times*, April 12, 1929.
89. Curitz, *Black Fury*.
90. *Pittsburgh Press*, September 30, 1929.
91. *Pittsburgh Press*, May 27, 1931.
92. Merovich, interview, 14.
93. *Pittsburgh Press*, February 19, 1937.
94. John Prucnal, quoted in *Pittsburgh Post-Gazette*, July 13, 2003.
95. *Pittsburgh Post-Gazette*, August 3, 1990.
96. *Pittsburgh Post-Gazette*, July 13, 2003.
97. *Pittsburgh Post-Gazette*, January 27, 1956.
98. *Pittsburgh Press*, May 7, 1956.
99. Ann Anuskiewicz, quoted in Cecil, *Our Coal-Mining Community Heritage*, 158.
100. *New York Times*, August 28, 1977.
101. *Pittsburgh Press*, July 9, 1974.
102. *Beaver County Times*, September 5, 2010.
103. ESPN.com, "Cup Ratings in U.S. up 41 Percent."
104. *New York Times*, June 28, 2010.
105. Kissell, "World Cup Final."
106. See Burstyn, *Rites of Men*.
107. National Soccer Hall of Fame, "Raymond Bernabei."
108. *Pittsburgh Post-Gazette*, July 13, 2003.
109. *Pittsburgh Post-Gazette*, May 7, 1956.
110. Waddington and Roderick, "American Exceptionalism," 39.
111. *Valley News Dispatch*, September 28, 2009.
112. Waddington and Roderick, "American Exceptionalism," 44–45.
113. *Pittsburgh Press*, July 9, 1974.

114. James Mihalke, quoted in *Pittsburgh Press*, March 8, 1978.
115. *Pittsburgh Press*, February 15, 1913.
116. *Pittsburgh Press*, April 11, 1920.
117. *Pittsburgh Press*, February 19, 1928.
118. *Pittsburgh Press*, May 29, 1967.
119. *Pittsburgh Post-Gazette*, August 3, 1990.
120. *Pittsburgh Press*, May 29, 1967.
121. *Pittsburgh Press*, February 6, 1913.
122. *Pittsburgh Press*, October 3, 1918.
123. *Your Carlynton*, July 15, 2010.
124. *Pittsburgh Press*, April 6, 1920.
125. *Pittsburgh Press*, June 16, 1918.
126. *Pittsburgh Press*, March 24, 1953.
127. Frommer, *Great American Soccer Book*, 18.
128. See Mulrooney, *Legacy of Coal*, 27.
129. Abrams, "'Inhibited but Not 'Crowded Out,'" 14.
130. Valletta, "'To Battle for Our Ideas,'" 320–324.
131. *Pittsburgh Post-Gazette*, July 13, 2003.
132. *Pittsburgh Press*, November 28, 1909.
133. *Pittsburgh Press*, November 5, 1911.

3: POACHED TROUT

1. Newell, *Portrait of an American Community*, 31. In September 2022, the US Geological Survey announced the removal of the derogatory term *squaw* from place names of federal lands and renamed this stream Sycamore Run. Panizzi, "Squaw Run Stream Renamed."
2. Pittsburgh Field Club, "Club History."
3. Sajna, *Days on the Water*, 26–27.
4. Colonel Thomas P. Roberts, quoted in Casner, "Acid Mine Drainage," 93.
5. Collins, Muller, and Tarr, "Pittsburgh's Three Rivers," 48.
6. Tarr and Yosie, "Critical Decisions," 70.
7. Collins, Muller, and Tarr, "Pittsburgh's Three Rivers," 47.
8. Collins, Muller, and Tarr, "Pittsburgh's Three Rivers," 53–59.
9. Margaret Penn Feame, quoted in Sajna, *Days on the Water*, 44.
10. *New York Times*, January 15, 1905.
11. *Pittsburgh Press*, June 26, 1898.
12. *Pittsburgh Press*, July 31, 1903.
13. *Pittsburgh Press*, June 26, 1898.
14. *Pittsburgh Press*, July 31, 1903.
15. McCullough, *Johnstown Flood*, 61.

16. Frank and Charles Semple Papers, MFF 2160, Senator John Heinz History Center, Thomas and Katherine Detre Library and Archives.

17. *Science News*, "1889 Pennsylvania Flood."

18. Whitman, "Voice from Death."

19. Isaac Reed, quoted in McCullough, *Johnstown Flood*, 250.

20. Herman, *Hunting*, 238–39.

21. Herman, *Hunting*, 199.

22. John Phillips, quoted in Kosack, *Pennsylvania Game Commission*, 21.

23. Hornaday, *Camp-Fires*, 1.

24. Hornaday, *Camp-Fires*, 172.

25. Hornaday, *Camp-Fires*, 46.

26. Hornaday, *Camp-Fires*, vi–vii.

27. Hornaday, *Camp-Fires*, 16.

28. Hornaday, *Camp-Fires*, 279.

29. Hornaday, *Camp-Fires*, 180.

30. Boys Scouts of America, "Awards Central."

31. Kosack, *Pennsylvania Game Commission*, 22–23.

32. Reiger, *American Sportsmen*, 146.

33. See Krausman and Mahoney, "How the Boone and Crockett Club Shaped North American Conservation," and Reiger, *American Sportsmen*, 146–74.

34. Phillips, quoted in Kosack, *Pennsylvania Game Commission*, 42.

35. Pennsylvania Game Commission, "Game Lands."

36. "Symbol of democracy": Miner, "Hardhat Hunters"; "state power": Warren, *The Hunters Game*, 48–70.

37. Sajna, *Buck Fever*, 211.

38. National Rifle Association.

39. Herman, *Hunting and the American Imagination*, 32.

40. William Penn, quoted in Kosack, *Pennsylvania Game Commission*, 5.

41. Herman, *Hunting*, 25.

42. Miner, "Hardhat Hunters," 43.

43. Hornaday, *Our Vanishing Wild Life*, 387.

44. Hornaday, *Our Vanishing Wild Life*, 260–61.

45. Report of the Department of Fisheries, 1889-90-91, Records of the Pennsylvania Fish and Boat Commission, Record Group [RG] 72, box 1, Pennsylvania State Archives, Harrisburg.

46. Herman, *Hunting*, 248.

47. *Pittsburgh Press*, April 19, 1911.

48. *Pittsburgh Press*, August 18, 1917.

49. *Pittsburgh Press*, September 27, 1919.

50. Henry William Herbert, quoted in Herman, *Hunting*, 175.

51. Shoemaker, *Pennsylvania Deer*, 40.
52. Shoemaker, *Pennsylvania Deer*, 84.
53. Warren, *Hunter's Game*, 65.
54. McCullough, *Johnstown Flood*, 62–63, and "Short History."
55. "Short History."
56. McCullough, *Johnstown Flood*, 63.
57. Julia Laktash, quoted in Cecil, *Our Coal-Mining Community Heritage*, 85.
58. Helen Babich Sabol, quoted in Cecil, *Our Coal-Mining Community Heritage*, 62–63.
59. Joe Fogel, quoted in Cecil, *Our Coal-Mining Community Heritage*, 106–7.
60. Don Bosnich, quoted in Cecil, *Our Coal-Mining Community Heritage*, 95.
61. Report of the State Commissioners of Fisheries for the Year 1896, Records of the Pennsylvania Fish and Boat Commission, RG 72, box 2, Pennsylvania State Archives, Harrisburg.
62. Report of the Fish Commissioners of the State of Pennsylvania for the Year of 1902, Records of the Pennsylvania Fish and Boat Commission, RG 72, Pennsylvania State Archives, Harrisburg.
63. Kalbfus, "Law of Pennsylvania," 27.
64. Hornaday, *Our Vanishing Wild Life*, 101.
65. See Warren, *Hunter's Game*, 21–47.
66. Sajna, *Buck Fever*, 74.
67. Laws of General Assembly of the Commonwealth of Pennsylvania 1903, 178–80.
68. Laws of General Assembly of the Commonwealth of Pennsylvania 1909, 466–69.
69. Kalbfus, "Law of Pennsylvania," 28.
70. Frederick W. Fleitz, quoted in Kalbfus, "Law of Pennsylvania," 29.
71. "Nolo contendere" is Latin for "no contest." A defendant in a criminal proceeding may enter this plea, which indicates he or she does not accept or deny responsibility for the charges but agrees to accept punishment.
72. Commonwealth v. Cosick, 44 Pa. Super. Ct. 109.
73. Report of the Game Commission, 1911. Records of the Game Commission, RG 39, Publications, Publications 1902–2000, carton 5, Pennsylvania State Archives, Harrisburg.
74. Report of the Department of Fisheries of the Commonwealth of Pennsylvania, 1907, Records of the Pennsylvania Fish and Boat Commission, RG 72, Board of Commissioners, Reports, box 5, Pennsylvania State Archives, Harrisburg.
75. Cecil, *Our Coal-Mining Community Heritage*, 96.
76. Lucas, "From Patsone and Miller to Silveria," 9.

77. Patsone v. Commonwealth of Pennsylvania, 232 U.S. 138.
78. "Aliens and Firearms."
79. Hornaday, *Our Vanishing Wild Life*, 102.
80. Hornaday, *Our Vanishing Wild Life*, 100.
81. Kalbfus, "Law of Pennsylvania," 32.
82. Report of the Department of Fisheries, 1913–1914. Records of the Pennsylvania Fish and Boat Commission, RG 72, Board of Commissioners, Reports, box 5, Pennsylvania State Archives, Harrisburg.
83. Laws of General Assembly of the Commonwealth of Pennsylvania 1915, 644–47.
84. "2 Charged with Poaching Deer."
85. *Pittsburgh Post-Gazette*, November 13, 2010.
86. *Pittsburgh Post-Gazette*, January 13, 2008.
87. *Pittsburgh Post-Gazette*, January 22, 2011.
88. See Fine, "Rights of Men."
89. Leo Luttringer, "Game Administration in Pennsylvania: Yesterday and Today," Records of the Game Commission, RG 39, Publications, Publications 1902–2000, carton 5, Pennsylvania State Archives, Harrisburg.
90. Sarah Speed, quoted in *Pittsburgh Post-Gazette*, June 12, 2011.
91. Evan Heusinkveld, quoted in *Pittsburgh Post-Gazette*, June 12, 2011.
92. U.S. Department of the Interior, *2011 National Survey of Fishing*, 4.
93. *Pittsburgh Post-Gazette*, June 12, 2011.
94. Pennsylvania Game Commission, "Hunting and License Sales."
95. Pennsylvania Fish and Boat Commission, "Pennsylvania Fishing License."
96. *Digest of the Game, Fish and Forestry Laws*, 1917, Records of the Pennsylvania Fish and Boat Commission, RG 72, Board of Commissioners, Reports, box 5, Pennsylvania State Archives, Harrisburg.
97. See Martin, "Apartheid."
98. *Pittsburgh Tribune-Review*, May 16, 2010.
99. U.S. Department of the Interior, *Participation and Expenditure Patterns*, 5–6.
100. U.S. Department of the Interior, *2016 National Survey of Fishing*, 4.
101. TribLive, "Minorities Scarce among Outdoor Media."
102. Casner, "Angler Activist."
103. See Duda, "Pennsylvania Sportsmen's Attitudes."
104. Sajna, *Buck Fever*, 198.
105. U.S. Department of the Interior, *Participation and Expenditure Patterns*, 27.
106. Shoemaker, *Pennsylvania Deer*, 49–50.
107. *Digest of the Game, Fish and Forestry Laws*, 1917.

108. Many of the records of Pennsylvania's Game Commission and license sales records were destroyed.

109. See Buni, *Robert L. Vann*; Pride and Wilson, *A History of the Black Press*, 137–40; Finkle, "Quotas or Integration"; Stevens, "Black Press"; and Lamb, "'What's Wrong With Baseball.'"

110. Bodnar, Simon, and Weber, *Lives of Their Own*, 20, 30–35.

111. Bodnar, Simon, and Weber, *Lives of Their Own*, 239.

112. Trotter and Day, *Race and Renaissance*, 39.

113. Trotter and Day, *Race and Renaissance*, 51.

114. Hardie, *Fox Chapel*, 96.

115. *Pittsburgh Courier*, June 12, 1926.

116. Hornaday, *Camp-Fires*, 13.

117. *Pittsburgh Courier*, June 12, 1926.

118. Hardie, *Fox Chapel*, 96.

119. For the rise of Black recreation in this period, see Alnutt, "'Negro Excursions,'" and Foster, "In the Face of 'Jim Crow.'" See also Young, "'Contradiction in Democratic Government.'"

120. Du Bois, quoted in Foster, "In the Face of 'Jim Crow,'" 138.

121. Du Bois, "Problem of Amusement," 28. See also Holland, *Black Recreation*, 165–69.

122. *Pittsburgh Courier*, March 13, 1926.

123. *Pittsburgh Courier*, October 13, 1928.

124. *Pittsburgh Courier*, August 13, 1927.

125. *Pittsburgh Courier*, August 31, 1929.

126. Alnutt, "Negro Excursions," 78.

127. See U.S. Fish and Wildlife Service, *Participation and Expenditure Patterns*, 6, 16. Seventy-three percent of African American hunters resided in the South, only 7 percent in the Northeast. Similarly, 64 percent of African American anglers resided in the South, 14 percent in the Northeast.

128. Gottlieb, *Making Their Own Way*, 96 (quote), 104–10.

129. See Bodnar, Simon, and Weber, *Lives of Their Own*, 250–51; Darden, "Effect of World War I," and Alexander, "Great Migration."

130. Gottlieb, *Making Their Own Way*, 8.

131. File of Council, City of Pittsburgh, Series 1924, File no. 217, Bill no. 621. Urban League of Pittsburgh Records, AIS.1981.11, Government Bodies, Pennsylvania, Display and Sale of Firearms, 1924, box 10, folder 447, University of Pittsburgh Library System, Archives Service Center [UPLS, ASC].

132. "Urban League Finds 214 Revolvers on Display in Ten Blocks." Urban League of Pittsburgh Records, AIS.1981.11, Government Bodies, Pennsylvania, Display and Sale of Firearms, 1924, box 10, folder 447, UPLS, ASC.

133. *Pittsburgh Courier*, April 19, 1930.

134. For the local evolution of fox hunting from a communal activity to an elite recreational practice, see Martin, *Killing Time*, 135–38.

135. *Pittsburgh Courier*, May 22, 1941.

136. *Pittsburgh Courier*, September 28, 1957.

137. *Pittsburgh Courier*, January 26, 1957.

138. *Pittsburgh Courier*, January 5, 1957.

139. Allegheny County Sportsmen's League.

140. *Pittsburgh Courier*, April 14, 1956.

141. Laws of General Assembly of the Commonwealth of Pennsylvania 1905, 261.

142. *Pittsburgh Courier*, May 18, 1957.

143. *Pittsburgh Courier*, August 31, 1957.

144. *Pittsburgh Courier*, August 22, 1959.

145. *Pittsburgh Courier*, September 30, 1961.

146. Pennsylvania Fish and Boat Commission, "State Issues Updated Fish Consumption Advisories."

147. Responsive Management, "Women's, Hispanics,' and African Americans' Participation," 16.

148. Giltner, *Hunting and Fishing*, 137–67. See also Montrie, *Making a Living*, 35–52.

149. Giltner, *Hunting and Fishing*, 2.

150. "Uncle David's Filosofy."

151. "Unkel David's Letter."

152. Wild Bird Protection. Records of the Game Commission, RG 39, Publications, Publications 1902–2000, carton 5, Pennsylvania State Archives, Harrisburg.

153. Hornaday, *Our Vanishing Wild Life*, 105.

154. *New York Times*, September 10, 1906.

155. *New York Times*, September 11, 2006.

156. *New York Times*, September 18, 1906.

157. *New York Times*, October 2, 1906.

158. *New York Times*, August 6, 2006.

159. *Pittsburgh Courier*, July 14, 1956.

160. *Pittsburgh Courier*, June 29, 1957.

161. *Pittsburgh Courier*, August 4, 1962.

162. *Pittsburgh Courier*, August 9, 1952.

163. Wideman, "Hunters," 17–18.

164. Wideman, "Hunters," 23.

165. Wideman, "Hunters," 25–26.

166. Herman, *Hunting*, 269.

167. *Pittsburgh Tribune-Review*, May 16, 2010.

168. Responsive Management, "Women's, Hispanics,' and African Americans' Participation," 17.

169. Carter, "Coloured Places," 281.

170. *Pittsburgh Courier*, July 25, 1964.

171. *Pittsburgh Courier*, February 8, 1958.

172. Trotter and Day, *Race and Renaissance*, 53.

173. Graves, interview.

174. *Pittsburgh Courier*, July 2, 1966.

175. Foner, *Forever Free*, 101.

176. The 2006 U.S. Fish and Wildlife Survey investigating African American hunting participation also noted that African Americans focus more on small game hunting.

177. For more on Harris, see Crouch, *One Shot Harris*; Westmoreland Museum of American Art, *Spirit of a Community*; and Finley, Glasco and Trotter, *Teenie Harris*.

178. *Pittsburgh Courier*, December 9, 1967.

179. *Pittsburgh Courier*, December 21, 1957.

180. *Pittsburgh Courier*, December 7, 1935.

181. *Pittsburgh Courier*, July 27, 1957.

182. *Pittsburgh Courier*, January 19, 1957.

183. Sajna, *Days on the Water*, 63.

184. *Pittsburgh Courier*, September 14, 1957.

185. *Pittsburgh Courier*, February 16, 1957. See Smalley, "'I Just Like to Kill Things.'"

186. *Pittsburgh Courier*, May 21, 1960.

187. *Pittsburgh Post-Gazette*, July 18, 2010.

188. *LancasterOnline*, "1 Out of Every 10 Hunters."

4: BASKETBALLS, BUNK BEDS, AND BRIDGES

1. Feldman, *Jewish Experience*, 5, 15–19.

2. Rodef Shalom Congregation.

3. Feldman, *Jewish Experience*, 70, 79.

4. For early history of the Pittsburgh Jewish community, see Burstin, *Steel City Jews*.

5. Feldman, *Jewish Experience*, 124–25.

6. President's Report to the Members of the Columbian School and Settlement, 1907. Jewish Community Center of Greater Pittsburgh Records, MSS #389, box 7, folder 5, Senator John Heinz History Center, Thomas and Katherine Detre Library and Archives [HHC, DL].

7. "Memories: A Dramatic Presentation," by Arthur Lassman and Sidney J.

Lindenberg, January 18, 1953. Jewish Community Center of Greater Pittsburgh Records, MSS #389, box 4, folder 5, HHC, DL.

8. *Jewish Criterion*, May 16, 1902.

9. "Memories: A Dramatic Presentation."

10. Crocker, *Social Work*, 5.

11. Eisen, "Sport, Recreation and Gender," 113.

12. Butera, "Settlement House," 25.

13. *Jewish Criterion*, May 13, 1904.

14. *Jewish Criterion*, May 12, 1905.

15. President's Report to the Members.

16. A Brief History of the Irene Kaufmann Settlement House, Jewish Community Center of Greater Pittsburgh Records, MSS #389, box 5, folder 2, HHC, DL.

17. Goodman, "(Re)Creating Americans," 22.

18. Annual Report, September 1914–September 1915, Kaufmann Family Scrapbooks Collection, 1920–1940, AIS.1998.32, box 4, University of Pittsburgh Library System, Archives Service Center [UPLS, ASC].

19. Annual Report, September 1913–September 1914, Kaufmann Family Scrapbooks Collection, 1920–1940, AIS.1998.32, box 4, UPLS, ASC.

20. Kellogg, *Pittsburgh District*, 307.

21. Kellogg, *Pittsburgh District*, 307.

22. Kellogg, *Pittsburgh District*, 311.

23. Kellogg, *Pittsburgh District*, 314.

24. Kellogg, *Pittsburgh District*, 237.

25. Kellogg, *Pittsburgh District*, 289.

26. Annual Report, September 1914–September 1915. Kaufmann Family Scrapbooks Collection, 1920–1940, AIS.1998.32, box 4, UPLS, ASC.

27. National Association of Jewish Community Center Physical Directors, *Jewish Center Physical Director* 1, no. 4 (May 1930), Jewish Community Center of Greater Pittsburgh Records, MSS #389, Young Men's and Women's Hebrew Association, box 46, folder 10, HHC, DL.

28. "Community Centers and Related Problems," 407.

29. Year Book, January 1, 1918, to January 1, 1919. Kaufmann Family Scrapbooks Collection, AIS.1998.32, box 4, UPLS, ASC.

30. Year Book, September 1, 1916–December 31, 1917. Kaufmann Family Scrapbooks Collection, AIS.1998.32, box 4, UPLS, ASC.

31. Annual Report, September 1913–1914. Kaufmann Family Scrapbooks Collection, AIS.1998.32, box 4, UPLS, ASC.

32. See Cavallo, *Muscles and Morals*, 88–106.

33. Year Book, September 1, 1916–December 31, 1917.

34. Annual Report, September 1914–September 1915. Kaufmann Family Scrapbooks, AIS.1998.32, box 4, UPLS, ASC.

35. Year Book, January 1, 1918–January 1, 1919. Kaufmann Family Scrapbooks, AIS.1998.32, box 4, UPLS, ASC.

36. Extracts from the Director's Report for the Twenty-Ninth Year (1924), Jewish Community Center of Greater Pittsburgh Records, MSS #389, Irene Kaufmann Settlement, box 4, folder 2, HHC, DL.

37. 1919 Yearbook. Jewish Community Center of Greater Pittsburgh Records, MSS #389, Irene Kaufmann Settlement, box 4, folder 1, HHC, DL.

38. *I. K. S. Neighbors*, January 15, 1925. Jewish Community Center of Greater Pittsburgh Records, MSS #389, Irene Kaufmann Settlement, Publications, box 8, folder 9, HHC, DL.

39. *I. K. S. Neighbors*, March 13, 1927, Irene Kaufmann Settlement, MS #78, Newsletters, box 1, folder 7, HHC, DL.

40. *Pittsburgh Press*, April 18, 1928.

41. *I. K. S. Neighbors*, March 13, 1927, Irene Kaufmann Settlement, MS #78, Newsletters, box 1, folder 7, HHC, DL.

42. Barry Paris, "Induction," *New Yorker*, January 7, 1991.

43. National Council of Jewish Women, *My Voice Was Heard*, 124.

44. *Jewish Criterion*, September 10, 1926.

45. Postal, *Encyclopedia of Jews in Sports*; Slater, *Great Jews in Sports*; Megdal, *Baseball Talmud*; Horvitz, *Big Book of Jewish Sports Heroes*; and Eliezer and Kupperberg, *Jew-Jitsu*.

46. *Jewish Criterion*, August 15, 1924.

47. *Jewish Chronicle of Pittsburgh*, March 18, 1982.

48. Stern, *What I Can't Bear Losing*, 37.

49. Stern, *What I Can't Bear Losing*, 38–41.

50. *New Yorker*, January 7, 1991.

51. Jenkins, *Hoods and Shirts*, 70.

52. Jenkins, "Ku Klux Klan to the Members," 121.

53. Gallico, *Farewell to Sport*, 325.

54. IKS Annual Report, 1914–1915. Kaufmann Family Scrapbooks Collection, AIS.1998.32, box 4, UPLS, ASC.

55. *Jewish Criterion*, August 15, 1924.

56. Eisen, "Jews and Sport," 231.

57. *Jewish Criterion*, June 6, 1926.

58. See also Borish, "Athletic Activities."

59. Report of President of Columbian Council School in *Jewish Criterion*, May 12, 1905, Jewish Community Center of Greater Pittsburgh Records, MSS #389, Irene Kaufmann Settlement, box 4, folder 1, HHC, DL.

60. Annual Report, September 1913–1914. Kaufmann Family Scrapbooks Collections, AIS.1998.32, box 4, UPLS, ASC.

61. 1919 Yearbook.

62. *Jewish Criterion*, August 15, 1941.

63. See Borish, "'Cradle of American Champions.'"

64. See Levine, *Ellis Island to Ebbets Field*, and Borish, "Women, Sport, and American Jewish Identity."

65. Eisen, "Jewish History," 490.

66. *Jewish Criterion*, August 27, 1926.

67. *Jewish Criterion*, September 3, 1926.

68. *Wisconsin Jewish Chronicle*, May 7, 1926.

69. Cohen, quoted in Gurock, *Judaism's Encounter*, 100.

70. Auslander, "Playoffs." *New Yorker*, January 15, 2007.

71. *Jewish Criterion*, February 8, 1924.

72. *I. K. S. Neighbors*, October 1925. Jewish Community Center of Greater Pittsburgh Records, MSS #389, Irene Kaufmann Settlement, box 8, folder 9, HHC, DL.

73. Smith and Manaker, "Pittsburgh's African American Neighborhoods," 159.

74. Lindenburg and Zittel, "Settlement Scene Changes," 563–64.

75. Lindenburg and Zittel, "Settlement Scene Changes," 566.

76. Nathaniel Spear, quoted in "Memories: A Dramatic Presentation."

77. The Farm School was discontinued in March 1918.

78. Teller, "Summer Camps and Their Relation to Community Health," May 26 and 27, 1932, at Pittsburgh, PA, Jewish Community Center of Greater Pittsburgh Records, MSS #389, Irene Kaufmann Settlement, box 4, folder 1, HHC, DL.

79. *Pittsburgh Courier*, November 22, 1941.

80. *Pittsburgh Courier*, August 28, 1926.

81. Wilson, *Fences*, 16.

82. Schwartz, "No Joshing."

83. Ruck, *Sandlot Seasons*, 157.

84. Ruck, *Sandlot Seasons*, 3.

85. *Pittsburgh Courier*, November 3, 1928.

86. *Pittsburgh Courier*, February 13, 1932.

87. *Pittsburgh Courier*, August 26, 1933.

88. *Pittsburgh Courier*, February 12, 1938.

89. *Pittsburgh Courier*, May 18, 1940.

90. See Lamb, "'What's Wrong with Baseball,'" 189–92, and Alpert, *Out of Left Field*, 133–57.

91. *Pittsburgh Courier*, July 20, 1946.

92. *Dearborn Independent*, September 10, 1921.

93. See Crocker, *Social Work*; Lasch-Quinn, *Black Neighbors*; Philpott, *The Slum and the Ghetto*; and Stuart, "Kingsley House Extension Program."

94. Butera, "Settlement House," 46.

95. *Pittsburgh Courier*, November 7, 1925.

96. Paris, *Children's Nature*, 62–63.

97. Paris, *Children's Nature*, 59.

98. The History of Camp James Weldon Johnson, 1938–1958. Urban League of Pittsburgh Records, 1915–1963, AIS.1981.11, Administrative Material, box 5, UPLS, ASC.

99. Camp James Weldon Johnson, 27th Annual Camping Season, 1965. Urban League of Pittsburgh Records, 1915–1963, AIS.1981.11, Administrative Material, box 5, UPLS, ASC.

100. Camp James Weldon Johnson, Fourth Annual Report, 1942. Urban League of Pittsburgh Records, 1915–1963, AIS.1981.11, Administrative Material, box 5, UPLS, ASC.

101. See Mishler, *Raising Reds*, 83–108.

102. Jenkins, *Cold War at Home*, 4.

103. Lasch-Quinn, *Black Neighbors*, 70–71.

104. Camp James Weldon Johnson, Fifth Annual Report, 1943, Urban League of Pittsburgh Records, 1915–1963, AIS.1981.11, Administrative Material, box 5, UPLS, ASC.

105. Camp James Weldon Johnson, Annual Report, 1940. Urban League of Pittsburgh Records, 1915–1963, AIS.1981.11, Administrative Material, box 5, UPLS, ASC.

106. Faye Lieberman Schwartz, quoted in Cecil, *Our Coal-Mining Community Heritage*, 139.

107. American Camping Association, "Establishing Racial Good Will," 9.

108. American Camping Association, *Camping*, 4.

109. American Camping Association, "Establishing Racial Good Will," 9.

110. Serotkin, "Experiments in Inter-Racial Camping."

111. "Some Characteristics of Soho Members as Determined by Economic, Social, Cultural and Racial Factors," June 1951, American Service Institute Records, AIS 1963.01, Local Organizations and Activities, box 7, folder 49, UPLS, ASC.

112. Serotkin, "Experiments in Inter-Racial Camping," 11.

113. Verbrugge, "Recreation and Racial Politics," 1208.

114. Consultation Camp Claudine Virginia Trees, July 22, 1949. American Service Institute Records, AIS 1963.01, Consultation of Camps and Miscellaneous, box 3, folder 8, UPLS, ASC.

115. Camp Claudine Virginia Trees, Intercultural Report, Summer 1949, American Service Institute Records, AIS 1963.01, Consultation of Camps and Miscellaneous, box 3, folder 8, UPLS, ASC.

116. Serotkin, "Experiments in Inter-Racial Camping," 12.

117. The History of Camp James Weldon Johnson, 1938–1958, Urban League of Pittsburgh Records, 1915–1963, AIS.1981.11, Administrative Material, box 5, UPLS, ASC.

118. Consultant's Record, Camp Claudine Virginia Trees, Pre-Camp Institute: June 1948, American Service Institute Records, AIS 1963.01, Consultation of Camps and Miscellaneous, box 3, folder 8, UPLS, ASC.

119. Consultant's Report: Camp Redwing 1949, American Service Institute Records, AIS 1963.01, Consultation of Camps and Miscellaneous, box 3, folder 11, UPLS, ASC.

120. See Deloria, *Playing Indian*, 95–127, and Paris, *Children's Nature*, 189–225.

121. Bland, "In the Evening by the Moonlight."

122. Consultant's Record, Camp Redwing, Pre-Camp Institute: June 1948.

123. Consultation—Camp Redwing, July 21, 1949. American Service Institute Records, AIS 1963.01, Consultation of Camps and Miscellaneous, box 3, folder 11, UPLS, ASC.

124. Paris, *Children's Nature*, 207.

125. Robert A. Woods, quoted in Kellogg, *Pittsburgh District*, 10.

126. William Penn, quoted in Jable, "Pennsylvania's Early Blue Laws," 108.

127. Pennsylvania State Reports for 1853.

128. Commonwealth ex rel. Woodruff v. American Baseball Club of Philadelphia, 290 Pa 136.

129. Extracts from the Resident Director's Report 1895—for the Twenty-Ninth Year—1924. Jewish Community Center of Greater Pittsburgh Records, MSS #389, Irene Kaufmann Settlement, box 4, folder 1, HHC, DL.

130. Community Cooperation Committee Irene Kaufmann Settlement, November 16, 1945, Kaufmann Family Scrapbooks Collection, 1920–1940, AIS.1998.32, UPLS, ASC.

131. Second Report to the Special Study Committee of the Health and Welfare Federation of Allegheny County on the Irene Kaufmann Settlement, March 27, 1950, Jewish Community Center of Greater Pittsburgh Records, MSS #389, Irene Kaufmann Settlement, box 5, folder 4, HHC, DL.

132. Annual Report of the Executive Director, 1948, Jewish Community Center of Greater Pittsburgh Records, MSS #389, Irene Kaufmann Settlement, box 4, folder 4, HHC, DL.

133. Trolander, *Professionalism and Social Change*, 102.

134. Annual Report of the Executive Director, 1948.

135. Summary of Background Data Considered by the Study Committee, April 14, 1950, Jewish Community Center of Greater Pittsburgh Records, MSS #389, Irene Kaufmann Settlement, box 5, folder 3, HHC, DL.

136. First Annual Report of President of the Irene Kaufmann Settlement. Kaufmann Family Scrapbooks Collection, AIS.1998.32, UPLS, ASC.

137. Annual Report of the Executive Director, 1948.

138. Second Report to the Special Study Committee of the Health and Welfare Federation of Allegheny County on the Irene Kaufmann Settlement, March 27, 1950, Jewish Community Center of Greater Pittsburgh Records, MSS #389, Irene Kaufmann Settlement, box 5, folder 4, HHC, DL.

139. *Pittsburgh Courier*, January 5, 1946.

140. Annual Report of the Executive Director, 1954, Jewish Community Center of Greater Pittsburgh Records, MSS #389, Irene Kaufmann Settlement, box 1, folder 3, HHC, DL.

141. Annual Report of the Executive Director, 1950, Jewish Community Center of Greater Pittsburgh Records, MSS #389, Irene Kaufmann Settlement, box 4, folder 5, HHC, DL.

142. Report to the Special Study Committee of the Health and Welfare Federation of Allegheny County on the Irene Kaufmann Settlement, November 14, 1949, American Service Institute Records, AIS.1963.01, Settlements, box 7, folder 46–47, UPLS, ASC.

143. Second Report to the Special Study Committee of the Health and Welfare Federation of Allegheny County on the Irene Kaufmann Settlement, March 27, 1950, American Service Institute Records, AIS.1963.01, Settlements, box 7, folder 46–47, UPLS, ASC.

144. James McCoy Jr. to Mr. J. D. Bayus, June 19, 1967, Jewish Community Center of Greater Pittsburgh Records, MSS #389, Irene Kaufmann Settlement, box 4, folder 14.

145. David Aronson, quoted in Gurock, *Judaism's Encounter*, 104.

146. J. W. Joselit, quoted in Sales and Saxe, "How Goodly Are Thy Tents," 15.

147. Untitled Report by Sidney Lindenberg to Members of Camping Services Committee, 1961, Jewish Community Center of Greater Pittsburgh Records, MSS #389, Emma Kaufmann Camp, box 2, HHC, DL.

148. History of the Emma Kaufmann Camp, Jewish Community Center of Greater Pittsburgh Records, MSS #389, Emma Kaufmann Camp, box 2, HHC, DL.

149. "Memories: A Dramatic Presentation."

150. Untitled Report to Members of Camping Services Committee.

151. The Program—Membership Study Committee Minutes, January 24,

1951. American Service Institute Records, AIS.1963.01, Settlements, box 7, folder 46–47, UPLS, ASC.

152. The Program—Membership Study Committee Minutes, January 17, 1951. American Service Institute Records, AIS.1963.01, Settlements, box 7, folder 46–47, UPLS, ASC.

153. Eleanor L. Ryder to Mrs. Lenore E. Rainey, February 20, 1951. American Service Institute Records, AIS.1963.01, Settlements, box 7, folder 46–47, UPLS, ASC.

154. Camp Redwing-Pre Camp Institute: June 1948, Consultant's Record.

155. Mimi Kaplan, quoted in Palmer, "Recognizing Racial Privilege," 151.

156. Palmer, "Recognizing Racial Privilege," 150.

157. Lane, "Search for the American Dream Home."

158. Bodnar, Simon, and Weber, *Lives of Their Own*, 193.

159. Bodnar, Simon, and Weber, *Lives of Their Own*, 71.

160. *Pittsburgh Courier*, January 13, 1945.

161. Report to the Special Study Committee, 11.

162. Wiltse, *Contested Waters*, 128.

163. *Pittsburgh Courier*, July 26, 1952.

164. CDC, "Drowning Facts."

165. Swimming Pool Committee Meeting Minutes, December 15, 1952, National Association for the Advancement of Colored People, Pittsburgh Branch Records, AIS.1964.38, UPLS, ASC.

166. See Jenkins, *Cold War at Home*, 77–81.

167. Schlesinger Petition to the Supreme Court of Pennsylvania, 367 Pa. 476.

168. William H. Matthews, quoted in Kellogg, *Pittsburgh District*, 97.

5: TERRIBLE TOWELS AND SIXTY-MINUTE MEN

1. *Pittsburgh Post-Gazette*, August 5, 2002.
2. Rose, "NFL Coaches Hired."
3. Varley, "Tomlin Takes Over."
4. *Cleveland Plain Dealer*, July 31, 2009.
5. Faires, "Immigrants and Industry."
6. *Toledo Blade*, March 2, 1952.
7. Francis, "Saga of Joe Magarac."
8. *Pittsburgh Post-Gazette*, April 18, 1951.
9. Riesman and Denney, "Football in America," 318.
10. Dinnerstein, "Backfield in Motion," 176.
11. *Lewiston Daily Sun*, December 7, 1905.
12. *Los Angeles Times*, July 18, 1990.
13. Zbiek, "Coal, Steel, and Gridiron," 217.

14. Patrick, "Joe Magarac," 55.
15. Kleinberg, *Shadow of the Mills*, 31.
16. Eastman, *Work Accidents*, 13.
17. Kellogg, *Wage-Earning Pittsburgh*, 25.
18. Kellogg, *Wage-Earning Pittsburgh*, 37, 73.
19. Eastman, *Work Accidents*, 64.
20. Kellogg, *Wage-Earning Pittsburgh*, 73.
21. Kellogg, *Wage-Earning Pittsburgh*, 41.
22. Kovacevic, "Who Murdered Joe Magarac?" 94.
23. Owen Francis, quoted in Gilley and Burnett, "Deconstructing and Reconstructing Pittsburgh's Man of Steel," 394.
24. Gilley and Burnett, "Deconstructing and Reconstructing," 397.
25. Sewald, *Gridiron and Steel*.
26. Wright, *Above the River*, 121.
27. Zbiek, "Coal, Steel, and Gridiron."
28. Riesman and Denney, "Football in America," 323.
29. *Trib-Live*, "Foreign Influx."
30. Danielson, *Home Team*, 9.
31. See Kraszewski, "Pittsburgh in Fort Worth."
32. *New York Times*, August 26, 1988.
33. Rich Koster, quoted in Ruck, Patterson, and Weber, *Rooney*, 367.
34. Ruck, "Art Rooney," 244.
35. Rooney, *Dan Rooney*, 21.
36. Gary Anderson, quoted in Mendelson, *Pittsburgh Steelers*, 68.
37. Lambert, "Reflections on the Pre-Renaissance Steelers," 67.
38. O'Brien, *Doing It Right*, 24.
39. *New York Times*, January 15, 2005.
40. *Washington Post*, November 26, 2004.
41. Mendelson, *Pittsburgh Steelers*, 194.
42. Michael Novak, quoted in Sewald, *Gridiron and Steel*.
43. Andy Kelly in *New York Times*, January 15, 2005.
44. Myron Cope, quoted in O'Brien, *Doing It Right*, 127.
45. *Pittsburgh Post-Gazette*, January 19, 2005.
46. Grossman, interview.
47. Gans, "Symbolic Ethnicity."
48. See Novak, *Rise of the Unmeltable Ethnics*.
49. Brignano, *Boundless Lives*, xxi.
50. Oral history interview with Al Vento Jr. and Al Vento Sr., 1999 (2002.0067), Thomas and Katherine Detre Library and Archives, Senator John Heinz History Center.

51. See Tuttle, "Christopher Columbus' American Lawyer."
52. *Pittsburgh Sun-Telegraph*, October 13, 1958.
53. *Sporting News*, November 22, 2004.
54. Crowley, *Politics of Place*, 8–89. See also Dietrich-Ward, *Beyond Rust*.
55. Pro Football Hall of Fame, "Profile: Ray Kemp."
56. Dinerstein, "Backfield in Motion," 170.
57. *Pittsburgh Post-Gazette*, May 8, 2014.
58. *New York Times*, October 29, 1997.
59. Mendelson, *Pittsburgh Steelers*, 209.
60. United Press International, January 29, 1982.
61. NFL Players' Association, "FAQs."
62. Raymond Sauer in *New York Times*, January 21, 2007.
63. Mike Webster, quoted in O'Brien, *Doing it Right*, 371.
64. *Pittsburgh Post-Gazette*, December 14, 2006.
65. Almond, *Against Football*, 7.
66. Kevin Henry and Najeh Davenport v. National Football League, Civil Action Complaint 20–4165, United States District Court for the Eastern District of Pennsylvania.
67. *New York Times*, January 25, 1996.
68. Mendelson, *Pittsburgh Steelers*, 12–13.
69. Elizabeth Shuler in *Pittsburgh Tribune-Review*, April 15, 2010.
70. Anderson, *Imagined Communities*.
71. *New York Times*, January 12, 2005.
72. *Press Enterprise*, January 31, 2007.
73. *New Pittsburgh Courier*, February 14, 2006.
74. Ciotola, "Spignesi, Sinatra, and the Pittsburgh Steelers," 272.
75. Waters, "Costs of a Costless Community."
76. Gans, "Symbolic Ethnicity," 435.
77. Vento, interview.
78. Waters, "Costs of a Costless Community," 289.
79. Dickerson, *Out of the Crucible*, 36.
80. Dickerson, *Out of the Crucible*, 101–2.
81. Dickerson, *Out of the Crucible*, 159.
82. Hinshaw, "Job Strategies," 70.
83. Epstein, "Negro Migrant," 63.
84. Kellogg, *Wage-Earning Pittsburgh*, 424.
85. Dickerson, *Out of the Crucible*, 224.
86. Hinshaw, "Job Strategies," 72.
87. Dickerson, *Out of the Crucible*, 185.
88. Dickerson, *Out of the Crucible*, 244–45.

89. Dickerson, *Out of the Crucible*, 250.
90. Hinshaw, "Review Essay."
91. King and Springwood, *Beyond the Cheers*, 39.
92. Michael Novak, quoted in Sewald, *Gridiron and Steel*.
93. Dinerstein, "Backfield in Motion," 183.
94. McCallum, "See No Evil."
95. Andrews, "Excavating Michael Jordan's Blackness," 178.
96. Tony Dungy, quoted in Rhoden, *Third and a Mile*, 31.
97. Joe Gilliam Sr., quoted in Rhoden, *Third and a Mile*, 36.
98. Stewart, "'You Know What I Heard???'"
99. Jacobson, *Whiteness of a Different Color*, 274–80.
100. Wideman, *Brothers and Keepers*, 41.
101. Marshall and Briggs, *Negro Participation in Apprenticeship Programs*, 23.
102. *Pittsburgh Press*, August 4, 1969.
103. Dubinsky, *Reform in Trade Union Discrimination*, 140–44.
104. Wideman, *Brothers and Keepers*, 40–41.
105. Wideman, *Brothers and Keepers*, 27.
106. *Los Angeles Times*, October 15, 2000.
107. Robinson, *I Never Had It Made*, 272.
108. *Pittsburgh Post-Gazette*, October 9, 2005.
109. *Syracuse Herald American*, November 17, 1996.
110. *Sports Illustrated*, January 24, 2005.
111. Jun and Lee, "Globalization of Sport," 104.
112. Lee and Ha, "Evolution and Symbolism."
113. Kawashima, "We Will Try Again," 125.
114. Jun and Lee, "Globalization of Sport," 106.
115. *Korea Times*, April 5, 2006.
116. *Chicago Sun-Times*, February 5, 2006.
117. *Pittsburgh Tribune-Review*, December 17, 2006.
118. See Thangaraj, Arnaldo, and Chin, *Asian American Sporting Cultures*.
119. Hollinger, *Postethnic America*.
120. Ashtulany, "Toward a Multiethnic Cartography," 145.
121. Adarand Constructors Inc. v. Peña, 515 U.S. 200 (1995).
122. *Korea Times*, April 4, 2006.
123. Ahn, "Rearticulating Black Mixed-Race," 397.
124. Korean language for 4-2-9 and Korean American community's term for the events.
125. *Central New Jersey Home News*, November 4, 2005.
126. *USA Today*, accessed November 3, 2006, www.today.com/browse/tag-hines_ward.

127. *New York Times*, May 30, 2001.
128. *Pittsburgh City Paper*, July 12, 2016.
129. *Pittsburgh Quarterly*, Fall 2012, 80; and *New York Times*, April 16, 2010.
130. *Pittsburgh Daily Post*, September 4, 1850.
131. *Jewish Chronicle*, February 9, 2006.
132. Gurung, interview.
133. Timsina, interview.
134. *Pittsburgh Post-Gazette*, September 3, 2012.
135. *Pittsburgh Post-Gazette*, May 6, 2000.
136. *Pittsburgh Tribune-Review*, July 30, 2007.
137. Steelers.com, "Tomlin Will Bring a Blue-Collar Approach."
138. *Pittsburgh Tribune-Review*, January 27, 2007.
139. Steelers.com, "What Do You Think of Tomlin?"
140. Ron Cook in *Pittsburgh Post-Gazette*, January 23, 2007.
141. Institute for Diversity and Ethics in Sports, "2019 Racial and Gender Report Card: National Football League," 27–30.
142. Institute for Diversity and Ethics in Sports, "2019 Racial and Gender Report Card: College Sport," 27.
143. Associated Press, February 28, 2007.
144. Institute for Diversity and Ethics in Sports, "2019 Racial and Gender Report Card: College Sport," 25.
145. *Pittsburgh Post-Gazette*, July 4, 2010.
146. University of Pittsburgh School of Social Work, Center on Race and Society Problems, "Pittsburgh's Racial Demographics 2015," 74.
147. Brink, "Asthma in Pittsburgh"; and *Pittsburgh Post-Gazette*, July 7, 2013.
148. *New Pittsburgh Courier*, February 22, 2007.
149. Savran, interview.
150. *Pittsburgh Press*, July 14, 1970.
151. *Pittsburgh Post-Gazette*, October 30, 1965.
152. Conrad v. Pittsburgh, 421 Pa. 492 (Pa. 1966).

BIBLIOGRAPHY

ARCHIVAL RECORD GROUPS

Senator John Heinz History Center, Thomas and Katherine Detre Library and Archives
    Irene Kaufmann Settlement, MS #78
    Jewish Community Center of Greater Pittsburgh Records, MSS #389
    Peter Merovich Papers and Photographs, MSS #0729
    Frank and Charles Semple Papers, MFF #2160

Pennsylvania State Archives, Harrisburg
    Records of the Pennsylvania Fish and Boat Commission, Record Group 72
    Records of the Pennsylvania Game Commission, Record Group 39

University of Pittsburgh Library System, Archives Service Center
    American Service Institute Records (AIS.1963.01)
    Brashear Association Records, 1891–1978 (AIS.1979.17)
    Kaufmann Family Scrapbooks Collection, 1920–1940 (AIS.1998.32), Kaufmann Family Scrapbooks
    Urban League of Pittsburgh Records (AIS.1981.11)

NEWSPAPERS AND PERIODICALS

Architectural Digest
Beaver County Times

Bridgeport Telegram
Carlisle Evening Herald
Central New Jersey Home News
Chicago Defender
Chicago Sun-Times
Chicago Tribune
Cleveland Plain Dealer
Daily Worker
Dearborn Independent
Evening Public Ledger
Field and Stream
The Guardian
Honolulu Advertiser
Jewish Chronicle of Pittsburgh
Jewish Criterion
Korea Times
Lewiston Daily Sun
Life
Logansport Pharos-Tribune
Los Angeles Times
Menorah
Neighbors
New Pittsburgh Courier
New York Daily News
New York Post
New York Sun
New York Times
New Yorker
News-Herald
Philadelphia Inquirer
Pittsburgh City Paper
Pittsburgh Commercial
Pittsburgh Courier
Pittsburgh Daily Post
Pittsburgh Dispatch
Pittsburgh Post
Pittsburgh Press
Pittsburgh Post-Gazette
Pittsburgh Quarterly
Pittsburgh Sun-Telegraph

BIBLIOGRAPHY

Pittsburgh Tribune-Review
Pittsburgh Weekly Gazette
Press-Enterprise
Reading Times
San Francisco Chronicle
Scribner's Magazine
Southern Workman
Spokane Chronicle
Spokesman Review
Sporting News
Sports Illustrated
Syracuse Herald American
Toledo Blade
USA Today
Valley News Dispatch
Washington Post
Wisconsin Jewish Chronicle
Your Carlynton

PRIMARY AND SECONDARY SOURCES

Abern, Martin. "Attack on the National Miners' Union Convention." In *James P. Cannon and the Early Years of American Communism: Selected Writings and Speeches, 1920–1928*. New York: Spartacist, 1992.

Abrams, Nathan. "Inhibited but Not 'Crowded Out': The Strange Fate of Soccer in the United States." *International Journal of the History of Sport* 12, no. 3 (December 1995): 1–17.

Adarand Constructors Inc. v. Peña, 515 U.S. 200 (1995).

Ahn, Ji-Hyun. "Rearticulating Black Mixed-Race in the Era of Globalization: Hines Ward and the Struggle for Koreanness in Contemporary South Korean Media." *Cultural Studies* 28, no. 3 (2014): 391–417.

Alexander, Trent J. "The Great Migration in Comparative Perspective: Interpreting the Urban Origins of Southern Black Migrants to Depression-Era Pittsburgh." *Social Science History* 22, no. 3 (Autumn 1998): 349–76.

"Aliens and Firearms," *Forest and Stream* 86, no. 23, June 10, 1911.

Allaway, Roger. *Rangers, Rovers and Spindles: Soccer, Immigration, and Textiles in New England and New Jersey*. Haworth, NJ: St. Johann Press, 2005.

Allaway, Roger, Colin Jose, and Dave Litterer, eds. *The Encyclopedia of American Soccer*. Lanham, MD: Scarecrow Press, 2001.

Allegheny County Sportsmen's League. Accessed December 12, 2011. http://www.acslpa.org/.

Almond, Steve. *Against Football: One Fan's Reluctant Manifesto*. Brooklyn: Melville House, 2014.

Alnutt, Brian. "The Negro Excursions: Recreational Outings among Philadelphia African Americans, 1876–1926." *Pennsylvania Magazine of History and Biography* 129, no. 1 (January 2005): 73–104.

Alpert, Rebecca T. *Out of Left Field: Jews and Black Baseball*. Oxford: Oxford University Press, 2011.

American Camping Association. *Camping: A Wartime Asset*. New York: Association Press, 1942.

American Camping Association. "Establishing Racial Good Will through Camping." ACA Workshop Report, April 1945. *Camping Magazine* 17–18 (1945–46): 1–8.

Anderson, Benedict. *Imagined Communities: Reflections on the Origin and Spread of Nationalism*. London: Verso, 1991.

Andrews, David L. "Excavating Michael Jordan's Blackness." In *Reading Sport: Critical Essays on Power and Representation*, edited by Susan Birrell and Mary G. McDonald, 166–205. Boston: Northeastern University Press, 2000.

Ashtulany, Evelyn. "Toward a Multiethnic Cartography: Multiethnic Identity, Monoracial Cultural Logic, and Popular Culture." In *Mixing it Up*, edited by SanSan Kwan and Kenneth Spiers, 141–62. Austin: University of Texas Press, 2004.

BBC. "I'm Sorry but No Regrets—Zidane." Accessed July 12, 2006. http://news.bbc.co.uk/sport2/hi/football/world_cup_2006/5169342.stm.

Beers, Paul B. *Pennsylvania Politics Today and Yesterday: The Tolerable Accommodation*. University Park: Pennsylvania State University Press, 1980.

Bieler, Stacey. *"Patriots or Traitors"? A History of American-Educated Chinese Students*. Armonk, NY: M. E. Sharpe, 2004.

Bland, James A. "In the Evening by the Moonlight." 1880.

Bodnar, John, Roger Simon, and Michael P. Weber. *Lives of Their Own: Blacks, Italians, and Poles in Pittsburgh, 1900–1960*. Urbana: University of Illinois Press, 1982.

Borish, Linda. "'Athletic Activities of Various Kinds': Physical Health and Sports Programs for Jewish American Women." *Journal of Sport History* 26, no. 2 (Summer 1999): 240–70.

Borish, Linda. "'The Cradle of American Champions, Women Champions . . . Swim Champions': Charlotte Epstein, Gender and Jewish Identity, and

the Physical Emancipation of Women in Aquatic Sports." *International Journal of the History of Sport* 21, no. 2 (March 2004): 197–235.
Borish, Linda. "Women, Sport, and American Jewish Identity in the Late Nineteenth and Early Twentieth Centuries." In *With God on Their Side: Sport and the Service of Religion*, edited by Tara Magdalinski and Timothy J. Chandler, 71–98. London: Routledge, 2002.
Boy Scouts of America. "Awards Central." Accessed July 2, 2022. https://www.scouting.org/outdoor-programs/conservation-and-environment/conservation-awards-and-recognitions/bsa-distinguished-conservation-service-award/.
Brignano, Mary, ed. *Boundless Lives: Italian Americans of Western Pennsylvania*. Pittsburgh: History Society of Western Pennsylvania, 1999.
Brink, LuAnn. "Asthma in Pittsburgh and Allegheny County, Current Information and Future Directions." Accessed February 12, 2021. https://www.heinz.org/UserFiles/File/AirWeBreatheConference/Brink.pdf.
Buni, Andrew. *Robert L. Vann of the Pittsburgh Courier: Politics and Black Journalism*. Pittsburgh, PA: University of Pittsburgh Press, 1974.
Bunk, Brian D. *From Football to Soccer: The Early History of the Beautiful Game in the United States*. Urbana: University of Illinois Press, 2021.
Burstin, Barbara S. *Steel City Jews: A History of Pittsburgh and its Jewish Community, 1840–1915*. Apollo, PA: Closson Press, 2008.
Burstyn, Varda. *The Rites of Men: Manhood, Politics and the Culture of Sport*. Toronto: University of Toronto Press, 1999.
Butera, Ronald J. "A Settlement House and the Urban Challenge: Kingsley House in Pittsburgh, 1893–1920." *Western Pennsylvania Historical Magazine* 66, no. 1 (January 1983): 25–47.
"Carry on Beadling." *Mount Lebanon Magazine* 15, no. 1. Accessed July 5, 2010. https://www.beadling.com.
Carter, Perry L. "Coloured Places and Pigmented Holidays: Racialized Leisure Travel." *Tourism Geographies* 10, no. 3 (August 2008): 265–84.
Casner, Nicholas. "Acid Mine Drainage and Pittsburgh's Water Quality." In *Devastation and Renewal: An Environmental History of Pittsburgh and Its Region*, edited by Joel A. Tarr, 89–109. Pittsburgh, PA: University of Pittsburgh Press, 2003.
Casner, Nicholas. "Angler Activist: Kenneth Reid, the Izaak Walton League and the Crusade for Federal Water Pollution Control." *Pennsylvania History* 66, no. 4 (Autumn 1999): 535–53.
Cavallo, Dominick. *Muscles and Morals: Organized Playgrounds and Urban*

Reform, 1880–1920. Philadelphia: University of Pennsylvania Press, 1981.
CBS News Pittsburgh. "Increase in Asian Population is Changing Region Culturally, Economically." Accessed February 12, 2018. https://www.cbsnews.com/pittsburgh/news/pittsburgh-asian-population-increase/.
Cecil, Jeanne Svitesic, ed. *Our Coal-Mining Community Heritage: Harmarville, PA*. Self-published, Homestead, PA, 2002.
Centers for Disease Control and Prevention (CDC). "Drowning Facts." Accessed February 8, 2021. http://www.cdc.gov/homeandrecreationalsafety/water-safety/waterinjuries-factsheet.html.
Chaffee, Zechariah Jr. "Company Towns in the Soft Coalfields." *Independent* 111, no. 3852 (1923): 102–4.
Chin, Gabriel J., and John Ormonde. "The War Against Chinese Restaurants." *Duke Law Journal* 67, no. 4 (January 2018): 681–741.
Cimino, Michael, director. *The Deer Hunter*. Universal Pictures, 1978.
Ciotola, Nicholas P. "Spignesi, Sinatra, and the Pittsburgh Steelers: Franco's Italian Army as an Expression of Ethnic Identity, 1972–1977." *Journal of Sport History* 27, no. 2 (Summer 2000): 270–89.
Cobb, Ty. *My Life in Baseball: The True Record*. Lincoln: University of Nebraska Press, 1993.
Collins, Timothy M., Edward K. Muller, and Joel A. Tarr. "Pittsburgh's Three Rivers: From Industrial Infrastructure to Environmental Asset." In *Rivers in History*, edited by Christof Mauch and Thomas Zeller, 41–62. Pittsburgh, PA: University of Pittsburgh Press, 2008.
Commission on Wartime Relocation and Internment of Civilians. *Personal Justice Denied*. Seattle: University of Washington Press, 1997.
Commonwealth ex rel. Woodruff v. American Baseball Club of Philadelphia, 290 Pa 136 (Pa. 1927).
Commonwealth v. Cosick, 44 Pa. Super. Ct. 109 (1925).
"Community Centers and Related Problems." *American City* 14 (April 1916): 407.
Conrad v. Pittsburgh, 421 Pa. 492 (Pa. 1966).
Couvares, Francis. *The Remaking of Pittsburgh: Class and Culture in an Industrializing City, 1877–1919*. Pittsburgh, PA: University of Pittsburgh Press, 1984.
Crocker, Ruth Hutchinson. *Social Work and Social Order: The Settlement Movement in Two Industrial Cities, 1889–1930*. Urbana: University of Illinois Press, 1992.
Crouch, Stanley. *One Shot Harris: The Photographs of Charles "Teenie" Harris*. New York: Harry N. Abrams, 2002.

BIBLIOGRAPHY

Crowley, Gregory J. *The Politics of Place: Contentious Urban Redevelopment in Pittsburgh*. Pittsburgh, PA: University of Pittsburgh Press, 2005.

Curitz, Michael, director. *Black Fury*. Warner Brothers, 1935.

Curry, Graham. "The Origins of Football Debate: Comments on Adrian Harvey's Historiography." *International Journal of the History of Sport* 31, no. 17 (November 2014): 2158–63.

Danielson, Michael. *Home Team: Professional Sports and the American Metropolis*. Princeton, NJ: Princeton University Press, 1997.

Darden, Joe. "The Effect of World War I on Black Occupational and Residential Segregation: The Case of Pittsburgh." *Journal of Black Studies* 18, no. 3 (March 1988): 297–312.

Deloria, Philip J. *Playing Indian*. New Haven, CT: Yale University Press, 1998.

Dickerson, Dennis C. *Out of the Crucible: Black Steelworkers in Western Pennsylvania, 1875–1980*. Albany: State University of New York Press, 1986.

Dietrich-Ward, Allen. *Beyond Rust: Metropolitan Pittsburgh and the Fate of Industrial America*. Pittsburgh, PA: University of Pittsburgh Press, 2017.

Dinerstein, Joel. "Backfield in Motion: The Transformation of the NFL by Black Culture." In *In the Game: Race, Identity, and Sports in the Twentieth Century*, edited by Amy Bass, 169–89. New York: Palgrave Macmillan, 2005.

Du Bois, W. E. B. "The Problem of Amusement." In *Du Bois on Religion*, edited by Phil Zuckerman, 19–28. Walnut Creek, CA: AltaMira Press, 2000.

Dubinsky, Irwin. *Reform in Trade Union Discrimination in the Construction Industry: Operation Dig and Its Legacy*. New York: Praeger, 1973.

Duda, Mark Damian. "Pennsylvania Sportsmen's Attitudes toward Global Warming." Responsive Management, 2006.

Duke, Benjamin. *The History of Modern Japanese Education: Constructing the National School System, 1872–1890*. New Brunswick, NJ: Rutgers University Press, 2009.

Eastman, Crystal, ed. *Work Accidents and the Law*. New York: Russell Sage Foundation, 1910.

Eisen, George. "Jewish History and Ideology of Modern Sport: Approaches and Interpretations." *Journal of Sport History* 25, no. 3 (Fall 1998): 482–531.

Eisen, George. "Jews and Sport: A Century of Retrospect." *Journal of Sport History* 26, no. 2 (Summer 1999): 225–39.

Eisen, George. "Sport, Recreation and Gender: Jewish Immigrant Women in Turn-of-the-Century America (1880–1920)." *Journal of Sport History* 18, no. 1 (Spring 1991): 1–24.

Eliezer, Rabbi Daniel, and Paul Kupperberg. *Jew-Jitsu: The Hebrew Hands of Fury*. New York: Citadel Press, 2008.

Epstein, Abraham. "The Negro Migrant." In Lubove, *Pittsburgh*, 60–65.

ESPN.com. "Cup Ratings in U.S. up 41 Percent." Accessed July 20, 2010. https://www.soccernet.espn.com.

Faires, Nora. "Immigrants and Industry: Peopling the 'Iron City.'" In *City at the Point: Essays on the Social History of Pittsburgh*, edited by Samuel P. Hays, 3–31. Pittsburgh, PA: University of Pittsburgh Press, 1989.

Feldman, Jacob S. *The Jewish Experience in Western Pennsylvania: A History, 1755-1945*. Pittsburgh: Historical Society of Western Pennsylvania, 1986.

Fine, Lisa M. "Rights of Men, Rites of Passage: Hunting and Masculinity at Reo Motors of Lansing, Michigan, 1945–1975." *Journal of Social History* 33, no. 4 (Summer 2000): 805–23.

Finkle, Lee. "Quotas or Integration: The NAACP versus the Pittsburgh *Courier* and the Committee on Participation of Negroes." *Journalism Quarterly* 52, no. 1 (1975): 76–84.

Finley, Cheryl, Laurence A. Glasco, and Joe W. Trotter. *Teenie Harris, Photographer: Image, Memory, History*. Pittsburgh, PA: University of Pittsburgh Press, 2011.

Foer, Franklin. *How Soccer Explains the World: An Unlikely Theory of Globalization*. New York: Harper, 2004.

Foner, Eric. *Forever Free: The Story of Emancipation and Reconstruction*. New York: Knopf, 2005.

Foster, Mark S. "In the Face of 'Jim Crow': Prosperous Blacks and Vacations, Travel and Outdoor Leisure, 1890–1945." *Journal of Negro History* 84, no. 2 (Spring 1999): 130–49.

Francis, Owen. "The Saga of Joe Magarac: Steelman." *Scribner's Magazine*, November 1931.

Franks, Joel S. "Asian American Baseball and Asian American Communities: The Early Twentieth Century on the Pacific Coast and Hawai'i." *Journal of the West* 53, no. 3 (Summer 2014): 51–59.

Franks, Joel S. *The Barnstorming Hawaiian Travelers: A Multiethnic Baseball Team Tours the Mainland, 1912-1916*. Jefferson, IA: McFarland, 2012.

Franks, Joel S. *From Honolulu to Brooklyn: Running the American Empire's Base Paths with Buck Lai and the Travelers from Hawai'i*. New Brunswick, NJ: Rutgers University Press, 2022.

Frommer, Harvey. *The Great American Soccer Book*. New York: Atheneum, 1980.

Galeano, Eduardo. *Soccer in Sun and Shadow*, translated by Mark Fried. London: Verso, 1998.

Gallico, Paul. *Farewell to Sport*. Lincoln: University of Nebraska Press, 2008.

Gans, Hebert J. "Symbolic Ethnicity: The Future of Ethnic Groups and Cultures in America." In *Theories of Ethnicity: A Classical Reader*, edited by Werner Sollors, 425–59. New York: New York University Press, 1996.

Gems, Gerald R. *Sport and the American Occupation of the Philippines: Bats, Balls, and Bayonets*. Lanham, MD: Lexington Books, 2016.

Gems, Gerald R. "Welfare Capitalism and Blue-Collar Sport: The Legacy of Labor Unrest." *Rethinking History* 5, no. 1 (2001): 43–58.

Gilley, Jennifer, and Stephen Burnett. "Deconstructing and Reconstructing Pittsburgh's Man of Steel: Reading Joe Magarac against the Context of the 20th-Century Steel Industry." *Journal of American Folklore* 11, no. 442 (Autumn 1998): 392–408.

Giltner, Scott E. *Hunting and Fishing in the New South: Black Labor and White Leisure after the Civil War*. Baltimore: Johns Hopkins University Press, 2008.

Goldblatt, David. *The Ball Is Round: A Global History of Soccer*. New York: Riverhead Books, 2006.

Goodman, Cary. "(Re)Creating Americans at the Educational Alliance." *Journal of Ethnic Studies* 6, no. 4 (Winter 1979): 1–28.

Gottlieb, Peter. "Black Miners and the 1925–28 Bituminous Coal Strike: The Colored Committee of Non-Union Miners, Montour Mine No. 1, Pittsburgh Coal Company." *Labor History* 28, no. 2 (1987): 233–41.

Gottlieb, Peter. *Making Their Own Way: Southern Blacks' Migration to Pittsburgh, 1916–30*. Urbana: University of Illinois Press, 1987.

Graves, Houston. Interview with author. September 20, 2011.

Grossman, Randy. Interview with author. December 31, 2008.

Gulick, Luther. "What the Red Triangle Stands For." *Association Men* 43, no. 10 (June 1918): 774, 809.

Gurock, Jeffrey. *Judaism's Encounter with American Sports*. Bloomington: Indiana University Press, 2005.

Gurung, Balaram. Interview with author. January 19, 2017.

Guthrie-Smith, Sayuri. *Transpacific Field of Dreams: How Baseball Linked the United States and Japan in Peace and War*. Chapel Hill: University of North Carolina Press, 2012.

Guttmann, Allen, and Lee Thompson. *Japanese Sports: A History*. Honolulu: University of Hawai'i Press, 2011.

Hardie, Frances C. *Fox Chapel: A History of an Area and Its People*. [N.p.]: Financial Press Corporation, 1987.
Hare, Geoff. *Football in France: A Cultural History*. Oxford: Berg, 2003.
Herman, Daniel Justin. *Hunting and the American Imagination*. Washington, DC: Smithsonian Institution Press, 2001.
Hinshaw, John. "The Job Strategies of Black Steelworkers in the 1960s and 1970s." *Pittsburgh History* 80, no. 2 (Summer 1997): 70–75.
Hinshaw, John. "Review Essay: Steel Communities and the Memories of Race." *Pennsylvania History* 60, no. 4 (October 1993): 517–18.
Hollinger, David A. *Postethnic America: Beyond Multiculturalism*. New York: Basic Books, 1995.
Hornaday, William T. *Camp-Fires in the Canadian Rockies*. New York: Charles Scribner's Sons, 1919.
Hornaday, William T. *Our Vanishing Wild Life: Its Extermination and Preservation*. New York: New York Zoological Society, 1913.
Horvitz, Peter S. *The Big Book of Jewish Sports Heroes: An Illustrated Compendium of Sports History and the 150 Greatest Jewish Sports Stars*. New York: SP Books, 2007.
"How to Tell Japs from the Chinese." *Life*, December 22, 1941.
Howard, Walter T. "The National Miners Union: Communists and Miners in the Pennsylvania Anthracite, 1928–1931." *Pennsylvania Magazine of History and Biography* 125, nos.1–2 (2001): 91–124.
Humes, Harry. *Robbing the Pillars*. Easthampton, MA: Adastra Press, 1984.
Institute for Diversity and Ethics in Sports. "The 2019 Racial and Gender Report Card: College Sport."
Institute for Diversity and Ethics in Sports. "The 2019 Racial and Gender Report Card: National Football League."
Jable, J. T. "Pennsylvania's Early Blue Laws: A Quaker Experiment in the Suppression of Sport and Amusements, 1682–1740." *Journal of Sport History* 1, no. 2 (November 1974): 107–21.
Jacobson, Matthew Frye. *Whiteness of a Different Color: European Immigrants and the Alchemy of Race*. Cambridge, MA: Harvard University Press, 1998.
Jenkins, Philip. *The Cold War at Home: The Red Scare in Pennsylvania, 1945–1960*. Chapel Hill: University of North Carolina Press, 1999.
Jenkins, Philip. *Hoods and Shirts: The Extreme Right in Pennsylvania, 1925–50*. Chapel Hill: University of North Carolina Press, 1997.
Jenkins, Philip. "The Ku Klux Klan in Pennsylvania, 1920–1940." *Western Pennsylvania Historical Magazine* 69, no. 2 (April 1986): 121–38.
Jerome, William, and Jean Schwartz. "Chinatown, My Chinatown." 1906.
Jun, Jong Woo, and Hyung Min Lee. "The Globalization of Sport and the

Mass-Mediated Identity of Hines Ward." *Journal of Sport Management* 26 (2012): 103–12.

Kalbfus, Joseph. "The Law of Pennsylvania Denying to Aliens the Right to Hunt or Shoot or Even to Be Possessed of a Shotgun or a Rifle in the Commonwealth." Sixth Biennial Meeting of the National Association of Game Wardens and Commissioners, Denver, Col. Boston: Wright and Potter Printing Co., 1913.

Kawashima, Kohei. "'We Will Try Again, Again to Make It Bigger': Japan, American Football, and the Super Bowl in the Past, Present, and Future." *International Journal of the History of Sport* 34, nos. 1–2 (2017): 121–38.

Kellogg, Paul U., ed. *The Pittsburgh District: Civic Frontage*. New York: Russell Sage Foundation, 1914.

Kellogg, Paul U., ed. *Wage-Earning Pittsburgh*. New York: Russell Sage Foundation, 1914.

Kevin Henry and Najeh Davenport v National Football League. Civil Action Complaint 20–4165, United States District Court for the Eastern District of Pennsylvania, 2020.

King, C. Richard, and Charles Fruehling Springwood. *Beyond the Cheers: Race as Spectacle in College Sport*. Albany: State University of New York Press, 2001.

Kissell, Rick. "World Cup Final Nets 26.5 Million Viewers in the U.S." *Variety*, July 14, 2014. Accessed June 10, 2018. https://variety.com.

Kleinberg, S. J. *The Shadow of the Mills: Working Class Families in Pittsburgh, 1870–1907*. Pittsburgh, PA: University of Pittsburgh Press, 1989.

Kosack, Joe. *The Pennsylvania Game Commission 1895–1995: 100 Years of Wildlife Conservation*. Harrisburg: Pennsylvania Game Commission, 1995.

Kovacevic, Ivan. "Who Murdered Joe Magarac?" *Folklore: Electronic Journal of Folklore* 59 (December 2014): 85–104.

Kraszewski, Jon. "Pittsburgh in Fort Worth: Football Bars, Sports Television, Sports Fandown, and the Management of Home." *Journal of Sport & Social Issues* 32, no. 2 (May 2008): 139–57.

Krausman, Paul, and Shane P. Mahoney. "How the Boone and Crockett Club Shaped North American Conservation." *International Journal of Environmental Studies* 72, no. 5 (October 2015): 746–55.

Kung, S. W. *Chinese in American Life*. Seattle: University of Washington Press, 1962.

Laderman, Scott. *Empire in Waves: A Political History of Surfing*. Berkeley: University of California Press, 2014.

Lamb, Chris. "'What's Wrong with Baseball': The Pittsburgh *Courier* and the Campaign to Integrate the National Pastime." *Western Journal of Black Studies* 26, no. 4 (Winter 2002): 189–92.

Lambert, Frank. "Reflections on the Pre-Renaissance Steelers." In Roberts, *Pittsburgh Sports*, 47–75.

LancasterOnline. "1 out of Every 10 Hunters in Pennsylvania Is Now Female." Accessed February 7, 2021. http://lancasteronline.com/news/local/out-of-every-hunters-in-pennsylvania-is-now-female/article_de6d94dc-ec95-11e6-94a7-f704a64386ae.html.

Lane, Jessica Marie. "Search for the American Dream Home: Race and Suburbanization in Post War Pennsylvania." Accessed January 10, 2012. http://www.phmc.state.pa.us/portal/communities/pa-suburbs/files/Discrimination_Paper_Lane.pdf .

Lasch-Quinn, Elisabeth. *Black Neighbors: Race and the Limits of Reform in the American Settlement House Movement, 1890–1945*. Chapel Hill: University of North Carolina Press, 1993.

Laws of General Assembly of the Commonwealth of Pennsylvania 1903.

Laws of General Assembly of the Commonwealth of Pennsylvania 1905.

Laws of General Assembly of the Commonwealth of Pennsylvania 1909.

Laws of General Assembly of the Commonwealth of Pennsylvania 1915.

Lee, Karam, and Jae-Pil Ha. "The Evolution and Symbolism of American Football in Korea." *Sport History Review* 48 (2017): 75–90.

Levine, Peter. *Ellis Island to Ebbets Field: Sport and the American Jewish Experience*. New York: Oxford University Press, 1992.

Light, Richard L. "Japan." In *Routledge Companion to Sports History*, edited by S. W. Pope and John Nauright, 472–86. London: Taylor and Francis, 2010.

Lindenburg, Sidney J., and Ruth Ellen Zittel. "The Settlement Scene Changes." *Social Forces* 14, no. 4 (May 1936): 559–66.

Litterer, David. "The History of Soccer in Pittsburgh." Accessed November 22, 2022. https://soccerhistoryusa.org/ASHA/pittsburgh.html.

Liu, Eric. *The Accidental Asian: Notes of a Native Speaker*. New York: Vintage, 1998.

Logan, Gabe. "C'mon, You Reds: The U.S. Communist Party's Workers' Soccer Association, 1927–35." *Journal of Sport History* 44, no. 3 (Fall 2017): 384–98.

Lubove, Roy, ed. *Pittsburgh*. New York: New Viewpoints, 1976.

Lucas, Roy. "From Patsone and Miller to Silveria v. Lockyer: To Keep and Bear Arms." *Thomas Jefferson Law Review* 26 (Spring 2004): 257–332.

Lui, Mary Ting Yi. *The Chinatown Trunk Mystery: Murder, Miscegenation, and Other Dangerous Encounters in Turn-of-The-Century New York City.* Princeton, NJ: Princeton University Press, 2005.

Luxbacher, Joe. Interview with author. July 30, 2010.

Magnusson, Leifer. "Employers' Housing in the United States." *Monthly Review of the U.S. Bureau of Labor Statistics* 5, no. 5 (November 1917): 35–60.

Mallinger, Alan. Interview with author. March 16, 2010.

Markovits, Andrei S. *Offside: Soccer and American Exceptionalism.* Princeton, NJ: Princeton University Press, 2011.

Marks, John. "The French National Team and National Identity: 'Cette France d'u "bleu mètis."'" In *France and the 1998 World Cup: The National Impact of a World Sporting Event*, edited by Hugh Dauncey and Geoff Hare, 41–57. London: Frank Cass, 1999.

Marshall, Ray F., and Vernon M. Briggs. *Negro Participation in Apprenticeship Programs.* Washington, DC: Office of Manpower Policy, Evaluation and Research, Manpower Administration, US Department of Labor, December 1963.

Martin, Derek. "Apartheid in the Great Outdoors: American Advertising in the Reproduction of a Racialized Outdoor Leisure Identity." *Journal of Leisure Research* 36, no. 4 (December 2004): 513–35.

Martin, Scott C. *Killing Time: Leisure and Culture in Southwestern Pennsylvania, 1800–1850.* Pittsburgh, PA: University of Pittsburgh Press, 1995.

McCallum, Jack. "See No Evil, Hear No Evil." *Sports Illustrated*, October 9, 2006.

McCart, Melissa. "America's Next Great Chinatown Takes Root in Pittsburgh." *Saveur*, October 21, 2015. https://www.saveur.com/how-pittsburgh-is-growing-americas-next-chinatown-chinese-restaurants/.

McCullough, David. *The Johnstown Flood.* New York: Simon and Schuster, 1968.

Megdal, Howard. *The Baseball Talmud: The Definitive Position-by-Position Ranking of Baseball's Chosen Players.* New York: Harper, 2009.

Mendelson, Abby. *The Pittsburgh Steelers: The Official Team History.* Dallas, TX: Taylor, 1996.

Mine Safety and Health Administration. "History of Mine Safety and Health Legislation." Accessed August 30, 2010. https://www.mhsa.gov.

Miner, Curtis. "Hardhat Hunters: The Democratization of Recreational Hunting in Twentieth Century Pennsylvania." *Journal of Sport History* 28, no. 1 (Spring 2001): 41–62.

Mishler, Paul C. *Raising Reds: The Young Pioneers, Radical Summer Camps, and Communist Culture in the United States*. New York: Columbia University Press, 1999.

Montrie, Chad. *Making a Living: Work and Environment in the United States*. Chapel Hill: University of North Carolina Press, 2008.

Mullan, Michael. "Ethnicity and Sport: The Wapato Nippons and Pre-World War II Japanese American Baseball." *Journal of Sport History* 26, no. 1 (Spring 1999): 82–114.

Mulrooney, Margaret. *A Legacy of Coal: The Coal Company Towns of Southwestern Pennsylvania*. Washington, DC: National Park Service, 1989.

National Council of Jewish Women. *My Voice Was Heard*. New York: KTVA, 1981.

National Rifle Association. Accessed December 13, 2011. http://www.nra huntersrights.org/Article.aspx?id=3156.

National Soccer Hall of Fame. "Raymond Bernabei." Accessed September 1, 2010. https://www.nationalsoccerhof.com/players/raymond-bernabei.html.

Newell, Nan, ed. *Portrait of an American Community O'Hara Township, PA*. Pittsburgh, PA: Township of O'Hara, 2008.

NFL Players' Association. "FAQs: NFL Hopefuls FAQ." Accessed March 9, 2007. https://www.nflpa.org.

Nomura, Gail. "Beyond a Level Playing Field: The Significance of Pre-World War II Japanese American Baseball in the Yakima Valley." In *Bearing Dreams, Shaping Visions: Asian Pacific American Perspectives*, edited by Linda Revilla, Gail Nomura, Shawn Wong, and Shirley Hune, 15–31. Pullman: Washington State University Press, 1993.

Nora, Pierre. *Realms of Memory: The Construction of the French Past, Vol. 1, Conflicts and Divisions*. New York: Columbia University Press, 1996.

Norwood, Stephen H. *Strikebreaking and Intimidation: Mercenaries and Masculinity in Twentieth-Century America*. Chapel Hill: University of North Carolina Press, 2001.

Novak, Michael. *The Rise of the Unmeltable Ethnics: Politics and Culture in the Seventies*. New York: Macmillan, 1972.

O'Brien, Jim. *Doing It Right: The Steelers of Three Rivers Stadium and Four Super Bowls Share Their Secrets for Success*. Pittsburgh, PA: Wolfson, 1991.

O'Neill, Brian. *The Paris of Appalachia: Pittsburgh in the Twenty-First Century*. Pittsburgh, PA: Carnegie Mellon Press, 2009.

Page Act of 1875, 18 Stat. 477, 43rd Congress, Sess. II, Chap. 14.

Palmer, Phyllis. "Recognizing Racial Privilege: White Girls and Boys at

BIBLIOGRAPHY

National Conference of Christians and Jews Summer Camps, 1957–1974." *Oral History Review* 27, no. 2 (Summer/Fall 2000): 129–55.
Panizzi, Tawnya. "Squaw Run Stream Renamed as Sycamore Run." *TribLive*, September 15, 2022. https://triblive.com/local/valley-news-dispatch/squaw-run-is-now-sycamore-run/.
Pardon the Interruption. ESPN, June 25, 2010.
Paris, Leslie. *Children's Nature: The Rise of the American Summer Camp*. New York: New York University Press, 2008.
Patrick, Kevin J. "Joe Magarac and the Spirit of Pittsburgh." In *Pittsburgh and the Appalachians: Cultural and Natural Resources in a Postindustrial Age*, edited by Joseph L. Scarpaci and Kevin J. Patrick, 53–63. Pittsburgh, PA: University of Pittsburgh Press, 2006.
Patsone v. Commonwealth of Pennsylvania, 232 U.S. 138.
Pennsylvania Fish and Boat Commission. "Pennsylvania Fishing License Sales Reports." Accessed December 21, 2011. https://www.fish.state.pa.us/licsales.htm.
Pennsylvania Fish and Boat Commission. "State Issues Updated Fish Consumption Advisories for 2011." Accessed January 11, 2012. https://www.fish.state.pa.us/newsreleases/2011press/consume_adv.htm.
Pennsylvania Game Commission. "Game Lands." Accessed July 2, 2022. https://www.pgc.pa.gov/hunttrap/stategamelands/Pages/default.aspx.
Pennsylvania Game Commission. "Hunting and License Sales." Accessed July 14, 2017. https://www.pgc.pa.gov/HuntTrap/LicensesandPermits/Pages/HuntingLicenseSalesReport.aspx.
Pennsylvania Historical and Museum Commission. "King Coal: Mining Bituminous." Accessed September 2, 2010. https://www.explorepahistory.com.
Pennsylvania State Reports for 1853.
Pew Research Center. "A Portrait of Jewish Americans." Accessed June 22, 2022. https://www.pewresearch.org/religion/2013/10/01/jewish-american-beliefs-attitudes-culture-survey.
Philpott, Thomas Lee. *The Slum and the Ghetto: Neighborhood Deterioration and Middle-Class Reform, Chicago, 1880–1930*. New York: Oxford University Press, 1978.
Pittsburgh Field Club. "Club History." Accessed August 8, 2011. https://pittsburgh.membersstatement.com/tour.
Pope, Steven W. "An Army of Athletes: Playing Fields, Battlefields, and the American Military Sporting Experience." *Journal of Military History* 59, no. 3 (1995): 435–56.
Postal, Bernard. *Encyclopedia of Jews in Sports*. New York: Bloch, 1965.

Pride, Armistead S., and Clint C. Wilson. *A History of the Black Press*. Washington, DC: Howard University Press, 1997.

Pro Football Hall of Fame. "Profile: Ray Kemp." Accessed March 2, 2007. https://www.profootballhof.com.

Reiger, John F. *American Sportsmen and the Origins of Conservation*. Corvallis: Oregon State University Press, 2000.

Responsive Management. "Women's, Hispanics', and African Americans' Participation in, and Attitudes toward, Boating and Fishing."

Rhoads, Edward J. M. "Asian Pioneers in the Eastern United States: Chinese Cutlery Workers in Beaver Falls, Pennsylvania, in the 1870s." *Journal of Asian American Studies* 2, no. 2 (June 1999): 119–55.

Rhoads, Edward J. M. "'White Labor' vs. 'Coolie Labor': The Chinese Question in Pennsylvania in the 1870s." *Journal of American Ethnic History* 21, no. 2 (Winter 2002): 3–32.

Rhoden, William C. *Third and a Mile: The Trials and Triumphs of the Black Quarterback*. New York: ESPN Books, 2007.

Richards, Elizabeth, and Charles Lee. "Bringing Children to Recreation." *Federator*, November 1943, 231–32.

Riesman, David, and Reuel Denney. "Football in America: A Study in Cultural Diffusion." *American Quarterly* 3, no. 4 (Winter 1951): 309–25.

Riess, Steven A. *Sport in Industrial America, 1850–1920*. Urbana: University of Illinois Press, 1989.

Roberts, Randy, ed. *Pittsburgh Sports: Stories from the Steel City*. Pittsburgh, PA: University of Pittsburgh Press, 2000.

Robinson, Jackie. *I Never Had It Made: An Autobiography of Jackie Robinson*. New York: Ecco, 1995.

Rode, Silvia. "Johann Georg Rapp." In *Immigrant Entrepreneurship: German-American Business Biographies, 1720 to the Present*, edited by Marianne Wokeck. German Historical Institute, Washington, DC. Accessed November 27, 2017. https://www.immigrantentrepreneurship.org/entries/johann-georg-rapp/.

Rodef Shalom Congregation. Accessed March 3, 2018. http://rodefshalom.org/about-rodef-shalom/history.

Rooney, Dan. *Dan Rooney: My 75 Years with the Pittsburgh Steelers and the NFL*. Cambridge, MA: Da Capo Press, 2007.

Rose, Donovan. "NFL Coaches Hired in the Last Decade: What the Data Says." *Cauldron*. Accessed February 12, 2021. https://the-cauldron.com/nfl-head-coaches-hired-during-the-last-ten-years-a-look-at-the-data-a41e2e68a1b6.

Ruck, Rob. "Art Rooney and the Pittsburgh Steelers." In Roberts, *Pittsburgh Sports*, 243–62.

Ruck, Rob. *Sandlot Seasons: Sport in Black Pittsburgh*. Urbana: University of Illinois Press, 1993.
Ruck, Rob, Maggie Jones Patterson, and Michael P. Weber. *Rooney: A Sporting Life*. Lincoln: University of Nebraska Press, 2010.
Sajna, Mike. *Buck Fever: The Deer Hunting Tradition in Western Pennsylvania*. Pittsburgh, PA: University of Pittsburgh Press, 1990.
Sajna, Mike. *Days on the Water*. Pittsburgh, PA: University of Pittsburgh Press, 1999.
Sales, Amy L., and Leonard Saxe. *"How Goodly Are Thy Tents": Summer Camps as Jewish Socializing Experiences*. Hanover, NH: Brandeis University Press, 2003.
Savran, Stan. Interview with author. January 12, 2017.
Schlesinger Petition to the Supreme Court of Pennsylvania, 367 Pa. 476.
Schwartz, Larry. "No Joshing about Gibson's Talent." Accessed, July 24, 2016. *ESPN.com*.
Science News. "1889 Pennsylvania Flood Was as Big as Mississippi River." October 21, 2009. http://www.wired.com/wiredscience/2009/10/1889-pennsylvania-flood-was-as-big-as-mississippi-river/.
Serotkin, Harry. "Experiments in Inter-Racial Camping." *Camping Magazine* 16, no. 5 (May 1944): 10–22.
Sewald, Jeff, director. *Gridiron and Steel*. Real as Steel Media Ventures LLC, 2001.
Seymour, Harold. *Baseball: The People's Game*. New York: Oxford University Press, 1990.
Sherman, Allan. "Hello Muddah, Hello Fadduh." Arista Records, 1963.
Shoemaker, Henry Wharton. *Pennsylvania Deer and Their Horns*. Reading, PA: Faust Printing, 1915.
"A Short History of the Millers of Sidman, PA." Accessed, July 2, 2011. https://webs.lanset.com/azazella/miller.html.
Slater, Robert. *Great Jews in Sports*. New York: Jonathan David, 2005.
Slavishak, Edward Steven. *Bodies of Work: Civic Display and Labor in Industrial Pittsburgh*. Durham, NC: Duke University Press, 2008.
Smalley, Andrea L. "'I Just Like to Kill Things': Women, Men and the Gender of Sport Hunting in the United States, 1940–1973." *Gender and History* 17, no. 1 (April 2005): 183–209.
Smith, Scott, and Steve Manaker. "Pittsburgh's African American Neighborhoods, 1900–1920." *Pittsburgh History* 78, no. 4 (Winter 1995/96): 159–62.
Steelers.com. "Tomlin Will Bring a Blue-Collar Approach to Coaching Steelers." Accessed January 24, 2007. steelers.com.

Steelers.com. "What Do You Think of Tomlin?" Accessed January 24, 2007. www.steelerslive.com.

Stern, Gerald. *What I Can't Bear Losing: Notes from a Life*. New York: W. W. Norton, 2004.

Stevens, John D. "The Black Press and the 1936 Olympics." *American Journalism* 14, no. 1 (Winter 1997): 97–103.

Stewart, Kordell. "'You Know What I Heard about Kordell Stewart???'" Accessed February 11, 2021. https://www.theplayerstribune.com/posts/kordell-stewart-nfl-football-pittsburgh-steelers.

Stuart, Paul H. "The Kingsley House Extension Program: Racial Segregation in a 1940s Settlement Program." *Social Service Review* 66, no.1 (March 1992): 112–20.

Tarr, Joel A., and Terry F. Yosie. "Critical Decisions in Pittsburgh Water and Wastewater Treatment." In *Devastation and Renewal: An Environmental History of Pittsburgh and Its Region*, edited by Joel A. Tarr, 64–88. Pittsburgh, PA: University of Pittsburgh Press, 2003.

Thangaraj, Stanley I., Constancio R. Arnaldo Jr., and Christina B. Chin, eds. *Asian American Sporting Cultures*. New York: New York University Press, 2016.

Thiessen, Marc. "Soccer Is a Socialist Sport." *American Enterprise Institute*. June 30, 2010. Accessed July 7, 2010. https://www.aei.org/society-and-culture/soccer-is-a-socialist-sport/ .

Thomas, Clarke. *They Came to . . . Pittsburgh*. Pittsburgh, PA: Pittsburgh Post-Gazette, 1983.

Timsina, Diwas. Interview with author. January 21, 2017.

TribLive. "Foreign Influx in Allegheny County at 'Tipping Point.'" *TribLive*. Accessed August 8, 2015. https://archive.triblive.com/local/pittsburgh-allegheny/foreign-influx-in-allegheny-county-at-tipping-point/.

TribLive. "Minorities Scarce among Outdoor Media." May 16, 2010. https://archive.triblive.com/local/local-news/minorities-scarce-among-outdoor-media/.

Trolander, Judith Ann. *Professionalism and Social Change: From the Settlement House Movement to Neighborhood Centers, 1886 to the Present*. New York: Columbia University Press, 1987.

Trotter, Joe W., and Jared N. Day. *Race and Renaissance: African Americans in Pittsburgh since World War II*. Pittsburgh, PA: University of Pittsburgh Press, 2010.

Tuttle, Cliff. "Christopher Columbus' American Lawyer: Michael A. Musmanno and the Vinland Map." *Pittsburgh History* 77, no. 3 (Fall 1994): 130–42.

"2 Charged with Poaching Deer at Rolling Rock Club." Accessed July 5, 2011. http://www.thepittsburghchannel.com/News/433281/detail.html.

"Uncle David's Filosofy." *Field and Stream*, March 1904, 988.

United States District Court for the Eastern District of Pennsylvania.

United States v. Wong Kim Ark, 169 U.S. 649 (1898).

University of Pittsburgh School of Social Work, Center on Race and Society Problems. "Pittsburgh's Racial Demographics 2015: Differences and Disparities."

"Unkel David's Letter." *Field and Stream*, January 1911, 893.

U.S. Department of the Interior, U.S. Fish and Wildlife Service, and U.S. Department of Commerce, U.S. Census Bureau. *2011 National Survey of Fishing, Hunting, and Wildlife-Associated Recreation, Pennsylvania.*

U.S. Department of the Interior, U.S. Fish and Wildlife Service, and U.S. Department of Commerce, U.S. Census Bureau. *2016 National Survey of Fishing, Hunting, and Wildlife-Associated Recreation, Pennsylvania.*

U.S. Department of the Interior, U.S. Fish and Wildlife Service. *Participation and Expenditure Patterns of African-American, Hispanic, and Women Hunters and Anglers: Addendum to the 1996 National Survey of Fishing, Hunting and Wildlife-Associated Recreation.*

Valletta, Clement. "'To Battle for Our Ideas': Community Ethic and Anthracite Labor, 1920–1940." *Pennsylvania History* 58, no. 4 (October 1991): 311–29.

Varley, Teresa. "Tomlin Takes Over." Steelers.com. Accessed January 24, 2007. https://news.steelers.com/article/73537/.

Vento, Al Sr., and Al Vento Jr. interview with Nicholas Ciotola, January 25, 1999.

Verbrugge, Martha H. "Recreation and Racial Politics in the Young Women's Christian Association of the United States, 1920–1950s." *International Journal of the History of Sport* 27, no. 7 (May 2010): 1191–218.

Waddington, Ivan, and Martin Roderick. "American Exceptionalism and American Football." *Sports Historian* 16, no. 1 (1996): 42–63.

Walker, Isiah Helekunihi. *Waves of Resistance: Surfing and History in Twentieth-Century Hawai'i.* Honolulu: University of Hawai'i Press, 2011.

Wang, Joan S. "Race, Gender, and Laundry Work: The Role of Chinese Laundrymen and American Women in the United States, 1850–1950." *Journal of American Ethnic History* 24, no. 1 (Fall 2004): 58–99.

Warren, Louis S. *The Hunter's Game: Poachers and Conservationists in Twentieth-Century America.* New Haven, CT: Yale University Press, 1997.

Waters, Mary. "The Costs of a Costless Community." In *New Tribalisms:*

The Resurgence of Race and Ethnicity, edited by Michael W. Hughey, 273–95. New York: New York University Press, 1998.

Westmoreland Museum of American Art. *Spirit of a Community: The Photographs of Charles "Teenie" Harris, An Exhibition*. Greensburg, PA: Westmoreland Museum of Art, 2001.

Whitman, Walt. "A Voice from Death." Yale Collection of American Literature, Beinecke Rare Book and Manuscript Library. Accessed December 9, 2011. http://www.whitmanarchive.org/manuscripts/transcriptions/yal.00060.html.

Whitsitt, Sam. "The Game America Refuses to Play." *Raritan: A Quarterly Review* 14, no. 1 (Summer 1994): 58–69.

Wideman, John Edgar. *Brothers and Keepers*. New York: Vintage Books, 1984.

Wideman, John Edgar. *God's Gym*. Boston: Houghton Mifflin, 2005.

Wideman, John Edgar. "Hunters." In Wideman, *God's Gym*, 17–26.

Wilson, August. *Fences*. New York: Theatre Communications Group, 2007.

Wiltse, Jeff. *Contested Waters: A Social History of Swimming Pools in America*. Chapel Hill: University of North Carolina Press, 2007.

Winston Holland, Jearold. *Black Recreation: A Historical Perspective*. Chicago: Burnham, 2002.

Wright, James. *Above the River: The Complete Poems*. New York: Farrar, Straus and Giroux, 1990.

Wu, Chien-shiung. "The Chinese in Pittsburgh: A Changing Minority Community in the United States." PhD diss., University of Pittsburgh, 1982.

Young, Terrence. "'A Contradiction in Democratic Government': W. J. Trent, Jr., and the Struggle to Desegregate National Park Campgrounds." *Environmental History* 14, no. 4 (October 2009): 651–82.

Zbiek, Paul J. "Coal, Steel, and Gridiron: High School Football in the Pittsburgh Area." In Roberts, *Pittsburgh Sports*, 214–42.

INDEX

Note: References in *italics* refer to figures and tables.

AAU. *See* Amateur Athletic Union
Abrams, Nathan, 69
ACA. *See* American Camping Association
Act 136 of Pennsylvania, 88–89
Adamson, D. C., 68
AFL. *See* American Federation of Labor
African Americans, 137–39, 231n127; employment discrimination in steel mills, 194–96; hiring for Pittsburgh Steelers, 186–87; literary production, 140–41; potentials in baseball game, 141–43; racial identities in sports, 196–99
African Americans in hunting and fishing, 97, 233n176; causes water pollution, 104–5; criminal behavior, 100–102; hunters in Hill District, *103*; paucity of Black participants in outdoor recreation, 94–95, 99–100; racism in print media, 105–10; social violence against, 110–12; sportsmen's clubs, 102–4. *See also* fishing and hunting in Penn's Woods
Ah Chuck, 8
Akana, Lang, 23–24
Albert, Nathan, 161–62
Allegheny Conference on Community Development, 184
Allegheny County Sportsmen's League, 102
Allegheny River, 72–74, 87, 104
Allen, Wellington, 97
Almond, Steve, 189
Amateur Athletic Union (AAU), 56, 128
American Bridge Company, 9
American Camping Association (ACA), 147–48

American Civil Liberties Union, 57
American Federation of Labor (AFL), 9
American Service Institute (ASI), 27, 148–51, 159
Anderson, Dave, 176
Anderson, Gary, 177
Andrews, David L., 197–98
Anna B. Heldman Center, 156
Anti-Coolie Labor Association groups, 7
Argonaut Club, 75, 78, 101
Armstrong, Louis, 16
ASI. *See* American Service Institute

Barkoski, John, 56–57
Barrett, John, 47
baseball in Pittsburgh, 19, 20, 167; Chinese baseball team, 18–20; Chinese Hawaiian baseball team, 21–25; Japanese baseball team, 20–21; Jewish communities influence on, 143–44; potentials of African Americans in, 140–43
basketball playing of IKS, 127–29; Jewish basketball clubs, 129–31; writings about Jewish identity and sports, 131–32
Beadling Club, 41, 42, 49, 51–52, 59. *See also* soccer in Pittsburgh
Beaver Falls Cutlery Company, 6–8
Beckenbauer, Franz, 43, 61
Benedict, Bertram, 127, 132
Benga, Ota, 107–9
Benswanger, William, 142
Bergman, Ray, 72
Bernabei, Ray, 54, 60, 61, 64, 69
Bettis, Jerome, 187
Bezdek, Hugo, 24

265

Black Construction Coalition, 199
"Black Headed Bill," 96
Bleier, Rocky, 190
Blount, Mel, 185, 186
Boone and Crocket Club, 81–82
Boone, Daniel, 80, 95
Boulware, J. H., 98
Boxer Indemnity Scholarship Program, 19
Braddock, Pennsylvania, 174–75
Bradshaw, Terry, 186
Brainin, Joseph, 130, 132
Brashear Association, 150
Bridger, Jim, 95
Broadway Joe. *See* Namath, Joe
Brooklyn Hakoah, 135
Bruce, Aubrey, 213–14
Bruegel, Pieter, 113
Bucktails Hunting and Fishing Club, 102, 103
Bunk, Brian, 47
Burleigh, R. Stanley, 44, 45
Burns, H. B., 45
Byrne, Stephen, 207

Caldwell, Mike, 192
Caliguiri, Richard, 18
Caminetti, Anthony, 25
Camp-Fires in the Canadian Rockies (Hornaday), 79
Camp Claudine Virginia Trees, 150, 152
Camp Emma, 27, 139–40, 158–59
Camp Fire Girls club, 124
Camping a Wartime Asset, 147–48
Camp James Weldon Johnson, 27, 145, 146, 158; ACA, 147–48; funding from Community Chest, 145, 146; issue of recruiting white staff, 149–50; permission for white children participation, 148; radical politics and racial plurality, 147
Camp Kon-O-Kwee, 148; issue of Black representation, 149; racial issues, 148–49
Camp Laurel, 158–59
Camp Redwing, 148, 150; racial tolerance promotion, 151–52

Carnegie, Andrew, 17, 58, 75, 78–79
Carnegie Library, stone façade of, 169
Carson, Rachel, 18, 104, 105
Carver, George Washington, 145
Carver House, 150
Castle Shannon (soccer team), 49
Chaffee, Zechariah, 53
Chinatown, Pittsburgh, 5–6, 16–17; absence of Chinese women, 26–28; card games in, 18; demolition of, 17–18; Downtown Project, 28–30; gambling houses, 18; history of Asians in, 4–5
Chinese-American Merchants' Association, 12
Chinese communities in Pittsburgh: Chinese Educational Mission, 19; Chinese Hawaiian baseball team, 21–25, 23; Chinese restaurants, 11–13; cross-cultural exchange of, 18–20; racial segregation, 8–10
Chinese Home Finished Laundry Company, 10
Chinese labors: Anti-Coolie Labor Association groups against, 7; issues in Beaver Falls, 6–8; women participation, 26–27
Chinese laundries in Pittsburgh, 8–9, 10; anti-Chinese activism, 9–10; decline of, 17–18; Geary Act, 11, 13; white women's participation in, 9
Chung, Mon, 25
Civil Rights Act (1964), 199
CJW. *See* Council of Jewish Women
Clairton Steelworks, 42
Clark, John T., 100
Coal and Iron Police, 54–58, 81, 90, 147
Cobb, Ty, 44
Coffey Club, 129
Coffey, John D., 129
Cohen, Armand E., 136
Collum, Robert, 32
Columbian Council School, 120–21
Committee of Inquiry on Coal and Civil Liberties, 53
Community Chest, 156
Conklin, J. E., 91

Conrad, Robert, 215, 216
Cope, Myron, 64, 178, 180, 181, *191*
Cosick, George, 89
Cossacks, 54, 55, 69
Coughlin, Charles, 131
Council of Jewish Women (CJW), 119–20, 121
Couvares, Francis, 41
Cowher, Bill, 186, 211
Craddock, Bob, 59–60
Crockett, Davy, 95
Crosby, Bing, 16
cross-cultural exchange of United States in sports, 18–25
Cvetic, Matt, 162

Dallas, Frank, 70
Danzilli, John, Jr., 183–84
Davenport, Najeh, 189
David, Ralph, 48
Dawson, Len, 176, 177
Deltier Club, 114
Dewar, Thomas, 42
DiOrio, Nick, 60
Ditka, "Iron" Mike, 171, 172
Djorkaeff, Youri, 36
Dobre Shunka fan club, 180–81
Donelli, Aldo "Buff," 48
Donora Steelworks, 42
Dorie Rod and Gun Club, 103
Douglass, Herb, 155
Dreyfuss, Barney, 21, 141–42
Du Bois, W. E. B., 98–99, 101, 109
Dungy, Tony, 191–92, 198, 211–12
Duquesne Lafayettes, 131

Ederle, Gertrude (Trudy), 133
Edgar Thomson Steel Works in Braddock, 174
Educational Alliance in New York, 122–23
Edwards, Herman, 192
Eisen, George, 132
Elling, Max, 131
Emma Farm Association, 139–40, 158
Emma Kaufmann Camp, 158

England, 47; right to hunt in, 83; soccer game in, 39–40
Enoch Rauh Club, 129
Epstein, Charlotte, 133
ESPN, 63, 64, 166, 202, 204

Fairfield, Harry, 48, 59, 64
Fairley, George E. A., 31
Federal Coal Mine Safety Act, 51
Federation of Jewish Philanthropies (FJP), 156
Field and Stream magazine, 106–7
Fisher, Claude, 97, 104
fishing and hunting in Pennsylvania, 74–75, 86; Argonaut Club, 75, 78, 101; as cultural practice, 87–88; fishing clubs, 75–76; grizzly bear hunting in United States, 79–80; hunting rights, 82–83; issues with poachers, 84–85; Johnstown Flood impact, 76–77, *76*; Lewis and Clark Club of Pittsburgh, 80–81; licenses for, 92–94; role of Game Commission, 81–82; slaughter of innocents, 88–92; social violence against African Americans, 110–12; South Fork Fishing and Hunting Club, 75, 77–78, 85–86, 91, 101; wildlife protection activities, 83–84; women hunters and anglers, 112–16, *115*. *See also* African Americans in hunting and fishing
FJP. *See* Federation of Jewish Philanthropies
Flores, Tom, 191
Flying Dutchman. *See* Wagner, Honus
Foer, Franklin, 38
football in Pittsburgh: as asylum for immigrant laborers, 171–72; development along with industrial society, 169; formalization of rules, 170; link with degenerative brain disease, 189. *See also* Pittsburgh Steelers
Ford, Henry, 144
Forest and Stream magazine, 91, 106
Fort Pitt Bridge, Pittsburgh, 118

Foster, Stephen, 151
Francis, Owen, 167–68, 171
Frick, Henry Clay, 75
Fujikawa, Fresa, 14

Gaetjens, Joe, 60
Galeano, Eduardo, 46
Gallico, Paul, 131
Gammage, Jonny, 200–201
Geary Act, 11, 13
Gefsky, Meyer, 29
Gems, Gerald, 19
Gibson, Josh, 141, 144
Gilliam, Joe, 186, 198, 211
Girl Scouts, 29, 147, 148
Gordon, James H., 107–8
Gottlieb, Peter, 100
Grant, Madison, 108
Great Steel Strike (1919), 171
Greenberg, Hank, 143
Greene, Joe, 179, 182, 186, 190, 211
Greenlee Field, 184
Greenlee, Gus, 141
Grimm, Russ, 166, 211
Grivnow, Steve, 60
Grossman, Julia, 132
Grossman, Randy, 180–81
Grove, David, 92
Guest, Edgar, 105–6
Gulick, Luther, 15, 124, 126
Gurock, Jeffrey, 136
Guthrie-Shimizu, Sayuri, 20

Ham, Jack, 180, 182
Hare, Geoff, 35
Harleston, Edwin, 96
Harmarville Hurricanes, 41, 49, 51–52, 59–61, *62*, 68–69, 87; second US Open Cup, 63; sponsorship from coal companies, 50, 58–59. *See also* soccer in Pittsburgh
Harmonie (Harmony) Society, 5, 7
Harris, Franco, 182–84, *191*, 199, 209, 211
Harris, Teenie, 113
HBCUs. *See* historically Black colleges and universities
Hebrew Hammer. *See* Greenberg, Hank

Heidelberg (team), 48, 49
Heinz, H. J., III, 31
Henry Kaufmann Foundation, 156
Henry, Kevin, 189
Henry, Thierry, 36
Herman, Daniel, 78
Heusinkveld, Evan, 93
Highland Park Bridge, Pittsburgh, 118, 161–63
Hinshaw, John, 196
historically Black colleges and universities (HBCUs), 184–85
Hitchcock, Edward "Doc," 15, 122
H. J. Heinz Company, 96
Holmes, Ernie, 181, 185
Holmes, Oliver Wendell, 90–91
Homestead Grays, 41, 141–42, 177
Homestead Rebellion, 171
Homestead Steel Works, 170
Hornaday, William, 79, 83–84, 88, 91, 104, 107–9
Horne, Durbin, 75
Houk, Seeley, 88
How Soccer Explains the World (Foer), 38
The Hunters in the Snow (painting by Bruegel), 113
hunting. *See* fishing and hunting in Pennsylvania

IKS House. *See* Irene Kaufmann Settlement House
intermarriage in Judaism, 3–4
Irene Kaufmann Settlement House (IKS House), 121, 137–39, 144; African Americans in, potentials of, 140–43; Anna B. Heldman Center, 156; basketball playing, 127–29; Camp Emma, 139–40; camping services, 144–52, 157–61; Centre Avenue site, new board for, 156–57; Highland Park, 161–63; integration process, 153–55; intergroup programming, 157–61; Jewish basketball clubs, 129–31; Jewish girls, 119–21, 132–37; legislation for practicing religious beliefs, 152–53; playground and gym recreation, 121–26; Squirrel Hill

extension, 155–56; writings about Jewish identity and sports, 131–32
Iso, Ariko, 208

James Weldon Johnson Camp Association, 145
Japanese migration to Pittsburgh, 14; educational system, 15–16; industrial development, 14–15
JCC. *See* Jewish Community Center
Jewish communities: Highland Park, 161–63; influence on sports in Pittsburgh, 143–44; Jewish basketball clubs, 129–31; Jewish girls, 119–21; women participation in sports, 132–37; writings about Jewish identity and sports, 131–32
Jewish Community Center (JCC), 4, 157
Jewish Criterion, 120, 129–30, 133, 135
Jewish Welfare Board (JWB), 157–58
Joel, George, 129–30, 132
Joe the Genie of Steel (comic book), 171
Johns, Harold, 113
Johnson, Jack, 23–24
Johnstown Flood (1889), 76, 76–77
Johnstown Tribune, 43
Jolson, Al, 16
Jordan, Jimmy, 64
Jordan, Michael, 197–98
Jung-Hwan, Ahn, 206
Jutsugyono-Nippon (Industrial Japan), 15
JWB. *See* Jewish Welfare Board

Kahn, Ziggy, 129, 130, 154–55, 181
Kalbfus, Joseph, 86, 107; Act 136, defending, 89; views on Black people hunting, 94–96; views on cultural hunting and fishing practices, 87–88
Kassam, Karim, 208
Kau, Apau, 24
Kaufmann, Henry, 119, 122, 156
Kaufmann, Isaac, 139
Kaufmann, Morris, 119, 139
Kaufmann's Department Store, 119
Kemp, Jack, 38–39, 169, 176
Kemp, Ray, 184
Kennard, Beulah, 124–25

Kennedy, Michael, 45
Kennedy, Stetson, 112
Kennywood Park, 161
Keystone League, 48
Kimura, George, 31
Kingsolving, Arthur, 32
Knights of Labor, 9, 10
Kopa, Raymond, 36
Kopaszewski, Raymond. *See* Kopa, Raymond
Kornheiser, Tony, 44–45
Kwan, Michelle, 207

Ladies Professional Golf Association (LPGA), 203
Lambert, Jack, 177, 188
Lee, Ah Jing, 33
Lee, Alvin, 25
Lee, Charles, 27, 29
Lee, Kin, 13
Lee, To, 13
Leland, George, 15
Le Pen, Jean-Marie, 36
Lewis, Marvin, 192
Lindenburg, Sidney, 138, 158
Lin, Jeremy, 205
Lipinski, Tara, 207
Litterer, Dave, 41
Liu, Eric, 4
Lloyd, Greg, 209
Loendi Club, 113
Long, Terry, 189, 209
Loving v. Virginia decision, 26
LPGA. *See* Ladies Professional Golf Association
Luxbacher, Joe, 38
Lynch, Wister I., 145
Lyster, Walter, 57

Madden, John, 202
Madden, Mark, 63
Magarac, Joe, 167, 170; Francis' narration of tale of, 168, 171; promotion stories of, 171–72; statue in Braddock, *172*, 173; Vittor's clay model of, 168
Magee, William A., 12
Major League Baseball (MLB), 141–43

Major League Soccer, 38, 63
Makélélé, Claude, 36
Making Their Own Way (Gottlieb), 100
Malinowski, Don "Pug," 60, 61, 69
Mansfield, William D., 57
Marasco, Anthony, 92
Markovits, Andrei, 40
Masloff, Sophie, 129
Mazeroski, Bill, 167
McClellan, George B., 109
McCredie, Walter, 3
McCullough, David, 75, 86
Mellon, Andrew, 14, 75
Mellon, Richard King, 184
Mellon, William Larimer, 14
Meloni, Dave, 66
Mennonites Society, 5
Menorah newspaper, 123
Meredith, William, 70
Merovich, Peter, 45–46, 58
Miners League. *See Press* League
MLB. *See* Major League Baseball
Mojack, Johnny, 59, 87
Monongahela River, 32, 73–74
Mordecai, Zipporah, 119
Morgan (team), 49
Morgan Community Center, 140
Morrison, Bill, 42
Musmanno, Michael, 56–57, 152, 162, 182, 215
Mussolini, Benito, 48

NAACP. *See* National Association for Advancement of Colored People
Naibu, Kanda, 14
Naismith, James, 124, 137
Namath, Joe, 5
Nantes, FC, (French soccer team) 37
National Association for Advancement of Colored People (NAACP), 145, 161–62
National Basketball Association (NBA), 38
National Federation of Settlements, 121, 144
National Football League (NFL), 38, 166, 213

National Miners Union (NMU), 55–56
National Park Service (NPS), 95, 147
National Rifle Association (NRA), 93, 103–4
National Tube, 42
NBA. *See* National Basketball Association
Negro History Contest, 145
Neighbors, 128, 129, 138
New Pittsburgh Courier, 113, 192, 213–14
New York Hakoah, 135
NFL. *See* National Football League
Nikkei communities, 30
Nisei, 16, 32
NMU. *See* National Miners Union
Noll, Chuck, 177, 180, 186, 211
Norboe, Mack, 83
North American Soccer League, 38
North, Lila Ver Planck, 125
Novak, Michael, 179, 197
Nozaki, Masao, 32
NPS. *See* National Park Service
NRA. *See* National Rifle Association
Nunn, Bill, Jr., 185–86
Nunn, Bill, Sr., 141

Ohno, Apolo, 206
Okabe, Heita, 16
Ökonomie (Economy) Society, 5
O'Neill, Bill, 35
"One Nation, One People" policy in Bhutan, 209
Organizing Committee against Community Exploitation, 156
"Orientals," 17, 22, 25
Our Vanishing Wildlife: Its Extermination and Preservation (Hornaday), 83, 107
Owens, Jesse, 214
Owens, Terrell, 207

Pacific Coast League (PCL), 23
Page Act (1875), 26
Paige, Satchel, 141
Palmer, Phyllis, 159–60
Palmer, Rich, 92

INDEX

The Passing of the Great Race (Grant), 108
Patsone, Joseph, 90–91
Patton, Robert, 45
PCL. *See* Pacific Coast League
Peacock, A. R., 120
Peduto, Bill, 208
Penn, Margaret, 74
Pennsylvania Deer and Their Horns (Shoemaker), 85
Pennsylvania Game and Fish and Boat Commissions, 95
Pennsylvania Game Commission, 79, 82, 110, 115
Pennsylvania Outdoor Writers Association, 95
Pennsylvania State Sportsmen's Association, 103
Pennsylvania Turnpike, 49, 96, 116
Penn, William, 82–83, 152
Perry, Lowell, 186, 191
Pettey, Walter, 97, 101, 104–5, 109
Philadelphia Spartans, 67–68
Phillips, Harriet, 150
Phillips, John M., 79–80, 139; Boone and Crocket Club, 81–82; Lewis and Clark Club of Pittsburgh, 80–81
Phipps, Henry, Jr., 75
Pinchot, Gifford, 54, 57, 81, 152
Pittsburgh Celtic team, 67
Pittsburgh Courier newspaper, 96–97; article about racism against Black people, 109; article about Teller's experience with IKS, 140; criminal behavior, report about African American's, 100–102; devoting space to outdoor sports, 98; and paucity of African Americans in hunting and fishing, 97–99; sportsmen's clubs, 102–4; about women hunters and anglers, 112–16
Pittsburgh Crawfords, 141, 184
Pittsburgh Cricket Association, 209
Pittsburgh Daily Post: article about impact of Chinese laundries, 9; report about Chinese laborers in Pittsburgh, 6–7; report on "picturesque" Chinatown demolition, 17
Pittsburgh Dispatch, 43–44
Pittsburgh Field Club, 72–73
Pittsburgh Penguins, 37, 214
Pittsburgh Pirates, 21, 44, 140, 142–43, 164, 167
Pittsburgh Post-Gazette: report about Chinese laundries, 18; support of soccer, 64–65
Pittsburgh Press: report about playing soccer during World War I, 46–47; report about soccer growth in western Pennsylvania, 47–48; report on decline of Chinese laundries, 17; soccer promotion in 1900s, 43–44; support for soccer, 64–65
Pittsburgh Riverhounds, 63
Pittsburgh Steelers, 3, 5, 48, 166–67, 175, 179–80, 208; Bill Cowher's role, 186–87; Bill Nunn's role, 185–86; bonding between white and Black players, 192; cultural anxiety about white ethnic identity, 181–82; evolution of hypocycloids symbol, 178–79; forgetting Black past, 192–99; Franco Harris' role, 182–84, 192, 199; Hines Ward's role, 202–7; influence of Rooney family, 176–78, 190; Jack Ham's role, 180, 182; Jerome Bettis's role, 187; Joe Greene's role, 179; Mike Tomlin's role, 210–12, 214; Mike Webster's role, 188–89; player's salary, 187–88; Rooney Rule, 212–13; Super Bowl media, 191–92; Three Rivers Stadium, 199–202, 214. *See also* football in Pittsburgh
Pittsburgh Survey, 8, 124, 125
Pittsburgh, United States, 166; Asian migrants in, 210; Chinese migration in, 5–8; with Civic Arena and Rivers Stadium Construction, *185;* migrants in professional sports, 207–9
Platini, Michel, 35
Posey, Cumberland, 142, 177
Prattis, P. L., 31
Press League, 48, 51

Prima, Louis, 16
Professional Club of Western Pennsylvania and West Virginia, 98
Prucnal, John, 59

Quong, Da, 10

Racing Club de Lens, 37
Rangers and Rovers, 42–43
Rapp, Johann Georg, 5, 7
Raritan (Whitsitt), 39
Reese, W. L., 11–12
Reeves, Henry, 6
Reeves, John, 6
Reid, Mary, 112
Resavage, George, 61, 63, 69, 171
Responsive Management, 111–12
Richard King, C., 196–97
Rickey, Branch, 142, 143
Robinson, Jackie, 142–43, 201
Robinson, James, 199–200
Robson, Jack, 45, 48
Robson, John, 51
Rocheteau, Dominique, 35
Rodef Shalom, 119–20
Rogers, Fred, 137
Rome, Jim, 44
Rooney, Art, 67, 176–77, 184, 186, 190, 191
Rooney, Dan, 177, 190, 212
Rooney Rule, 212–13
Roosevelt, Teddy, 19, 81, 168, 169
Ruck, Rob, 141, 177
Rusch, Paul, 16
Russell Sage Foundation, 8
Ryder, Eleanor, 159

Sabol, Helen Babich, 87, 90
Sacco, Nicola, 56
Sajna, Mike, 88, 95
Same Old Steelers (SOS), 166
Savran, Stan, 214
Scalia, Antonin, 205
Schenkel, Gary W., 30, 31
Schlesinger, Hymen, 162
Schoenfeld, Julia, 122, 126
Schwab, Charles, 42

Schwartz, Morris, 147
Scribner's Magazine, 168
Seals, Ray, 200, 202
Senator John Heinz History Center, 75
Sengstacke, John, 113
Shell, Art, 192
Shoemaker, Henry, 85, 96
Silent Spring (Carson), 105
Sinatra, Frank, 183, *191*
Sing, Yee Wah, 10
Smith, Clara, 114
Smith, Lovie, 191, 211
Smith, Wendell, 143
soccer in Pittsburgh: 49–50, 69–70; Bhutanese contribution, 209–10; Chinese teams, 19–20; emphasis on establishing American credibility, 68–69; ethnic divide, 67–68; familiarity in suburban areas, 37–39; fatalities in mining industry, 50–51, *51*; influence of coal operators, 52–53; limited narratives of American soccer, 66–67; Pittsburgh Riverhounds, 63; racial and ethnic segregation in Harmarville, 53–54; sponsorship from coal companies, 51–52; viewership growth of American soccer, 63–64; violent nature of soccer, 65–66; as workingman's game, 39–49. *See also* Harmarville Hurricanes
Solender, Sanford, 161
SOS. *See* Same Old Steelers
South Fork Fishing and Hunting Club, 75, 77–78, 85–86, 91, 101
Sport Club Hakoah, 136
Springwood, Charles Fruehling, 196–97
Squaw Run, 72, 73, 92, 98
Squirrel Hill, 4, 33, 155–56
Stagg, Amos Alonzo, 16
Stallworth, John, 185
Stargell, Willie "Pops," 164
Steel Army, 63
steel mills in Pittsburgh: development, 168–70; employment discrimination against Black workers, 194–96; industrial accidents, 170

Stern, Gerald, 130
Stewart, Kordell, 198
Strzelczyk, Justin, 189
swimming, Jewish woman participation in, 133–35
Synagogue Council of America, 136

Tan, C. L., 19
Taylor, Harry, 42
Teller, Sidney, 126–28, 140, 145, 153, 157, 163
Three Rivers Stadium, *185*, 199–202, 214, 216
Thuram, Lilian, 36
Tin, Lai, 22–24
Tittle, Y. A., 167
Toledo Blade, 168
Tomlin, Mike, 166, 192, 210–12, 214
Trezeguet, David, 36
Triphammer Gun Club, 102, 103, 113
Trout (Bergman), 72
Twyman, Levi, 53

UMWA. *See* United Mine Workers of America
Unitas, Johnny, 176
United Labor League of Western Pennsylvania, 43
United Mine Workers of America (UMWA), 55, 56
United States Football Association, 68
United States Steel Corporation, 178
United Steel Workers of America, 195
URA. *See* Urban Redevelopment Authority
Urban League of Pittsburgh, 100–101
Urban Redevelopment Authority (URA), 18, 184
US Fish and Wildlife Service (USFWS), 93, 95, 111

Vann, Robert Lee, 97, 145
Vanzetti, Bartolomeo, 56
Vento, Al, 182, 183, 205
Vento, Al, Jr., 193
Verner, Samuel Phillips, 108
Vieira, Patrick, 36

Vienna's Hakoah club, 129–30
Vinland Map, 182
Viti, Marcel, 90
Vittor, Frank, 168; clay model of Joe Magarac, 168; statue of Christopher Columbus in Schenley Park, 182

Wagner, Honus, 44
Walker, C. J., 99
Walls Laundry Grays, 19
Ward, Hines, 202–7
Warhol, Andy, 18
War Relocation Authority (WRA), 30, 31
Washington, Booker T., 109, 145
WASP culture, 39
Waters, Mary, 193
Watson, Diane, 207
Watts, Harold, 57
Webster, Mike, 188–89
Wedge, Will, 24
Weil, A. Leo, 120
Western Pennsylvania Football Association, 43–44
Western Pennsylvania Interscholastic Athletic League (WPIAL), 66
Westinghouse Electric Corporation, 14
Whisenhunt, Ken, 211
Whitman, Walt, 77
Whitsitt, Sam, 39
Wideman, John Edgar, 110–12, 199, 200
Will, George, 169
Williams, Joe, 47
Wilson, August, 141
Wolf, Irwin, 153, 161
women: absence of Chinese women in Chinatown, 26–28; hunters and anglers in Pittsburgh, 112–16, *115*; Jewish girls, 119–21, 132–37; participation in fishing and hunting, 95–96; participation in swimming, 133–35
Women's Swimming Association, 133
Woosnam, Phil, 38
WPIAL. *See* Western Pennsylvania Interscholastic Athletic League
WRA. *See* War Relocation Authority

Wright, James, 171
Wyoming Paris, 131

Y-IKC. *See* Jewish Community Center
Yakopec, Lou "Skip," 60, 66
Yakopec, Lou "Sonny," 60, 66, 69
Yakopec, Mike, 70
Yee, Tang, 12

Young Men's Christian Association (YMCA), 15, 28, 56, 104, 145–49, 153, 161

Zidane, Zinedine, 35–37
Zimbicki, Ed, 60
Zittel, Ruth Ellen, 138
Zullinger, Melody, 92

www.ingramcontent.com/pod-product-compliance
Lightning Source LLC
Chambersburg PA
CBHW031409290426
44110CB00011B/321